THE
FLATT FAMILY
STORIES

ERNEST ALLEN FLATT, SR.

 page vision

228 Hamilton Ave.
Palo Alto, CA 94301

FOREWORD

Believe it or Not- from Ernest Allen Flatt, Sr.

I am writing this for my present family and my family to come. Understanding I am not a great writer, I am telling The Flatt Family Stories as a combination of family stories, as I have been told, as I was growing up, or moments that I lived myself. The Stories are told of the Flatt Family on my Dad's side, and the Griffin Family on my mother's side. These stories are based on facts set forth in my memory also in the memory of the one that told them to me. Some events, and incidents, are as they were told to me, True or False. I am not saying any of my family did not tell the truth, it is just the way they remembered the events. Sometimes the stories were told to me by the person involved in the story, sometimes by someone who observed or heard about it. Some personal events and incidents are remembered and slanted by personal opinions of how things happened. You may find someone that was evolved that does not agree with what was told to me. Some technical info, chronological dates, places, or names have been changed where the memory is dim, and it doesn't matter to the story. While this story is a dramatization of actual events; certain names, incidents, order of events, and dialogue have been fictionalized to round out the story and make it more interesting than just saying you know <u>what's his/her name</u>*.*

I believe someone should tell the story of at least one line of the Flatt Family. I would like to see other lines of the Flatt Family also written for future generations to read. Since I know the most about myself it is written in the line of myself, Ernest Allen Flatt, Sr. I hope you enjoy this story of the struggles, and conquests of the Flatt Family. These stories are told of the past, and just gone by present events. May this story also be continued by my children, grandchildren, and great grandchildren for generations to come.

The Flatt Family has always been a great believer in that GOD comes first, then a close second is family or, should I say," We may agree, we may disagree, but we are always The Flatt Family". The first/main part of the Flatt Stories is written for family as well as the reading public. The Family Trees at the end are mainly for The Flatt and Griffin Families Future offspring.

<u>*We live by a creed:*</u>

We do not lie to family members. We don't cheat a family member. *No-one outside the family comes between one family member, and another. And because family members can upset you more than anyone else, physical confrontation with a family member is a last resort, and a no, no. Although this has happened before it was usually brought on by drink. Therefore, the Flatt Family members need to beware of alcoholic drinks, and hard drugs.*

CONTENTS

PICTURES

01. 1898-THE GRIFFIN SIDE OF THE FAMILY-RUFFORD GRIFFIN.

Rufford Griffin was a young man born in Kentucky, on 08/04/1881, and that he had grown up faster than his years, was not unusual. He was a 17-year-old, older than his years, stern young man. He was a man that meant what he said and said what he meant. He was a man that would not start a fight but had no problem with finishing one. A man with grit, as course as 60 grit, 01. emery cloth backed, sandpaper.

Rufford had started out with a traveling soul. As a teen Rufford carried himself and acted older than he was. After lying about his age at fourteen and joining the army he had completed a two-year stint in the military where he had learned a lot about taking care of himself. Then Rufford had traveled by horseback from Kentucky finding his way to east Texas where he had taken a job as a lawman with the Texas Rangers. Rufford had looked older as a young teen but then somewhere around 16 years of age he began to look younger for his age but acted very much older than his age.

As Rufford came riding into a small Texas town he was riding the gray/white appaloosa horse that had been furnished by the Texas Rangers once his own horse had died. He was here to pick up a prisoner from the local sheriff. The prisoner he was to pick up had been captured by the sheriff almost accidentally and was now being held in the sheriffs' town jail. The sheriff had the prisoner waiting for the Texas Rangers to come and get him and carry him to Bowie County Texas, Texarkana on the Texas side to be put on trial for murder. As he rode up to the jail Rufford got down off his horse and tied it to the hitching post in front of the jail.

Rufford was about 6 foot tall and would have been slim if not for the beginnings of a belly. He wore a dark gray, sweat stained, short brim hat, with the brim turned down in the front and up in the back. He wore blue jeans trousers, a long sleeve dark green shirt that buttoned up the front, without a collar. Over his left pocket there was pinned a Texas Ranger badge. There was a brown leather holster swinging from his right hip. Sticking out of the holster was the plain, walnut, wooden handles of a Colt, caliber 38, six shot revolver pistol.

Rufford looked up and down the small Texas town street. There were a couple of horses tied on both sides of the small main street. The small town did not look like much but seemed to be a peaceable enough town he thought to himself. Maybe that is why Frank Union felt he could hide out here. Frank Union had killed a man in Bowie County Texas a couple of months ago. The town of the killing was better known as Texarkana on the Texas side. Frank Union may have been able to hide out here if he had not gotten arrested for public drunkenness. Just so happened the sheriff had a wanted poster that had just been brought in by mail on him.

Rufford stepped up the two short steps that lead to the front porch of the sheriff's office and jail. There was a strong, heavy, wooden door with large hinges that went about halfway across the door.

Rufford banged on the door and heard a voice from inside say "Come on in"! Rufford opened the door and stepped in. There was a large fat man sitting behind a desk. He was dressed in an army shirt with a badge over his heart.

As Rufford walked across the floor to the desk, the fellow behind the desk gave him the once over.

"Can I help you", spoke the fat man behind the desk.

Rufford answered, "My name is Ranger Rufford Griffin". "I have been sent by the Texas Rangers to take a prisoner named Frank Union to Bowie County Texarkana to stand trial for murder". "Here are my papers" handing the papers toward the sheriff. "Are you Sheriff Fields"? Rufford asked.

"Yes, I am," said the Sheriff as he took the papers from Ranger Griffin. "Well, your warrant looks in order"! "When do you want to take the prisoner"?

"Well, I have been traveling for quite a while; me, and my horse could use some rest, and something to eat before we head out", said Rufford. "How about in the morning after breakfast", Rufford added, not really asking for the sheriff's permission?

"Works for me" said the sheriff. "But I tell you, I will be glad to get rid of this fellow, he is bad news. He has tried to escape two times. I think he will try anything to get loose. He's a real asshole too"! "You better watch yourself on your way back to trial". "Are you by yourself", the Sheriff asked Rufford?

"Yeah, but I can handle him" said Rufford in a dry tone.

"I don't mean any offense, but you look kinda young" said the sheriff, almost apologetic.

"I have heard that before, but I have got a lot of experience, and can handle the job just fine" said Rufford with a cold stare at the sheriff.

"Well, if the Rangers say you can do the job, and trust you, I guess I should too", said the sheriff. "No offense meant"!

"None taken, but don't let my age fool you", Rufford lied to the sheriff. The fact is Rufford did not like being judged by his age. He felt he had paid his dues and deserved respect and would have it. Even by a fellow lawman!

"How did you catch him if he is so bad", said the ranger in a sarcastic tone to the sheriff?

"Well, to be honest with you, he was drunker than "Cooter Brown", and I just slapped the cuffs on him. "He was so-o drunk"! "He could hardly stand up". "I barely could walk him back to the jail". "Man, he was sick the next day too"! "Puked everywhere in the cell"! "Stunk so badly"! "When we tried to clean it up, it was the first time he tried to escape"! "So now, if we open the cell door, he's got cuffs on first". "You know he still tried to strangle my deputy with the cuffs chain"! "That was the second time he tried to escape"!

"Well, how about I take a look at this prisoner", asked Rufford dryly.

"Sure, follow me down the stairs to the back where the cells are" grunted the fat sheriff as he wobbled toward the back.

The sheriff opened the door leading back to the cell area with his key. They made a left turn down a set of steps that landed in front of the first of three cells. To the right there was a 6-foot wide, hallway in front of the cells which led to an inside cell barred door. On the other end of the hallway there was a wooden entrance/exit door which led outside. Each of these doors needed a key to unlock once closed just like the cell doors and the one at the top of the stairs. This is where the prisoners were brought in and out to avoid the stairs and the sheriff's office. The jail was built on the side of a hill and the Office where Rufford came in was on the second floor, but almost even with the street.

Frank Union was in the first cell. He was also the only prisoner being housed in the jail cells at this time. As the two lawmen came down the steps and came into view, the prisoner sat up and stared at them with a snarl.

"Hello, you fat son-of-a-bitch" he growled looking straight at the sheriff with fire in his eyes. "You know you wouldn't never have arrested me if I hadn't been drunk, you lazy ass, fuck face! Poor excuse for a sheriff"! "Why don't you open this cell and let me show you how to be a man"?

"See what I mean," said the sheriff turning to Rufford?

"Who the hell is this kid" shouted the prisoner!

"This is the ranger which came to take you to trial, Frank, you asshole", spit back the sheriff!

"No Shit"? "This must be my lucky day" laughed Frank! "The rangers must be pretty hard up if they are signing up children"! Again, Frank laughed a deep belly laugh out loud while staring straight at Rufford.

Rufford starred straight back without blinking an eye.

Ranger Griffin stepped toward the cell and said, "Mister you don't know me, don't let my looks fool you". "I will get you to trial"! "We're goanna leave in the morning after breakfast heading back to Texarkana in Bowie County so you can stand trial for murder"! "Understand that if you give me any trouble, I'll shoot you"! "If you try to run, I'll shoot you"! "If you give me any shit whatsoever, trial will be held right there on the fucking trail between here and Bowie County"! "Do we understand each other"? Rufford asked this without blinking an eye and starring straight in the eyes of the prisoner.

"Well Texarkana is a longways off ranger" smiled the prisoner Frank Union.

"Well just so you know that I'll do what I have to do". "I'll hog tie you and drag you back if need be" snapped back Rufford!

"What's your name ranger", demanded the prisoner?

"You can call me ranger, that's good enough", Rufford snapped back! "Sheriff, let's get out of here, I've been about as friendly as I want to be with this piece of shit", snapped Rufford as the ranger stomped up the steps the sheriff right behind him with the key.

"You'll have a hell of a time getting' me back to Texarkana ranger", shouted Frank Union. "A hell of a time"!!!

After stabling his horse at the livery and getting some supper Rufford got himself a room at the hotel and laid down for a rest.

The next morning came. As the rooster crowed down the street Rufford woke from a sleep he was sure would be the best he would get for several nights. Cause today he would be heading back with the killer waiting for him at the jail. As he lay there in the bed, he began to plan his day. First, he would have breakfast, a good one, with steak and eggs, biscuits and black coffee. Then his plan would be to go to the livery to retrieve his horse and buy one for Frank Union to ride back to his hanging. It was going to be a long ride back to Texarkana with a killer like Frank Union looking to get free every minute of the ride.

Rufford came in the front door of the jail looking all around. "Good morning sheriff, has my prisoner eaten his breakfast yet"?

"Yeah, we took it down to him about a half hour ago, Ranger". "We also opened the outside door". "We'll take him out that way". "It gives us more room if he acts up, rather than going up the stair steps" said the sheriff.

"Good, let's go get him then, I need to get going toward Texarkana," Rufford said lightly".

Down the steps went the ranger and the sheriff. The sheriff told Frank to stick his hands through the cuff hole, where he placed the cuffs on the prisoner's wrists.

"We don't need these, sheriff," said Frank!

"Now, Frank, you know we are not gonna open this cell door without you having cuffs on," said the sheriff.

"Yeah, cause you both are chicken shit", growled Frank at Rufford and the Sheriff.

Rufford stepped forward toward the cell door, and said in a low growl back, "Frank I am telling you now if you give me any shit, or try to run away, I won't think twice about shooting' your ass". "Do you understand", asked Rufford with more of a statement in his voice than a question?

"Yeah, Ranger I am gonna be the model prisoner", Frank answered sarcastically with a smile.

The sheriff stuck the key in the cell door and turned it. As he opened the door Frank stepped out into the hallway. Without a word Frank swung his cuffed hands over Rufford's head and around his neck. At the same time, he put a steak knife he had hid in his shirt sleeve to Rufford's neck.

"Give me your gun ranger or I'll kill you shouted Frank"!

At almost the same instance the sheriff fired a wild shot at Frank Union. He may have missed because he was running up the stairs to get away. He did not hit him, but it was enough to cause him to loosen his grip on the ranger. Rufford grabbed his gun out of his holster. Frank dropped the steak knife someone had smuggled into him. But because he was off balance both men went down while they were wrestling over the ranger's gun. The gun went sliding across the floor. It just so happened; the gun was closest to Frank. But to go for it Frank had to release the chain around Rufford's neck. As Frank was going for the gun, Rufford got loose.

"Run sheriff he's got my gun", shouted Rufford. The Sheriff went up the steps lick-a-tea-split.

Rufford jumped to his feet and ran for the door leading outside at the end of the cell hallway. Frank reached the gun and shot at Rufford just as he went outside on the run. The bullet hit the door facing right beside the Ranger's head.

Rufford now was outside, but because of the shot fired at him was not able to close the outside door. Knowing Frank would be coming with his own gun, the Ranger ran for the front of the jail. As he got to the corner another shot rang out. Frank had fired at Rufford again but missed again. There was the sheriff in full sprint just ahead of Rufford running for his life. Rufford ran after the sheriff, and being a younger, slimmer, quicker man, caught him just as the two of them reached a small wooden white fence, about 3 foot tall. Another shot rang out. It was another miss. The two lawmen jumped the fence together, side by side. While they were in the air Rufford reached over and grabbed the sheriff's gun out of his holster. As they landed on the other side of the fence Rufford turned and fired at the murderer.

Bam! The shot rang out! As if in slow motion the killer fell to the dry dirt ground. Then everything went quiet.

The sheriff spoke softly almost in a whisper, "I believe you got him". "But watch him ranger, keep the gun on him, he might be playin' possum"! Both men stepped back over the fence. Rufford held the gun on him as each man walked slowly, and cautiously back toward the un-moving Frank Union.

Rufford pushed him with his foot and the engineer boot he wore, all the time pointing the sheriff's gun at the motionless prisoner on the ground. Then Rufford kneeled and checked for any signs of life. Rufford checked the pupils in his eyes. They were dilated and fixed.

"He's dead", said Rufford to the sheriff!

The sheriff reached down into the dirt to pick up Rufford's gun that the prisoner had dropped when Rufford shot him.

"Wow, you shot the sight off your own gun", said the sheriff. "But you got him, he would have killed us for sure", stated the sheriff. "You saved our lives for sure, Ranger", he said with a corked smile! "Guess you do know what you're doing"!!

"Well, I guess my ride to take him back to Texarkana will be a quiet one after all", spoke Rufford in a matter-of-fact way.

Rufford decided to not re-up with the Texas Rangers when his time came.

He was beginning to get home sick and longed to go back home. Rufford Griffin came back to Kentucky. The area was called Jackson County. Rufford had begun to get tired of all his traveling and was getting the feeling he needed to settle down, get some land, and raise crops and maybe a family.

Rufford was told by a friend of his that there was a barn dance taking place that Saturday night in a nearby town in the next county. Rufford did not dance. He never had learned or even tried. He just had not felt there was a need to know how.

John Brandenburg, Rufford's long time school friend asks "Rufford why don't you go with me to the barn dance? There will be some good bluegrass music, tasty food, and lots of pretty girls to dance with".

Rufford answered in a dry tone, "Well John I like good Hoedown Music, and you know I like to eat, but I don't dance. I never learned".

John answered with a big smile on his face, "Well, hell Rufford! I cannot dance either. I just shuffle around the floor in a square and try not to step on the lady's feet with my big feet". "They don't like that. Stepping on their feet that is" said John with a big laugh that came all the way up from his belly.

"You do like girls don't you" ask John?

"Of course, I do" answered Rufford. "But, John, I never met a man I was afraid of, but women just get me all tongue tied. Sometimes I sound like a fool around them". "But I do like Hoedown Music and good food" smiled Rufford. "And Girls, Well, I ain't no quire", grinned Rufford!

"Then we will go Saturday night" said John Brandenburg with a large smile.

Saturday night rolled around and John and Rufford put on their best Sunday go to Meetin' bib overalls and got on their horses and rode over to the next county. Rufford did not carry his 38 on his hip, but he did have his 2 shot 38 Derringer in his pocket. People did not carry guns out in the open in Kentucky like they did in Texas, but you can bet most everyone had one hid on their person somewhere. Rufford was no exception, nor was John Brandenburg.

The two young men came riding up to the barn and tied up their horses in the corral. They could already hear the music coming from inside. It was a nice spring evening, and the weather was perfect.

"Big foot up, little foot down makes that bigfoot jar the ground" was heard coming from inside the barn as someone was calling a square dance already in progress.

John looked at Rufford and said with a smile "This place is jumpin' Rufford. This is going to be great".

Rufford looked around and could see some couples already necking outside the barn in the shadows. Over in one corner there were some young men passing around a bottle and getting louder and louder with each drink.

The light from several coal oil lamps was shining through the cracks of the big double doors at the front of the barn. There was one small door standing open just around the corner from the big double doors. The light from the small door lit up a large area outside which caused shadows to each side.

As John and Rufford walked through the small door a man came up to them that was standing just inside and said, "Fellows that will be a nickel a piece, if you will". John and Rufford looked at the man up and down and John said, "We thought this was going to be free"! It was not that the men minded paying the nickel, it was just they were not going to be hood wicked out of a nickel. And they did not know this fellow.

"Well, the dance eats, and ladies are free, but we need to get something for the band", said the man at the door with a smile. "It's just a nickel; these guys are famous in these parts and had to come from a way away". John started to say, "Wait a minute" --. Rufford spoke up its "OK John, I got this. The music's has come from a long way. That's fair enough."

Rufford was not being so kind hearted as it was that he wanted to impress the young dark-haired girl that he saw out of the corner of his eye. She had noticed that someone she did not recognize had walked in and was paying close attention to Rufford. Rufford was also paying close attention to her. Although he was trying to act like he had not noticed her. She was short, not as big as a pound of soap with long dark hair and blue eyes. She was standing behind a table off to the side of the barn not far from the door that Rufford and John had entered. She was drinking some sweet tea out of a small mason jar and patting her foot to the music. She was from time-to-time filling mason jars with sweet tea on the table in front of her with a metal dipper. Guests would come up and get some now and then.

People were sitting, standing, and talking all around the edges of the barn. There was a stage at the far end of the barn with a 5-piece acoustic band playing a hoedown and a 6th man calling square dance moves. In the middle of the barn there was a group of young men and young women doing those square dance moves. As the band played, the man called the moves, and the group of people smiled and danced the moves like clockwork.

"Swing your partner"! "Doe-see, doe to your right"! "Ala-bam left"! "Kick up your heels, but don't you fight"! Yelled the square dance caller in perfect rhythm.

After Rufford paid the man at the door the ten cents, Rufford and John went over to the drink table to get some sweet tea.

'Bring back your mason jars, and I will fill them up when you need it", said the cute little dark-haired girl that had been looking at Rufford.

"Thank you", said John. But Rufford just tipped his hat and smiled without saying anything as they walked a few feet away to drink their tea.

Every time Rufford would look her way she would look another way. But she could not stop her eyes from wandering back. Rufford's eyes would catch hers, and he or she would look away. This went on for several minutes.

Finally, John said, "Well hell Rufford, why don't you just go say hi to her, you two can't keep your eyes off each other".

"I don't know what you're talking about", said Rufford.

"Yea, sure you don't", laughed John!

Rufford stood looking around for several minutes. Then he turned to John and said, "Do you know what her name is"?

John said with a big grin, "Who"?

"Well, now John, who the hell do you think I am talking about", snapped Rufford.

John began to laugh and slap his leg and danced in a circle.

"You want me to go ask her what her name is", ask John? John was grinning from ear to ear.

"You're having a good time with this, ain't you John", ask Rufford?

"To be honest with you, --yea", smiled John!

"I am going to find out what her name is for you," said John.

"You owe me", John said as he walked away toward the sweet tea table.

"No-o-o"! "Come back here" whispered Rufford with a growl.

But John did not listen; he went straight over to the young Lady and asked her what her name was.

Then he turned and pointed at Rufford. As the young lady turned to look at Rufford, Rufford felt he could just die. Rufford turned beet red. He wanted to crawl under a table.

John turned and came right back over to Rufford and said with a smile, "Her name is Nancy Elizabeth Sparks, and she wants to meet you". "Come on I'll introduce you, John said.

Rufford followed behind him like a puppy dog but looked like he had the wind knocked out of him.

As the two men approached the young lady, John swung his hand in a gallant jester toward Rufford and at the same time did a small bow and said, "Miss Nancy this is Rufford Griffin and Rufford this is Miss Nancy Sparks". John was smiling from ear to ear as Rufford gave him a menacing glare.

As John walked away Rufford whispered in his ear "You asshole".

John walked away snickering.

"What did you say to him", said Nancy with a smile.

"I uh, I uh, spoke to, I told him he was very bold", stammered Rufford trying to look at Nancy, but only able to look away in embarrassment.

Nancy spoke in a soft sweet voice "I saw you come in and wondered who you were. I don't think I have seen you around here before". "Have you been here long", she asks?

"Uh, no, I have been gone, out west for a while", Rufford finally spit out with an awkward smile.

Nancy asked again, trying to keep the conversation going "Do you live around here", then she smiled.

"No, my family lives over in the next county", smiled Rufford back." Jackson County"! "What about you," asked Rufford as he dropped his eyes from her blue eyes?

"Yes, my family lives here in Estill County, guess they always will. But I got relatives that live in Jackson County, around Kerby Knob", said Nancy.

Rufford's eyes suddenly lit up. "That's around where my folk are from", smiled Rufford. That seems to be the thing that broke the ice for Rufford.

"And where do you come from in Estill County", ask Rufford?

"You probably never heard of it, it is so small it's not on a map, it's called Barns Mountain just south of Ravenna and Ravenna is just south of Irvine", explained Nancy.

"Yea, I know where Irvine is"! smiled Rufford, glad he finally recognized a place she had mentioned.

"Yea, Irvine is on the map", smiled Nancy. "Would you like to dance?", asked Nancy, realizing that Rufford was not going to ask on his own. "I can get someone to fill in for me here at the tea table", smiled Nancy. She had come hoping someone would ask her to dance. She liked to dance.

Rufford's face went sour. "I, uh, I uh, don't know how", Rufford finally admitted.

"It's just a slow dance", Nancy explained! "I'll show you how", grabbing his hand as she heads for the middle of the barn.

"John said you are MISS Nancy Sparks, does that mean you're not married", ask Rufford in a shy way, looking down?

"No, I am not married", smiled Nancy as she took his hand to dance.

John stood at the side of the barn laughing. He could not believe that she had actually got Rufford out on the dance floor. But there he was! And he was dancing. Dog-gone it, thought John. But he could not believe his eyes. Though he could see Rufford and Nancy were stricken with each other.

As it turned out Rufford and Nancy danced every slow dance the rest of the evening until the last song of the evening.

Just as Rufford and Nancy were about to dance the last dance of the evening, a young man came from outside and tried to cut in on Rufford and dance with Nancy.

"Hey, fuck face you been dancing with her long enough. I do not even think you are from around here. Get the fuck out of the way", the young man said as he shoved Rufford aside.

Rufford swung around in a split second and was in the young man's face.

"Watch your language around the lady mister", snarled Rufford right back in his face.

The young man stepped back. "What lady asshole, I've known Nancy all my life", shouted the rude young man.

"Mister, I know you're not trying to stand here in my face and tell me that she is not a lady"? "Well, are you" asked Rufford as he stepped forward toward the young man? Rufford could smell the whiskey on the young man's breath. But his hand had already gone into the right front pocket of his bib overalls where his hide away gun was.

Suddenly John was at Rufford's side and spoke up, "Mister, I know you've had a little too much of the bottle". "I can smell it on you". "You better bring your voice down, apologize to Nancy, and go home".

"Everyone has had a good time here tonight and we don't need any trouble", spoke John softly glancing at Rufford, hoping he would not lose it on the fellow.

"What's the matter mister you think I can't kick this hillbilly's ass, just because I have had a few drinks", ask the young man weaving unsteady where he stood?

"Mister, I not only think you can't, kick his ass if you were sober, I think you would not be leaving here standing up right if you keep pushing this", snapped John! "I have known Rufford for a long time, and it's not a matter of kicking someone ass, Rufford don't play that game"! "It is a wonder you ain't dead already"! "Go home", said John, getting louder!

About that time the Sheriff came in the barn and came straight to where the men were getting louder. "I told you William, not to be drinkin' and causing any trouble, you're going to jail for public drunkenness", the Sheriff said!

As the Sheriff put the cuffs on the drunken young man and took him away, the Sheriff said, "Sorry folks, go back to the party".

"Awe, Sheriff, let me kick this stranger's ass first", said the drunken William.

Rufford never took his glaring eyes off the drunken man, or his hand out of his pocket and was still staring after the young man as he was being led away by the sheriff.

Rufford turned to Nancy and said, "I am sorry about that, how about that last dance"?

"Too late" said Nancy, "they have started putting the music's away".

"Well can I call on you sometime" ask Rufford?

"I would like that, but you would have to come and ask my Daddy", said Nancy with hope in her eyes. "Can you find Barns Mountain", ask Nancy?

"I'll find it. If it can be found", smiled Rufford.

"You can ask anyone up in that area where the Sparks Family lives and they can tell you", smiled Nancy.

"What's the name of your daddy", ask Rufford.

"My daddy's name is Solomon Sparks and my mother's name Sarah Jane Moore Sparks, and as I said we live on Barns Mountain, Kentucky just past Doe Creek, Kentucky in Estill County. My grandpa on my daddy's side is Daniel Sparks, and my grandma is Louise. On my mother's side my grandpa is John Moore, and my grandma on my mother's side is Linda Horn Moore" explained Nancy with a light in her eyes.

"Hold it", explained Rufford! "I got it", he said with a smile. "I'll find it"! "Doe Creek"!! "Barns Mountain"!!! "I know where it is", said Rufford as he walked away smiling.

Then all sudden Rufford turned around and said," Do you think your daddy would mind if I came up next Friday after I get off from work"?

Nancy's face lit up like she just became a Christmas tree." Oh, I think he won't mind as long as you come up and talk to him first, when you get there", said Nancy with a smile on her face.

She followed Rufford all the way to the door. Rufford went outside to retrieve his horse and swung up into the saddle. He turned in the saddle tipped his hat and gave Nancy one last smile before he rode away.

Nancy was still smiling from the doorway when someone from inside said "Come on girl we gotta get this stuff cleaned up". It was Solomon Sparks, Nancy's dad. Solomon Sparks was a farmer, and a strong man. He wore bibs just like most country people did at that time who lived on farms. He had brown hair that was streaked with light gray.

"Who's that young man you were talking to just a minute ago", said Solomon.

"Oh, he's only the man I'm going to marry", said Nancy with a smile on her face.

"Oh, I knew there was some reason why I didn't like him", said Solomon.

"Well, you better learn to like him, because I believe he's coming next Friday to ask if he can court me", smiled Nancy with a dreamy look in her eyes.

Suddenly, Nancy looked at her Dad with a serious look on her face. "Please daddy, say you'll say yes, and don't scare him away", begged Nancy.

"Well, we'll see after I have gotten to know him a little better. And any man that can be scared away ain't much of a man", spoke Solomon with a stern voice!

"By the way have you ever met him before the dance", ask Solomon?

Nancy just shook her head no, smiled, and began to sing as she cleaned up the table that she had overseen. "Ala-bam left, Ala-bam right", she sang!!

Nancy knew it was going to be a long week until the next Friday came around.

03. 1901-RUFFORD GRIFFIN COURTS NANCY SPARKS.

Rufford had been waiting for the week to go by. Each day seems to just go slowly by. He was looking forward to the Friday coming around that he could go and talk to Solomon Sparks about being allowed to court Nancy. Oh, he hoped he would say "yes". Rufford did not know it but Nancy was looking forward to the day just as much as he was. But the days drug by for both Rufford and Nancy. Finally, the day came when Rufford knew once he got off from work that he would be able to saddle up his horse and ride over to the Spark's farm. Hoping to be able to ask Solomon Sparks if he could come courting, his daughter Nancy Sparks. All day long Rufford had been looking at his pocket watch. Didn't those hands ever move, thought Rufford?

Rufford had never met a man he was afraid of, but he knew that to be able to court Nancy he would have to try and get Solomon to like him. He had brought along with him his Sunday go to meetin' bib overalls, and a clean dress shirt. He would stop somewhere along the way and change into the clean clothing when he was closer.

Finally, the time had come when Rufford could saddle up his horse and head over to the Spark's farm. He had been talking to friends and coworkers all week long and had gotten directions several times from several different people. He believed he had a fairly good idea where the Sparks farm was.

Rufford found the Sparks farm with no problem. Once he got there he rode right up to the front door and tied up his horse. Walked up and knocked on the door. Rufford knew someone was home because he had seen someone looking out the upstairs window from within the farmhouse as he rode up. Rufford did not know it, but Nancy had been watching for over an hour for Rufford's arrival. Her heart jumped when she saw him riding up the road to the house from the bedroom window.

She ran to inform her daddy of Rufford's arrival. "Daddy it's him, when he knocks, let him in", hollered Nancy from upstairs to her daddy downstairs!

"OK! OK!" hollered back Solomon. "You stay upstairs, this is man's business", said Solomon as the knock came at the door.

Solomon opened the front door. And said "Yeah"!

Rufford stood there with his hat in his hand and said with a lump in his throat "Mr. Sparks, I am Rufford Griffin. I came to ask your permission to court your daughter"!

Solomon just looked at him and said, "Well I see you are a man who likes to get right to the point. I suppose we could see about that, but I would have to get to know you better.

"Yes, sir your daughter told me that there would be a requirement," said Rufford.

"Well first we have to ask her if she wants to court you. If she says yes, then you can court her here at the house for a while. Then we will think about courting away from the house later. You know, at a later date, once I have got to know you better", stated Solomon. "Those are the terms"! "Do you understand, and agree", ask Solomon?

"Yes sir, Mister Sparks" smiled Rufford with his hat twirling in his hands, and glad things were working out so well.

"Well come on in the house" said Solomon!

Rufford stepped into the living room.

"Have a seat" said Solomon.

Rufford took a seat in a big leather chair, with his hat still in his hands.

"Would you like to see my daughter now, young man", ask Solomon?

"Yes sir" answered Rufford as he sprang to his feet again.

"Sit down son! Relax, and I will go get her"! Then we can find out if she agrees with you about having you come to call", smiled Solomon turning to leave the room.

Nancy had been listening from upstairs and was so excited. When she heard her daddy say he would go to get her, she turned and ran back into her room to wait for her daddy. She did not want him to know she had been eavesdropping at the top of the stairs. But she waited, and waited, and he did not come. Finally, she tiptoed back out of her room to the top of the stairs to ease drop again. This is what she heard.

Solomon re-entered the living room, and turned and said, "Come on in here girl, don't be so shy".

Nancy was confused. Who was her Daddy talking to? He had not come up stairs where she was.

In through the downstairs door came a young girl about 4 years younger than Nancy. She had been slopping the pigs and some of it was on the clothes she was wearing. Her hair was a mess.

"How did you meet my daughter", ask Solomon with a grin on his face pointing to the girl that had just come in?

Rufford sprang to his feet. "Who is this" asked Rufford?

"Well, this is my daughter", said Solomon. "You said you wanted to court her" exclaimed Solomon!

Rufford looked confused. "Sir, I-- ah, I-- ah, don't know who this girl is. I've never"! "Who is"? "I have never seen her before", stuttered Rufford!

Malinda, Solomon's other daughter looked very confused.

"This is my daughter"! "Malinda Sparks" explained Solomon! "You said you wanted to court her", Solomon smiled!

"Stop it Daddy! A voice came from the top of the stairs. "You know perfectly well he came to see me", said Nancy as she came down the stairs. Nancy had on a new, beautiful, blue, print dress, with a yellow scarf around her neck, and Rufford, though confused, thought she was gorgeous.

Solomon began to laugh a deep belly laugh. Then said, "I am sorry for tricking you son, but you didn't say which daughter"!

Rufford looked back and forth from one daughter to the other still confused.

Then Rufford began to understand. It was a joke! Then he began to laugh also. "Well sir, Malinda is pretty, but Nancy is the one that I met at the barn dance and came to see" said Rufford with a laugh. "That was a good one, sir. I came here all nervous and that has certainly gone away now"!

Well, it is good to see you got a sense of humor, smiled Solomon with a big, crooked grin!

Malinda, still confused, said "You all are crazy", as she stomped out of the room still not sure what was going on.

Everybody now was laughing except Malinda.

(Just for the record as time goes by, Malinda Sparks later marries James Griffin, Rufford's brother)

Rufford came back many times to court Nancy. Slowly Solomon began to allow them to go places together.

One day Rufford came in and asked Solomon if he could marry Nancy.

Solomon's answer was simple.

"Rufford", said Solomon, "If you want to marry my daughter, Nancy, you must get together enough money to buy some land and build a house. I would like for it to be in this area so that her mother and me and all her brothers and sisters can still see her from time to time. This is the requirement".

From that time on Rufford began to search for a piece of land to buy. Rufford had already saved up some money from his military and ranger days. He knew what he wanted. He wanted a piece of land away from everyone else. A farm so he could grow a lot of his own food for him and his family. Also maybe sell some.

One day when Rufford was over at the Sparks farm to see Nancy, Solomon called Rufford and Nancy aside.

Solomon said, "Rufford I understand you have been looking around for a piece of land, have you found one yet"?

Rufford answered, "No sir, not yet. Not one I can afford with enough acreage".

Solomon looked at Rufford and said, "Well, I don't know how much money you have yet, but I know a fellow that has a piece of land that he might consider selling really cheap. It is good land. The problem is it is way back up in a hollow a long way from the road. The reason why he is willing to sell it so cheap is that it does not have a road front, or any road in, and out, to it.

"Well how would I get in, and out, to it", said Rufford?

"Well, that is what I am about to tell you, I have a friend named Green Roberts that owns a piece of land right next to the piece I am telling you about. Green Roberts owes me some money and he cannot afford to pay me. He is a good friend, but he does not have the money. I have known him a long time and he is not trying to cheat me he just does not have it. But he is willing to give me the deed to a road passage from the main road all the way up to this property that is for sale. Now, no one knows about this, but Green Roberts, me, and now you. This also is including the man that owns the property for sale, I was just telling you about".

"You would have to clear out a wagon wide road back up into the hollow. It would have to have 2 creek crossings and up two large hills. You would have to build a walking bridge across each creek crossing in case a flood blocks you in with your wagon. The banks of the creek are too low for a wagon bridge without a lot of cost. But at least you could get across the creek if you were flooded in. So, you would have a lot of work ahead of you".

"How much would you want for the deed to the entrance property", said Rufford thinking all the time he did not mind the work.

"Well how about $10.00 a mile. Just to get back the money that is owed to me. And since you and Nancy are going to get married you can pay me on time if you need to", said Solomon. "We can work that out".

"How many miles is it", said Rufford?

"About 3 or 4 miles", answered Solomon.

"Now here is the rub, this fellow that owns the land for sale is a crook", spoke Solomon. "He has been a crook for a long time. He has a farm on part of the land that has a road front. He has been trying to find a sucker he could sell this back side of his property to. Basically, anyone that buys this land would lose their butt, because there is no way in, or out. He thinks he will be able to charge them a lease to go through his property. Then he will slowly raise the lease price a little at a time. He will want to shake hands on the lease for the in, and out, so nothing is on paper. So, he is selling it cheap to try to catch a sucker. It has got a creek, and a freshwater spring perfect for a house. Now there is a holler, but there is also a lot of good land that can be farmed. Also, there is a lot of lumber to build a house, barn, smoke house, or whatever".

By this time Nancy is dancing for joy. Solomon and Rufford both look at Nancy; she is smiling and dancing.

"Hold on Nancy" said Solomon. "First Rufford has got to go see this fellow, look at the land, and decide if he wants to take this on".

Rufford spoke up and said, "Agreed"! "How many acres is it", ask Rufford?

"About 300 acres you can farm, more than that counting all of it", answered Solomon. "He owns the whole mountain. This part is over the back side of the mountain on the very back side of his property. He never uses it. You would never have to see him" winked Solomon.

"When you go meet him remember he doesn't know that you are aware about the entrance property. Try and talk him down. He will think he can make it up on the lease in and out. Play dumb or say something like you just are assuming he will let you have in, and out, privileges," smiled Solomon.

"I can't set this up for you because he knows I know what he is up to, said Solomon. But this fellow deserves whatever he gets. And you are not doing anything illegal, as a matter of fact you are keeping someone from being cheated. By buying this property you are doing a win for everybody. That is except the crook", smiled Solomon. "What do you think", asked Solomon?

"I think I need to talk to this fellow and look at the property", said Rufford.

"I'll have a neighbor who will take you to his farm, you just say you heard he had some land for sale, but don't say where you heard it", smiled Solomon.

"What is this fellow's name", asked Rufford?

"Oh the man that has got the property"? "Luke Brand," said Solomon.

"I suppose this means I will have to keep an eye on this fellow if I do this", Rufford asked looking at Solomon?

Solomon smiled and said, "Oh, sure he will be mad once he finds out you know me, and you have made a deal for your own entrance, but I checked into you son and I don't think he is anything you can't handle; besides, you will have a whole mountain between you".

"Oh, he doesn't scare me. I was just thinking I do not want to have to kill this fellow if I do not have to. Maybe he will leave me alone", spoke Rufford solemnly. "Anyway, I need the land". "Go ahead and tell your friend to set it up".

About 2 weeks later Rufford met up with Solomon's friend Bill Collins, and they rode up to Luke Brand's farm. As they rode up to the farmhouse Luke Brand came out. He had been expecting them.

After all the introductions and hand shaking was over Luke looked at Rufford and said, "Well Mr. Griffin I hear you want to buy some property. What kind of property are you looking for" ask Luke?

Rufford looked straight into Luke Brand's eyes and noticed that he had that same look in his eyes that the crooks he had to arrest in the past when he was a Ranger used to have.

"Well, Mr. Brand, I would like to buy a chunk of land to have a small farm on and maybe someday start a family. I heard you have got a piece of land for sale. If it is what I am looking for and we can agree on a price I may be interested", said Rufford.

"Well, I got a great piece of land on the back side of my property that I never use and am interested in selling. But I would have to like the person because we would be neighbors. Some of my neighbors are not so friendly, and that is especially important to me", smiled Luke with an evil smile.

"Yes, that would be very important to me also", smiled Rufford right back at Luke.

"Could we take a look at it", ask Rufford.

"Yeah, we have to get on our animals because it is around the other side of the mountain, too far to walk. Let us go", said Luke.

"Let us go", "Is there a road to it" ask Rufford

"No, just a cow path, through the woods", answered Luke.

Rufford was thinking great! Not having to deal with this crook on a daily period because of the distance between the lands.

Bill Collins spoke up and said, "You fellows you don't need me I will leave you two to do business. Have a good day".

"Sure, that would be fine", smiled Luke. Thinking how he did not want Bill mudding up the deal by maybe saying the wrong thing. Also, he did not want another witness even though it would all be put on paper. This way he could imply what he wanted about the entrance to the property.

When Luke was not looking Bill winked at Rufford as if to say, I am on your side.

Just a few minutes later the two men rode off to see the property, as Bill Collins turned his horse back down the road, he and Rufford had come in on.

Rufford and Luke rode along through the woods making their way around and up the mountain. Finally, they were at the top of the mountain and working their way down to a valley/hollow that had a creek running through it. Then they were on the side of the creek that had a flat land that was at the bottom of another hill. Luke showed Rufford a nice freshwater spring and a large area that could be a nice pasture for grazing cattle, with plenty of room for a house, barn, and other buildings. Rufford liked what he saw. He could envision a farm being built here. The spring could be dug out to keep milk cold, in a capped milk bucket or a jug cold and fresh. Now he had to work a deal with Luke to keep him from getting suspicious.

"How much do you want for this land", ask Rufford?

"Well, I am, wantin', to sell this land because I don't really need it and don't use it. So, I am willing to make you a deal", said Luke. "How about $20.00 an acre", smiled Luke.

"How many acres is it", ask Rufford?

"About 500 acres", said Luke.

"Is all of it farmable", ask Rufford? "Where does the line begin and end", Rufford asked very sternly?

"Top of this mountain, all the way to the top of that hill over there", pointed Luke.

"Look Mr. Brand, I am wasting my time and yours, I don't have that kind of money", said Rufford.

"Well how much do you have, son", ask Luke?

"Mister Brand I may have been born at night, but it wasn't last night", Rufford said as he looked at Luke stern. "I heard you had a deal on this land. 200 acres of it I can't even farm," Rufford said as he looked around.

"Well how about $15.00 an acre", asked Luke?

"Can't do it Mr. Brand, 200 acres I can't even farm", spoke Rufford in a firm voice.

"We might as well go", said Rufford as he turned and started walking toward his horse.

Both got on their horses and began to ride back across the creek and up over and around the mountain. Both rode in quiet, without saying a word.

Once they arrived back at Luke Brand's farmhouse Luke spoke up and said,

"Rufford I really want to sell that property to you, how about$10.00 an acre, and that is my final offer", said Luke.

"I tell you, I would like to buy the property but I can't go that much" spoke Rufford in a straight voice.

Well, I can't go any lower than $10.00 an acre, snapped Luke!

"Also how am I gonna get in, and out, to the land", replied Rufford.

"Well, we can work a deal for a lease for you to get in, and out. Like a wagon trail, say $5.00 a month lease", said Luke. "We will shake hands on the lease for $5.00 a month. You got my word it is as good as gold", smiled Luke.

"Well, here is the best I can do, I will give you $3.00 a month on the right of way in and out and I will give you $10.00 an acre for the 300 acres that I can farm, and you throw in the 200 acres of hill land that no one wants, or cannot use, for free. Now that is my last offer. Take it, or I get on my horse, and ride out", said Rufford. "Take It, or leave it", Rufford said at the same time turning his head away.

"Let me see that would be $3000.00, do you have that much", ask Luke with his mouth getting wet as he thought of the $3,000.00. "Would that be cash", he asks?

"Yes sir, we meet at the Estill County Bank in Irvine and draw up the papers, and the deal will be done. But I expect you to give me a one-month free lease so I can build a wagon trail in"! "OK", ask Rufford?

You're a hard man to deal with Rufford", said Luke. "But it's a deal", Luke said with a grin! "I'll meet you at the bank in Irvine at 9:00 in the morning".

"Deal" said Rufford! "But we will of course have to get a surveyor to survey the land we have agreed on, and we will walk it with him. And the deal can be done the next day after that at the bank. I think the surveyor that the bank uses will be fine". "Do you agree", ask Rufford?

"Agreed", said Luke!

04. 1902-RUFFORD GRIFFIN BUYS THE HOLLOW AND BUILDS A HOUSE.

The next week Rufford and Luke placed the wooden steaks with the surveyor on the land and the survey was completed and done by the end of the week.

Rufford and the surveyor met Luke at the bank in Irvine with the survey papers the next day after the completion of the survey. The banker helped them draw up the papers and once it was notarized, Rufford paid Luke, and was given a free and clear deed to his land.

The next week Rufford began to cut timber from the land that supposedly no one wanted. This was to build Nancy and his house, a barn, a smokehouse for smoking meat, and a workhouse. Not to mention a two hole outhouse. Rufford had decided on the spot where to put his house. It was right next to a spot where you could walk out on a big flat stone and stand looking out over the hollow, and down toward the creek. The creek was a long downhill walk from the place where the house would sit. That way Rufford thought he would not have to worry about the creek flooding the house. The mountain spring was just up a path a short way from house for convenience. Rufford decided to dig it out so he could dig a small dipping pond for filling up water buckets while he was working and to carry back to the house once the house was built. Also, because the water was very cool coming out of the mountain you could store milk in the cool spring in a closed container with a lid on it overnight for next day use. Everybody liked cool milk better than warm milk and the milk would last longer.

Rufford could imagine where the smoke house, and workhouse would be in a triangle from the house around the yard, which he would clear before he began to build. The barn would be a distance from the house the other direction from the house as to where the spring was. This was to keep from smelling the animals and contaminating the spring water. And the hogs in the hog pin that he would slaughter for meat once a year was down by the barn away from the spring. He would build the outhouse on the side of a hill lower than the spring and away from the other buildings for privacy, and so the rain would wash away some of the waste.

Finally, after Rufford had it all figured in his mind, Rufford started on the house by digging out a cellar for storing canned goods. This is where he would stay for now with a tarp over it to keep the rain out until it was dried in. Then he built the house right over the cellar where you could enter the cellar from the lowest floor of the house. The house was built on a hill. The second floor was even with the ground at the back entrance of the house. The front entrance of the house, or first floor was about 3 feet off the ground at the front entrance of the house. It ended up being a 5-room house with 3 large bedrooms, and a cellar. The largest room on the second floor was a combination bedroom and living room. Then there were 2 more bedrooms on the second floor. The kitchen, and dining area was on the first floor. The kitchen had a large iron wood stove to cook on, with a biscuit warmer on top. This warmed the whole downstairs. The second floor had a big pot belly stove in the center of the combination, living room and bedroom. This kept the house toasty when both stoves were heated up in the winter. For lighting they would use kerosene lamps at night. In the daytime there was plenty of light through the windows, if it was not a dreary day.

Rufford wanted a place to keep his horse so he began to build a barn at one end of the property with a corral. He had intentions of also getting a milk cow and some hogs later on when he had time to take care of them. After the barn he realized if he was going to marry Nancy, he was going to need an outhouse. Men could go about anywhere but women needed an outhouse. That would be his next project. The workhouse and smoke house could wait. He would build them like a frontier building and less fancy than the house. More like the barn. But the house had to be nice for a woman like the houses in town were. With wallpaper and such. But Nancy will decide the color and such.

05. 1902-RUFFORD RUNS AWAY WITH NANCY TO GET MARRIED.

Rufford finally had everything in place to go ask Solomon if he could marry Nancy. When Rufford got to the Sparks farm he asked Solomon if he could talk to him in private. Solomon took him into the big room used for what we call now a days a living room.

"Mr. Sparks I have come to ask you for Nancy's hand in marriage," said Rufford as bold as he could. "I have land with your help," he smiled, and I have built a farm with a house, a barn, a smoke house, and a workhouse. I believe it is a place where Nancy and me can be happy and raise a family".

"Do you love her Rufford" ask Solomon?

"Yes sir," exclaimed Rufford?

"Do you believe she loves you", ask Solomon once again?

"Yes sir", said Rufford with a puzzled look on his face. "You can ask her, sir," said Rufford, very confused.

"Rufford you will take good care of her and never hit her, right", ask Solomon?

"Of course, Mr. Sparks", explained Rufford. He thought there would be no problem since he had done everything Solomon had mentioned since they had last talked. Rufford explained, "Sir you can come and see my property, and see for sure that I have a good place for Nancy, and I will never hurt her. I want only the best for her".

"Rufford there is a problem; her mother thinks she is too young and should finish school before she gets married. She is afraid that as a young girl she might change her mind", explained Solomon.

"Sir I have done everything that was asked of me, because I love Nancy and want to build a life with her. Also, she tells me she wants to build a life with me, now I find out that there is a wrench put into the plans, I am terribly upset sir", snapped Rufford.

"Rufford, I am sorry nothing has changed. But you have got to give me time to convince Mrs. Sparks. Son I have got to live with the woman. I never thought there would be a problem, seeing as how this is the way things have been handled for years past", explained Solomon.

"Sir I can understand your problem, but it is your problem, the problem should not be mine", snapped Rufford.

"Well, Rufford, it seems as so, it is your problem if you want Nancy's parents' blessing over this marriage. Give me some more time son, to bring her around", begged Solomon in a stern voice.

Rufford turned and stomped out, without saying a word.

Solomon whispered under his breath, "Young people are so impatient"!

Rufford got up on his horse to ride away. He had only got to the entrance of the farm at the big road, when he heard a voice calling "Rufford, Rufford, wait"! It was Nancy running after him. "Rufford where are you going", asked Nancy?

"I am going home, your dad, or rather, your mother won't let us get married", explained Rufford.

"Well, are you giving up on me that easy", asked Nancy with tears welling up in her eyes?

Rufford jumped down off his horse, "Oh no, Nancy I couldn't, and would never give up on you" he said as he took Nancy in his arms and kissed her for the first time by the road.

"Well then take me home with you", she stated.

"Nancy you know I would take you in a minute, but ONLY as my wife. I love you way too much, to not make an honest woman of you. And your folks are saying No", spoke Rufford.!

"Rufford can't we get married without them", ask Nancy?

"Not in this county, without your daddy's signature", spoke Rufford.

"Is this the only county we can get married in", ask Nancy?

"Well,", thought Rufford out loud. "I do know where we can get married in another county. Over in Jackson County, that is where my folks live. There is a Justice of the Peace who owes me a favor over there".

"Well let's go" smiled Nancy. Rufford climbed back on his horse, studied for a second, cocked his head and then Rufford looked at Nancy and asked, "Are you sure you want to go against your folks"?

"Rufford, I want to be with you, that is, if you want to be with me" spoke Nancy softly. "And, since we can't go back to daddy, and mommy's house, I would need to get some clothes at a store to last until I can come back and get some of my things."

"Ok", said Rufford, "let us elope! Climb up here and let us go get married"!

Nancy climbed up behind Rufford on his horse, and the two of them rode away to Jackson County Kentucky and got married that night.

Then Rufford took Nancy to the hollow for their Honeymoon and the beginning of their new life together. After Rufford had taken Nancy up to the farm in the hollow Nancy was so incredibly happy. She loved everything about the hollow farm. She picked blackberries, and began to can jams, and jellies, and put them in the cellar that Rufford had made under the house. She put up wallpaper to make the place her own just as Rufford had planned she would. Rufford bought a cow, and they had fresh milk, and Nancy would churn butter. He also bought a rooster, and several hens to furnish eggs, and meat for the table. They also bought a sow and boar hog to raise pigs. They would butcher them and hang meat in the smoke house for smoked hams. When planting season came Rufford started planting some crops. Nancy also started a small vegetable garden behind the house. She had sweet corn, turnips, green beans, potatoes, carrots, etc. Life was so very wonderful for the newlyweds.

But Nancy still missed her mom and dad. They were still angry for her running away to get married. Although Rufford and Nancy had tried to talk to them they were still angry, but Rufford and Nancy felt they would eventually come around after they got over being angry.

06. 1907- RUFFORD THROWS AN AXE AT THE NEIGHBOR.

About 5 years had passed Rufford and Nancy had mended fences with Solomon and Sarah. Maybe manly because Nancy had given birth to 2 children and they wanted to be able to see their grandchildren.

Rufford had a couple of arguments with Luke Brand, the man that had sold him the hollow. But mainly the arguments had been mostly because Luke Brand had thought he would be getting lease money from Rufford for a wagon trail leased right-of way in, and out, of the property he had sold Rufford. But Solomon had gone behind his back, and sold Rufford the property in, and out of, the hollow that he had gotten from Green Roberts. The same side of the mountain where Rufford Property was. This was all on the other side of the mountain from Luke Brands property. Luke felt cheated, when in fact he was trying to cheat Rufford. Luke did not even know that Rufford knew Solomon Sparks or that Solomon had got the right of way, property from Green Roberts until after the deal was made and it was too late to do anything about it. So, Luke had a grudge with Solomon, Green Roberts, and Rufford Griffin, even though they were neighbors. But they did not see each other very often. And the thing that bothered Rufford the most was that Luke from time to time was cutting lumber on property that was on Rufford's side of the line. But so far Rufford had not been able to catch him at it.

Rufford and Nancy had just come outside of the house after eating a noon day meal. It was on a nice Sunday afternoon.

Rufford was smoking his pipe when he looked at Nancy and said, "Hold It, Mama, listen"! Off in the distance you could barely hear, chop, and chop, of an axe echoing across the valley. Rufford with a mad look on his face, cocked his head to listen and said, "Mama, that Son of a Bitch is choppin' wood on my property across the creek toward the top of the hill", snarled Rufford.

"Aww, don't worry about him Daddy", said Nancy.

"Mama if I don't do something about it, he will keep on till we ain't got no more lumber", snapped Rufford.

"Well, what are you gonna do", asked Nancy?

"I am gonna go over there and stop him", said Rufford. As he headed out, he looked back and said, "I'll be back in a while. I am gonna put a stop to this. It's also against the law"!!

"You be careful", called Nancy after him.

Rufford just shook his head OK as he was walking. Rufford and Nancy's house was in a valley between two Kentucky Mountains covered with a Forest of trees. The axe sounds were coming from the opposite side of the valley where the creek ran, at almost the top of the mountain. So Rufford had to walk down to the creek, cross it, and then walk up to the top of the mountain on the other side of the valley. Rufford was being incredibly quiet through the trees.

Finally, Rufford came to the area where he was hearing the axe sounds.

"What the hell you doing choppin' trees on my property", shouted Rufford?

Luke was startled in med swing and dropped the axe. As he turned to see who it was he backed up.

Luke looked at Rufford and lied, "I'm not cutting on your property. The property line is 30 yards further down the hill".

Luke was backing further up toward the mountain top all the time. He had heard about Rufford's reputation as a stand his ground no nonsense man. He had also heard that he had killed a man when he was a Texas Ranger lawman.

"Like hell it is", snapped Rufford. "Luke you know good and damn well I had this land surveyed before I bought it" glared Rufford. "The surveyor walked the property line with me and you. And, right back, over there, is one of his markers. You are 40 yards over my property line. You got several trees fallen here and you are planning on coming back and dragging them out with your mules. You are a lying son of a bitch".

"Like hell I am", snapped Luke backing up all the time! "You're the lying son of a bitch. You cheated me. You were supposed to give me lease money for a right of way in, and out, of this property"!

Rufford said, "Yeah you thought you would cheat me by selling me a piece of land without an in, and out, and I was able to buy a right of way from a neighbor! So why would I want to pay a stinking lease"? "You're just angry because I got the best of your deal", continued Rufford staring straight at Luke without blinking.

"Well, you're the cheating, lying, son-of-a- bitch", shouted Luke still backing up as he reached down and picked up a spear size tree limb. Then he pitched the tree limb at Rufford, but Rufford sidestepped the spear. This was the wrong thing to do. This only made Rufford angrier. Rufford reached down and picked up the axe Luke had dropped.

Rufford shouted "You call me a son of a bitch, a cheater, why I'll chop your fucking head off, and leave you right here"!

Rufford began to chase Luke with the axe in hand. Luke began to run back toward his land. Rufford noticed that Luke had made it back to his side of the property line. So Rufford stopped running and threw the axe at Luke. It missed and stuck in a tree right beside his head.

Luke turned and shouted at Rufford, "I'm going' to get my shotgun"!

Rufford shouted back, "OK, I'll go get my shotgun and meet you back here, you son of a bitch"!

Luke disappeared over the top of the mountain, and into the trees.

Rufford was so mad he went down the mountain at almost a run dodging trees and limbs. The thorns were scratching him but Rufford kept going. Down the mountain he went, splashing across the creek, and back up the hill to his house. By the time Rufford got to the house he was bleeding from thorn scratches, covered in sweat, and wet up to his knees. He went into the house and got down his Remington, double barrel shotgun. He put his hunting bag over one shoulder. He took out 2 shells from a box of shells and loaded the shotgun. Then he poured the rest of the box of shells into the hunting bag and headed for the door.

Nancy asks him, "Daddy, what's going on and where are you going"'?

"That son of a bitch called me out, mama", snapped Rufford!

"Who", shouted Nancy?

"Luke Brand! That tree stealing son of a bitch", shouted Rufford! Out the door he went.

"Daddy be careful", called out Nancy from the back door! The back door everyone used as the main door because it was only one step higher than the ground. The front door was about 3 or 4 steps off the ground. This was because the house was built on the side of a hill, but still level. Nancy walked out into the yard and watched Rufford till he was out of sight. She had never seen him this angry. Even with the drunken man at the barn dance when they first met.

Rufford went back to the top of the mountain and sat there on a stump with his shotgun across his legs, listening for every sound, bird, squirrel, and cricket until past dark. He was waiting for Luke to return. Luke never came back! Luke also never stole lumber, or anything else from Rufford again. Most people agree that by not coming back, Luke had most likely, saved his own life. The axe that Rufford threw at Luke stayed where it was stuck in the tree for over 15 years after that. When asked why he didn't take it down, Rufford just answered, "It's not mine, and it's not on my land". Then he would grin and say, "Guess the owner doesn't want to come back after it"!

07. 1917-RUFFORD GRIFFIN GOES TO TOWN AND FINDS OUT WORLD WAR 1 HAS BROKEN OUT.

In 1916 Rufford and Nancy had pretty much settled into their country way of life up in the hollow. The farm had been doing well. Both Rufford and Nancy had been doing well and were incredibly happy. They had 5 children at the time.

Here is the order they had been born up to this time:

Ellen Griffin	bd-3/05/1903-would have been about 14 years old, she later dies 11/24/1918-at the age of 15 years old
Cleona Griffin	bd-9/06/1905-was 12 years old.
Providence Griffin	bd-11/11/1907-was 10 years old
Grant Griffin	bd-12/12/1910-was 07 years old
Solomon Griffin	bd-9/02/1915-was 02 years old

Rufford had some fellows that worked part time for him on the farm. It was getting into fall and most of the farm work was done, and crops were stored. There still were some crops that needed to be taken to market. So Rufford had still not let the farm help go for the season. He was looking forward to the children getting to be old enough to do some work around the place and maybe not have to put out money for farm help. The two older girls helped around the house with chores and did do a few small things around the barn and such. But couldn't do much hard man work although if you had asked them, I'm sure they would have disagreed. Rufford hoped he would have boys first, but as it turned out some of the girls came first and the boys were still too young to help much. Rufford loved all his children but thought like a farmer of the old days. Sons could help more around the farm. The girls that were old enough were ready to go back to school. Which Rufford thought for a girl was just plane nonsense. After all he was not able to read and write very well. Oh, he could read a wanted poster, or simple stuff, but anything difficult he would have Nancy look at it or a law person. Sense Nancy could read, she insisted that all her children at least learn to read and write. So Rufford agreed, with the insisting of Nancy, for all the children to go to grade school.

Rufford was not a highly educated man, but by no means was he dumb. He had a lot of common sense. Also, Rufford was a very patriotic man. He believed in his country, the United States, and his patriotic duty. As also did Nancy.

I remember Grandma Griffin was very patriotic (this was long after Grandpa Rufford had died, he died when I was not quite two years old.) and she came to stay with Mom (Daisy Griffin, Flatt) and Dad (Joe Allen Flatt) one summer in Ohio. Grandma did not have a television at home (or even electricity), but we had a black & white console TV. The President of the United States (I believe it was John F. Kennedy at the time) came on the TV to give a *fellow* talk, He said, "My Americans", and immediately Grandma Griffin stopped her chores she was doing, and stood at attention, and made all us children hush until the president was done talking. She said, "Listen children, we may be going to war"!

Back to the story about Rufford and World War 1.

Rufford went to town to sell some of his crops. Once he got to the town of Irvine, Kentucky in Estill County, he found out that World War 1 had broken out. Everybody was talking about the World War that was raging in Europe. There were so many countries involved. A lot of people were afraid it would cross the ocean and end up on American soil. Rufford heard that war was raging, and it was especially important to stop the Kaiser from taking over countries before he tried to take over land in the United States. So Rufford felt time was very urgent to stop the German Kaiser right away. And Rufford did not believe in anybody doing his fighting for him. Rufford sent money and a verbal message back to the hollow by a trusted friend.

The message was simply "Gone to fight the German Kaiser, be home as soon as I can. If we do not stop him, he will be here next".

He then went and joined the army to go fight. Rufford was gone for almost a year. Nancy had heard nothing from him. She did not know if he was alive or dead. Grandpa was too proud to ask someone to write a letter for him because he would have to admit that he could not read and write.

A year later after being gone to fight, Rufford would not talk much about the war, but from what has been told he fought in Somme, France in the trenches. Rufford would only say he got as much from the Germans as he gave. He said they were good fighters. Best he had ever fought against.

But when Rufford finally did come back, Grandma Nancy would not let him move back in the house. Grandma Nancy made him court her for 4 months before she would let him move back home. Rufford would come with hat in hand and take Grandma Nancy out on a date just like he was a boyfriend, and she was his girlfriend. It was funny because they had five children at the time. This goes to show you how much respect and love Rufford had for Nancy. Rufford was a strong big man, and Nancy was a small woman. But what she said was the law for him and his children. Rufford also promised Nancy he would never leave again without talking to her first. Not long after Nancy allowed Rufford to come back home, Nancy found out she was pregnant with my Aunt Emma.

Then Ellen became extremely sick and died in November 1918. Rufford and Nancy were devastated that they had to bury their oldest child. I am not sure what she died of, maybe Smallpox? I am not sure!

08. 1923-JOE ALLEN FLATT IS BORN.

It was February 17, 1923 in central Kentucky. There was a coal oil lantern giving off just enough light so the old country midwife could see to deliver the baby that was about to be delivered on the wooden kitchen table. The baby's head was crowning. But the old woman was worried about the health of the mother. The mother was trying to bring into this world the youngest of 3 children. But it had not been, and was not being, an easy birth. The old mid wife knew something was not right.

With encouragement from the old woman, one last sharp contraction, and one final push, the young mother cried out in pain as the baby was pushed out onto the table. The old woman slapped the newborn on the behind and the baby gasped his first breath. The baby began to cry with strong loud lungs. The child is born. It is a boy.

The old woman begins to clean the child off with towels that had been set aside for the occasion. She wraps him in a new baby blanket that Mattie, the mother, had stitched by her own hand, just as soon as she found out that she was expecting. The old woman smiles a big smile at the baby boy as she lays the child next to the mother's breast. The child begins to suck. It is a boy! This will be Mattie's second boy and 3rd child.

But the old woman who was filled with joy suddenly became alarmed. There is too much blood, she thinks to herself. She begins to wipe with more towels. But the blood will not stop!

"God help us," the old mid wife speaks softly as she tries in vain to stop the flow of blood.

The mother in her weakness asks, "Is it a boy"?

"Yes Mattie, it is", speaks the old woman in a dry tone.

The weakened mother says "Then he will be Joe! Joe Allen, Joe Allen Flatt", whispers the very tired and weak Mattie. Then she noticed the worried look on the mid wife's face. "What is the matter", Maddie says above a whisper to the old woman?

The old woman has a look in her eyes of despair and helplessness. "I can't stop the blood honey", says the old woman with a break in her voice. "I get it stopped, and then it starts again," she says more to herself than to the weak mother. Mattie asks with a whisper, "is the baby bleeding"? Then she loses consciousness.

Through the days and nights that follow the old woman can get the flow of blood to slow, but then it will start again. The mother begins to fade, going in and out of consciousness, getting weaker with each passing day. This goes on for several days and nights. Then the day arrives Little Joe Allen is left on this earth without a mother. He has been alive just nine days. So, things started out for Little Joe Flatt kind of ruff!

On February 26th, 1923 Mattie L. Grider, Garner, Flatt passed away due to complications of childbirth. Just 9 days after the birth of her 3rd child and 2nd son, Joe Allen Flatt.

My Aunt, Noreen Garner, later married a man with the last name Carter, was Mattie's first child, by another husband named Garner. I am not sure what happened to Mr. Garner, I assumed he died before meeting Francis Flatt. Not many people got divorced in those days. My how things have changed now a days!

Orlie was Mattie's second child, but her first child by Frances Flatt. Joe was her 3rd child, and second child by Frances Flatt.

FYI-My Dad (Joe Allen Flatt) had 2 half-sisters that were no kin at all. My Dad's first half-sister, Aunt Noreen Garner, (who my sister, Rita Noreen Flatt was named after), was born by Mr. Garner to Mattie. The second half sister (Aunt Geneva) was born to Frances Flatt, and his second wife. Grandma Pearl Flatt-not sure what her maiden name was. I am not sure that my half-aunts even ever met each other, but most likely did, sometime, somewhere along the way.

Grandpa Francis (Frank) Flatt, the newborn baby's daddy stood on the old front porch of the small wood tenant house. The funeral was over. He had seen to it that Mattie received as decent a burial as he could afford. Mattie had been laid to rest, buried in the Flatt Family cemetery, in Creoles Burl, Kentucky. Francis was slim, not an excessively big man, about 5'9". He wore Sears and Roebuck, bib overalls, and a fedora hat most anytime he was awake, or not eating. Almost black hair stuck out from under the front of the old fedora hat. He wore dirty black construction boots that stuck out the legs of the blue jean bib overalls. How would he be able to take care of an infant and still work, he thought?

Noreen was 5 years old. Orlie, the first child of Mattie, and Francis, was out of diapers and 3 years old. Frances could get a babysitter for the other 2 children, in the daytime while he was at work. But a baby, ask Frank to himself? How would he ever work and take care of a baby? He was not sure he could even take care of a baby, by himself anyway. Mattie had always taken care of the house and children. Let alone how would he work and make a living on the oil wells around the area? He could get the children sent off to the babysitter and then go to the oil rig till supper time. But how would he take care of baby Joe? Finding someone to watch him in the day would not be easy, let alone at night. He could not afford to give up the job, because people were having trouble finding jobs at this time. The economy was going down, and jobs were hard to find. It did not pay much, but at least it was a job to put food on the table, clothes on their back, and a roof over their head. What was he going to do with "baby Joe"??

As Frank stood on the old front porch smoking his pipe, walking back and forth, thinking about the situation he was in. What was he going to do? Then a thought came into his head. Maybe he could get Will, and Deelee Grider to take care of Joe for a while. Hmmm! Maybe just until he started school. Will Grider was Mattie's brother. Will and Deelee had kids! None of them were babies. Maybe they could handle one more? And after all we are family, by marriage. Tomorrow he would ride his mule over to Willow Grove, TN. and talk to Will and Deelee. See if they would take "Little Joe" in for a while. Frank knew he would be taken good care of, if Will, and Deelee would take him. They could do better for him, much better than he could do.

And of course, he thought, I will even mail over some money to help with food and clothing. Yes, that is what he would do. It sounded like a good plan. Deelee would be sure to like having a baby around. As a matter of fact, he thought, I will take Joe with me. The weather is mild for February and if she lays eyes on him it will be harder for them to say "no". She will see what a pretty baby he is. Also, if they say yes, I can leave Joe with them. I need to get back to work anyway. The boss had said he could have off as much as he needed, but it is without pay.

The next morning Frank hitched up his old mule, wrapped baby Joe in a warm blanket. He had been given an army nap sack with straps that he could hang baby Joe on his chest. He would be safe and warm.

Frank tied a bag of supplies on to the saddle and headed toward northern middle Tennessee. Just across the border of Kentucky there was a small town called Willow Grove. Willow Grove, Tennessee was about 36 miles across the Tennessee/Kentucky border, part of the Dale Hollow Dam Project that would later take place. Phones were not very plentiful in those days so Will and Deelee had not an idea that Frank was on his way with the surprise he held to his chest in the nap sack.

The sun was just going down behind the hills when Frank, baby Joe, and the mule arrived. The winter days did not last long, and he had to stop several times during the day to give baby Joe a break. He had been lucky to find places he could get some warm milk along the way. They arrive with a clop, clop, clop into the edge of Willow Grove's only brick street. But Will and Deelee's rented farm was just about 3 or 4 more miles outside of the other side of town. It would be past supper time before they reached the small farmhouse. So, if there was an eating place open in town, Frank thought maybe him, and Joe would stop and get something to eat. Little Joe had liked the clopping, and swaying of the mule ride, but the child had become restless in the last half hour since they had stopped for a break. So, a diaper change, some milk, and some supper would be good. If the diner was still open, he thought. As he got closer, he could tell the small dining hall was dark. He thought to himself, no lights on, the diner is closed. He sighed to himself, "Oh well"!

An old man using a walking cane was just walking down the side of the country street, just as Frank rode up in front of the dinner.

"Hey, mister! Where could I get some milk and something hot to eat"? "My son and I have been traveling for a while".

"Well, the diner is closed" said the old man as he stopped and scratched his head".

Frank could not help but smile a little. It was not hard to tell the diner was closed.

"There's a bar down the street where you may be able to get a bowl of chili, but I don't know about the milk". "They may have some," he said. "But Mister it is a rough old saloon, I don't know if you would want to take your son in there".

Then Joe began to whimper. "How rough", said Frank? "We're awful hungry"!

"Well, I have heard the Farmer Brothers hang out in there and will rob their own grandmother if they think there is a dollar in it". "Be careful if you go in there," said the old gentleman.

"Thanks for the warning and the information", smiled Frank. "Where did you say it was at"?

The old gentleman warned, "be careful sonny" as he pointed south with his cane down the street. Frank looked down the direction he pointed. "Have a good evening sir", Frank said as he tipped his hat and looked for a second time down the street.

"Well come on mule, we'll take a look before we decide".

As the mule clopped, clopped down the brick street an old store with a porch came into view. It had been turned into a tavern. Frank noticed a light inside and a beer sign you could hardly read in the dim light. Well, it did not look too bad, he thought. Just then Joe began to whimper, again. Joe needed to be changed and he needed something to eat. So, Frank decided to give it a try. He turned the mule into the side of the street. A few people were driving those new horseless carriages, but there were still hitching posts around. There was a water trough, and the mule began to drink right away. Frank got down off the mule and tied him up to the hitching post. Francis reached into the bag he had tied to the saddle and pulled out a blue Smith & Wesson 38 caliber, six shot revolver. After checking to make sure it was loaded, he stuck it in his right front pocket, and pulled his wool navy peacoat down over it. Well, just in case, thought Francis. He reached again into the bag and got out another smaller bag, and inside he pulled out a glass baby bottle wrapped in a clean cloth diaper.

"Well Joe, let's go get something to eat". "Huh"? "And get you changed," he said looking down at the army nap shack and baby Joe.

Frank walked through the front door of the old tavern, just as a big, bald, fat man was beginning to wipe off the bar. Frank, then slowly uncovered baby Joe's head that was covered by the blanket. In the center of the bar room there was a big pot bellied stove. It still had a red glow from the heat of the fire. Over in the corner there were 3 unpleasant looking men playing a card game. Everyone stopped what they were doing and gave Frank, and the baby Joe, a callous look. Frank thought to himself, they do not see many strangers coming in this bar, especially holding a baby.

"Howdy, folks"! Frank said turning to everyone in the room with a smile. "My son, and me, have been traveling for quite a while, I was wondering if you had some milk, and something to eat that I could purchase" Frank asks toward the bartender? The bartender spoke up and said, "Yea I can get you some milk". Do you have a bottle"? Sure, do said Frank as he stepped toward the bar and placed baby Joe and the knapsack on the bar.

Frank then unwrapped the bottle from the extra diapers. As he handed the bottle to the bartender, the bartender said "Whey! You need to change that baby". He waved his hand in front of his face as if to wave away the smell.

"Yea, which was another thing I stopped in for" smiled Frank. "If you don't mind, I'll change him over here away from everybody".

"Well, I will go warm some milk and fill the bottle". "Will a bowl of chili and some crackers do for you," smiled the bartender? "I think I got some sweet tea left too".

"That would be great" said Francis with a smile in return.

"I'll get it while you change the baby", said the bartender as he started for the back. "Be right back".

Frank took baby Joe over to a table in the far corner of the bar room away from the men playing cards and began to change baby Joe.

The bartender came back with the baby bottle of milk just as Frank finished changing baby Joe and said, "The chili will be out in just a minute".

"Thanks for your kindness, said Frank as he fed baby Joe.

When Frank was finished feeding and rocking baby Joe the bartender came back with a nice big bowl of chili on a plate surrounded by crackers and a big glass of sweet tea. "Enjoy," said the bartender. Frank sat there at the table rocking baby Joe on his shoulder with one hand and eating the chili, crackers, and drinking the sweet tea with the other. Just as Frank was finishing the chili, crackers, and tea, baby Joe had fallen asleep.

"How much do I owe you," said Frank to the bartender? "5 cents for the milk and 15 cents for chili should do it, forget the tea" spoke the bartender. "I make that for myself anyway." Frank paid the 20 cents for the meal and thanked the bartender again. Francis had walked back over to the bar. as he covered baby Joe with the blanket and placed him back in the nape sack. Strapping Joe and the nap sack once again to his chest he turned toward the door.

As Frank started to leave one of the men from over at the card table came across the room, spoke up and said, "Hold it"! "You didn't pay your bill, mother dear"!

Frank turned to look at the bartender and could tell the bartender was looking extremely nervous.

"Yea, I paid him the twenty cents for the food," said Frank.

"No, you don't understand, you owe us money, mommy". "You owe us $10.00", said the hard looking man as he walked toward Frank about halfway before stopping.

"What do I owe you $10.00 for," said Frank?

"Well, mommy you owe us for having to smell baby shit, or we're going to take it out of your ass."

"You know what I mean"? he said as the other men began to snicker and laugh.

"Hum"! "Hum"! "Hum"! he said as he made hunching motions.

"Look I don't want any trouble", said Frank. "We just stopped in for some food".

"Well, then sweetie pie, you better come up with 10 bucks"! "Or else"! The man looked dead cold at Frank.

"Else what," said Frank?

"Else we are going to take it out in trade". "All three of us," he said as they all laughed.

"Farmer you need to leave this stranger alone", said the bartender nervously as he came out from behind the bar.

Just then the hard man, who had been doing the talking, knocked him to the floor with his fist. Just then the other two men jumped up and began to kick him as he lay on the floor. After kicking the bartender, the other two men then turned their attention toward Francis. Stepping up right behind their brother.

"Well, what's it going to be" said the hard looking man that was doing the talking? "10 bucks or else"! Then he reached inside his coat and pulled out a bowie knife. "I still can smell that stinking baby shit". "My brothers are going to hold you while we take turns with you". "Now you got the $10.00 or not".

"How do I know you are going to let me, and my son go if I give you $10.00", said Frank as calm as an undertaker.

"You don't," said the lead faced man with a grimace.

"Ok," said Frank, "it is in my pocket". "I'll get it". "Just don't hurt my boy", Frank whimpered.

Francis reached into his right front pocket. In one smooth move Frank pulled his Smith & Wesson revolver out of his pocket and fired. The nasty man with the knife was struck right between the eyes. He fired a second shot which struck the 2nd man in the thigh of the right leg. He went down with a surprised look on his face. By this time baby Joe was awake and screaming. The 3-rd. shot struck the 3-rd. man dead in the heart, spinning him around till he fell on the floor. By this time, the 2nd man which had been shot in the leg was getting up off the floor where he had grabbed the knife his brother had dropped. He made 2 steps toward Frank and drew the knife back as if to throw it. "You son of a bitch, you shot me," he screamed at Frank. As he drew the knife back to throw it, Frank fired again hitting him in the mouth just below the nose. Down he went in a bundle. Now things were quiet, except for baby Joe's crying.

Frank walked over to where the bartender was lying unconscious. Frank poured some drinking water on him. The bartender came to life.

"What happened," said the bartender looking around at the blood and bodies?

"I had no choice," said Frank. "One of them pulled a knife".

"Are they dead", said the bartender with his eyes wide?

"Yeah, I believe so", calmly said Frank as he replaced the revolver in his pocket.

"Look mister, I am glad they are gone, but they have family all around here". "You take your son and get gone".

"What about the bodies," said Frank?

"I'll take care of them". "You have done me a favor". "Those fellows have had everybody around here on edge for years". "They have been running off my customers for years". "You just get on out of here"! "I'll tell the sheriff it was somebody totally different"! "They got what they deserved"! "It was just a matter of time until they picked on the wrong man" said the bartender! "You take your boy and go"!

Frank covered the head of the crying baby Joe in his blanket, patted him lightly on the behind, turned and slowly walked out of the old country tavern, which was now turned into a bloodbath. He reached up, grabbed the horn on the saddle, put his left foot in the stirrup, and swung up into the saddle. Looking up and down the street from the top of the mule, Frank said "calm down Joe". Then he patted the baby on his behind once again and pulled him to his chest with one hand. Looking up and down the street one last time, Frank said, "Come on mule, let's move on", as they headed slowly south. Clop, Clop, Clop went the mule's hooves on the brick. This would bother Frank for the rest of his life. But he would not talk much about it unless he had a few drinks.

09. 1923-A NEW HOME FOR LITTLE JOE ALLEN FLATT.

Francis Flatt and little Joe Allen Flatt came riding up to the outer edge of Willow Grove, Tennessee after dark. It was late by farmer time, by the time they arrived on the back of the mule to Will and Deelee Girder's farmhouse. Frank climbed down off the back of the mule and patted little Joe on the behind. Joe had now become very restless. "Hold on Joe. We'll have a place to rest in a while", said Frank.

As he walked up on the porch he called out, "Will! Deelee! It is Francis"! Someone must have heard the mule come up because a flicker from a coal oil lamp came on in a front bedroom and moved into the living room. Finally, the front door came open.

Now everybody in the family called Frank, Francis! But in everyday life, on the job he went as Frank. Short for Francis!

"Francis! Lordy! Lordy! What are you doing way down here"? said Will Grider. Deelee called out from inside the house, "Come on in, you'll catch your death in that night air"!

Frank walked into the living room of the four-bedroom country farmhouse.

"Is everything OK? Are you all hungry" ask Deelee?

"No thank you", said Frank. "Me and Joe stopped and ate in Willow Grove", explained Franck!

"Well, something must be pretty important for you to ride all the way down here", said Will. "We hadn't seen you since Mattie's funeral, but you say everything is OK", he asked Francis?

"Well yes, but that can wait until tomorrow if you will put Joe and me up for the night", said Frank. Frances did not want to put too much on them at once. "Can I put my mule in your barn and give him some your oats or grain" ask Frank?

"Of course, you can! I'll change the baby" said Deelee. "I got some clean diapers put away in a dresser somewhere. You put your mule away".

"Need any help! I'll get some boots on" offered Will?

"No! That is OK, you're already for bed, it will not take me long", smiled Frank. "You go on back to bed and we'll talk in the morning" suggested Frank. "Just tell me where you want me and Joe to bed down".

"Just use the back bedroom, there is a baby bed Joe can use, I'll double up the kids in the other bed" said Deelee.

Frank went back outside and took the mule by the bridle. "Come on mule! I guess you are a tired old boy. Bet you're hungry too? Well, we are about to take care of that. You did real good getting Joe and me down here. But you rest because you are gonna get me back. Or, maybe Joe, and me? Don't know what we are gonna do if Will, and Deelee won't help me out with Little Joe for a while", Frank spoke softly to the mule as he was putting him away for the evening.

The next morning just before daylight, Frank heard pots and pans clanging in the kitchen when he woke up, and he smelled bacon cooking. So, Frank got up to take care of Little Joe. But Joe was not in the baby bed. Frank walked through the house looking for Little Joe. When he walked into the kitchen there was Deelee holding Joe on her left chest with one hand and cooking breakfast with the other on an old wood cooking stove.

"Deelee does he need changing", ask Frank?

"No, taken care of, Francis", smiled Deelee. "He has already guzzled down a bottle of milk too," Deelee smiled again.

"I'm sorry Deelee, I guess I was more tired than I thought," apologized Frank. "You want me to take him"?

"No, we're getting along OK," smiled Deelee again while cooking eggs with one hand and patting Joe on the behind with the other.

"Where is Will", ask Frank?

"He is taking care of the stock and getting water," replied Deelee.

"Well, then if you are OK with Joe, I'll go help Will," ask Frank? "That is unless you need some help"?

"No, you go on Francis, I've done this before, and Will could probably use some help. Tell him to bring the water and some more eggs," smiled Deelee once again patting Joe on the behind.

Frank walked out into the farmyard looking for Will. He found him in the barn whistling an ole gospel song.

"Will, good morning, Will"! "Deelee said she wants some water and some more eggs. What do you need help with," ask Frank? "How about I get the water"?

"Well, the buckets are over there Francis, and you know where the pump is. I'll get the eggs, that old roster is a mean son-of-bitch" laughed Will. "We call him "Big Cock", because he thinks he is", laughed Will out loud again. "One of these days I'll kill him and put him in a pot", chuckled Will. "When you come back help me spread some hay in the stalls and feed mine and your mules. When we get done with that breakfast should be ready. I'm hungry as hell", laughed Will.

"Sounds like a plan, but don't kill that son-bitch-roster yet". "Big Cock"! ``laughed Frank almost in a whisper as he picked up the buckets and went off to the pump to get the water.

After Frank got the water and Will got the eggs the two men jumped in together to spread hay in the stalls and feed the mules. Frank was spreading the hay with a pitchfork while Will was throwing hay down from the hay loft. Then they began to talk.

"Francis, my curiosity is getting the best of me", said Will. "What are you doing all the way down here, and with a baby", ask Will? "What is wrong" he asks without stopping his work?

"Well, Will I have a big favor to ask? I was going to talk to you, and Deelee both, at the same time- but here goes. I need some help with Little Joe. I cannot work and take care of a baby at the same time. I love him, but until I can find someone to help, I cannot work, and take care of him too. No one can prepare for the death of a wife, let alone suddenly having a baby child to raise. Noreen, and Orlie are not old enough to take care of themselves, but I can get a babysitter for the daytime for them, until they start school. I will send money, and contribute to his raising-and it would only be for a little while until I can make better arrangements. But I have thought, and thought, and I just do not know what else to do. Can you help me for just a little while"?

Will stopped spreading the hay and was in deep thought.

"Well Francis if you're willing to send some money, one more mouth in our house won't make any difference to me. But you know the final decision will have to be Deelee's. You know that", Will asked? "She is the one who will be most responsible to take care of him".

Frank began nodding his head. "Sure, that is the way I had it figured", answered Frank.

"But you see Will, I am between a rock, and hard place", said Frank.

By this time both men had just about completed their work and were leaning on their pitchforks.

"Yes, I do see Francis. Let us finish up here, go get some breakfast, and you can speak to Deelee and see", said Will.

The men finished up spreading the hay and started for the house just as Deelee came out on the back porch and hollered, "Breakfast is ready"!

Will and Deelee's children had already eaten and gone off to school.

Frank and Will came into the kitchen/dining room and sat down at the table. Breakfast was eggs, gravy, bacon, and country biscuits. Both men were full when they finished eating the breakfast that Deelee had prepared for them.

Deelee was rocking Little Joe in an old country rocking chair, as he was about to doze off.

"Well,", Deelee said "what is this big secret you have to tell us, Francis"? "My curiosity has got the best of me," said Deelee.

"Well, Deelee it's not a secret. Will has already pulled it out of me. I just wanted to ask you something" responded Frank.

Well let me put Joe down, he is asleep, and we will talk, said Deelee with a puzzled look on her face.

After coming back from putting Joe in the baby bed Deelee sat down.

"Well, Deelee I got a really big favor to ask," said Frank. "I need help raising Little Joe. I cannot work and take care of Joe at the same time. I love him, but until I get married again, or can find someone to help, I cannot work and take care of him too. I was not prepared for the death of Mattie, as I am sure none of us were, let alone suddenly having a baby child to raise by myself. Noreen and Orlie are not old enough to take care of themselves, but I can get a babysitter for the daytime until they start school. But to get a babysitter for a child in diapers is not so easy. But Joe must always have adult supervision until he starts school. I can, and will, send money, and contribute to his raising-and it would only be for a little while until I can make other arrangements. But I have thought, and thought, and I just do not know what else to do. Can you, and Will help me for just a little while"?

"Like I said, I will buy food, clothes, diapers, whatever he needs. If you cannot help me, I just don't know what I am gonna do. It would not have to be any longer than when he starts school. Maybe sooner, if I can find a babysitter that will take a child in diapers to help", begged Frank.

"How do you feel about this?" Deelee asked, looking at her husband Will.

'Francis, and I talked about this in the barn, and I told him it would be up to you. If he is going to send money for the things the baby will need, I do not think another mouth is a problem, but you will be the one most involved with taking care of him. So, it is up to you", answered Will.

"As you have seen Deelee, Joe is not a fretful baby" said Frank trying to convince her. "He made the trip down here, and hardly cried".

"Yes, I noticed he is a good baby", said Deelee "and cute as a button". "When do you have to head back", ask Deelee?

"I need to head back tomorrow morning so I can get back to work, and I got a lady watching Noreen and Orlie while I'm gone temporarily", Frank answered.

"Well, you spend the day, and night, relax, and I will make my decision in the morning", said Deelee.

"Come on outside, and bring your pipe Francis", said Will to Frank, "and we'll sit out under the shade tree and smoke".

The two men sat under the shade tree and smoked their pipes.

"Will, do you know some fellows named the Farmer Brothers in Willow Grove?" ask Frank.

"I don't know them, but I have heard about them", answered Will. "I hear they are a real mean family". "Why do you ask Francis", questioned Will?

"I had some trouble with them yesterday evening in Willow Grove", answered Frank.

"What kind of trouble Francis", ask Will?

"Well, I killed 3 of them in self-defense at a bar on my way through Willow Grove yesterday", said Frank without blinking. "One pulled a knife, and it happened so quick I just reacted. I shot him, and then the other 2 came after me. So, I shot them" said Frank staring off in the distance.

"Did you call the sheriff Francis", asked Will?

"No", said Frank. "The bartender said he would take care of it and tell them someone else did it. I was so shaken up, I just took Joe and left. I didn't want to say anything in front of Deelee". "I just stopped in to get something for me, and Joe to eat, and things got way out of hand", explained Frank!

"Well, you might have done the right thing, that family is dangerous, said Will. They will be looking for you. Well, you should probably go around Willow Grove on your way back, and I wouldn't tell anyone else about this if I was you", said Will. "Try just to forget it if you can", cautioned Will.

"I don't know if I can", replied. Frank. "Do you think that bartender will do as he said", ask Frank. "He said he would say someone different did it", added Frank.

"I have bought a jug or two from him, Francis, and he was definitely afraid of them boys, but he is known to do what he says he will do", replied Will. "Who knows", added Will!

"Well Francis once you find out what Deelee is gonna do, I would stay away from this area for a while if I were you. Cause the sheriff will not be able to stop these folks if they find out you did it. They're a mean bunch," said Will.

"Well, do you think the bartender will break under pressure from the family", ask Frank?

"Well, he was afraid of the other 3 men", replied Will. "Who knows"?

The next morning started pretty much the same as the one before. Deelee fixed breakfast and they gathered at the kitchen table for a talk.

"Francis, I have thought about it hard and here is the deal", started out Deelee.

"I am going to take Little Joe to raise because he was Maddie's son. He is family. But only under one condition! You are not going to have me raise that boy, love him, and then get attached to him. Then just show up one day and say I have come to get him! That would break my heart! So here it is! If I take him, then it is for good! You can come see him. And when he is older, you can even come take him to your place for some visits. But this will be his home until he grows up enough to leave on his own. If you cannot agree to this, then you need to figure out something else. Because if I take him, it is gonna be for good to raise him. I will raise him as my own. Now that is my decision. What is your decision"?

Frank thought for a while then said, "Well, I guess I don't have another decision to pick from. If I can visit, and like you said, when he is older, come get him for visits. Then I agree! I know he will be better off here with you and Will. It is agreed! You, and Will, are going to raise him," said Frank trying to fight back the tears.

Frank reached in his wallet and gave Deelee some money. "I'll send some more each time I get paid," said Frank with a big lump in his throat. Frank saddled up his mule, went in, and kissed Little Joe goodbye, and rode away before the tears began to flow.

But Frank took Will's advice and did not go back through Willow Grove. He took the long way around.

Frank kept his promise, and even after he remarried, and had children, Joe Allen Flatt stayed on the farm with Uncle Will, and Aunt Deelee Grider. He would go to visit with his dad, Frank, his new wife Pearl Flatt, and his half-brothers, but he always returned to his real home on Uncle Will and Aunt Deelee's farm.

Joe Allen Flatt loved Uncle Will, and Aunt Deelee, and they loved him. But it bothered him all his life that he never got to know his mother. But he only talked about it when he had too much alcohol to drink.

FRANCES FLATT- in later life.

10. 1924- RUFFORD KILLS A MAN AT A PARTY.

Several years had passed and it was now 1924. Rufford was now 43 years old. Rufford and Nancy had now had 4 more children. This made a total of 9 children. But Ellen had died on November 24,1918. The latest children to be born were:

Emma Griffin	bd-2/24/1918
Etta Griffin	bd-11/30/1920-d-4/23/1990
Anna Marie	bd-7/24/1922-d-2/18/1998
Ben F. Griffin	bd-6/30/1924-d-3/01/1991

Rufford and Nancy had decided to have a party at their house in the hollow. Several people were invited. It was mostly family and good friends. They butchered a pig and there was going to be plenty to eat. Each visitor brought a covered dish. There were a few people that showed up that were not invited. But Rufford and Nancy wanted to be sociable and everything seemed to be OK. There was plenty to eat.

Then there was a man who showed up that was drinking too much. Rufford and Nancy did not want drinking at their home, and they were not serving alcohol drinks. Rufford was turning the pig on a spit over a fire and basting it.

Then Nancy came to him and said, "There is a man drinking inside that is being rude to the women.

Rufford looked at Nancy and asked, "Well now mama is he being rude or is the women just insulted because he is drinking"?

Nancy said, "Well, Rufford he told one of the ladies that he would like to see her panties.

"What do you think", she asked? "He also is being very loud and annoying", she added.

"You met him a long time ago. His name is William Young".

"Where did I meet this William Young", asked Rufford of Nancy?

"You remember the night we met, at the barn dance, the drunken fellow that tried to cut in on you while we were dancing, do you remember", ask Nancy?

Rufford thought back and said, "Oh, yeah, the loudmouth drunk"!

"Well daddy, it's the same loudmouth drunk, snarled Nancy.

"Who invited him", ask Rufford?

"Darn if I know", shrugged Nancy!

Rufford thought kind of out loud to Nancy, "The fellow is most likely just feeling his oats, but I best check it out. Maybe I can get him to settle down. Can you go get someone to watch, and turn this pig for me", ask Rufford of Nancy.

"Yes" said Nancy as she turned to go find someone.

She went and got Green Roberts. He came out, and asked "Rufford you need some help"?

"Yeah, I got a visitor that has had a little too much of the jar", laughed Rufford, "I guess Nancy wants me to see if I can calm him down a little". Rufford laughed again.

"Sure Rufford, what do you need", ask Green? "Watch this pig on this spit for me and keep it turning until I get back", said Rufford. "Should not take long, he's just feeling his corn squeezin', smiled Rufford again.

"Hold it, Rufford", said Green, "If it's the fellow I saw a while ago, he is from over in the next county. I don't know how he ended up here, but I hear he is a bad hombre. A no shit taker, and a starter of trouble. Watch yourself"!

"Yeah, I had some dealings with him once before, a long time ago", said Rufford.

"But thanks for letting me know, I sure will do just that", answered Rufford.

Rufford turned and headed for the house. As Rufford turned and stepped up into the living room of the house, he noticed that everybody was standing around the room facing the man as if he was the center of attention. Rufford knew from his lawman days that before breaking up a fight it was always a good idea to check out the room and see what was going on. The women were all looking at the visitor in disgust, and fear. Rufford noticed the stranger was healthy looking, about 6 feet 2 inches tall, and strong enough to take seriously. Yeah, he was the same fellow from the dance just a little older. He was not sure though that he would have recognized him if Nancy had not reminded him who he was. The fellow had a smile on his face and was telling the whole room what a stud he was.

The stranger smiled and said in a loud voice, "I know all you women want some of this, and I ain't had no pussy in a long, long time.

At this point Nancy stepped forward and said, "Well, William with your manners, I can understand why. That is also why; I am asking you to leave my home at this very moment"!

The stranger turned and looked at Nancy and smiled and said, "Well maybe you would like to go with me"! "Maybe to the barn", he added, "I got enough that I can please you good", he continued with his insults.

At this point Rufford had, had, enough! Rufford stepped toward him and asked, "Sir what is your name"? "My name is William Young", answered the man turning toward Rufford like he was proud.

"Who the hell are you", he asks back at Rufford?

Rufford stepped forward again. "I am the man that owns this house, and property", spoke Rufford in a stern voice without ever taking his eyes off the stranger.

"Well, woopty doo", said the bold man. "Is that supposed to make me scared", shouted the party crasher.

"No sir, that is supposed to make you stop long enough to realize what an ass you are making of yourself in someone else's home", Rufford spoke slowly and sternly.

"Are you calling me an ass", he said looking back at Rufford.

"No sir, my mule has got more sense than to go into someone's home and act the way you are. But you take it any way you want to Mister Young! But one thing is for sure, I am losing my patients with you, and you better leave just as my wife has asked you to. And pretty damn quick", said Rufford, his eyes narrowing, and a blaze!

Rufford had noticed the outline of a small handgun in William's pocket.

"Oh, you're the one that married Nancy, and everybody thinks you're a badass. And you used to be a Texas Ranger", laughed William Young. "And just what if I don't leave", ask the impolite intruder?

"Then I will have to make you leave, but leave you will", spoke Rufford with narrowing, blazing eyes.

"You think you can whip me", smiled the intruder. "I might have a gun hideaway"!

"I most likely could whip you, but for trash like you I will not dirty myself. I know you would not fight fair. I think, I'll just get my shotgun, and by the time I get back you better be gone, I have had enough", snarled Rufford!

Rufford went into the next room and came back out with his double barrel 12 gauge shotgun.

Rufford cocked both barrels and said "Now William Young get the hell out of my house. This makes the third time you have been told". "Also keep your hands away from your pockets", warned Rufford!

William said, "Ok I am leaving, you do not have to get so upset. But I got a gun hid out in the brush and I will be back, then we will see who the chicken shit is"! "Then I'll kill your ass" shouted William!

When he got to the front door it was standing open. He grabbed the door, turned and called out to Rufford,

"Hey Texas Ranger, you're a motherfucking son of a bitch, and you can keep that whore Nancy too"! Then William grabbed the front door of the house which was behind him. Rufford saw him reach for his front pocket where the gun was, and with a big fuck you smile on his face, and a middle finger in the air, he slammed the door to use it as shield.

Rufford would have most likely let him leave if he had not called Nancy a whore and reached into his pocket for the hide away. And, making a threat to kill a man in his own home in those days was not tolerated. But calling the mother of his children a whore in his own house was just too much. Also, reaching into his pocket for the gun Rufford believed he was gonna use the door for a shield and shoot back by opening the door. Understand that men in those days did not even curse in front of women, except in battle with another male. It was considered very, very, rude.

Rufford pulled the trigger on both barrels. BOOM!!!!

The 12-gauge double 00 buck shot blew a hole in the door big enough you could have put both of your fists through.

William Young was blown backward being hit square in the chest.

Rufford was not actually trying to kill Walter, just run him off. So, he shot to the right of the doorknob close to the hinges. Walter had stepped backward right into the line of fire while pulling his pistol. Rufford had double aught (00) buck shot in his shot gun just like most lawmen of those days would use for home protection or going after a bad hombre. That made the shotgun almost a cannon.

Rufford pulled open the door and there lay William. William was gasping for breath with blood running out his mouth. There was some gurgling of blood as he tried to breath. This did not last long. Then he stopped gasping. Rufford knelt down and checked for life. Rufford checked his eyes. They were fixed and dilated. He died without saying another word.

Nancy screamed, "Oh, Rufford you have killed him. What are we going to do"?

Then there was no sign of life. William had been hit square in the left side where the heart was. He still had the small 38 caliber hide away gun in his hand. If he had gone out the door and took one step to leave to the right, he would still be alive. As it was, must have backed up while getting the gun out to make another attempt at coming back through the door.

Green Roberts came running. All the women were crying out loud.

Green told Rufford, "We can bury him here on your property Rufford, and no one will ever know the difference. No one here will say anything".

Rufford said, "No, Green, I have got to take him into the sheriff, and also turn myself in". "I learned a long time ago you can't run from the law", said Rufford sternly!

Rufford carried the body with him on horseback and went to town and turned himself into the sheriff.

At the trial, the door to the house was brought in as evidence, and all the visitors at the party testified as to what happened. Rufford was found guilty of Manslaughter instead o murder, since William was in Rufford's house, and William had a gun in his hand. But, because Rufford shot him through the door, he was guilty of Manslaughter.

After the trial, Rufford did a little over a year in prison for shooting William Young through the door. Although William had a long record with the law, and everybody including the judge said he probably deserved it.

In those days you had to respect another man's home. Now these days Rufford might have got more time. But in those days justice was much swifter and handed out on the spot a lot of times. After all it was unusual that Rufford did not have a gun on him at the time. But William still did not leave even though Rufford, left the room to go get his shotgun and told him so. William could have left then, but he did not. There were a lot of people who thought Rufford got the raw end of the deal, but William Young's family had a little money, and knew people in high places.

The door that Grandpa Griffin shot through was kept up in the attic of the house for many, many years. Even after Grandpa Griffin passed away, and I was just a young boy, the door was in the attic. I guess the door burned up with the house after Grandma sold it years later. Grandma sold the house, and land, to a lumber company, and divided the money among her children. The lumber company rented it out to some hippies. There was a fire, and the house burned down.

11.   1929-DAISY GRIFFIN IS BORN.

The year was 1929 the year of the Great Depression. 5 years had passed since Rufford had killed William Young. Rufford was back home with his family. Rufford and Nancy now had a total of 10 children born to them. Although Ellen had died in 1918, so there were nine.

Here is the order they were born:

Ellen Griffin	bd-03/05/1903 died-11/24/1918
Cleona Griffin	bd-09/06/1905 died-12/12/1964
Providence Griffin	bd-11/11/1907 died-11/29/19??
Grant Griffin	bd-12/12/1910 died-12/27/1948
Solomon Griffin	bd-09/02/1915 died-02/07/1979
Emma Griffin	bd-02/24/1918 died-??/??/????
Etta Griffin	bd-11/30/1920 died-04/23/1990
Anna Marie	bd-07/24/1922 died-02/18/1998
Benjamin F. Griffin	bd-06/30/1924 died-03/01/1991
Daisy Griffin	bd-05/09/1930 died-04/04/2000

Daisy (my mother who later marries Joe Allen Flatt) was the last to be born of the Griffin children of her generation. She also, just like all the rest, was born in the holler at home with one of Nancy's kin helping with the birth. She was born in the holler, at the Griffin farmhouse on, May 09, 1930.

Being the youngest of all the children she was also a beautiful little girl right from the beginning. She was a country gal and not afraid of anything except snakes. She hated and feared snakes of any kind.

Finally, Daisy got old enough to go to school. She loved school. She liked learning about different places and wanted to learn more. And hoped, someday she could travel to some of those places.

Daisy went to a two-room schoolhouse called Doe Creek Elementary School. One room had 1st grade through 4th grade. The other room had 5th grade through the 8th grade. Doe creek Elementary was just like out of the book, and TV show "Little House on the Prairie". The school had outside toilets, and all. Daisy did so well in school that she skipped the 7th grade and went straight from the 6th grade to the 8th grade.

FYI-I went to this same 2 room schoolhouse that my mother went to in the 3rd. grade.

She was so excited when she finished the 8th grade because she would now be going to High School in the 9th grade.

Daisy was growing and became a feisty young girl. She was feisty manly from trying to keep up with her older brother Benjamin Griffin which was 5 years older than her.

By now, it was 1942, and times were still tuff and money was short because of the slow recovery from the depression. Daisy needed new shoes to start High School. Rufford did not have the money, and he was the head of the house. He had kept his promise to Nancy, and all the children had gone to school, and learned to read, and write.

Times were hard, and the only money Rufford had was the money he saved back for seed to plant crops. If he did not use the money for seed, they would not have any crops, and would go hungry the next year.

Daisy was 12 years old, when she had to drop out of school because they didn't have the money for a pair of shoes for winter. So, Daisy stayed home and worked on the farm. When she got older, her and one of her girlfriends began sneaking out at night to go to Irvine, KY the closest town. Of course, Grandpa, and Grandma Griffin did not know about her sneaking out at night. She would always get back before, especially Grandpa, found out she was gone.

Times were extremely hard during the depression. Times never got any better until after World War II was over.

12. 1935-JOE ALLEN FLATT BECOMES "ALL TERMINATE" IN HIGH SCHOOL BASKETBALL.

Joe Allen Flatt was 12 years old when somebody told him he could get drunk if he mixed rubbing alcohol with water, half and half, and drank it. Joe had to go to the store one morning on a Saturday and he had a little money and decided to try it out and see if it would work.

Joe told the storekeeper "Aunt Deelee needs a bottle of rubbing alcohol, how much does it cost"?

The storekeeper reached and got a bottle and said, "It's 3 pennies". Joe reached into his bib overalls and pulled out the 3 cents and gave it to the storekeeper. "Thank you" said the storekeeper as he rang up the register.

Joe left the store and started home. On the way back Joe stopped by a creek, where he poured half of the rubbing alcohol out on the ground. Then he found a small waterfall and ran water in the bottle to fill it back up. Joe then took a big drink. It took his breath away. It was awful tasting stuff. So, he decided to sit under a tree, and drink it slowly, but it tasted so bad. He was getting a buzz, and finally just guzzled it down.

The next thing Joe wakes up under the tree with his mouth full of cotton. He looks around and thinks, where am I at? Then Joe realized where he was, and remembered what had happened. Suddenly, Joe realized it was almost dark. He had been asleep all day long. He realized that he was in big trouble. He had missed lunch, and supper. He was also not supposed to be out after dark. Joe began to try, and run home, but he only staggered home.

Once he got home, he climbed a tree, and went into his bedroom window. His thinking was that he would pretend he was asleep in his room. If they had not looked up there for him, he might get away with it. Joe went down to the front room, and as he entered, he yawned excessively big.

"We hollered for you for supper a little bit ago, you were sleeping' ", said Uncle Will.

"Yeah", said Joe as he yawned again making sure to stay away so they could not smell his breath.

"Well, we done took up the leftovers after hollering several times", said Aunt Deelee.

"I even hollered come and get it, or I'm gonna give it to the pigs", snapped Aunt Deelee!

"I ain't very hungry anyway" said Joe as he yawned big again.

"You getting' sick", ask Aunt Deelee? "You look a little peaked"!

"No," said Joe, realizing that it just might work. "I'm just tired, think I'll go back to bed", answered Joe, as he turned to go back to his bedroom with a smile on his face. This was the first time Joe ever got drunk.

It was July the 4th 1935. Joe had made it through most of his grade school years pretty much the same as any other child. Joe had been a normal kid going to school and working on the farm. His grades had been good, but not great, but he was by no means a dumb child. It was just a matter of getting Joe to apply himself.

His Aunt Deelee, and Uncle Will Grider had been hard on him, but not any harder on him than their own children. He called them pap and mam.

He worked hard on the farm when not going to school. He was slim, tall for his age, a light-haired boy, but his hair was getting darker all the time. He was now a dark brown-haired boy with deep blue eyes. He loved to play basketball, or any sport such as baseball, or horseshoes.

Joe would be starting High School in the fall at Willow Grove High School, and he was planning on joining the basketball team.

Dad told me a story one time when he was loaded on booze, or he maybe would not have told me. But dad liked to tell jokes, so who knows, if it was true?

When Joe turned about 13 years old, he began to think about girls, and sex. But he did not have a girl to have sex with, but he was "Horney", and a country boy!

So, one day Uncle Will told Joe to put away the mare in her stall. She was named "Dolly". Joe was putting away the mare horse into its stall. He noticed the mare was in season. He got the idea that if he could get up high enough, he could have sex with the mare, and get himself off. He thought for a minute and went over into the other side of the barn, and got the milking stool, and came back, and put the stool up behind Dolly the Mare. Joe pulled his pants down, and got up on the stool, and began to have sex with the mare. Joe was enjoying himself because of the warmth of the mare. Well Joe wasn't big enough to pleasure the mare, but as he began to have sex with the mare something must have got good to Dolly the Mare. The Dolly the Mare horse began to want more than Joe had to give, and began to back up, and pinned Joe up against the barn wall. She was beginning to crush Joe up against the wall in an effort to feel more. Joe began to smack the mare on the back side, and holler "get up". But the mare just kept backing up, pushing Joe up against the barn wall more, and more. Joe was feeling the weight of the horse more, more, and more!

"DOLLY GET UP"! "DOLLY GET UP"! Joe kept hollering and smacking the horse on the backside. Just about the time that Joe thought he was gonna be crushed by the horse, Dolly the Mare stepped forward, and Joe jumped down off the milking stool, and from in between the horse and the barn wall.

"Whoa"! Said Joe as he grabbed a big breath and pulled up his pants. After pulling up his pants, he went into the house to clean up for supper.

As the whole family sat down for supper, Uncle Will was sitting at the end of the table reading the newspaper. Aunt Deelee came from outside into the house with a bucket of fresh milk to replace the cold milk they were going to use up for supper. They would put it in a jar with a lid and store it overnight in the cool spring to get it cold.

Aunt Deelee spoke up and said, "Will, how did the milking stool get over into Dolly's stall?

As Aunt Deelee went on about her chores in the kitchen, Uncle Will pulled the side of the newspaper away from the front of his face. Then looking around the newspaper, stared straight at Joe, and said "I DON'T KNOW"!!

Joe turned beet red in the face!

Then Uncle Will pulled the newspaper back in front of his face and went back to reading.

Joe said, he believed Uncle Will put two, and two, together in just an instance, and knew what had happened. But did not wish to discuss it, with Aunt Deelee in the room.

13. 1939-JOE FLATT & FRIENDS, BLOW UP A TREE STUMP.

Joe Allen started his freshman year in High School year and just like everyone expected, Joe was so good at basketball that he started off on the Varsity team the first year. Joe's grades weren't great, but Coach Williams of the basketball team was a good teacher and helped Joe make it through English. There were times that Uncle Will and Aunt Deelee believe Joe only stayed in school to play basketball. And Coach Williams demanded passing grades of "C" or better. Joe knew this.

Joe's first year of high school Willow Grove's high school basketball team only lost one game all season. The next year Joe's sophomore year they lost 2 games. Joe said he was tired of coming in second, and in his junior year they went undefeated. But they lost the State Championship by one point.

Joe's senior year they went undefeated again and won the State Championship by one point. Joe won All-Tournament in basketball his senior year of high school.

Joe had worked hard over the winter and earned enough money to buy himself an old Model A Ford. It ran fairly well when it started, but sometimes it just did not want to start. So, Joe would always park it on a hill at school, and at home, that way he could push it off the hill and pop the clutch in second gear to get it started.

Basketball was over, and as usual Joe had come to school, but did not want to be there. Coach Williams, as everyone called him, had kept Joe interested in school for as long as he could with basketball, but now Joe was showing less, and less, interest in school.

Coach Williams said, "Everyone hand in your homework from last night". Everyone made their way up to Coach Williams' desk to hand in their homework. That is everybody, but Joe. Coach Williams noticed that Joe had not moved from his seat.

"Joe where is your homework paper", ask Coach Williams with a stern look?

"It's out in my car", answered Joe.

Well, for all the interest you are showing in this class you might as well be out there in your car and drive off" snapped Coach Williams.

"Excuse me", added Coach Williams in a sarcastic tone, "not drive off, because it won't start, PUSH IT OFF"!

Everybody in the class laughed, except Coach Williams and Joe.

Joe got up and slowly started walking to the classroom door.

"Where are you going Joe", ask Coach Williams?

Joe turned and said, "Well you said I might as well be out in my car for all the interest I was showing". Joe then turned and started out the door.

"Wait a minute Joe", said Coach Williams followed after Joe out into the hall. "Wait a minute Joe, I am sorry if I embarrassed you, come on back in class. You don't have much, only 2 more 6 weeks sessions to go"!

Joe turned and said, "No Coach, I'm done"! "It's not about you embarrassing me; I am gonna get me a job and go to work. Maybe join the service. I've had enough", said Joe as he continued to walk away!

"Come on Joe, you, you just got a short time to go", begged Coach Williams as Joe went out the door shaking his head no. Coach Williams went by the Grider farm several times trying to talk Joe into coming back to school. But it did no good. Joe never returned.

Joe regretted for the rest of his life that he did not finish school. But as you will see all Joe's children will finish High School. Mainly, because my mom required it, and Joe backed her up to see that it happened.

Joe tried hard to get himself a job, but everything he found did not last, or didn't pay much.

Finally, Joe decided he may join the Navy because he might get drafted anyway. He had heard that the Navy had good food and if he joined, he could choose the one he wanted. And so Joe decided to possibly join the Navy, and he was about 19 years old.

Two of his buddies Chief Billy Rider, and Jess Couch were planning on possibly joining the service also. Not because they wanted to, but because there were just not any jobs, and they were tired of working on their family farms. They had played ball in grade school together, and in High School together.

Joe and some of his buddies were meeting tonight to go skinny dipping down at the gravel pit. Their folks did not know they were meeting, but all of them were old enough that they were hard to control. Uncle Will, and Aunt Deelee still tried to keep Joe from getting in trouble. But they had all made up some lie to tell their folks to get out of the house so they could meet and run around together.

The government was building several dams; it was an attempt to make jobs and control flooding. It was called the Wolf Creek Dam, but later was renamed the Dale Hollow Dam Project. The idea was to dam up the Obey River and flood the valley. This would create a large man-made lake. It was a project that would take many years to complete and they had just started preparing the area to start building the dam. But the project had caused a good swimming hole to happen down at the gravel pit where the construction company would blow up rock with dynamite, to get stone, to grind up to make gravel for their project. Then they would truck it to where it was needed. The boys would go down there on holidays, weekends, and Sundays while the construction crew was not around to swim. And this just happened to be a July 4th Holiday and the construction crew was off. The young men were going to swim under a bright full moon. The moon lit up the sky to the point that they could see very well without a lantern.

There were 3 of them, Joe Allen Flatt, Chief Billy Rider, and Jess Couch. When Joe got to the gravel pit Chief Billy Rider was waiting for him.

"Hey Joe, where is Jess at", ask Chief Billy?

Chief Billy was a black headed, full blooded, Cherokee Indian that was not as tall as Joe but was just about the same size. Both boys were tan, but Chief Billy was much darker than Joe, because of his Indian blood. No one knew if Chief Billy was a chief or not, but it was spoken that his bloodline was in line with the famous Cherokee Indian Chief, Chief Doublehead. Anyway, the name stuck, and Chief Billy didn't mind being called Chief.

"I don't know where Jess is at", said Joe. "I thought he would be with you, Chief"!

About that time two figures appeared up on the ledge, one much taller than the other.

"Hey fellows", called out Jess Couch! "I got a friend with me", shouted Jess.

Jess was a Skinny, gangly, clumsy looking boy not quite as tall as Joe, with blond hair that always seemed to have a cow lick that stuck out over his left ear. Which made it look like the wind was blowing his hair always to the left, even when it was not.

"Who's your friend Jess", ask Chief Billy

"This is my cus' on my mother's side", said Jess Couch. "He just got out of the Army". "His name is Sam Bell, and he is 20 years old". "Sam, I want you to meet Chief Billy, and Joe Flatt". "Joe was our top player on the basketball team this last year of school". "Joe, Chief Billy, meet Sam Bell", introduced Jess. Then everybody reached to shake hands.

"Hello fellows, just wanted to come down and swim a little with you, if you don't mind? It sure has been hot today", smiled Sam!

"Did you really just get out of the Army", ask Chief Billy.

"Yea, only it was more like getting thrown out", snickered Sam. "It just wasn't for me"!

"What did you do", ask Joe?

With a big smile Sam said, "Well they said, I was drinking too much". "But I didn't think so".

"Well shit, let us go get wet, shouted Chief Billy.

"Last one in," shouted Joe!

With this all 4 started to strip off their clothes and race toward the water to dive in.

After a good hour of horseplay swim the young men got their clothes back on. While sitting on the bank talking, and having a smoke, they began to talk.

Chief Billy looked at Sam and asked, "Sam what did you do in the army"?

"I was studying to be a demolitions expert", smiled Sam.

"That's where you blow things up, right", ask Jess?

"Yea", said Sam. "I was doing pretty good too until they caught me drinking", smiled Sam.

"So, you can blow things up", ask Joe?

"Yea, if I had some munitions'", said Sam.

"What about Dynamite", ask Chief Billy?

"Yea", said Sam, "I know how to hook it up, and make it work".

"Come here" said Chief Billy. "Look at this"!

They all walked over to a small shack.

The shack sat off by itself, and had a sign on it with bright red letters, that read,

DANGER EXPLOSIVES
DYNAMITE
DO NOT TOUCH
DO NOT ENTER
BY ORDER OF FEDERAL LAW

Joe looked at the shack and the sign and said, "Let's blow something up"! "After all it is the 4th of July" shouted Joe.

"What would we blow up?" said the Chief.

"How about that old tree stump over there" ask Jess? They could barely see it in the moonlight.

Everyone turned and looked at the old tree stump that had been sawed off flat about 2 feet of the ground. It was about 200 yards away from the shack.

"Yea", said Joe, "Blow the shit out of it".

"Ok", smiled Sam, "but we can't tell anyone about it". "They will hang our asses out to dry", cautioned Sam.

"We're just celebrating' the 4th of July", shouted Chief with a smile!

Jess spoke up and said "Well, we sure got to be a long way away before it goes ka-boom".

"Can you make it Sam, to where we can be long gone before it goes off", ask Joe?

"Yes, but we need to get into the shed and see if there are any primer caps and fuse. And fellow's we must be long gone, or behind something before it goes off", said Sam with a little worry starting to wrinkle his brow.

Joe reached down, grabbed a big rock and walked over to the shed and began to strike the lock on the door with the rock. One time, two times, three, times.

"Damn", "Be careful Joe", shouted Sam. "Dynamite, don't like sparks"!

About that time the lock broke on the door of the shed.

Joe turned and smiled at the other fellows. "Well, let's see what's in here" said Joe with a crooked smile.

They went into the shed and Sam found a roll of fuse, and some blasting caps.

"How much dynamite are we gonna use?" said Jess.

"Well, that would be up to Sam", said Joe.

"How much are we gonna use, Sam", ask Chief?

"Well let's use enough to blow the shit out of that stump", laughed Joe.

"Bring out a case", said Sam.

As Jess brought out a case of dynamite Sam followed and said, "Put it on that stump, and Joe get me that crowbar I saw in the shed". Joe brought out the crowbar and handed it to Sam.

Sam opened the top of the case of dynamite that was sitting on the tree stump. Has somebody got a pocketknife ask Sam?

Joe got out his pocket knife and gave it to Sam. Sam began to hook up the blasting caps and fuse to the dynamite.

"Oh, shit we're really going to do this ain't we", shouted Jess?

"If Sam really knows what the hell, he is doing we are", replied Joe with a grin.

"He knows what the hell he's doing", shouted Jess in excitement. "He learned it in the Army"!

Sam had finished loading the fuse and blasting caps to the case of dynamite.

Just then Jess asked so excited he barely could get it out, "Are we gonna use a whole case"?

"Joe just said for us to blow the shit out of the stump didn't he", asked Sam with a grin. "So, we're gonna blow the shit out of it"! "Who's got a light"?

"I do", said Joe reaching in his pocket. He pulled out a match and handed it to Sam.

Sam lit the fuse.

As the fuse began to sparkle, everyone took off running just as someone hollered "Oh Shit, Run"!!

The 4 ran wide open, and ran, and ran, and ran some more. They had run so long that they were all breathing extremely hard. Finally, the 4 young men came to a ditch. They all fell down in the ditch and covered their heads with their hands. They waited, but nothing happened! They waited some more, still nothing happened! It was as quiet a time you could hear the crickets singing. Still nothing! Some more time passed. Still nothing!

Finally, Chief raised up in the ditch, and sat right straight up, and said, "Shit Sam you don't know what the hell you're doing, that thing ain't going' off-f-f.

"BOOOOM"!!!

Chief fell back down in the ditch, someone maybe Sam hollered" get down, put your hands over your head"!

The earth shook so hard, it was like an earthquake. Then rocks, gravel and earth were raining down upon the 4 men to the point that they had to cover their heads with their hands again. It was beating them like someone had dumped a dump truck full of rocks and dirt upon them.

When the rocks, gravel, and earth finally stopped raining down, the boys got up wide eyed, and headed for home each one did not expect how powerful, and loud it would be. Even Sam had not ever lit that much off, even in the army. None of them were ready for that big of a blast. It was talked about all over the county for months. The law said they would fully prosecute them to the fullest extent of the law if they ever found out who did it. The Feds sent the FBI, or one of the federal law agencies into the area to try and, investigate the explosion. The word was, there was a hole in the ground where the stumps used to be, big enough to park a pick-up truck in, and cover it up with dirt.

Each boy warned the others several times.

"Don't you tell anybody about it" each one told the other.

Each boy was scared because the Construction Company, Clay County Sheriff, and Federal Government had placed a reward out for information leading to the arrest and conviction of the people responsible. The construction company also hired a night watchman every night to watch the construction site from then on. They also built a 10 ft. fence around the explosives shed.

It was now1941 and times were tough. Joe had no idea just how tuff. Since the Great Depression had already taken its toll on the country. Although it had not yet been named "The Depression", the stock market crash was causing the American economy to sink lower and lower. As a matter of fact, Joe and his Aunt and Uncle, all his cousins, and Francis Flatt his dad, did not know much about what a stock market was. They just knew the times were hard, and there were not many jobs to be had. The Griders barely made a living on their farm growing crops to eat and selling a bit of their crops for money or for seed. Or any of the things they could not grow for themselves. There was a lot of trading going on because money was hard to come by. But when you do not have much, maybe it is not as easy to notice, when not having anything comes sneaking around the corner. It reminds me of the old story about the cook dropping a frog into the pan of boiling water, and the frog just hops right back out. But the cook puts the frog in the pan of cool water and slowly turns the heat up a little at a time. By the time the frog realizes that the water is hot it is too late for the frog to jump out and he cooks to death.

14. WILLOW GROVE-A GHOST TOWN-A TOWN UNDERWATER.

Part of Chapter #14 was taken from an online article about Willow Grove, Tennessee written by Darren Shell.

Willow Grove, the Town That Drowned
By Darren Shell
http://www.lrn.usace.army.mil/history/dale_hollow.htm

Clay County, TN. about 13 miles north of this close-knit town construction for the Wolf Creek Dam. Started. The project was completed in 1943 and was also the year this town drowned. Some seventy-four families lived in the town's 441.54 acreage area and more in the area outside the town.

Cordell Hull, Secretary of State under President Roosevelt, is said to have attended school there before moving on to Celina. The people of Willow Grove were not for the dam and lake. They held town meetings to discuss the building of the dam. The people could not get any action taken against the project. They did not know how to fight the government, and the government was determined to build the dam. As time went on, the people realized the dam was going to be built. They had to prepare to move their belongings, their families, and even their cemeteries to new locations. Most of the people moved several of their belongings by truck and drove their cattle and livestock in herds. The hardest thing for the people was digging up the graves from all the cemeteries. They moved most of the graves to St. John's Cemetery and Fellowship Cemetery. If they could not find anything under the grave markers, they would take a bit of dirt and rebury it at one of the other cemeteries. Willow Grove was a town nestled in the Obey River valley and on the eastern side of Iron's Creek. It was located thirteen miles from Celina, the county seat. Willow Grove was said to have gotten its name from a grove of willow trees, which surrounded a spring. Willow Grove was founded as a settlement by five families from New York. Four of the five families were the Edward Irons family, the Hill family, the Barber family, and the Sprowl family. They bought their land from the Cherokee Indians. The Cherokees were a very peaceable tribe. The chief of the tribe was Knettle Carrier, son of Chief Obed and brother of Chief Doublehead. There is no specific record of when this land was bought, but it was before 1785. Willow Grove was a town with a proud history just like any other small town. It had its own school system, churches, stores and small businesses, service stations, and a post office. There is no record of the first school in the area, but the town did have a grade school and a High School.

On July 18, 1942, the people of Willow Grove met as a whole for the last time on the school grounds. Dr. Clark gave his heart touching farewell speech to the community.

They did not tear down the buildings, High School, etc. The government just backed up the water. I found my information at the following website where there is a lot more history on this town: http://www.lrn.usace.army.mil/history/dale_hollow.htm

**This is Willow Grove Before Water Back Up & Being
Buried Under Water/ black & white picture**

**taken fromWillow Grove, the Town That Drowned *By Darren Shell* online
at http://www.lrn.usace.army.mil/history/dale_hollow.htm**

Not unlike the fabled city of Atlantis, the old town of Willow Grove, Tennessee, is now under a lavish blanket of water. The murky depths of Dale Hollow Lake still house the shadowy foundations of what was once a beautiful and thriving valley town. The winding and crystal-clear waters of the Obey River wound through many small communities and towns as it meandered its way toward the Cumberland.

Willow Grove sat along the banks of Irons Creek and was lovingly named from the Willow trees that grew along its shores. For its day, this little town was not so little. It had service stations, churches, general stores, and one of the largest school buildings within miles. It even had a large gymnasium, where children rode horse-back to basketball games. A large grist mill sat in the middle of what is now Willow Grove Campground, and it overlooked the bustling Tennessee Highway 53 that cut through the center of town. The clip-clop of hooves echoed through the streets as wagons were drawn by horses and mules, and the chuckles of children scampering through the streets filled the air. The crisp, clean air smelled of freshly cut hay and the wisps of smoke from the fires burning in the kitchen cook stoves. And life was grand.

And then it happened. The year was 1943. The once cheerful and quaint valley town of Willow Grove was now forlorn and solemn. Aside from the sad sights of the town's men marching off to World War II, the residents faced a horrific and depressing dilemma. The government was forcing the families and friends of this closely-knit community to move away. The United States government was buying their property. It was demolishing their homes and businesses…to build a dam. The farm fields tilled by their forefathers were now dozed clean of fences and barns. The ever-incessant sounds of chainsaws hummed day in and day out. Bonfires were kindled in every field and the loud claps of dynamite shook the earth. And the beautiful little valley town of Willow Grove now looked like a war zone.

Despite the anguish in their hearts, the community gathered one last time before the move. On July 18, 1942, the people of Willow Grove united at a town picnic. The Corps of Engineers set it up and made certain that county agents were on hand to help the townspeople with the inevitable move. Amid the anger and sadness, one of the town's most beloved members gave a particularly moving speech. Dr. Edward Clark convinced the people of Willow Grove to press forward and offered hope to those forced to move. His words softened the blow of moving. And for the people of Willow Grove, Father Time pressed on, and the water did rise.

In the years that followed, the rough terrain around the lake began to take shape. Marinas were built where the old roads entered the lake. Tiny wooden boats dotted the shores and people all over the country were beginning to love this special lake named Dale Hollow, in remembrance of the Dale family that owned the large tract of land that now houses a giant chunk of concrete that holds back billions of gallons of water. Dale Hollow Dam now stands in remembrance of William Dale and the hundreds of his descendants that now populate the surrounding communities.

The people of old Willow Grove still get together once a year for a reunion. On Sunday of Labor Day weekend, once again the familiar voices of the townspeople fill the air as memories flow and laughter helps heal the hearts of those that still mourn the loss of their old hometown.

So, when your feet dangle in the cool, clear water of Dale Hollow, and your face is warmed by the brilliant colors of the setting sun, give a little thank you to the people of old Willow Grove and its surrounding communities. Say a little prayer for those who endured the hardships of this lake's making. And remember in your heart…that these shores contain so very much more than just water.

Darren Shell is the Owner/Manager of Willow Grove Resort and local author.

15. 1941-JOE FLATT JOINS THE NAVY.

Joe was 19 years old. Joe was about to get drafted so he joined the Navy and went through training and was stationed at a very cold place. World War II had not started but it was believed that the United States could be entering the war very soon if Hitler was not whipped soon.

Then on December 7, 1941 Japan bombed Pearl Harbor. The United States then entered the war. Joe had just joined the Navy.

One day Joe came in for chow, Joe had learned that his ship was leaving out in a few days. It was very cold outside when Joe entered the chow hall. He was standing in line for chow and a big gas heater that was hanging from the ceiling and was blowing down on Joe. Suddenly Joe found himself flat on his back on the chow hall floor. The chief came over and would not let him get up. He wanted him checked out at the sick bay.

Joe protested but the chief said "Sailor you stay on your back until the medics get here. You're going to the sick bay, like it or not".

Joe was carried to the sick bay. The Navy doctors ran every test on Joe they could think of to find out what was wrong with Joe. But still they found nothing wrong with him.

Joe continued to protest, "Nothing is wrong with me, I just fainted because of the heater"! But the Navy doctors would not listen. The doctor kept Joe in the sick bay for 2 whole weeks.

In the meantime, Joe's ship sailed out without him.

Joe later found out that his ship had been torpedoed and had gone down with all hands lost. The doctors never did find anything wrong with Joe, but still would not give him a good bill of health. Because of this Joe could not be transferred to a ship. So, Joe began to train for boxing. Joe later became fleet champion. To celebrate Joe had 2 boxing gloves tattooed on his right forearm with the fleet champion tattooed under them. Joe also learned from a fellow seaman how to play the guitar. They started a band while in the Navy and Joe found out he was pretty good at singing and he sounded very close to Ernest Tubb. So, Joe learned all of Ernest Tubb's songs. At that time Ernest Tubb was on top in the country music business. Everybody told Joe he needed to go to Nashville to sing and record. Joe liked the sound of that.

Joe had never fainted before and never fainted again the rest of his life like he did in the chow line in the Navy. But as it turned out it saved his life. But Joe began to drink very heavily, but only when on leave at first while they were playing music in the seaman's club and the night clubs in the area.

Joe had been caught so many times for disorderly conduct and drinking while on duty that it was not unusual that he was standing once again before the Captain for disciplinary reasons. But this time Joe was in real trouble. It seems Joe and his only full brother Orlie (who was in the army) had stolen a deuce and a half truck load of military beer. Orlie was on leave which turned into a.w.o.l. from the army and was being sent back to his camp in handcuffs.

Joe and Orlie had met up while on leave and got drunk together. Then when they ran out of money, they got the idea to steal a truck load of beer. Once they had stolen the truck load of beer they went on a real bender. They took the truck load of beer and went out onto a country road under a tree and drank beer until they both passed out. When they woke up, they were both surrounded by MP's with their guns pointed straight at them.

Orlie said, "Oh shit Joe the drinking party is over"!!!

Both were arrested, for public drunkenness, grand theft, and being a.w.o.l. and sent to jail.

Time passed and now Joe was standing in front of the Captain for discipline.

The Captain said while looking at Joe. "Seaman Flatt it is my job to get you to agree to an Undesirable Discharge. We are going to let you out of the Navy. We are not going to Dishonorably Discharge you, but we are going to do the next best thing. But you have got to agree to it, or you will be Dishonorably Discharged. That is why it is called an Undesirable Discharge".

Joe spoke, "OK sir"! "But what is the difference, sir", ask Joe?

"Well, the difference is Seaman Flatt, about 48 months in the hole and court martial. That is what the Dishonorable Discharge will get you", spoke sternly, the Captain looking Joe dead in the eyes. "You apparently want out of the Navy, and the Navy doesn't want you. Also, the Navy does not even want to waste the time or money, giving you a court martial or the cost of keeping you in the hole", snapped the Captain. The Navy does not think you will learn anything by serving 4 years in jail and it would be a waste of money for the Navy. Is that right, is this what you want", ask the Captain again.?

"Yes sir", snapped Joe at attention.

"You understand that you will not get any benefits Seaman, is that OK with you", ask the Captain?

"Yes sir", snapped Joe still at attention.

Well sign right here Sailor and you are a civilian again, the Captain said pushing a form across the desk toward Joe. Joe signed the form.

The Captain looked at Joe and said, "Get out of here and don't come back, you got 3 hours to get your things and to get off this naval base" snapped the Captain one more time.

Joe snapped to attention and saluted the Captain.

"Get out of here Flatt"! "You aren't in the Navy anymore, I only salute Sailors," snapped the Captain! Then he turned his chair back toward Joe as if he were disgusted.

Joe got out of there. In less than 2 hours Joe was on a bus back to Tennessee.

16. *1942-JOE FLATT GETS A JOB DRIVING A TAXI BETWEEN TOWNS.*

Joe finally got back to his hometown of Willow Grove, TN. only to find that the town was about to be flooded with water. Joe did not know it then, but the lake would not make it all the way to the farmhouse.

Dad (Joe Allen Flatt) and I (Ernest Allen Flatt) went back for a reunion in 1964 almost 20 years later, you could see the lake off in the distance from the farmhouse where he grew up. But the whole town of Willow Grove, TN. was flooded under water, out to the edge of town.

After looking for a job he finally found one with a taxi company in Livingston, TN. After he worked a few weeks driving a taxi Joe found himself an apartment in Livingston. Livingston was a bigger town not as big as Nashville, but much more like a city than Willow Grove. The biggest part of Willow Grove would be underwater due to the Dale Hollow Dam project in a year. The river was dammed up and the water would be backed up to make a big lake which it still is today. Joe would drive taxis around Livingston and from time to time he would get a fare to another town. Joe worked a lot of hours and got a lot of tips. Then Joe began to play music in the Honky Tonks around Livingston and other towns close by.

Joe began to drink so much that he would not remember the night before. One morning Joe woke up in a motel and there was a woman lying beside him he did not remember. He had been so drunk last night that he only remembered being in a nightclub drinking and that is all. Joe thought well I am already here. I will just wake her up and get some more before I go.

As Joe nudged the naked lady beside him, she turned over and smiled and said, "Hey Joe we sure had a great time last night"!

Joe was aghast at what he saw. The naked woman lying next to him was incredibly good looking, built very well, but had a 2-inch gorget on her neck. In those days they called it a gore-der. This was not uncommon in those days because there was not a medical/surgical procedure to take care of it. Joe would have been embarrassed for any of his friends to have seen him with her. Mostly, because they would have teased him about her. Joe did not remember taking her to the motel, or who may have seen him with her. Also, Joe did not want to insult her by leaving abruptly. Plus, it was Sunday, and they had a full bottle of Kessler's Whiskey to finish. So, Joe thought what the hell I am already here with her now. So, they had sex several times that day as they finished the bottle. Also, Joe determined because other men had felt like he did about her affliction, that she had not been touched sexually very many times. She was particularly good in bed.

Finally, it began to get dark outside. Joe said his excuses, and goodbye to the young lady. As Joe went out the door, he looked both ways to check and see if anyone was around to see him. Then he went quickly to his car. Hoping no one would see him coming out. He drove away quickly, and never looked back.

The next day was Monday and Joe came to work to pick up his cab. The boss told him there was a fare to Celina if he wanted it. Joe knew that it would be a good fare and maybe a good tip. So, Joe said that he did want it.

To get to Celina you had to take the Celina Highway that ran between Livingston and Celina. Joe's boss said that he was not able to take the fare because of an appointment, and would give it to Joe because he would have to be gone most all day. And the other important appointment he could not get out of. Also, he wanted Joe to take his brand-new taxis. It was a 1942 4 door sedan, Buick, Roadmaster. The fare/trip was for an important person in Livingston that Joe's boss would normally take himself. Joe's boss told him it was for some high dollar people, the Mayor of Livingston, and an especially important Medical Doctor from the Livingston Hospital. Joe went and picked the fares up. The fares for the mayor and the Doctor were because they did not want to drive. They wanted to talk business about getting a new hospital built in Livingston. They were working on a deal where the Celina Hospital would finance a smaller hospital in Livingston. The hospital in Celina got most of the business from Livingston anyway. But the hospital was so far away that patients were sometimes lost due to the distance away. Joe's job was to get them to Celina safely and return if they did not need him anymore the rest of the day. Joe was hoping that the business would go quick so he could get back to Livingston because he had a date with a young lady.

The trip over to Celina was without event. The Mayor and the Doctor just talked among themselves in the back seat discussing the importance of Livingston getting the hospital, while Joe drove his best, smooth ride. Once they got to the Celina Hospital Joe pulled up and let the two gentlemen out. It seems Joe had determined from their conversation that they had a meeting with the head of the hospital there at Celina. It seems the deal was for Celina to build a hospital and run it for the land and tax deferrals. This would get Livingston a hospital far bigger, and better than what they had already. Livingston's hospital was nothing more than a clinic.

They arrived in Celina at about 11:00 am. Joe got out and went around and opened the rear door to let the men out just like a chauffeur would do.

The Mayor spoke to Joe and said "Just hang around Joe till this afternoon. We are going to all go to lunch and then have the meeting. If we are not done by 3:00 pm or so, we may stay the night. And if so, you can come back and get us tomorrow. We will know by 3 which way we need to go. Be out here at 3:00 pm and I will come out and let you know what we are going to do".

"OK", said Joe, a little disappointed that he had to spend most of the whole day in Celina.

"Don't worry Joe, we are gonna make it worth your while, tip and all", smiled the Mayor.

This made Joe feel a little better, but he had a date with a nice young lady at the end of the day. Joe was wondering if he may need to call long distance and cancel the date. He decided to wait and see if the Mayor and Doctor were coming back with him. He could travel a lot faster above the speed limit if they were not with him. So, he would wait and see before calling his date.

Joe hung out all day in Celina and was back at the hospital by 3:00 pm as he was commanded by the mayor. The mayor came out and told Joe that the meeting was still going on. That they had more to talk about and were going to stay the night to see the lawyers. That Joe could go on back to Livingston and come and get them tomorrow afternoon at 3:00pm. Joe was glad to hear that, because he could drive his speed to hurry up and get back to Livingston for his date.

Joe took off toward Livingston from Celina on what everybody called Celina Highway. He knew if he were swift enough, he could still make his date. Joe thought, man this car could sure run fast. It was a brand new, straight 6 cylinders motor, and had a lot of power. Joe was taking the curves with tires squalling. Sometimes Joe would get the car sideways in a four-wheel drift. But he would straighten it up. Joe was a particularly good driver. Joe was about 4 miles from Livingston when it began to mist rain, he went into a curve and cut the curve to short and got in some gravel that was piled on the right-hand side of the road. The big heavy Buick began to slide in the gravel when the right tires lost traction. Joe was fighting the big heavy vehicle, but it still began to slide to the left side of the road. There was a red dirt bank about 15 feet tall on the left side of the road. The Buick slid over across the road to the red dirt bank, then the car left the road. It rolled on its left side over toward the red dirt bank. The Buick turned over and over 3 times and ended in the middle of the black top road on its top facing the direction Joe had been coming from. Joe had been knocked unconscious and when he came to there were 2 or 3 cars and people stopped all around to check on him.

"Are you OK!" asked a man that was on the ground looking in at Joe? Joe was lying on the inside top of the banged-up Buick taxi.

"Yeah", replied Joe! "At least, I think I am", mumbled Joe as he began to crawl from the wrecked taxi. Once Joe was on his feet the man that had been on the ground got to his feet also, and asked, "What is wrong with your head"?

Joe reached up and said "what"?

Immediately, Joe thought he felt what he believed was brain matter on his head in his hair. Joe was very scared. Joe was afraid to look at the matter in his hand but did anyway. It was moist red dirt clay. There was mud in his hand that he had just reached up and got from the hair on his head. Joe blew a quick breath of relief as he found out what it was in his hand. His head had gone out the open driver's window and hit the soft red dirt clay bank when the Buick had rolled over. Joe was sure relieved. But he still had to go over to the ditch and sit down for a while to recuperate. He felt sick at his stomach. The brand new, Buick, Roadmaster taxis was a wreck. There was not one side of the brand-new Buick taxi that was not banged up. All the windows were broken and had fallen out. All the doors and fenders were bent and mashed in. The car was totaled. Joe was a little sore but OK. Needless to say, Joe lost his job with the taxi company.

Joe had got him a girlfriend named Ruby. They had been going together for some time. But Ruby had some news for Joe. It seems that she was pregnant by Joe. Ruby had gone to the Doctor and was close to 2 months pregnant. So Ruby and Joe got married. But both were too young and not ready to be married. They argued all the time.

Joe wanted to play music for a living, and she was very jealous of Joe. Joe would travel several towns over with the band and get home late. They had a small upstairs apartment. Joe would come home, and they would argue. Ruby would say he was running around because she believed she was fat and ugly.

She was over 8 months into her pregnancy when she laid down the law and told Joe that he could not go to play the music jobs that he and the band had already booked. She was accusing Joe of running around. But Joe was not. No matter how hard he tried to convince her she would not believe Joe.

Joe was leaving to go to a music job on a Saturday Night when she began to argue with Joe again. They were on the landing at the top of the stairs.

Ruby told Joe, "One of these days you won't come back home". Joe started to leave and stopped on the 3rd step and turned and said, "If you don't stop being so jealous one of these days I just might not come back".

Ruby stepped to the edge of the landing and said, "You son of a bitch, you have been thinking about leaving me haven't you".

Ruby took a big swing at Joe. Joe sidestepped, and Ruby tumbled down the flight of stairs.

Joe could not believe what had just happened. He checked her and she was breathing but he could not wake her up. She was unconscious, so Joe ran next door to some people who had a phone and called an ambulance. They took Ruby to the hospital. Once they got to the hospital Ruby was still unconscious and went into labor.

The doctor came out and told Joe, "Joe, Ruby had twin boys, but both have died. Still born at birth". The doctor said that he was going to keep Ruby unconscious because she was so weak and needed the rest. The doctor asked him what he wanted to name the twins. He would need to put names on the birth/death certificates. They were going to bury them right away while Ruby was still unconscious. The doctor said as weak as she was he didn't think she could handle the funeral. Since he could not talk to Ruby about it, Joe had to name them. They had not talked about a name, let alone 2 names. Joe thought for a while. Joe had just seen a movie last week with a couple of movie stars, Tyrone Powers and Henry Fonda, playing Frank and Jesse James. He had liked the movie. So he named the oldest one Frank Flatt and the youngest one Jesse Flatt.

Ruby and Joe did not stay married exceedingly long after the death of the boy's. They got a divorce and went their separate ways.

Dad had a tattoo on his left arm even with the shoulder that was faded. It had a name written in the ribbon, but I could not read the name. I asked who it was, and he told me about his first wife Ruby, and the boys. Dad told me the story about Ruby and the boys but had me promise never to mention it in front of Mom. He said she was very jealous about the tattoo. I never did.

Somewhere we have two half-brothers named Frank Flatt and Jesse Flatt. Wish I could find the graves, but I don't even know where they are.

17. 1945-JOE FLATT BECOMES ALLEN FLATT.

Joe was looking for a job. Finally, a musician friend told him about a job with a famous Bluegrass Singer and Recording Artist. Bill Monroe needed a stagehand to help move his tent show from place to place. Bill Monroe had a tent show that traveled from town to town around Kentucky, Tennessee, West Virginia, Virginia, North and South Carolina. The tent was carried on a semi flatbed trailer and pulled by a semi-tractor truck once the crew got to the field, they had rented from a farmer the trailer would be jack knifed to use the trailer for the stage. Then the tent was set up around the flatbed trailer with the semi-tractor truck sticking out of the tent. Bill Monroe also carried a diesel generator to furnish electricity for the public address system and lights to light up the tent. They would sing on the PA, but the instruments were all acoustic and the singers sang into microphones connected through the PA system. This was the beginning of what is called Kentucky Bluegrass Music of today.

Joe was given a job as a stagehand and Truck driver. Joe could back the tractor in and jackknife the tractor just perfect to set up for the show. The tent is then unfolded off the trailer, and the diesel generator unloaded with a small lift carried on the instrument truck. Then the tent is set up around the flatbed trailer and the tractor is sticking outside the tent. The generator is set far enough from the tent so that the sound of it running would not interfere with the performance.

Joe was doing such a good job that Bill Monroe took a liking to Joe. When he found out that Joe could play and sing, he asked if he wanted to audition for the show. Joe was allowed to come into the tent after practice and sing a couple of songs with the band. Joe did great.

Bill called Joe into the tent on payday and said, "Joe I have room for and need for another act on my show. Would you be interested in auditioning for me and taking on a job of setting up the tent, driving the truck that hauls the tent, and doing a couple of songs on the show? There will be a small raise and a chance to become a regular on the show. Are you interested"?

Joe said, "Yes" almost shouting.

Bill said "Well you got it! I will give you a 20 dollar raise a week and a new Stetson hat, and a western shirt, once we get to the next big town where I can get one. Do you have a nice pair of trousers you can wear on stage", ask Bill? "Yes sir Mr. Monroe, I even have a pair of good-looking boots", smiled Joe.

"Call me Bill", smiled Bill. Bill was usually a very stern-faced man. "As you already know Joe, if you need an advance on your pay don't be afraid to ask me" Bill said looking Joe in the eyes.

Joe nodded and smiled. Joe found out that Bill never wrote down any advances on pay, but never forgot when someone borrowed money on their pay. Everybody was amazed how Bill could remember even the smallest advances.

"Joe you may already know you sound a lot like Ernest Tubb, so much so that it is amazing, so I want you to do regular country songs and the band will play as close to regular country as they can with acoustic instruments, understand? You are gonna break up the beginning and end of the show. We will put you in the middle. Give them something different. How's that"?

"Great", said Joe, almost ready to dance for joy.

"You will practice with the band and I will tell them what I want them to play behind you", said Bill speaking all business.

"Yes sir" exclaimed Joe?

The next day the show drove to a farmer's field just outside of Greenville, South Carolina. In the afternoon, after the tent was set up and it was time to practice. Joe felt important being introduced to all the Smoky Mountain Boys. Most of all to Lester Flatt and Earl Scruggs which were members of Bill Monroe's Smoky Mountain Boys at this time. This was before they went out on their own. Joe and Lester Flatt began talking about family members. They determined that they were about 3rd cousins on Joe's side. The entire band made Joe feel right at home. And wow, they could play great music. If they were not moving from town to town all they did was play music. Even over in the corner backstage before the show. Even straight country music was not a problem. Lester even loaned Joe an extra guitar to play when he was performing on the show.

Lester said "Joe your old guitar will not stay in tune. So, you can use my old Martin-D-28. It is a little scratched and bumped from road use, but it will stay in tune". Joe was thrilled to get to play a professional guitar like a Martin-D-28. As far as Joe was concerned it was not scratched, or bumped, hardly at all. Joe could not believe that Lester had such a good ear. All you had to do was give him and e for the first string on a guitar, and then he would just move up the strings. He would hit each string once, then tune, then move to the next string. Hit it once and tune, then move to the next string, and so on. Then he would hand the guitar off without even hitting a chord, and it would be in perfect tune. Joe thought that is why they are with Bill Monroe, they were such great fellows, and so tight they could play with anybody in Nashville.

Later that night it was time for the show. Joe was very nervous and paced back and forth. He wanted to do a good job and have Bill and the crowd to like him. They had a full tent and a great crowd. Finally, it was time for Joe to be introduced. (The announcer for the show, Bill Monroe, and Joe had talked it over and decided to have Joe use his middle name, Allen.

The announcer and Bill felt that Allen Flatt rolled off the tongue better than Joe Flatt. (Maybe it was because the number of syllables)

The announcer which was a disc jockey from the nearby town and all very professional stepped up to the microphone and said,

"Ladies and Gentlemen, here is the newest member of the Bill Monroe Traveling Tent Show let us give him a good, warm, welcome! Make him feel good, for the first time tonight. Put your hands together for Al--Len -- Flatt", shouted the announcer! The crowd burst into more applause than Joe had ever experienced before. Allen had to tell himself to put one foot in front of the other.

"Is he really introducing me", thought Allen?

As Allen was making his way to the center of the stage, Lester Flatt put his guitar up to the microphone and kicked off the beginning notes to Ernest Tubb's Walking The Floor Over You.

Allen forced himself to the microphone and began to sing, "I'm walking the floor over you. I can't sleep a wink that is true". The crowd began to cheer and applaud. Allen was on cloud nine. In a blink of an eye the song was over. Allen began to introduce his second song.

"Folks you have made a country boy feel right at home", Thank you so very much", continued Allen.

"I want to thank also Mr. Bill Monroe for giving me this chance to come out and try to entertain you" spoke Allen. "he'll be out in just a few to sing all his hits for you"!

Again, the crowd burst into applause again.

He was sure that the crowd could hear the shake in his voice.

"Here is another song. This is one that I wrote, called "A Broken Heart and A Glass of Beer". The fiddle man stepped toward the microphone and kicked the song off. Allen began to sing, and the crowd went wild. The song had never been recorded or played on the radio, but the crowd loved it.

The Flatt Family Stories

"I got a broken heart, lord a glass of beer. My cow's been dry for over a year. My mail man died, my phone won't ring, and the landlord kicked me out in the rain, with a broken heart and a glass of beer". The crowd whistled and cheered as the dobra player stepped up to the microphone and took a half of a solo break, then the fiddle player finished the solo break.

Allen stepped back to the microphone and sang, "My Ford won't run, I stripped her gears, that's all I have, before me here. I was wild and wooly lord full of flea's, but I've ended up down on my knees with a broken heart and a glass of beer.

By this time, the crowd was on their feet.

Allen received a standing ovation as he left the stage. The announcer came to the microphone and said, "give him another big hand"! The crowd gave him another large round of applause. "You want to hear him sing another song, ask the announcer? Let us bring him back. Allen came back out to another round of applause with a confused look on his face. Then he sang another song. "I'm just drivin' nails in my coffin, every time I drink a bottle of booze", Allen sang.

At the end of the show Allen was happy, but just a little ashamed. After all, it was Bill Monroe's show. And he was a grand ole Opry star.

Lester Flatt came and got him and said, "Bill wants to see you Allen".

Allen's heart sank into his boots.

Lester looked at him and gave him the thumbs up and said, "You did fine tonight son".

"I hope Bill thinks so," said Allen with his head low.

Allen found Bill in the equipment truck behind his small desk that he used as an office to do business.

Allen walked in and said "Bill, I'm so sorry. I didn't know that the announcer was going to call me back out for another song". "I wasn't trying to be a hog" Allen apologized.

"No, you got it all wrong Allen", began Bill. I am very happy with your performance tonight. As a matter of fact, I was the one that told the announcer to have you do another song". Bill smiled as Allen's shoulders stopped being slumped and he said, "Allen we are out here to give the people a good show. Word of mouth is better than all the radio advertising we can buy. And it doesn't cost us anything".

Allen looked at Bill and said, you do not think I was trying to steal the show?

Bill smiled again, "Allen you make me laugh more than anyone on this show. No, if we can give the people a good show then we <u>had</u> a good show. We are professionals. Tonight, was your night, maybe tomorrow night will be Lester's, and the next night will maybe be mine. But we all make the show work". "Right", ask Bill.?

"Never be ashamed of putting on a good show. Only amateurs get jealous. I believe you would do good telling a joke now and then. I have listened to you tell jokes with the crew and band; you got a talent. Course we do have to be careful to keep it a family show. You will have to be careful to clean up your jokes if you take them to the stage. You may get so popular that I will have to get me another truck driver, tent man, some day. I was wondering how you might go over sounding so much like ET, but tonight my doubts went away. You just keep on doing what you are doing. As a matter of fact, I was wondering if with your bass voice if you wanted to do some gospel songs with our quartet. Lester does the lead singing, and you would have to do bass. What do you think" ask Bill?

"Well, I don't know", said Allen. "I have never sung bass harmony before.

"Well, you think about it," said Bill, "and let me know. I am sure Lester can help you out as to what to sing. He has got an excellent ear. He is also after me to get a bass singer to complete the gospel quartet".

"I'll think about it", said Allen.

Allen never sang bass because he was afraid, he could not do it, and they hired someone else. He mentioned several times, years later, that he wished he had given it a try because they had several hit gospel records. And, when Lester Flatt and Earl Scruggs left Bill Monroe and went out on their own, they might have taken Allen with them, because the quartet gospel group was a big part of their show just like it was with Bill's show. As a matter of fact, Bill continued the gospel quartet songs after Lester and Earl left Bill.

Allen stayed with Bill Monroe a little over six months and then the season was too cold. So, they took a break from the tent show for the season. While he was with Bill Monroe Allen met a Carnival, country show promotion man named Will Beck, which also had a Country Music tent show.

He said, "Just call me Will the Carney Man"! He told Allen he would like to hire him if his contract ran out with Bill Monroe. Allen did not tell him that he did not have a contract except verbal with Bill Monroe. Will the Carnie Man said, "We go south and west in the wintertime and north in the summertime! I can make you a star. I like what you do. Also, you will be doing real country music. Here is my phone number at my office. I keep in touch with my secretary, and she can always get in touch with me in a couple of hours. And Allen we go all year round." smiled Will.

Allen liked the sound of the way the man was talking. Of course, Will was a Carney and a very good salesman to the bone. Carney's have a bit of a used car salesman approach to their business. Allen thought it sounded good.

When Bill Monroe's show stopped for the winter, Allen pulled out the phone number.

Allen called the number and talked to the secretary, she said she would get in touch with Will Beck and have him call Allen back. Allen waited on pins and needles till Will called him back.

Will said "Glad to hear from you son. Come on down here to Florida and we will talk turkey". Can you get here with no problem" ask Will the Carney Man.

Allen said "yes". Allen promised to meet him in Tampa Bay, Florida.

When Allen got to Tampa Bay, Florida he went to Will's place.

"Allen we are getting ready to go south west for the winter", said Will the Carney Man.

"Here's the way our show works. We travel with the Carnival it is called the Beck Shows and Amusements. Here is the poster that we are going to put up outside the tent".

Beck showed Allen a great big Poster. On the poster it said in great big letters in person **ERNEST TUBB** tonight.

Allen looked at the poster in confusion. He read the poster again. It read.

BECK SHOWS & AMUSEMENT

In Person Tonight
ALLEN FLATT
Sounds like

ERNEST TUBB
8:00PM TO 10:00PM
EVERY NIGHT EXCEPT SUNDAYS

Allen explained, "Will, the people are going to think they are going to get to see Ernest Tubb when they read this poster".

"The poster Allen is just to get them in", smiled Will.

"But they will be mad at me when they find out I ain't Ernest Tubb", explained Allen.

"Look Allen, I have heard you and you sound more like Ernest Tubb than anyone I have ever heard, and you're a good entertainer. You give these people a good show and I promise you that they will be happy. We are gonna give them such a good show for the money that they will leave happy", smiled Will.

Allen had a; I am not so sure look on his face.

"Allen, we have got you a top-notch band from right out of Nashville. Trust me. I am going to get you and the band some fancy western clothes for your performances, and we have got a professional sound system that will help to make you sound like a million bucks. Allen just trust me", explained Will with a big smile on his face. "I have been in this business for many years. And I promise you the people will love you. All I am asking you is to trust me. We are gonna give them such a good show for their money that they would be ashamed to complain. People don't complain about having a good time." explained Will.

"OK, I'll trust you Will. "I just hope they don't jump up on stage and beat me to death", explained Allen.

Both men then had a great big laugh.

"Son, your lessons on being in show business and being a Carney is just beginning. I am also going to give you some lessons on how to operate some of our Games so you can fill in at times in the daytime and make some extra money" said Will.

"Talking of money, what are we talking about", ask Allen.

"Well Allen I figured we would get around to that", smiled Will.

"How about $50.00 dollars a week" ask Will?

"Well, how about $80.00 dollars a week, countered Allen?

"Well, I can see you are learning already". "How about $60.00 a week for the shows that is $10.00 a day for each show, and $30.00 a week, that's 5 dollars a day for being a fill-in on the games. I promise you will not have to do rides or set up for the tent. I do not want you to be tired for the shows. How is that", ask Will?

"Let me understand", said Allen. "I'll make $90.00 dollars a week between the two jobs.

"Yes", said Will. "And all you can shortchange people. I am going to show you how to shortchange people, so you can get away with it, while you are doing the games", smiled Will. "You can usually make around $5.00 bucks a day doing that," smiled Will. But do not ever get caught, and you will not if you follow my directions, smiled Will again. If that is OK with you, we will do a contract for 1 year. Of course, we can't say anything about the shortchanging. If you do not like it after one year we will be done. But Allen I want you to be happy. You will do a better show if you're happy", spoke Will to Allen.

Then Will hollered for Jean his secretary and told her to make up a contract with the agreed pay and time.

Allen was taught how the shortchange scam worked. If someone paid you with dollars you always gave them change back. For incidence if someone paid you $5.00 and the game was $1.25 you did not give them back 3 dollars & 3 quarters. You would give the 3 dollars and then, 2 quarters, 1-dime, and 5 pennies and a nickel. Then you had just shortchanged the customer out of a nickel if he or she did not notice. This may not sound like much but over a days' time or even a week it counts up. Allen learned that it was amazing how many people would not stop to count their change but would count their dollars. And if they noticed the short you just apologized and gave them the shortchange back. But never cause a disturbance even if they called you a cheat. The more complicated the change, the more chance of getting away with it. Allen got so good at it; he would still shortchange the customer even if they noticed. Then he would still get them for a penny in the final exchange.

Will came to Allen and said, "Allen you need to slow down on the shorts changes, you're doing so damn good, I am afraid you're gonna get caught", warned Will.

Allen was knocking down an average of $40.00 a week total on shorts changes.

One of the games that Allen sometimes filled in on was a table with an arm that stuck out. On the end of the arm was a string that hung down. At the end of the string was a wooden ball. On the table was a bowling pin. The idea was to swing the ball on the string out and make it come back and knock over the bowling pin.

Allen would say, "Step right up folks and knock the bowling pin over and win a Teddy Bear for your girlfriend"! "It only cost 25 cents a try", shouted Allen. "Look how easy it is", Allen would say.

Then Allen would swing the ball out and "thump"! It would knock over the bowling pin. Then a customer would step up, pay a quarter, swing the ball on the string out and, "swoosh", it would miss.

Then Allen would say "Sorry partner you lose"! "Do you want to try again", Allen would ask"?

The trick was, unless Allen placed the bowling pin in just the right spot, no one could knock it over. The ball would just pass next to the curve in the neck of the bowling pin, but not touch it let alone knock it over. And Allen had been taught just where to sit the bowling pin. But Allen had changed the price to 36 cents, because this gave him a chance to shortchange the customer. Allen even began to let the customer win a few times, to entice them to gamble on the side with him. Of course, the customer never realized the game was rigged. But once the customer got greedy and the gambling started, and Allen had got the gamble high enough, they would begin to lose.

Will told Allen, "You are a natural at this, but be careful, or we will get caught". "OK", asked Will?

Allen smiled and said, "OK Will, I'll slow down and be careful".

"Now go do your show", smiled Will.

Allen had done even better with the show than the games. The crowds loved him. And Allen was amazed, but Will was right, no one ever complained.

Like Will said, "We will give them such a good show they will go away happy".

And Allen had added more jokes and their show was just as top notch as any Nashville show. Allen had even learned to tell some ornery joke and clean them up enough that people were not offended. Even after being introduced as Allen Flatt, some people still thought he was Ernest Tubb. Why Allen was even told once in a while that he sounded better than Ernest Tubb.

Allen also got a lot of women hanging around that wanted to go out with him. He had a big share of dates. In one town Allen woke up one morning and went to take a "p". Wow his penis burned like fire.

One of the older musicians in the band named Jim, just laughed and told Allen, "son you got the clap"!

Allen just looked at him in a worried state and asked, "What do I need to do to get rid of it Jim"?

Jim, the older more experienced musician looked at Allen and smiled then said, "Just make an appointment and go to a doctor. He will give you a shot of penicillin. Then you'll be alright".

"How long does it take to make it go away", ask Allen.

"Ah, it will start getting' better by the end of the day, or the next. But you will not be able to have a woman for about a week. The doctor will tell you", said Jim.

Allen looked in the phone book and found a doctor. He made the call to make an appointment.

The lady on the phone said, "and what is the reason you want this appointment for Mr. Flatt"?

Allen stuttered, "I well, it's personal, could I speak to the doctor"?

"Well Mr. Flatt, I am the nurse and will have to know the reason. The doctor is busy right now", said the nurse.

"Well, I think, well I know, I have got the drip, disease", stuttered Allen.

"Oh", said the nurse. "Can you come in right away", ask the nurse.

"Yes, as soon as I can get there", answered Allen.

Allen arrived at the doctor's office after borrowing a pick-up truck from Will the Carney Man.

Allen was embarrassed at first. Once Allen went inside, he told the nurse who he was. After filling out the paperwork for the office, Allen asked in a whisper, "How long will it take to get well"?

The nurses ask Allen, "Has one of our girls in town been bad to you", with a little chuckle?

Allen said, "No actually it was in the last town. I am with the carnival country music tent show". This got all the nurses in the office excited. Allen was answering questions about the show.

Allen invited all the nurses to the show that night. All of them said they would be there.

That night after a couple of songs Allen looked and sitting on the front seats were the 3 nurses.

Allen said, "Folks I want to introduce you to 3 ladies I met today from your town. They are sitting right on the front seats". Allen then pointed to the front row. All the ladies started snickering and punching each other with their elbows.

Allen said, "Let me have them all stand up"! All the nurses stood up. Allen said, "I'd like to dedicate a song to them. They did me a great favor today"! All the nurses began snickering and shoving each other again.

"Here's a little love song called, I Ain't Goin Honky Tonkin' Anymore"! All the crowd burst into applause and the nurses sat down just laughing their heads off while shoving each other. Also, the band could hardly play from laughing at the inside joke.

The audience was just applauding very loud and whistling.

Allen talked to the nurses after the show. The one that he had talked to at the doctor's office was extra cute. Allen asked her if she would like to go out and get a late supper.

She smiled, and said, "See me the next time you come to town. Maybe you'll be well then".

Allen just grinned and said, "Well I see your point, but I feel better".

"Not good enough, there's not been enough time for the shot to cure you. Maybe next time", smiled the nurse.

Allen never saw the nurses again.

JOE ALLEN FLATT-at about 24 years of age

DAISY GRIFFIN-at about 18 years old.

18. 1946-ALLEN MEETS DAISY GRIFFIN AT THE COUNTY FAIR.

By the time Daisy was 16 she was sneaking out of the house with her neighbor girlfriend Reyna. Reyna had a boyfriend with a car, and she did not mind Daisy going along. They would go to the movies, and different places such as the county fair and this is how she met Allen Flatt.

The Beck's Shows and Amusement Carnival came up from Florida to Kentucky, and because it was the beginning of the spring season it would close down for 2 weeks for repairs before starting up for the run all through the summer then it would hold up in Florida and south west for the winter. The carnival would operate the rides in one spot for 1 month. The tent show would be closed down so that the crew could make repairs or replace the big tent Allen performed in. This gave the musicians and performers a chance to rest and go home for a short spell.

Allen was performing in the tent show and by now was a real professional. He put on a show that was just as good as any Nashville act. They were in Richmond, Kentucky for one week. Allen met lots of women coming to the fair and to the Country Tent Show. It never occurred to Allen he would meet a young woman that would shake his world. But during one of the shows he saw a young lady that he thought was the most beautiful person he had ever seen. So, when the show was over, he went and found her.

"Hi my name is Allen, what's your name", said Allen as sure of himself as he could be.

Daisy turned and saw who was speaking to her. She immediately recognized Allen from the show inside the tent. She thought he was cute when she was watching the show.

Allen weighed about 195 pounds, and was 6-foot, 1 inch tall. He had almost black hair with deep blue eyes, and when dressed in his stage clothing, he was most striking.

Allen looked at Daisy once he was up close and she was even prettier than she was from a distance. She had light blond hair with green eyes. Daisy weighed about 110 pounds, fully figured with a waist that Allen could almost imagine putting his hands around from thumb to middle finger. Daisy had a small mole on the right side of her nose up toward one of her eyes, but it did not take away from how beautiful she was. Her figure made her look more mature than she was. Allen thought she was a knockout. She was very beautiful and looked like her early 20's even though she was still just a teenager of 17years. Because of her intelligence she also acted older than she was also.

"My name is Daisy Griffin", said Daisy with a smile.

Allen looked at her with a smile and said, "I can get us on free, would you like to ride some rides with me"?

Daisy looked into Allen's blue eyes and said "sure". "But I will not ride anything that goes high, like the Farias Wheel. I am afraid of heights". Daisy had vertigo. She could stand on a chair without having a problem, but anything above about "6 foot tall" and as she put it, her head would swim.

So the couple went to the Carnival Midway hand in hand. They rode every ride at the Carnival except the high ones.

Daisy had never had enough money to ever ride more than a couple of rides. She was just overwhelmed with Allen's confidence, and good looks. It was love at first sight.

Allen also bought some hot dogs, cold drinks with ice, and waffle cakes.

Daisy had to finally start refusing his offers to buy food, because she was full to the brim.

Allen then took her to some of the games because he wanted to impress her.

He took her to the basketball throw and of course he won her a teddy bear. Then he took her to the string, ball and bowling pin game that he sometimes operated.

Allen leaned over to the operator and whispered, make me look good and I'll make it up to you". The operator smiled and winked at Allen. Allen won almost every game he played making himself look very good in Daisy's eyes.

By the end of the night when Daisy had to leave, it had been a wonderful night. Allen was trying to get Daisy to come back again tomorrow night. But Daisy told him she could not get out tomorrow night. Allen told her that he wanted to see her again.

"Where do you live", ask Allen?

"I live in Estill County Kentucky", answered Daisy hoping that Allen would not give up. But she did not want to tell Allen just how far back in the sticks she lived and that she had snuck out.

"I have a car, I can come and get you", said Allen.

"Well, you would have to first meet my daddy", said Daisy. "He is kind of old fashioned", said Daisy, a little embarrassed.

Allen must have noticed she had turned red. He said, "Oh don't feel ashamed, my family is kind of that way too", as he smiled back at her.

"Well, Allen my family lives way back in the sticks, just outside of Irvine, Kentucky. We live in a place called Doe Creek. Doe Creek is south of Ravenna. Ravenna is just outside of Irvine. Then you take the main road toward Doe Creek and Barns Mountain. Doe Creek is just before you get to Barns Mountain. If you blink you will miss Doe Creek. All we have is a store, a schoolhouse, and a couple of churches. Then you have to get off the big road at our mailbox that says Griffin and take the small road; and cross the creek twice and up several hills' way back up into the holler to Dad and Mom's house. You can drive a wagon and team of horses' right up to the house. But you cannot drive all the way to the house with a car. That is unless you have one of them 4-wheel drive cars, or a big truck" smiled Daisy. "Allen, we are poor country people that really live back in the woods" admitted Daisy.

Allen looked at her and suddenly understood.

As Allen spoke to her he was ashamed. He had put on the dog so much trying to impress her, with her, he said, "Daisy darling, I come from a poor family also. Understand that times were hard when both of us were born. My mother died when I was 9 days old, I was born in Middle Kentucky and I was raised by my Aunt Deelee and Uncle Will in a small town called Willow Grove, Tennessee. I come from a poor family also. I am really attracted to you and you don't need to worry about me thinking bad about you or your family. Cause I understand how being raised poor is".

Daisy looked at Allen and suddenly liked him even more than she had before.

"In that case you can come to visit me at my family's house. But you will have to ask my daddy about 'courting' me. My parents are very old fashioned", said Daisy.

"No problem", said Allen. "I will be over next Thursday to talk to your daddy", smiled Allen.

The next Thursday Allen drove over to Estill County. Allen had borrowed a used 4-wheel drive army jeep from the carnival because of what Daisy had told him about the road. Allen left Irvine, past Ravenna across a small river, on a 2-lane blacktop road going toward Doe Creek.

Allen decided to stop at a feed store to ask directions. It seems that the clerk at the feed store knew Rufford Griffin. Why he even knew Daisy Griffin and right where they lived.

"The farm is sure enough way back up in a holler", said the feed store clerk.

"It's not hard to find once you have been there", smiled the clerk. "But if you miss the mailbox you will miss the road going back up into the holler where they live. The name on the mailbox says R. Griffin", said the clerk. Take the big black top road till it turns into a big gravel road, once you get to a Y in the road, there is a store at the Y in the road. Then you are at Doe Creek. Take the right hand of the Y and watch for the mailbox. At the mails box, turn right up the small wagon path road", said the feed clerk. "You can't miss it once you are on the small wagon path road if you stay to the right. But the road does not have any cut offs if you stay to the right at the one Y in the road it has, and the road ends right at Rufford's house way back up in the holler. And there ain't any other houses you can end up at unless you go to the left at the Y. If you do go to the left then you will end up at the Roberts Family farmhouse", explained the feed store clerk. "But don't go to the left, go to the right", continued the feed clerk. "Right up the hill", added the clerk.

"Thank you", said Allen. Allen believed he could talk all day, but he was glad for the directions.

Allen left Irvine on the big black top 2 lane road, then suddenly it was no longer blacktopped. It just turned into a big gravel road, like the county had run out of money. Allen was on the big gravel road for about 5 miles when he came to a mailbox on the right-hand side of the road that had R. Griffin on the side of it. I would hate to try and find this place in the dark thought Allen.

Allen turned right on the small wagon road at the mailbox that said, "R. Griffin".

The road was just 2 worn tracks that look like they were made by a car's wheels, or better yet, wagon wheels. After turning right on the small road Allen finally came to a creek. It seems to Allen that he had gone about 1 mile before coming to the creek. Allen put the jeep into 4-wheel drive and eased down and across the creek and then up the other side of the creek bank. The water came up to about the middle of the wheels and tires. But the jeep pulled on through. After crossing the creek Allen eased on down the small wagon path for about another 2 miles then he came to another creek crossing. As it turned out it was the same creek. It was just where the creek wound around and the road crossed it again. This crossing had a small waterfall right next to it that poured over a big flat stone that the road went across. Again, Allen eased across the creek crossing. This time the water was not as deep because of the water crossing over the big flat rock. Then the water poured over the small waterfall just to the right of where the road crossed the creek. It was not as deep because the big flat stone that acted as the road's foundation, had kept it from being dug out. It made like a hard bottom for the creek crossing. But then suddenly there was a small hill coming up out of the creek bed so that Allen had to give it some extra throttle and spin his wheels. But the jeep just pulled up on to the other side of the creek bank where the road continued.

Now the little Army jeep was back on level ground and the small 2-wheel wagon road again.

Finally, Allen and the jeep came to a fork in the road just as the clerk had said back in Irvine. The left fork looked flat and smooth. The right fork went up a very steep hill just like someone had built the road up the hill because they had to for some reason. Allen did not know about the way Rufford had acquired the land for the right of way road. Allen backed up, put it in low gear, 4-wheel drive-, and built-up speed, changing gears until he was in 3rd gear. Just as he started up the steep hill his wheels began to spin so he had to downshift spinning his wheels. All the 4 wheels were spinning. Finally, he crests the top of the steep hill and the road flattened out again.

For the next 3 or 4 miles the little road was mostly flat and wound back and forth next to a creek going farther and farther back into the forest and hills. It would go up some small hills and down some small hills, sometimes close to the creek and sometimes farther away from the creek. Allen didn't know it, but it was the same creek that he had crossed 2 times before on the way in from the big road.

Finally, Allen and the army jeep came to the bottom of another steep hill that the wagon path road went up. Again, Allen backed up and took a running start to build up speed. As he started up the steep hill the tires again started to spin. Allen was down shifting, and slowly climbing the steep hill where the wagon road went.

It looked like at the last Rainstorm, the rainwater had run down the hill, and gorged out some ruts in the small road. While washing away some of the foundation of the road to the point that the little jeep bounced from rut to rut. Finally, at the top of the hill Allen could see a house, just a little further up the hill. Maybe that was it, the Griffin house he hoped. After all he was told the Griffin house was the only one up that way.

It was coming on about 30 minutes before sundown when the army jeep came into site from the house. Rufford, Nancy, and Daisy could hear the jeep coming up the holler before they saw it. The other Griffin children were gone, married, or off working. The little army jeep exhaust was making a lot of noise in the quite woody hollow where things could be heard for miles. Sometimes the Griffins could hear cars all the way over to the big gravel road. But they were not use to having vehicles coming all the way up the holler to their house. Because, it was very unusual for a vehicle to come, or to be able to even make it up to their house.

They were all outside standing on the big flat rock looking down the holler, when Allen came into view with the jeep.

Ben had brought a vehicle up to the house once or twice before; it was a 4-wheel drive, ¾ ton, pick-up army truck he had borrowed, but this was not the normal everyday thing.

"Rufford", said Nancy. "Who is that coming up the holler"?

"I don't know", said Rufford. "Is anybody expecting anyone", ask Rufford? "Or do I need to get my shotgun", ask Rufford?

"I don't know could it be Ben", ask Nancy?

Daisy did not know for sure because the jeep was still too far away to see who it was driving it, but she thought it could be Allen if he really did come like he said he would.

"Daddy, it may be a friend of mine. Please do not get your gun, you might scare him away", said Daisy.

"What friend", ask Rufford?

"If it is him, he is a friend I met at the fair that plays music at the country music show", explained Daisy.

"Well why is he coming' up here Dump", ask Rufford looking at Daisy? No one knew why Rufford gave Daisy the nickname of Dump.

"Daddy, please don't call me Dump", ask Daisy. "Well daddy, if it is him, he wants to ask if he can, a-a-a", stuttered Daisy.

"He wants to court you, right", ask Nancy with a stern voice, while staring at Daisy?

"Well, yes", answered Daisy.

"You sneak out, then want me to let some fellow come up here", snarled Rufford?

"Daddy I told you I was sorry for that, I just wanted to go to the fair", spoke Daisy about to cry. "Please be nice and don't embarrass me if it is him. Please daddy", begged Daisy.

"Embarrass you, I might shoot him", snapped Rufford!

"Wait a minute daddy", broke in Nancy. "Let's just calm down and see if it is him", added Nancy. "Daisy maybe you might want to go get on another dress and fix up in case it is him. Go on to the house", said Nancy.

Nancy said this to get Daisy out of the way so Rufford and she could talk.

Daisy said with a smile, "Thank you momma" exclaimed Daisy as she ran to the house! After all she had been slopping the hogs.

Once Daisy was out of sight in the house, Nancy said, "Daddy let us wait and see what this fellow is like. After all he has sure made a ruff trip; he must be interested in Daisy".

"I don't care who--", said Rufford as Nancy cut him off!

"Daddy stop and think", as Nancy cut Rufford off. "You remember what she did, sneaking off. Well stop and think, I knew a couple of young people that ran away when their folks said they could not get married or be together. Let us meet this fellow and see what he is like, and maybe she won't run away with him", said Nancy with a look at Rufford.

"I remember", studied Rufford. "And I see your point", said Rufford as he was thinking over remembering Nancy and him running away. "We don't want her to run off in the night", explained Rufford. Then Rufford studied looking down toward the wagon road.

Nancy and Rufford stood on the big flat rock that was at the edge of the yard overlooking the road that came up out of the valley between the mountains. The noise of the army jeep was getting louder all the time.

Finally, the army jeep came up the last hill and was moving toward the front yard of the house.

Allen could now see the house good with Rufford and Nancy standing out in front looking his way.

Rufford and Nancy could now also see the jeep crawling up the wagon road toward the house. The road went past the house and circled around by the water spring and came back to the house on fairly level ground. If Allen had continued past the spring the wagon road would have taken him to one of the pastures. But he had already been told that the Griffin house was the only one up this road. So, Allen turned and went toward the house at the spring. Allen pulled up into the front yard; the jeep came to stop as he turned off the motor.

Allen stepped out of the jeep.

"Hello folks is this where the Griffin Family lives", Allen asks with a great big grin and a King Edwards cigar sticking out of his mouth?

"Yeah, you got the right place", said Rufford with a short remark. "It's sure strange to see one of those contraptions coming up to our place", said Rufford with a stern stare. "Most of them vehicles won't make it all the way up here", snapped Rufford.

"Well, I can sure believe that", said Allen with a smile. "There were a couple of times on the way up here when I thought I might not make it myself", Allen said with another big grin.

"Everybody around here knows they can believe me. They know they can count on my word", snapped Rufford. Rufford snapped so short that Allen took a step back.

Nancy spoke up and said, "What's your name stranger"?

"I am Allen Flatt, actually Joe Allen Flatt", spoke Allen in a timid tone while looking at Rufford.

Allen stuck his hand out to shake Nancy's hand and she shook it back. And then Allen reached for Rufford's hand. Rufford did not extend his hand back in the same manner, he just stared at Allen.

"I am Nancy Griffin, and this is Rufford Griffin my husband", said Nancy.

"Mr. Flatt what can we do for you, that brought you all the way up here", asked Nancy?

Still glancing over at Rufford, Allen asked "Are you the parents of Daisy Griffin", ask Allen? He was beginning to think this might not have been a good idea.

"Yes, we are", spoke up Rufford.

Then he hollered toward the house, "Dump come out here"!

As we said before, no one knew why Rufford nicknamed Daisy "Dump". Daisy did not like it, but it still did not stop Rufford from calling her that. Allen had a strange look on his face when Rufford called her Dump.

"Well, sir, I met your daughter over at the county fair a few nights ago and I asked her if I could come callin', to court her. She told me I had to come and get your permission, so I am here to ask permission", blurted out Allen.

"My daughter, Dump, told you that", asked Rufford, surprised, giving' Allen the up and down stare? Rufford was enormously proud of his daughter Daisy because he had not told her of this rule but was very much in agreement with it. "Yes, that's the rule", lied Rufford.

"Well, what do you say Mr. Griffin", ask Allen? "Is it OK"?

Rufford's face turned from an almost smile to stern again.

"Well young man, I just met you. Her mother and I do not know you. We may want to get to know you a little bit first before we give our permission or not", said Rufford sarcastically.

"But let me tell you one thing young man, so we get off on the right step, if you ever hurt my daughter, there will not be a place far enough away, or back in the woods far enough that, that, contraption can take you, that I won't find you. Do you understand", asked Rufford.

"Yes, sir I would never hurt her", answered Allen.

About that time Daisy spoke from the door of the house.

"Hello Allen, have you met my parents?" she asks, trying to be up town.

"Yes, we were just getting to know each other, Dump", answered Allen with a smile.

"Daddy you know I don't like that name", said Daisy as she turned toward Rufford.

"And you", turning toward Allen, "most definitely can NOT call me that and keep me happy", she said looking at Allen with a stern look.

Allen smiled but got the message. Rufford even almost grinned.

After some small talk went by things began to loosen up.

"Daddy you should hear Allen sing", smiled Daisy trying to lighten the mood some more. "Allen Daddy likes Ernest Tubb and Bill Monroe, and Flatt and Scruggs", said Daisy.

"Mama, can Allen stay for supper", ask Daisy?

"Well yeah, if he likes corn bread, ham hocks, and beans", said Nancy not being sure how uppity Allen was.

"Yes, Mrs. Griffin, I was raised on cornbread, ham hocks and beans, and love them", smiled Allen trying to let them know he was from a country family.

"Then let's go get ready for supper and get to know each other", said Nancy. Everybody was smiling except Rufford. Rufford still was not sure of Allen and he was going to take his time to get to know him.

"Allen while mom and I get supper ready would you sing us some songs", ask Daisy?

"Sure", smiled Allen, "It's kind-a like singin' for my supper, and it just so happens I got my guitar in the jeep. I'll go get it".

As Allen went out to the jeep to get his guitar, Daisy said, "Thank you daddy for being so polite to him".

"Well, the jury is still out on that", answered Rufford, "but I'm trying, Dump".

Allen came back in and began to sing songs.

After a couple of songs, Rufford spoke up and said, "Daisy your right he does sound just like that fellow Ernest Tubb on the radio. It's just like listening to the Grand Ole Uproar on our battery radio".

This was the start of Rufford warming up to Allen. Plus, Allen had a knack for getting everyone to like him. Also, it did not hurt that Allen began to do requests. Allen of course knew all of Ernest Tubb's songs, and several Bill Monroe and Flatt and Scruggs songs, it did not hurt that he also did several Gospel songs that Nancy requested.

Nancy grinned and said," It's just like going to church or having' a party right here at the house"!

When Rufford found out that Allen worked for Bill Monroe and was a 3rd cousin to Lester Flatt the ice really started to melt. People were always asking Allen if he was any kin to Lester Flatt. This also still happens for Allen's children today. Being distant cousins always makes for a good story and ice breaker. Allen and Rufford talked that evening and had a good time.

"Well, I guess I had better be heading on back home", said Allen.

Rufford spoke up and said "Maybe you should stay the evening, that road is pretty dangerous and tuff after dark. Do you have to get back to work", ask Rufford?

"No sir, I am off for the next 2 weeks, while the carnival is shut down for repair and maintenance", answered Allen.

Well, there it is", said Rufford, "It is settled then, we will set you up a pallet on the floor. Then we will have breakfast in the morning".

Daisy was just smiling because she knew she would get to spend more time with Allen.

Rufford put Daisy in a bedroom right next to him and Nancy, and Allen had a pallet on the floor in the kitchen.

This way Rufford knew there would not be any hanky-panky between Allen and Daisy, because they would have to go past his bed to reach each other. Rufford slept light because of his days when he would carry prisoners for the Texas Rangers.

The next morning Allen woke up when he heard Nancy getting ready to start breakfast.

Allen asks, "Mrs. Griffin, is there anything I can do to help"?

Nancy turned and looked at Allen and said, "Why sure, how about going to the spring to bring in a bucket of water, and the glass jug of milk we got cooling in the spring". "Also, you can start calling me Nancy".

Allen said, "Yes Miss Nancy".

About that time Daisy came to the kitchen, spoke up and said, "I'll show him where the spring is Momma".

Nancy smiled and said, "Well if you think he can't find it by himself but hurry up I need that water and milk right away".

Allen had seen the spring as he drove in, but he liked the idea of getting to take the walk with Daisy, so he did not say anything.

Nancy knew how to make a good country breakfast that would stick to a working man's ribs. She made milk gravy, biscuits, and eggs. For meat they had some of the last of their bacon from their own home grown hogs they had butchered, smoked, and salted, and hung in the smoke house the year before. If you went away from Nancy's table hungry it was because you did not eat.

Rufford and Allen were talking at the breakfast table and it came up that Rufford needed to go to town. Allen offered to drive him into town in the jeep. Rufford could make the trip to town much, much faster in the jeep than on horse, or wagon so he agreed to let Allen take him. Rufford had never learned to drive a vehicle. Daisy spoke up and wanted to go with them.

Rufford asks, "Mama do you want to go with us to town"? "You haven't been to town for a long time", said Rufford.

Nancy answered, "After you take care of business, I could visit with some of the ladies, while you smoke and whittle at the courthouse".

"Yeah, and with Allen's contraption we won't have to leave so early to get back before dark", said Rufford.

"Yeah", said Allen!

"Yeah", said Daisy!

"Agreed", said Nancy!

Irvine was just like most country towns in those days, it had a town square with a CourtHouse in the middle where a lot of the people would meet. The men would whittle, and tell ornery jokes, and the women would gossip about all the other women that were not there. This happened every Saturday. All around the town square were different types of stores. Allen and Daisy went shopping and to a movie while Rufford and Nancy were taking care of business and buying a few supplies. Allen bought Daisy and Nancy a nice Sunday Dress, and some groceries like bread, and some cheese. A thing like, store bought bread (was called light bread by the Griffins) was so special it was like cake. Everybody only got one piece at a time because it cost hard cash which came slowly. After coming back from the movie, Allen went and whittled a little with the men, while Daisy went and sat with the women. Allen had a Tree Brand Bowker pocket knife that could shave the hair off a person's arm. Allen told some good ornery jokes with the men. Allen was an excellent joke teller. Maybe it was because of his music and show business background, but he had a way of telling a joke to make it funny even when no one else could. Plus, he seems to be able to remember jokes for a long time so that he knew the latest jokes that others had not heard. He heard new jokes at the carnival all the time. The jokes sometimes could get real nasty in language and subject. If women were within sound distance that they could hear, the men would whisper the nasty words. In those days' men treated women with respect. If they would not say it in front of a child, then they would not say it in front of a woman. That is unless there was an argument or fight among men. Then everyone was on their own.

All in all, the day was a good one. Finally, they loaded back up in the jeep and headed back to Doe Creek. By this time Rufford had begun to like Allen a lot. Allen was the kind of fellow that most all people liked. It was like Allen never met a stranger. Rufford agreed to let Allen come over when he could and visit with Daisy. Rufford just insisted that Allen remember that Daisy was his youngest, and what he had told him when he first met him about never hurting her. Allen did not have to go back to work right away so he stayed with the Griffins and helped Rufford do some work around the farm. Rufford liked to have a man help with the chores.

One day Allen came in with a big grin on his face holding a 10-foot snake that he had killed in the barn.

"I killed this big old snake in the barn", Allen smiled with pride to Rufford.

"Damn it! Son of a bitch! I put him in there", cussed Rufford. Allen could see that Rufford was terribly upset.

Nancy spoke up and said, "Allen that's the barn snake. As long as it is around, poisonous snakes will not stay around. As much as I hate snakes, we prefer ones that are not dangerous".

Rufford spoke up in a very loud voice, and said, "Also it eats rats and creatures that eat my corn and grain"!

"Allen do you know it took me over six months to buy that snake. I put out a message to all farmers at the courthouse in Irvine that I needed a black barn snake. It will take me months to replace it", explained Rufford.

"Well don't I feel stupid", explained Allen. "Rufford, I am very sorry. All I could see was that it was a snake. I could not see the color. I just knew Daisy hated snakes.

Guess I thought I was being a hero or something. I am sorry! I will be glad to pay for a new one", apologized Allen.

"Well first I gotta find one", said Rufford. "But I'm sure you meant no harm, but until I find one you all need to watch yourself in the barn for poisonous snakes, copperheads, rattle snakes, and such", warned Rufford.

Finally came the day that Allen had to leave to go back to work at the Carnival show.

Everybody was sad to see Allen go, but most of all was Allen and Daisy. As Daisy, Nancy, and Rufford waved goodbye from the big flat rock in the front corner of the yard that overlooked the road, there were tears in Daisy's eyes. Mostly because she was afraid, she would never see Allen again. Although, he had promised to see her as soon as he could.

2 months went by, and all this time Daisy was missing Allen. Allen was also missing Daisy.

Ben had married Evelyn and had promised to stay close to help Rufford and Nancy. Ben had an automobile he drove to work at Avon and would give them rides to town and church. When he could get Rufford to go to church, but Nancy went every Sunday, morning and a lot of evenings. Rufford had given

Ben (Daisy's older but youngest brother) a parcel of land right beside the wagon type road. It was about three quarters the way between the Big Gravel Road and the Griffin House. It was just across the creek that ran beside the little road. Ben had built a bridge across the creek from bank to bank, he parked his car on the roadside of the creek, but the house was on the other side of the creek. He had electricity and a TV, but still used an outhouse and had to pump water from a well. The electricity wires stopped at Ben's house. Ben would from time to time raise a couple hogs and put out a vegetable garden. But he worked at a place called AVON in Richmond, KY. It was a good drive but a good job.

Then one day Daisy. Nancy and Rufford heard in the distance the sound of an automobile engine. If the vehicle were not 4-wheel drive and sat high off the ground it could only get past Ben's house to the bottom of the last hill before reaching Rufford and Nancy's house all the way back up in the holler. You had to drive to that point and then park and walk the last ½ a mile or so to the house. The last hill always was washed out with big ruts up and down the hill where the road ran, and it took a 4-wheel drive vehicle or a big truck to make it.

Daisy, Nancy, and Rufford stopped their chores and listened. Yeah, there was a vehicle coming up into the holler.

Nancy asks, "That doesn't sound like Ben's car, wonder who that could be"?

"Your right Nancy, it does not sound like Ben's car. Anyway, he would most likely walk up here unless he was in a hurry for some reason. It sounds like whoever it is has stopped down at the foot of the last hill though", explained Rufford.

Nancy, Rufford, and Daisy all went to stand on the big flat rock at the front end of the house looking down toward the little road where it topped the last steep hill. All of a sudden, they could see someone walking up toward the house. From a distance they could not tell who it was.

'Well, there comes someone", said Rufford. "But I can't tell who it is at this distance", explained Rufford. "Looks like he is carrying something", said Rufford as he strained to see. All three of them were straining to see who it was walking up the road while standing on the big flat rock.

Suddenly Daisy made a big yell and took off down off the big flat rock that they all used for a landing that was even with the ground around the house. Over the hill to the road went Daisy at a run, hollering, "Allen, Allen"!

Daisy ran up to Allen and threw her arms around his neck and gave him a big kiss. Normally she would have been concerned about Rufford watching, but this time she did not care.

Allen had a package in his arms that he had dropped. He picked it up and took Daisy's hand and headed for the house with Nancy and Rufford watching from afar. They had a great evening talking and fellowshipping.

Allen spoke up and said, "Folks I didn't come just to visit, I came to ask you, Rufford, and Nancy, for Daisy's hand in marriage. If it is OK with you, we will go to town tomorrow and get married at the courthouse", asked Allen?

Rufford was not saying a word.

Looking at Rufford Allen said, "Sir I can't live without Daisy. If she will have me, and it is OK with you folk, I have got her a job with the carnival. And I am going to take her with me"!

"Oh, please daddy, I love him so much", said Daisy almost at a shout!

"Well, Dump, you could at least act a little hard to get", smiled Rufford.

"Miss Nancy, I want you to come to the wedding, and of course you too Rufford, you got to give her away. Miss Nancy, I got you and Daisy a brand-new dress in this package I have here. And Rufford I got you a new pair of bib overalls and a nice Sunday "gotomeeting" suit jacket to wear. Daisy I also got you a new pair of shoes to go with the new dress. It's not white, but I hope you will like it".

"Oh, I am sure I will", said Daisy without even seeing the dress.

Rufford spoke up and said, "Well son they now require you two to get a blood test and a license to get married now".

"Yes sir, I checked into it and we can get it done first thing in the morning and then go to the courthouse and get married. Daisy and I got to be back to the carnival by Monday morning. So, we will have to leave on Sunday", said Allen.

Allen looked at Nancy and could see tears whaling up in her eyes.

"I'm sorry Miss Nancy, I know this is kind of fast, but I promise I'll take good care of her. To be honest I thought Rufford would be the one I would have the hardest time convincing", explained Allen.

"No, Allen I know Daisy cannot stay here in this holler, but she is my youngest child. You got to promise me you will bring her back to visit from time to time", said Nancy almost crying.

"I will, you got my word", said Allen.

Daisy gave Nancy a big hug while both cried and wiped tears from their eyes.

Then they all went into the house to make ready for the morning and the wedding. They all tried on their new clothes, they all fit. Nancy and Daisy used the old solid metal irons that were heated on Nancy's cooking stove to iron all the clothes and hung them up for the morning.

The next morning after breakfast they all walked down to Allen's car and drove to town. They went to the doctor to get a blood test, then over to the courthouse where Allen bought him and Daisy a marriage license. Then Nancy took them to a preacher's house she knew that was all the way back to Doe Creek. On Saturday, August 03,1946 Allen, and Daisy, got married in Estill County Kentucky. After the ceremony Allen took Rufford and Nancy back up to the holler. Allen said they were going to spend their marriage night in a Hotel, but not before promising Nancy that they would come back up to the holler for breakfast, and Church before leaving for the carnival the next afternoon. Nancy had got in touch with as many of the Griffin children and their family that she could. They were all going to come up for breakfast and church or at least supper before Allen and Daisy headed out.

Allen and Daisy were so happy after dropping off Rufford, and Nancy. Allen stopped and bought some moonshine from a fellow on Barns Mountain before heading back to Irvine. He had met this fellow at the courthouse the last trip. Then he stopped at the store and got RC cola to mix with it for Daisy. They had a wonderful night.

The next morning Allen, and Daisy, went back up to the holler to have breakfast and spend some time with Rufford, Nancy and the family before leaving.

Daisy said on the way back to the holler, "I am a little ashamed".

Allen looked over at her as he drove along, "Why", said Allen?

"Because they are gonna know what we did last night", answered Daisy.

Allen began to laugh and ask, "Well how do you think they got you"?

"I know", said Daisy, "but it was the first time and just last night".

"Don't worry honey, you don't say anything, and they won't", Allen smiled at her and hugged her close with one arm while driving with the other. Allen was right no one brought the subject up, and they had a wonderful time at their folks house the first time as husband and wife. The family all seem to like Allen, especially the brother in laws. That afternoon there were tears from the women and hugging before leaving. Allen and Daisy headed off to the carnival so they could be at work on Monday morning. Everybody stood and waved on the big flat rock at the edge of the yard.

Allen and Daisy worked at the carnival for 1 year before the carnival closed and suddenly, they were out of work. Allen rented a car so they could get back to the holler. Finally, Allen realized that he had kept the car too long and that he could not afford to pay the rental bill. The car being parked up in the holler makes

Allen believe that maybe the rental company will not be able to find the car, or him. But, at last the rental company sends a sheriff to arrest Allen because he did not take it back. Allen goes to jail, and then court. They send him to LaGrange Kentucky Prison where he receives 11 months and 29 days for grand theft auto. Daisy visited him as often as she could get a ride. Daisy got a job in Irvine at a restaurant as a waitress to save enough money to buy a car, so she could visit Allen at the prison more often. Finally, Allen got out of prison on good behavior; Allen and Daisy lived up in the holler with Rufford and Nancy and worked in Irvine. Allen was on parole so him and Daisy decided as soon as Allen was off parole they were going to move to Nashville. They would get jobs and try Allen's hand in the music business.

ICTU

19. 1948 ALLEN AND DAISY MOVE TO NASHVILLE, TN.

Finally, Allen and Daisy had saved enough money, and Allen was off parole. Allen had fixed the old car up that Daisy had bought while Allen was in jail to make sure it would make the trip. So, they loaded up their old 1939 Ford to move to Nashville. After saying goodbye to Rufford and Nancy they hit the road across Kentucky west then south to Nashville, the home of the Grand Ole Opry.

Allen got a job at Firestone changing semi-truck tires. Hard work, but Allen did not mind if he could get started in the music business in Nashville. Sometimes he would work later in the day, and sometimes he would work starting in the morning. This gave him time to push for a recording contract.

Daisy got a job as a waitress at a small restaurant. One of those restaurants that cook burgers and home cooked meals like most cities such as Nashville and other larger cities have.

Allen finally got him a radio show on WLIX in Nashville 5 days a week, Monday thru Friday. He would go do the radio program and then put on his uniform and go to Firestone and change truck tires. After about 6 months Allen put together a band called Allen Flatt and the Night Owls. This made his radio program better. Then he was able to get another radio program at WLAC in Gallatin, TN. It was also 5 evenings a week, Monday thru Friday. Allen's fan base soon increased to a large crowd. Daisy would help him read his fan mail and answer it back. Allen would do most of his radio commercials but occasionally the radio would do a commercial and this gave Allen a short break.

One day while Allen was doing his evening radio show Daisy gave him a note that said there is a man here who wants to talk to you. He said he is from Ernest Tubb. Allen smiled and whispered to her, "Well he is most likely full of it, but tell him I will talk to him after the radio show is over". Allen looked at Daisy and winked, "Just in case he is telling the truth", smiled Allen at Daisy.

When the radio program was over Allen went out to the front in the hall and there stood a man fairly normal looking except that he wore a cowboy hat. As Allen walked up to him, he put out his hand and said, "Hello, I am Allen Flatt! My wife said you wanted to talk to me".

"Yes sir! My name is Bill Wheeler. I am Ernest Tubb's brother-in-law. ET sent me over to give you a message. He reached into his pocket and pulled out a note and handed it to Allen. Allen looked at the note, on it was a phone number and written under it was signed Ernest Tubb.

"Mr. Flatt", said Bill Wheeler.

"Call me Allen", said Allen.

"OK, Allen, ET wanted me to ask you to call him at that number. That is his home number. He said maybe you two could have some fun".

"Have some fun", ask Allen?

"Don't know, I guess he will tell you when you call", smiled Bill.

Try calling him tomorrow morning Saturday, between 6 am and 11 am. He doesn't sleep late, but after about noon he starts doing his chores for the day and going down to 16th avenue to the record company, then he would perform on the Grand Ole Opry, and of course the radio show on WSM after the Opry the "Midnight Jamboree". "Oh, and he said if his phone is busy keep trying".

Allen followed him out to the front of the radio station and there sat a Big, Black, limousine Cadillac, with a luggage rack on top. In those days most of the country stars traveled in a limousine. This was before they started using the converted Greyhound bus to travel in.

Allen thought to himself maybe this fellow is on the up and up. Bill went around to the driver's seat of the big, black limousine. He got in and honked as he drove away.

Allen became shaky as he realized that he may get to talk to his hero, Ernest Tubb in person. He will find out tomorrow. What could he want with me, thought Allen? Is he going to cuss me out for sounding like him, Allen asked himself silently? Guess I will find out tomorrow.

Allen could hardly sleep that night he was so excited. The next morning Allen was up at the crack of dawn waiting for 6 am. But Allen thought maybe I should not act too excited. Maybe I should wait until 7 am. Wonder if that fellow Bill is pulling a joke on me. Finally, it was 7 am Saturday morning.

Allen had to walk up to the phone on the corner. In those days, most people did not have a phone. Allen and Daisy had been talking about getting a phone because he had now become so busy in the music. Allen picked up the phone, put the nickel in the phone and with a shaking finger dialed the number on the note signed Ernest Tubb. The phone rang on the other end. It rang again. Then all of a sudden, a deep bass voice on the other end of the phone said "Hello"?

Allen knew immediately who he was taking to. He could recognize that voice anywhere.

"This is Allen Flatt, is this the number of Ernest Tubb", ask Allen?

"Yes, sir it is", boomed the voice on the other end.

"Do you know a fellow named Bill Wheeler, ask Allen?

"I sure do. He is my brother-in-law, answered ET. Allen knew at once the man Bill Wheeler was on the up, and up.

Ernest Tubb said, "Yeah, Allen I sent Billy over to you. I know this is late notice, but I've been listening to your radio show whenever I am at home from the road. I was just wondering would you be willing to come down tonight and perform on my radio show. The Midnight Jamboree right after the Opry. As you may know we have guest performers from time to time. If you can come on down, we will have some fun".

"Tonight, I sure can, would love to, explained Allen trying not to sound too excited but professional

"If you can get there around 11:00 pm tonight we will run through the songs you are going to do with the Texas Troubadours. I have got a little surprise and we can have some fun. Just come through the record shop and on to the back and then backstage. I will have the people doing security watching out for you. I'll be looking forward to meeting you", said Ernest Tubb.

"Yes sir Mr. Tubb, I mean I'd love to", said Allen so excited that he could hardly talk.

After they hung up Allen was dancing for joy. He went home and told Daisy, "Ernest Tubb wants me to perform on his Midnight Jamboree radio show tonight".

After Allen had told Daisy all about the phone call, they were both excited.

Daisy asked, "Well what did he say actually"?

"Well, he wanted me to practice with the Texas Troubadours. So, I guess he wants me to sing? He said we were gonna have some fun, that's all", replied Allen to Daisy.

They both now had a confused look on their face.

Daisy said, "We need to go down to Hank and Audrey's Corral and get you a new western shirt to wear".

Hank and Audrey's Corral was a Western Wear Store just down on 724, Commerce St. in Nashville. The Ernest Tubb Record shop where the Ernest Tubb, Midnight Jamboree radio show on WSM Radio 650 AM on the dial, took place, was on Commerce Avenue at that time also. Much later the Ernest Tubb Record Shop moved to Broadway where it had been ever since. Hank and Audrey's Corral was a western clothing store that was owned by Hank Williams and Audrey Williams. They also had a radio show that took place there at their western store on Saturday afternoons on WSM radio 4:30 to 5:30 pm. Allen, and Daisy, had both been down before to see the radio show's at "Hank and Audrey's Corral" and the "Midnight Jamboree" at Ernest Tubb's Record Shop. The Ernest Tubb Midnight Jamboree at the Ernest Tubb Record Shop came on right after the Grand Ole Opry at midnight on WSM radio station 650 AM. And it is still going on today.

After going shopping Allen, and Daisy, went to get something to eat at the restaurant that Daisy worked at.

That evening Allen, and Daisy, went to the Ernest Tubb Record Shop just as planned. After parking they walked up Commerce Avenue and entered the record shop. The record shop was so full of people that Allen, and Daisy, could hardly get through to the back where the stage was. They walked all the way to the back of the record shop through a sea of people to where there was a stage. There was a man standing beside the stage looking to be on guard duty.

Allen walked up to him with Daisy and said, "Hello, I was told to come down here by Ernest Tubb. My name is Allen Flatt. This is my wife Daisy".

"Oh, yeah, you know how many times I get told that in an evening" he said in a rude police officer voice. Allen had a look on his face of what the hell am I gonna do.

"No just kiddin'," smiled the officer. Then he said, "ET told me to be expecting you. Would you come right this way", said the security man as polite as could be.

Allen and Daisy followed the security man back beside the stage and turned through a door into a big room. There were people standing all around. Some tuning instruments, and practicing, others just talking or telling jokes. Suddenly Allen saw him, his hero, there he was, Ernest Tubb. He was tall, skinny, with jet black hair, in western clothes, boots, and cowboy hat. The security man walked right up to him and whispered something in his ear. Suddenly he quit talking, took the cigarette out of his mouth with his left hand and stepped toward Allen, and Daisy. He stuck out his right hand and shook Allen's hand.

"I'm Allen Flatt, I talked to you on the phone", smiled Allen

"I am Ernest Tubb" he said in an announcer's voice with a Texas drawl. "I am so glad to meet you. I am glad you could come down here tonight. We are gonna have some fun this evening. I want you to kick off the program tonight just like you were me. Use my theme song, Walking the Floor Over You. I want you to sing it, take my guitar. As soon as the song is over, I will step up to the mic and take over".

Allen was in amazement while trying to put the Custom Martin D-45, 6 string guitar around his neck that Ernest Tubb had just handed to him. The guitar had Ernest Tubb on the neck, in mother of pearl, with a tooled leather strap. It fit exactly right.

"Who is this pretty darling lady you got with you Allen", ask ET looking at Daisy with a smile.

"Oh, excuse me Mr. Tubb, this is my wife Daisy", answered Allen.

Well, some people have all the luck, you sure got a pretty, and darling wife, smiled ET as he shook Daisy's hand. (from that time on he always called Daisy, Darling)

"By the way Allen, call me Ernest, or like a lot of my friends do, call me ET", smiled ET.

"Billy, come over here", waved ET to Billy Byrd, his lead guitar player. Ernest Tubb was one of the first country artists to have an electrified guitar player. All the other instruments except the steel guitar were acoustic.

Billy Byrd walked over to where they were standing.

ET said, "Allen is going to sing Walkin' The Floor Over You and I want you to come in with the lead".

"What key Allen", ask Billy looking confused?

ET spoke up and said, "Just like you were doing it for me, same key and everything".

Billy looked confused again. It was very unusual for a guest to sing a star's hit song. But ET was the boss. Then Billy hit into the song.

Allen sang, "I'm walking the floor over you", "I can't sleep a wink that is true"!

Billy looked still confused but smiled a big smile.

ET smiled and said, "We are gonna have some fun tonight".

Billy said, "What are you up to, ET"?

ET said with a smile, and once again, said "We are gonna have some fun tonight"!

ET looked at Billy and said, "Also run through a song that he wants to do also and learn the kickoff. Just do a turnaround in the middle".

Billy asks, "What song do you want to do of your own Allen"?

Allen looked at Billy and said, "I AIN'T GOIN' HONKY TONKIN' ANYMORE". Then Allen asks, "do you know it"?

Billy said, "Do just a little of it for me".

Allen sang just a verse and chorus of it and Billy said, "That will be fine. What do you have a verse, and chorus, turnaround, and another verse and chorus"? "Then do you do a tag", ask Billy Byrd?

"Yes, I do", answered Allen. "What about the rest of the band", ask Allen?

"Oh, they'll get it just fine, they watch me, I'll lead them", explained Billy.

"Well, I guess that's why you fellows work for a star, you know what you are doing", smiled Allen.

"Yeah, that's just part of the job, learning' stuff fast", answered Billy with a smile.

After almost an hour had passed it was getting close to program time. Allen was still holding Ernest Tubb's guitar. He was afraid to set it down. Afraid he would get it out of tune or scratch it.

Billy walked over and said, "Allen let me have ET's guitar for a second to check the tuning. That is part of the job too", he smiled.

Allen handed the beautiful Martin D-45 to Billy. Billy played each string one at a time until all six had been tuned. He never played a chord, just handed it back to Allen.

Allen could not believe he could tune it so fast without even playing a chord. Then Allen remembered that Lester Flatt used to do the same thing. Allen had heard it called perfect pitch. Allen played some chords, and it was perfectly in tune. This amazed Allen.

"Get ready fellows," said the announcer.

"Allen you go on out with the band", said ET with a smile.

Allen and the band walked through the door out to the record shop and up onto the small barroom size stage.

The announcer was looking at his pocket watch counting the seconds and they were listening over the speaker system to the Grand Ole Opry which played live just before the Midnight Jamboree. Roy Acuff was finishing up the Opry for the night. Roy Acuff as he was saying good night he said, "Ladies and gentlemen stay tuned for the Ernest Tubb's, Midnight Jamboree coming up next on WSM clear channel 650, on your dial".

All at once the announcer pointed at Billy Byrd, and Billy kicked the song off with the famous 3-part lead in, that starts the guitar vamp, that opens the theme song of the Ernest Tubb show. Allen knew every note by heart and sang,

"I'm walkin' the floor over you; I can't sleep a wink that is true.

I'm hopin' and I'm prayin' till my heart breaks right in two,

I'm walkin' the floor over you".

Allen sang just like Ernest Tubb would do. He had heard Ernest Tubb do it a thousand times, and had it memorized.

The audience began to applaud, as the announcer stepped up to the microphone very confused. Looking toward the door to the back room wondering where ET was. The announcer began to speak into the microphone as the music kept playing.

"Ladies and Gentlemen, welcome to the Ernest Tubb, Midnight Jamboree on WSM, 650, clear channel on your dial. Ladies and Gentlemen here is your host of the Midnight Jamboree, Er--nest Tubb and the Texas Troubadours" introduced the confused announcer!

Ernest Tubb stepped through the door from backstage, laughing and waving at the crowd. As the crowd burst into another big round of applause.

Allen continued to sing until the song was done and the Texas Troubadours brought the song to a big end.

ET stepped up to the microphone and said, "Ah, Thank You, Friends and neighbors Thank you"! As the crowd applause died down, ET began to speak, "Ladies and Gentlemen I want you to write in and let me know how many thought that was me singing' Walkin' The Floor Over You. If you thought it was me just let me know. If you thought it wasn't me tell me so also".

ET later told dad that the mail was about 75 % thought it was ET singing the song.

"Now I want to introduce the fellow that was actually singing Walkin' the Floor Over You just a minute ago", continued ET. "Ladies, Gentleman here is fellow that has a wonderful radio program Monday thru Friday on a different radio station here in Nashville singing' a song for you called, AIN'T GOIN' HONKY TONKIN' ANYMORE" announced Ernest Tubb, "Here is Al---Len Flatt"!!! "Let's give him a big hand" as he motioned to the crowd by clapping his hands above his head and waving toward the stage.

Billy Byrd kicked the song off with perfect perfection although it had been over an hour earlier that he had learned it.

The crowd loved it and gave Allen a big round of applause.

After the radio show was over, ET told Allen, "Come on down any Saturday night and if there is room on the show, I will put you on. Also, you can park around back where the musicians, and I park, and just come in the back door like we all do. Everybody knows you down here now, just knock on the back door, and someone will let you in".

Allen came down to the record shop and would hang out backstage and tell jokes almost every Saturday night that he was not playing a show of his own somewhere.

Allen got to know some up and comer recording artists, and musicians on a first name basis, and they would hang out and come perform on Allen's radio programs. Some of them became Grand Ole Opry Stars. Allen became friends with Hank Williams, Sr., Carl Smith, Carl Butler, Little Jimmy Dickens, Hank Thompson, Red Sovine, and many others. Allen even taught Ernie Ashworth to play the guitar. As a matter of fact, after Ernie Ashworth learned to play guitar, he played rhythm guitar on Allen's morning radio show. Later, after Allen had left Nashville and got out of the music business Ernie Ashworth got a big hit called "Talk Back Trembling Lips".

Allen was down at the record shop on Saturday night when ET asked, "Allen what record label do you record on"?

Allen answered, "ET, I have tried all over Nashville to get a recording contract and cannot get anyone to sign me because they say I sound too much like you. I'll be honest with you I don't know how to sound any other way", smiled Allen.

"Is that right", ask ET? All the while he studied the wall behind Allen.

"Allen would you mind if I made a phone call Monday to someone I know at a label", ask ET?

"Oh, of course not", answered Allen. "I would be glad for any help I can get", smiled Allen.

ET added, "Well this label is not a big one, but it is run by some good fellows I know. The label is called Tennessee Jubilee Records. I believe it would be a good start for you. I need to call them early Monday morning and see if they will be interested. So, give me a call at home around 9:00 am, that will give me time to call them and talk to 'em. I will give you the name, and number of who to get in touch with when you call me. They also have a publishing company for the songs you write. I have heard some of your songs and they sound good".

"Thanks, ET, I sure appreciate this", said Allen as he shook ET's hand.

Monday came around, and Allen called ET form work on break. ET answered and told Allen that he should go over to Tennessee Jubilee Records for a meeting and gave him the address. Tennessee Jubilee Records had an artist on it by the name of Benny Martin, who played the fiddle. After work Allen went to the record company and the A&R man had him sing a couple of songs. Allen signed a 1year contract and had his first recording session set up for the next week.

One phone call from the Grand Ole Opry legend Ernest Tubb broke down all the doors Allen was not able to get opened on his own for over a year.

20. 1949-ALLEN BECOMES FRIENDS WITH THE LEGEND, HANK WILLILAMS, SR.

Allen would hang out at Hank and Audrey's Corral (Hank Williams, Sr. and Audrey Williams western wear store down on Broadway). Allen had met Hank at the Midnight

Jamboree and Allen and Hank became friends right away. Both like to have a drink now and then, and both liked to tell dirty jokes to each other.

Funny thing though Dad (Allen) made the remark to me one time when the movie "Your Cheatin Heart" about Hank Williams Sr., came out starring George Hamilton, that he had never seen Hank, Sr. drunk when he knew him.

Allen came into Hank and Audrey's Corral one day and Hank was sitting in the back behind his desk with his boots up on the desk. Audrey was sitting over to the side at another desk writing in what looked like a ledger.

Hank asks, "Allen how the hell are you doing"? Hank as usual was dressed totally in his western apparel.

"Just great, Hank, how are you", answered Allen.

"Well, I have a problem. You may be able to help me. Are you busy right now", ask Hank?

"No, what you got in mind Hank", asked Allen.

"Well, Audrey's folks are coming in on a plane at the airport today. We were supposed to pick them up at four o'clock, but I've got a recording session I got to go to, and Audrey has got to go down to the bank to take care of some business at the same time they are supposed to be picked up", said Hank. "Could you go pick them up for us", ask Hank looking over at Audrey?

"Sure Hank, be glad to help any way I can", said Allen.

"Audrey you drop me at the session with my car and Allen you go over here to the garage and get Audrey's car. It's full of gas and here is 80 bucks" said Hank.

"Once you pick them up at the airport stop off and get them something to eat. That will give us time to get everything done. Just keep the change", said Hank.

"No, Hank you don't owe me anything for doing a favor", said Allen.

"No, Allen, you keep it. You are helping us out of a jam. Take that pretty wife of yours out on the town tonight", smiled Hank at Allen.

"I'll call over to the garage and tell them to let you have Audrey's car, just ask for it when you get there", said Hank.

Allen always wore hat and western clothes just like Hank when he was not at work at Firestone. Allen went to the garage where Hank and Audrey always parked and asked for Audrey William's car. The man got on the public address system and announced, "bring up Hank William's Cadillac to the front".

The people that were in the garage at the time all looked toward Allen. Allen could see people whispering and looking his way. Finally, the valet pulled up with a brand-new Baby Blue, Convertible Cadillac. He got out and Allen got in and drove out of the garage feeling like he was somebody important. Allen picked up Audrey William's dad and mom at the airport and took them to a nice restaurant explaining that Hank and Audrey were tied up with business and would meet them later back at the western store later that afternoon. Allen went by and picked up Daisy who had gotten off of work, and they all went to a nice restaurant and had drinks and a great meal. They had a great afternoon with Allen and Daisy. Allen had a way of getting people to like him right away. Allen and Daisy for that matter, never met a stranger. They both made friends extremely easy. After the meal they drove back to the western store. Allen had $65.00 left over even though he had not spared any expense just like Hank said. Allen offered the money back to Hank when no one was around.

Hank said, "no Allen, that is for you and Daisy. You folks use it for whatever you need. I knew they would have a good time with you, and you would take good care of them. You're maybe one of the few people I could trust to do this for me. You really did me and Audrey a favor I won't forget it".

Allen did not get any hits when on Tennessee Jubilee Records. When his contract ran out, he was offered a contract with a major recording company that had decided to get into Country Music in Nashville. Allen signed a recording contract with Mercury Record of Nashville. He got a $500.00 dollar contract signing advance from Mercury Records. On his first session Chet Adkins who was playing sessions at that time as well as playing with the Carter Family on the Grand Ole Opry played guitar for Allen. Also Moon Mullins, another great session musician, played piano on his recordings. Both these fine musicians went on to become legends in country music. Allen recorded "Vacant Lot Where My castle Use To Be", and "Cheat, Cheat, Cheatin" on his first session with Mercury Records. He went on to record 14 more sides.

Allen and Daisy could use the money. At the end of the year in 1949 Allen and Daisy found out that Daisy was pregnant, and the doctor had said she would have to stay off her feet. The waitress job she had was a definite no, no, until after the baby came. There was too much walking and staying on her feet at the café. So she would have to be a housewife until I was born. Dad took on a truck driving job at Garrett Construction. We lived at 2411 Eugenia Avenue, Nashville, TN. Dad was 27 years old, and mom was 21 years old and Christmas was coming on.

21. 1950- ERNEST ALLEN FLATT IS BORN.

Allen was supposed to perform and was hanging out at the Midnight Jamboree on a late Saturday night August 12, 1950.

Suddenly the record shop manager came to the backstage room, that we now a days call the green room.

"Allen I just got a call to give you a message ", said the record shop manager, "they have just taken your wife, Daisy, is in a cab, to the hospital. They think the baby is coming"!

Allen and ET who had been talking stopped, turned and faced the record shop manager.

"Which hospital", ask Allen?

"I think they said Vanderbilt", answered the manager.

Allen said, "Well gotta go ET".

ET said, "Sure you go be with your family. "Can you drive OK", ask ET?

"Sure", said Allen. "My parts are already done, it was the easy part", laughed Allen sticking his big cigar in his mouth. Not wanting everyone to know how nervous he was.

Everybody laughed, including ET and the manager.

Allen puffed on his cigar as he started for the door.

ET called out, "Allen if it's a boy name it after me"!

"Will do", said Allen as he went out the back door to where the musicians parked.

Allen arrived at the hospital and went to the emergency room. The nurse said they had already sent her up to the maternity ward, to be prepared for birth.

Allen made his way to the maternity ward where a nurse put him in the father's waiting room. In those days a dad did not go into the birth room during birth.

That Sunday morning at Vanderbilt Hospital in Nashville, TN. In room #4407 at 6:12 AM o'clock I was born. Allen was finally allowed to see Daisy after a few hours. After spending some time with Daisy, the nurses allowed Allen to go outside the big window and see his first-born son. I was 7 pounds 6 ounces and 19 ½ inches long. There I was, hair so white I looked bald. But, strong lungs, and crying loud while kicking up a storm dad said.

Dad talked to mom and she agreed to the agreement Dad had made to ET, but my middle name would be Allen. Dad did just as he had promised Ernest Tubb.

I was named Ernest Allen Flatt. Ernest was after Ernest Tubb, and Allen was after Joe Allen Flatt. My generation of our family had started.

The next Saturday night on the Midnight Jamboree, Mr. Ernest Dale Tubb sent out a song to his new name sake, Ernest Flatt son of Joe Allen Flatt and Daisy Flatt. Also, Mom and Dad told me about a package coming to the Vanderbilt Hospital where I was born from Ernest Tubb to Ernest Flatt. Mom opened the package; in the package was a Baby Blue Snowsuit and a note that read "For when the cold weather comes". Signed Ernest Tubb. Mom later was going through a store and found the same snowsuit. The purchase price was $60.00 dollars. That was a lot of money to my parents back then.

Allen Flatt was working an exhaustive schedule. He would get up in the mornings and go to WLAX for a morning radio show, called Allen Flatt and the Night Owls. The show was 5 days a week. Then he would go to work at Firestone Tires downtown Nashville the rest of the day for 8 hours, 5 days a week. Then in the evening he had a radio show 5 evenings a week in Gallatin, Tn. just north of Nashville. Usually if he was not doing a personal appearance with his band somewhere, he was backstage at the Grand Ole Opry sharing jokes with all the stars. Then later Saturday Night he was at the Ernest Tubb Midnight Jamboree on Saturday nights hanging out and sharing jokes. If Mr. Tubb needed him, or someone did not show up, he would put Allen on the air for a couple of songs.

Mom and Dad said I was healthy but had to get a blood transfusion because I was an anemic in my blood.

I do not know the names or all the facts of the incident, but about this time my Uncle Orlie, Dad's only full-blooded older brother was married to his first wife. Uncle Orlie was doing a stretch in the Army. They had two boys. Uncle Orlie's first wife was running around on him. She was with her boyfriend and he ran a stop sign at the corner of Morgan Avenue and Clover Street. A Dayton City Transit bus hit them. It killed both the boys that were with them, but the boyfriend and Uncle Orlie's first wife lived.

(Later on, when I was about 14 my family moved to a house about 2, or 3 houses from that same corner. This is where we lived when I graduated High School. Although it was many years later, looking back I now realize how it must have felt for Uncle Orlie each time he would visit us at that house.)

Back to the story, Uncle Orlie was called home from wherever he was at in the service. When he got home, he found out that the boy's were dead. Uncle Orlie came to Nashville to visit Mom and Dad; he had begun to drink a lot at this time. He wore a phonograph needle through one of Dad's records that Dad had given him. The recording. was called "Cheat, Cheat, Cheatin"!

The first line of the words went; Little bird told me you been Cheat, Cheat, Cheatin', little bird told me just who you been meetin', He kept plucking on that Daisy, tellin' me that I was crazy, and at last my eyes are dry, and I'm tellin' you good-bye.

Sometime later on Uncle Orlie met Aunt Lillian and pulled his life back together and lived in Dayton, Ohio. They had 3 children. Gary, Danny, and several years later on, Debbie. Gary, and Danny grew up with Terry, and I. We spent a lot of time together going to movies and the Boys Club on a regular basis. We were almost like brothers though actually Gary, and Danny were 1st. cousins to Terry, and I.

22. 1951-DAISY LEAVES NASHVILLE AND ALLEN BEHIND.

Dad was getting very popular around Nashville for someone who had not broken out into stardom yet.

Mom would go to the radio stations with Dad most of the time if she did not have to work a shift at the restaurant where she worked, to help with small things, and to answer his fan mail he got at the radio station. This was something that was not dad's cup of tea, so he really liked the help and mom did not mind.

Allen was on the air doing his show one morning when he looked over at the desk where Daisy was opening some fan mail when he noticed that Daisy's face had turned beet red. So as soon as he finished the show and got off the air, he went over to her and said, "Daisy what's wrong"?

"Read this," Daisy growled at Allen as she threw a letter and envelope, she had just opened at him.

Allen picked up the letter and envelope off the floor and began to read.

The letter was from a man in a nearby town.

It read:

> I am the father of Mindy Mars in Gallatin; TN. Mindy had a child by you on August the 16th. 1950. If you do not bring in some money for diapers, bottles and milk, I am going to go to the Sheriff and file a warrant on you.

Allen felt like he was hit with a baseball bat. His knees were weak. He had to pull everything that he had together to look at Daisy.

Allen kept looking at the letter even though he had long stopped reading it. He kept looking at the letter and this gave him time to think.

Allen finally looked up from the letter at Daisy. She had fire coming out of her eyes.

Allen looked at her and said, "Aw Daisy this is just a bunch of bullshit. I have been getting popular and they think they can get some money out of us. Little do they know we ain't rich" Allen said with a grin.

Daisy seemed to calm just a little and said, "So this ain't true? Allen are you sure you ain't been running around on me? Do you promise me"?

"Yes, I promise you I ain't been running around on you! I Love you and Little Ernest"!

Daisy said, "Well then what are we gonna do"?

Allen studied and said, "Well if it gets any worse, I guess we'll get a lawyer, but I don't want to waste any money we don't have on a lawyer if we don't have to. I'll go and talk to this fellow".

Daisy gave Allen a cold stare. Daisy was not stupid, but she wanted to believe the man she loved.

Allen knew he did not want this thing to go any farther. So, he made plans to take some money up to Gallatin the first chance he got alone. He would make sure that they did not go to the sheriff.

So, Allen took money up to the child, young lady, and her father. Allen could talk his way out of just about anything.

About 2 months went by and Allen was at the radio station doing a show and as usual Daisy was there answering the fan mail. Just as Allen got done with his show and the musicians were putting up their instruments Daisy looked up and saw a woman come through the front door and sat down in a chair with a baby in a bundle. The woman saw Daisy and turned her head. Daisy hollered, "You, just a damn minute"!

Just then she jumped up and ran for the front door. At the same time Allen saw Daisy going after the woman and went to intercept Daisy. Allen knew Daisy was not a woman to mess with. She would fight in a minute. The woman had stopped and turned, and it was plain she was scared of Daisy. Allen got between Daisy and the woman holding the baby.

Daisy reached around Allen and said, "Wait a damn minute woman, I want to see that little bastard", shouted Daisy while reaching for the bundle. The woman was so scared she let Daisy pull back the blanket and look at the baby in her arms. Daisy became silent as she looked on the face of a cute little baby boy. Daisy knew in an instant that she was not mad at the baby anymore. Tears filled her eyes as she looked at the baby. Then with tears streaming down her face she turned and looked at Allen and said, "He looks just like Ernest, I'll take a cab home you take care of your bastard"! Then she turned with tears in her eyes, gathered her purse, and things and started walking to the cab stop up the street. Allen was calling "Daisy please, I'm sorry, I'm sorry I hurt you. But Daisy did not turn around. She just kept walking.

When Daisy got home, she went next door to the babysitter and got Ernest. She packed their clothes, got in the cab she had kept waiting, went to the bus station to catch a bus, and went back to Dow Creek, Kentucky without Allen. This was January 1951.

Allen was very lonely in Nashville without Daisy and Ernest. He began to drink even more than he had in the past. He drank a lot in the past but kept it under control. Now he was beginning to lose control.

Allen had begun to get popular and the girls had begun to flirt and chase him, and he flirted back. But somewhere along the way he forgot it should only be an act so he then could go home to his family.

But Allen had a few drinks at one show in Gallatin and went out with the young lady Mindy Mars. As they say it only takes one time to make a baby. Whether Allen actually went out with Mindy more than once is not known. Mindy got married not too long after the incident with Daisy at the radio station and Allen lost track of her. He was told the man that married her adopted the child she had had with Allen.

But the fact is Allen really loved Daisy, and Daisy really loved Allen.

It was now the beginning of December just before Christmas. Allen and Daisy had been separated for just over 10 months. There were no phones up in the holler, and Daisy had not answered back to any of the letters Allen had sent. He was missing his family terribly. He wanted so bad to go to the holler and see if Daisy would consider taking him back and coming back to Nashville and their empty apartment. Did she miss him like he missed her and Ernest? Allen knew he would have to do a lot of apologizing to Daisy if she would even begin to think about coming back to him. Allen knew he would also have to face Rufford and Nancy. He did not look forward to facing any of them. Rufford had a temper and would have to be walked around cautiously even though he was getting some age on him. Daisy could have a temper also and was not afraid to tell you just what she thinks. Allen knew he had messed up by cheating on Daisy. He knew it was not an excuse, but he was known to do things he would not normally do when he was drinking.

Allen was called to the record company and he was informed that they had a royalty check for him. It seems Hank Thompson had recorded one of his songs called "A Broken Heart and a Glass of Beer". He had written it after Daisy had left him. The record and publishing executive handed Allen a $500.00 royalty check from BMI (BMI collects money for Writers and Artist). The executive also handed Allen another check to resign with the label, and for his royalties on his own recordings. It was for $1600.00. Allen could not believe his eyes. The executive said they wanted him to resign with them because a larger label (Mercury Records) was interested in him and wanted to buy his contract. The executive said it was just about a done deal and the record company Tennessee Jubilee would finally get their investment in Allen back. Of course, this was good for Allen to sign with a major label and Mercury was a major and up and coming label. Allen left the executive's office on cloud nine. He thought only if Daisy and Ernest could be here then everything would be great. At that moment Allen knew what he had to do. He would first go buy a better car, and go back to the hollow and beg, plead, Daisy and to come back to him in Nashville with Little Ernest.

"GOD, I Hope she will", said Allen out loud.

Allen went over to the used car lot he knew about. There was an almost like new black, 1948 Ford sedan with low mileage. He talked the fellow down to $700.00 by offering cash. The dealer filled it up with gas for him and Allen went by his apartment and packed his bags. Then he went by Firestone and explained he was going to get his family and he needed time off or he would have to quit. They gave him 2 weeks off without pay. They said they did not want to lose him. Allen didn't care that it was without pay, because if they had said no, he would have quit. His mind was made up. He hit the road headed to Doe Creek Kentucky which was on the north eastern end of the state from Nashville

Allen had been driving for over 8 hours and was finally getting close to Irvine, Kentucky in Estill County. Irvine was not a large town, but it was the closer town around from Doe Creek. He still had to drive a way to get to Doe Creek which was just below Barns Mountain, 15 miles give or take from Irvine. He was sure looking forward to seeing Little Ernest and of course Daisy. But he knew it was not going to be easy. He had a lot of talking and apologizing to do if he even hoped she would take him back and come home to Nashville. But he knew the fault was all his and he had to try to get Daisy to forgive him. He had heard the story about Nancy making Rufford court her for several months when he came back from World War 1 and Daisy was cut from the same cloth as Nancy and Rufford.

Allen got to the holler at about midnight. It had been raining and he could only drive his newly purchased car to the bottom of the last hill just before getting to Rufford's and Nancy's house. So, he had to get out with his flashlight and walk the rest of the way.

Finally, he got to the house and the 2 family dogs started to bark and raise Cain. They were country hound dogs, but they did not like anyone they didn't know coming around in the middle of night. Allen had to stop away from the house waving his flashlight because of the dogs.

Rufford came out with his double barrel shotgun and a flashlight.

He said in a loud voice, "Who's out there"? Shining his flashlight on Allen

Allen answered, "Rufford it's me, Allen. Can you call the dogs off, Rufford"?

Rufford called the dogs and got them by the collars while giving Allen a harsh look.

"Sorry I got her so late, been driving all night", said Allen.

"Well, I don't know how good of a warm welcome you're gonna get", said Rufford holding the dogs. "Maybe for you, it would be better if I turned the dogs loose on you," said Rufford.

"Well, Rufford I messed up. I was wrong. It was all my fault. But Rufford I love Daisy and Little Ernest from the bottom of my heart", said Allen. "I wish I could take it back, but I can't. But if I can ever get Daisy to forgive me it will never happen again" said Allen.

"Allen did you hit her", ask Rufford? "Cause if you did", ---said Rufford with a stern look.

Allen suddenly realized that Daisy had not told Rufford what had happened.

"Oh, no Rufford I didn't hit her"! "I did something much worse. I hurt her in her heart, awfully bad", explained Allen.

Rufford studied and then said, Yea, I know about that, I hurt Nancy one time, and spent a while trying to make it up to her". "Don't know if I ever did", said Rufford, "Still trying I guess".

"But you know who you got to convince," said Rufford.

Allen just nodded his head.

About that time Nancy hollered from inside the house, "Rufford who is it"?

"It's Allen", answered Rufford. "He wants to see Daisy", said Rufford.

Well, Daisy and the baby are asleep, he will have to wait till morning", snapped Nancy.

"I'll get some bedding, and he'll have to sleep in the barn", said Nancy after a long pause and some whispering. Rufford, and Allen, both knew that the dog's ruckus most likely woke up everybody but maybe Little Ernest. He could sleep through a storm!

Rufford reached and got the covers that Nancy was handing through the door.

Rufford turned with the covers, and looked at Allen and said, softly in a whisper with a smile, "Well at least they didn't shoot you"! "Here's the cover. See you at Breakfast" said Rufford.

Allen took the bedding and went to the barn. After taking a look around for Rufford's barn snake, or any other creatures, Allen made himself a nice bed in the corn crib and settled down for a rest. He was very tired from the drive, and the stress of thinking what he would say to everyone when he got her. So far it seems to be going good with Rufford, he seems to understand, but he may change his mind after he hears the story. It seems Daisy had not told at least Rufford what had happened.

The next morning Daisy came into the barn and woke Allen up. Allen could tell she had fixed herself up to speak to him. Maybe this was a good sign.

"Allen, what are you doing here", asks Daisy as she handed him a cup of coffee. He was glad to get it and would need it.

"Well Daisy", he said after a sip of the hot coffee. "I miss you and Ernest something awful, and I just had to come here and see if you will forgive me", said Allen.

"Allen you have broken my heart and I don't know if I am **able to** forgive you", answered Daisy. "Dad said it was up to me if I let you stay or not", added Daisy looking down at the ground.

Allen looked at the ground also and nodded he understood.

"But Daisy I wish you would let me stay long enough to try and talk this out. Daisy I have got a little money from my record royalties and if you will let me stay, I will try and make it up to you", pleaded Allen.

"I don't know Allen, you hurt me a lot, and you can't buy your way out of this", said Daisy.

"I know that money is not the answer, now Daisy, and I am so very sorry", said Allen almost about to cry. "But if you will let me stay, we can go to town and we will buy Christmas gifts for Ernest and us, so we can have a good Christmas. And we will talk and have a good Christmas. I can't stand a Christmas without you and Little Ernest".

"Let me show you what I got," said Allen as he reached into his pocket and pulled out a bunch of money.

"There is over $500.00 dollars here in cash and I got more in the bank and we could all have a good Christmas". "Rufford and Nancy too", said Allen.

Five hundred dollars went a long way at that time.

Suddenly Daisy began to cry.

Allen asks her, "Daisy honey, why are you crying"?

Daisy said, "Let me show you what I had for Ernest for Christmas". Daisy reached into her purse and pulled out a little 3-inch-tall plastic cowboy boot full of corn candy. With tears in her eyes Daisy said, "This is all I could afford for Christmas for Ernest". Allen looked at the little plastic cowboy boot with the corn candy, and big tears came into his eyes. Allen reached out to Daisy and with tears rolling down his face he said, "Daisy I am so ashamed of myself"

"If you will let me, we will go to town, and Ernest is going to have a big Christmas, as a matter of fact all of us are gonna have a great Christmas".

They both cried and held each other in the barn.

After they got done crying Allen asked, "Can I go to the house and see Ernest"?

"Yes". "You will see he is growing like a weed. Mom and Dad are most likely waiting for us for breakfast anyway", smiled Daisy.

"But there is something you should know, Allen, if we get back together, I am not moving back to Nashville. If we are going to make this work then we must talk and live somewhere else", said Daisy. "You can still record and do music, but Ernest and me are not moving back to Nashville, and I better never hear you have anything to do with that woman again". "Those are my terms", said Daisy straight to Allen.

"OK", said Allen with his head down looking at the ground. I don't know if this is a good time to bring it up, but I was told She got married to a fellow, and he adopted the child, and moved away from Nashville", said Allen softly. "But you are the one I have always loved".

"No, this is not the time", Daisy spoke softly.

"OK", said Allen.

Allen and Daisy walked back up the path from the barn to the house hand in hand.

They got back to the house and breakfast was waiting. Ernest was now about 16 months old. When Allen came into the house with Daisy, Allen noticed Nancy was a little cold, but polite. Ernest was at the kitchen table in a highchair Rufford had built, and Rufford was feeding him some baby food cereal or cream of wheat.

Allen was so happy to see Ernest. He gave him a great big kiss on the forehead.

Allen sat down at the kitchen table next to Ernest and Rufford on the other side.

Rufford smiled and said, "Bet you have been missing him, ain't you"?

"I sure have Rufford, and Daisy too, answered Allen.

Rufford winked when no one was looking and said, "Yeah I made a few stupid mistakes in my time, so I know how it feels".

Allen nodded his head, yes. Nancy just gave Rufford a stern look at his remark.

Nancy began to serve them Bacon, Gravy and Homemade Biscuits. Nancy sat down and said the grace over the meal, and then everyone began to eat. After the breakfast was over Allen took Ernest in his lap and said, if you all don't mind, I would like to get something off my chest, said Allen.

Allen took a deep breath and began, "I want to say how sorry I am for my actions. First to you Nancy, and then to you Rufford. But most of all to Ernest, and Daisy here. I was wrong, I made a big mistake. I know it is gonna be hard for you to forgive me. But I ask each of you to forgive me".

Rufford spoke up and said, "Well Allen I have made mistakes to. But it seems Daisy is the one you got to convince to forgive you. Daisy has not told us what you did, and maybe Nancy and me, don't need to know, because this is between you two. But you should know that Nancy, and I could tell that whatever you did sure hurt Daisy's feelings".

"Yes, I know I was stupid, and I will be spending a lot of time to make it up to you, Daisy", said Allen nodding his head in agreement toward Daisy.

"But please, Daisy, understand I am sorry, and I love you very much. I am so sorry for the hurt I caused you", said Allen with tears forming in his eyes while looking at Daisy.

Daisy began to cry, and said, "Allen no one could ever make me believe, because I loved you so much, that you would ever hurt me the way you did. I do not know if I CAN forgive you. But I do love you, and I want to try for my sake, and Ernest's sake. I want Ernest to grow up with his daddy". "But I will have to work hard on getting past this. But you can never hurt me like this again. But I do want to try to get past this. It may take a while", said Daisy with tears in her eyes.

There was a big quiet pause for Daisy to get her breath.

"But you should understand as I said before at the barn, I will never live in Nashville again", said Daisy.

There was another long silence.

Allen looked up from looking at the floor and said, "Well that's a start"!

"How about we all load up, and go to town, and get some Christmas presents for everybody", ask Allen.

"You don't know how it broke my heart to find out what Daisy was able to afford for Ernest for Christmas. And that is all my fault. I really have let my family down. But this part I can fix, because I just got a Royalty Check for some of my record sales, and song writing. So, let me please take everyone to town, and get a turkey, or ham, or both! Let me start trying to make it up to you all. Let's have a good Christmas Dinner, and get some presents for everybody. In the next few days Daisy, and I can talk some more, and try to work it out. I have made a bad mistake because of my drinking", said Allen.

They all went to Irvine, and Allen bought everybody several presents, and a turkey and a smoked ham and enough trimmings to last a month. Ernest got clothes, a rocking horse, toy guns, and many other more age-related toys. Some of them, Allen, and Daisy, knew he was too young for, but it was OK. He could grow into some of them. Allen bought some baby formula, baby food, bottles and new cloth diapers. They did not have the throw-a-way kind then. Daisy had been using rags to make diapers for Ernest. Allen, and Rufford, went to the woods, and cut down a small pine tree, and put Christmas Decorations on it. They could not put lights on it because the Griffins did not have electricity back in the holler. But they had bought many decorations in Irvine to make it look great. Christmas Eve it began to snow, and they all sat around the red-hot stove and Allen played guitar and lead in Christmas songs. Everybody had a great time that evening and on Christmas Day. I could not walk yet but they bought me a thing they could put me in, and I could push with my legs and move around in. Dad said Santa bought me a toy with 2 wheels that I could push around, and it made a popping noise. Dad said, as I got older, and could walk, that I just about drove everybody crazy with the popping noise toy all through the house. Back and forth I went from one end of the house to the other. The grown-ups finally had to hide the popping noise toy.

Santa also brought me a hobby horse, with a big spring at each corner that fastened to the corners of the stand that sit on the floor. It came in a big box, and Dad had to put the horse together. But all I wanted to play with was the box it came in. Dad told me the story. "Your Grandpa Rufford looked at me and said", as Dad began the story, "Allen you could have saved some money, and just left the horse at the store, and bought him the damn box, and he would have been just as happy", said Grandpa as they laughed out loud! Grandpa Griffin did have a sense of humor, at times! Santa also brought me a Black Motorcycle Jacket with zippers all over it. Dad and mom said I would not take it off and they had to put me to bed with it still on. They said I wore it the next day, and the next day and for several days after that. They made me take it off to take a bath, but I would put it right back on once the bath was over.

All the family came over on Christmas Day and they had a big dinner.

Ellen Griffin-Had died back on November 24, 1918.

Providence Griffin (they called her Provy), died November 29, 19??. Grant Griffin died December 27, 1948. Cleona Griffin, Solomon Griffin, Emma Griffin, Etta Griffin, Anna Marie, Ben F. Griffin, and of course, Daisy Griffin were all there to celebrate Christmas. The children that were born were there and of course the husbands and wives, of the ones that were married by this time.

DAISY GRIFFIN-FLATT-in her early 20's

If you notice, Mom has a small chip on her front tooth in this picture,
she said she got that because as a toddler, I accidentally flung a
glass baby bottle toward her that hit her in the mouth. FYI.

23. 1952-GRANDPA RUFFORD GRIFFIN GETS VERY SICK.

Allen (Dad) told me a story of what happened. On Easter 1952. I am going to tell it just as Dad told it to me when I was older. Grandpa Rufford had become attached to me, Ernest. Mostly because we were living there with him and Nancy and he saw me every day. Everyone had gathered at the Griffin house in the holler for dinner and fellowship. The reason they had come together was Rufford had been getting more, and more, sick. None of the doctors (when you could get him to go) knew what was wrong. But he was getting weaker and weaker and more, and more, frail all the time. He was losing weight and it was happening fast. No one knew what was wrong. Rufford would not talk about it, but everyone was worried about him. He had always been such a strong man.

Rufford would just only say when the subject was brought up, "Aw don't worry about me. I just got a bug. I'm not worried about it". But everyone knew something was going on because Rufford had allowed Nancy to talk him into going to church regular. This was something that had never happened before. This made everyone believe Rufford was more concerned than he acted.

All the Griffins and In-laws were there and all their children. The children were being children running around the house. In, and out, slamming the doors. Every time they went out, and in, or in, and out they would slam the door shut. Even though the family was trying to keep the children outside they still ran in, and out. Finally, Rufford's nerves had enough. One of the children came running through the house and went out the door and slammed the door again.

Bam!! Went to the door.

Rufford spoke up in a rough voice and said, "you children are going to tear the damned house down"!!!

All the parents began to send the children outdoors and make them stay out.

Just when things had settled down once again, I came wobbling through the house at 19 months, (I walked early for my age, most likely because of all the attention I got being the oldest child). Once I got to the door, I could barely reach the doorknob. I opened the door after several tries, and slowly went out the door. The adults including Allen (Dad) were sitting and talking about something.

BAM!!!! Went the door, that I had slammed.

Dad jumped up, and opened the door, and said, "Ernest stop coming in and out and slamming this door you'll tear it off the hinges"!

Rufford spoke up and said in a loud voice, "that's OK!! If he tears it off the hinges PAW-PAW will put it back up again"!

Dad said this embarrassed him a lot, because Rufford had just raised cane about the children slamming the doors. Now he was making a big difference in that Ernest could get away with it while the others were not allowed.

Dad said he apologized to the others later on when Rufford was not around. They told him not to worry about it. They knew how Rufford was. They also knew he was not feeling good most of the time.

Later that month Rufford became bed ridden. He could not get out of bed. Mom later in life said Rufford was throwing up dark, smelly vomit.

Rufford asked Nancy if she would get the preacher from church to come to the house.

Rufford said to Nancy, "I have something I wish to ask him".

The preacher came up in the holler to the house.

"Rufford what can I do for you", said the tall lanky preacher with the deep voice leaning over the bed so he could hear Rufford.

Rufford asked the preacher in a voice that could barely be heard, "Will God forgive me for the men I have killed even though they needed it? If so, could I be baptized, I feel the end is near "?

The preacher smiled with tears in his eyes and said, "Yes Rufford, God will forgive you of your sin if you truly ask for forgiveness. But Rufford, we will have to tie you to a chair and carry you to the creek because you're too weak to stand to be baptized".

That would be OK, the Lord has told me it is time to ask for forgiveness and be baptized", whispered Rufford.

"When do you want to do this", ask the preacher?

"As soon as we can get the family together, right away. I don't have much time", whispered Rufford again.

"I will help Nancy get the family here right away, you just hold on and give us time, Rufford", said the preacher.

"Nancy come here", hollered the preacher to the next room. When Nancy came in, the preacher explained Rufford's request. Nancy threw her hands up and shouted, "Praise GOD"!!!

"Now let us pray for the Lord's help with the time we need to get this done", said the preacher as he held Rufford's and Nancy's hand. Then they kneeled by Rufford's bed to pray.

Rufford was baptized in a chair in the deepest part of the creek. It took only 2 sons to carry him to the creek because he had lost so much weight. Then the preacher got them down in the creek with him for support so that when the time came to lean him back in the chair and raise him back up again, they could do it with ease. After speaking the correct words Rufford was tilted back in the chair until he was submerged under the water with a handkerchief over his mouth and nose. Rufford was then raised up out of the water still tied to the chair. Rufford had a great big grin on his face.

Later that month on May 16, 1952 Rufford Griffin my Grandpa went home to be with the LORD.

I do not remember him except in the stories my family has told me. But I believe he was a man I would like to have known. Down through the years I have heard these stories you have just read.

My mother Daisy Griffin Flatt who later worked 33 years as a Nurse's Aide said, "looking back I believe Dad had cancer. His vomit looked and smelled just like some of the patient's that I took care of who had cancer at the hospital where I worked. But back then the doctors did not know what cancer was".

I personally want to Thank GOD for giving Grandpa time to turn his life over to Jesus. I will get to see him again someday in heaven and this time I will get to remember and know him forever.

RUFFORD GRIFFIN & NANCY GRIFFIN-in later years

24. 1953-ALLEN CUTS A MAN WHEN GOING FOR MOONSHINE.

Allen was still working in Nashville, but he would only go down whenever he had a recording session. Allen was beginning to drink quite a bit on the weekends when he was not working. He had also shown up in Nashville for recording sessions so drunk that the recording producer had to postpone the session till the next day because Allen was too drunk to sing on key or up to his standards. Dad told me he believes that is why the record label eventually did not sign him back on.

One day Allen and a friend named Walter Young were drinking together and both were very much three sheets to the wind. They had run out of something to drink and it was on a Sunday. Back then you could not even get beer on Sundays in Kentucky.

Walter told Allen, "I know where we can buy some moonshine if you want to drive back into the mountains. Barns Mountain"!

Allen said, "Yeah, OK, I could drink some good moonshine. But first we will have to stop and get some gas over her at the station in Doe Creek".

The two men got in the car and went to the little country store in Doe Creek that was also a gas filling station. A little country store with a porch and gas pumps. People would hang out at this store and talk and tell jokes.

Allen pulled up to the pumps and this was when someone would still pump the gas for you, check your oil, and wipe your windshield off.

Allen said from the front seat of the 1940 Ford Coupe, "Frank give me $2.00 worth of high test and check my oil".

Frank wore dirty, greasy, overalls and had been working pumping gas for years it seemed to Allen. Back then $2.00 worth gas would be about ½ a tank of gas depending on how much your car would hold.

Walter got out of the car and slurred, "Allen, (hick up!) I am going in and getting a ham sandwich, you want one"?

Allen slurred back, "No, I'm OK, Walter"!

Both men were feeling their oats from all the booze they had drank today. They really did not need anymore. But they had run out and wanted more. Allen paid the man called Jesse for the gas and about that time Walter came back eating a ham and cheese sandwich.

"Allen", said Walter, "look what I found for sale in the store". Walter pulled out of his pocket a brand-new flashlight. "This is the same kind a cop carries when he is on patrol. It is the best you can get, as far as flashlights are concerned".

"Let me see it", said Allen reaching for the flashlight.

Allen was a big joker when he was drinking.

"Damn, Walter, that is a damn good flashlight" said Allen pretending to be excited and holding the flashlight. "I think I'll just keep it," said Allen pretending to put it in his pocket.

"The hell you will", said Walter with a snarl while grabbing the flashlight back out of Allen's hand. Walter stuck the flashlight in his back-work pants pocket away from Allen.

Allen just laughed as he started the car and put it in gear and said "I'm gonna get that flashlight before the day is over, Walter"!

"The hell you will", said Walter with another snarl!

Allen and Walter drove along toward Barns Mountain, then Walter told Allen where to turn.

The 40' Ford Coupe moved along an old wagon path up into the woods. Finally, they came to a large open spot where cars had been parking. Although there were not any cars parked there now you could tell someone had been parking there from time to time.

Walter told Allen, "just park here we have to walk the rest of the way to the moonshine still".

Allen parked the car at one end of the opening. The men got out of the car. Both were staggering to some degree. Allen began to follow Walter. As they walked, they had reached the other side of the open area of the woods. They were starting to enter the woods up a path to the still. Allen noticed Walter had the new flashlight sticking out of his back pocket. Allen was a big joker, so he reached up and wiggled the flashlight in Walter's pocket.

Allen said jokingly, "I told you I was going to get that flashlight"!!

Walter whirled around and came out of his pocket with a pocketknife. He opened it and said, "I'll cut your fucking head off. I told you, that you weren't getting my damn flashlight".

Allen was surprised and stopped with his hands in his pockets.

"Relax, Walter. I was just joking with you", Allen tried pleading with Walter. But Walter kept coming with his knife drawn stepping toward Allen. Cursing and threatening to cut Allen's head off. Allen was backing up with his hands in his pocket. Walter did not know it, but Allen was trying to open his Tree Brand Bowker pocket knife while in his pocket with one hand. While trying to calm Walter down the whole while he was backing up.

Walter had backed Allen up all the way across the open parking area. But Walter just kept coming.

All the while Allen was saying, "Walter calm down I was just joking with you, I thought we were friends", pleaded Allen.

But Walter just kept cursing and threatening to cut Allen.

At last, Allen was backed against the 40 Ford coupe and could go no farther. He was thinking, what am I gonna do.

About that time Walter got his legs tangled up in a fallen tree branch that was blown out of a tree by the last windstorm and was now laying on the ground. Down went Walter to the ground.

Everything that happens next happens extremely fast.

Allen saw his chance and pulled his knife out of his pocket where he could use both hands to open it. Allen kept his Tree Brand Bowker as sharp as a razor. It was a German knife and had exceptionally good metal. Normally when he sharpened it he wasn't happy until it would shave the hair off his arm. Allen made sure Walter could see he now had his knife in his hand.

"Don't get up with that knife Walter, or I'll cut you", shouted Allen!!

"You son of a bitch, I'm gonna cut you first", shouted Walter back at Allen!!

Once Walter was half up on his feet, he lunged at Allen with his knife in a stabbing sweeping motion. Allen stepped aside. He missed Allen, and then, Allen stepped to the side, and cut him down the left arm from the shoulder, to his forearm. The blood flew. Walter still did not drop his knife which was in the other hand.

Allen pleaded, "Hell, Walter put down the knife, before I have to kill you"!!

Walter kicked at Allen with his right leg trying to kick the knife out of Allen's hand.

Allen cut him again across the thigh leg. Again, the blood flew. This time Walter went down and dropped his knife. Allen grabbed Walters knife off the ground.

Walter said, "Oooo shit! You're trying to kill me"!!!

Allen said, "No Walter, I was just trying to keep you from killing me. Hell, Walter, we have been friends for a long time. What in the fuck is wrong with you"? Allen continued, "I was just teasing' you about your flashlight"!

Allen saw how much Walter's arm, and leg, were bleeding, and was worried he might bleed to death.

"Get in the car and let me take you to the hospital Walter. Your bleeding bad", begged Allen.

"Fuck you" said Walter, "you tried to kill me, you son of a bitch"!!

Walter began to walk back to the main road which was about a hundred yards away. He put his belt around his leg to slow the bleeding and was trying to hold his arm shut that was trying to gap open.

Allen had sobered up and became scared that Walter might die for loss of blood. He was bleeding a lot. Allen followed with his car talking to Walter trying to get him to get in the car so he could take Walter to the Hospital. But all Walter would do was keep walking and cussing Allen.

"Walter please get in the car so I can take you to the hospital", begged Allen.

"You tried to kill me you mother fuckin' son of a bitch.

Finally, Allen had had enough of the insults and said, "Well the hell with you then. I'll just let you bleed to death, you stubborn asshole".

Then Allen drove away in a cloud of dust. Allen drove down the double wide gravel road for several miles and then thought he should go back and try again to get Walter to let him take him to the hospital. After all, he did not want him to die. When Allen got back to where he had left Walter, he could not find him. He was either hiding from Allen or had got himself a ride. Allen thought he could have collapsed. So, he watched for him along the side of the road all the way back to the turn off to the holler that led to the Griffin place. Then he turned off the main road and took the wagon path that led back up into the holler to the Griffin house.

Allen finally reached the place where everyone parked and then got out to walk the rest of the way to the Griffin house.

As Allen walked all the way to the Griffin house, he began to wish Rufford was still alive so he could talk to him about this situation. Rufford would know what to do. Suppose Walter died Allen thought. Finally, Allen reached the house. No one was home but Nancy and Ernest. Allen decided to talk to Nancy after all; she was married to Rufford for many years and Rufford had been in trouble a few times. Allen walked into the house.

"Nancy, can I talk to you? I got problems" shouted Allen through the house.

Nancy came in from the kitchen wiping her hands on her apron and said, "Allen what's going on. Why are you shouting"?

"Sit down and let me tell you what has happened", said Allen.

Allen told Nancy the whole story from beginning to the end. Nancy sat listening, hardly blinking until Allen was finished with the story.

"Is he dead", ask Nancy in a somber tone?

"I don't know", said Allen. "I went back to find him but couldn't find him. I don't know if someone picked him up, or he fell in a ditch and I just couldn't find him, or what". "Nancy, what would Rufford have done in my place", asks Allen.

"Well, Allen, every time Rufford got himself into a fix he would always go turn himself into the Sheriff". Rufford always said that they look better upon you when you turn yourself in instead of having to hunt you down", answered Nancy with a shrug of her shoulders and her palms turned up.

Allen agreed he would wash up, change clothes (his clothes still had some blood on them) and go turn himself into the sheriff in Irvine.

At the same time as Allen was talking to Nancy, at the hospital in Irvine Solomon Griffin, one of Daisy's brothers, was there to get a hearing test.

Solomon was a big man, balding, about 38 years old. In a lot of ways Solomon was like Rufford his dad. That's when the doors of the emergency room flung open and in came an orderly pushing a gurney. On the gurney was Walter Young with blood all over him and a tourniquet tied around his left arm and right leg. The bleeding had been slowed, but he had some bad knife cuts that still needed stitches.

Solomon said, "Damn Walter what happened to you"?

As he was being wheeled by on the gurney to a room, Walter said, "that brother-in-law of yours tried to kill me! He cut me for no reason! Two times! I think that both sides of the family are crazy sons of bitches"!!

Solomon turned and followed the gurney to the room.

"Which brother-in-law" asked Solomon.

"Allen Flatt" shouted Walter back at Solomon. I knew the Griffins were no good, killing sons of bitches, but now I know, the Flatt's are no good killing sons of bitches too", shouted Walter at Solomon.!!

"Well, it's a good thing it wasn't a Griffin you got into it with", said Solomon.

"And why is that", shouted Walter at Solomon.

Solomon stuck his head in the door of the emergency room looking straight at Walter in the eyes and said,

"Cause if it had been Griffin, he would have cut your fucking head off, so you can't hand out bull shit anymore".

About that time the doctor said, "Solomon you are going to have to leave so I can stitch this man up".

"Put some stitches across his fuckin' mouth doc, maybe it will shut him up", said Solomon as he pulled his head back around the door and left.

Later on it was told that Walter had 50 stitches on the inside of his arm and over a hundred on the outside of his arm. It was also told that Walter got on his leg about 30 stitches on the inside of his leg, and 75 on the outside of his leg. It was also told around that Walter was never able to raise his left arm, past just below his shoulder ever again. Walter went around for a long-time making threats that he was going to get Allen back for cutting him. It was also told that Walter and his sons were going to get Allen good.

From that time on Dad went everywhere in Irvine with his snub nose 38 in his pocket.

One day Allen was going into the feed and grain store at the Y in the road just past the bridge outside of Irvine, when suddenly at the door Allen was face to face with one of Walter's sons. Bill Young

Allen looked at Bill and said, "Bill, I ain't got nothing against you, or your brothers, or Walter for that matter, but if we need to get this settled now is as good a time as any. I am tired of looking over my damn shoulder".

Bill looked at Allen, and said, "Allen what happened out there on Barns Mountain that day"? "I have heard dad's version", said Bill Young looking at Allen as they stepped outside away from the door.

Allen stared at Bill with his hand in his pocket on his 38-snub nose, and began, as he told Bill the whole story. Even about going back after Walter and not being able to find him.

Bill looked at Allen and said, "Allen I know how bad dad's temper is, you got nothing to worry about from me or my brothers. But I would still watch my back around dad, he still holds a grudge".

The two men shook hands and went their separate ways.

To the best of my understanding Dad and Walter never met up again.

About this time, I got sick and had to go to the hospital for tonsillitis. They were gonna take out my tonsils and adenoids, but Mom said the doctors said I took a turn for the worse in the operating room and stopped breathing on them. So, they only took out my tonsils that were inflamed, and left the adenoids.

25. 1953-ALLEN, DAISY, AND ERNEST, HAVE A CAR WRECK.

Mom and Dad and I moved out of Grandma's house and rented a house on the property where Uncle Ernie Roberts and Aunt Rea lived. The house was so bad you could see the dogs under the house between the floorboards. The snow would blow through the walls. It had an out

side toilet, no plumbing or electricity. We used a pot belly stove for heat. The house was in bad shape. We did not stay there long. Grandma's house did not have electricity, or plumbing but was solid and strong, and kept the weather out. It was heated by a pot belly stove and had outside toilets, but the house as I said was built exceptionally good. Grandpa had made sure of that.

Dad, Mom and I moved from Irvine, KY. to Lexington, KY just a short time later after that. That was most likely the best thing. We would still visit Grandma Nancy, and all the Griffins from time to time, but the only time that we ever moved there again was just us children moving down to the holler for summers.

Dad still had the black, 1940 Ford coupe. I was an old car but in good shape, ran and looked good. Dad and mom had gotten off work and decided to visit Grandma Griffin. We were traveling on a back, two lane, blacktop, road just outside of Lexington, Kentucky going back to Irvine, Doe Creek, Estill County Kentucky to visit Grandma and all the Griffins.

I don't remember any of this, but Dad and Mom told me all about it down through the years when I was old enough to understand. This is what I was told:

Dad had stopped and picked up an old man that was hitch-hiking along the side of the road and needed a ride. In those days it was normal to give people you felt you could trust a ride especially in Kentucky. We were driving along, singing a song, Dad was driving, and mom was sitting on the passenger's side. I was standing up in the front seat between them, as I often did. In those days there were not any seat belts in a car. Mom and dad would just automatically stick their arms out to grab me if something happened. The old man was sitting in the back seat just passing the time with mom and dad. It was now getting past dark. Dad told me they were driving the speed limit about 55 or 60 miles per hour when they came to a rise in the road. Dad told me the last thing he remembers is he saw headlights coming at him. Before he had time to react the two cars collided head on. It was an awful crash.

The wreck was a head-on collision at about one hundred and forty miles an hour between the 2 cars. I have been told in a head on collision you take the speed of each vehicle and add them together and this is the speed of the head on crash. We had been hit head on by a 1953 Oldsmobile. Witnesses said he was running about 80 miles an hour, passing on curves, and passing on rise that were no passing zones. He was passing on a rise when he hit us. He was under acceleration and hit us without ever applying his brakes. Dad said he did not think he had time to react to apply our brakes either. The impact was so great that the Oldsmobile's rear end came off the ground and landed on the truck he had just passed.

Dad hit his forehead on the top of the car, or the windshield and received a cut in his forehead.

The next thing he remembers he was sitting on the opposite side of the road with his feet in the ditch. Witnesses said he got out of the car and staggered over to the ditch and sat down.

The doctors later determined he had received a concussion to the head. That is why he did not remember getting out of the car. He also had 8 broken ribs from slamming up against the steering wheel. The steering column broke or else he could have been propelled by it.

I hit the metal dashboard of the 1940 Ford with my face and bit my tongue off. Mom said it was just hanging from a piece of skin. My nose was broken flat against my face, and of course I was crying. I also most likely received a concussion also.

Mom (Daisy) got the worst of it all. Mom went through the windshield and back through again. The windshield glass cut her very badly about the head and face. Mom ended up with over a hundred stitches in her head and face from the broken windshield. Mom said she remembers looking and seeing the Oldsmobile that had hit us was on fire. She was afraid the fire would spread to our car. So, she grabbed me and made one step, when her left leg buckled under her, and she and I went down on the road shoulder and then into the grass. Mom did not know it, but her left leg had been broken in two places in the car wreck. When she stepped on the broken leg it shattered. But even as we were falling down Mom held me above her and took the full fall up on herself. When good Samaritans/witnesses got to us, I was crying with my tongue dangling almost severed with blood coming from my broken nose and swollen mouth. The blood was running down all over my little shirt.

Mom was also covered in blood to her waist from all the glass cuts to her head and face and her leg was mangled and dangling. The fall had knocked her barely conscious. But she never let go of me. The witnesses said they had to talk her into letting me go when they got to us. Mom said she did not know how long it took for the ambulance to get there because she kept going in, and out, of consciousness. But mom would not go, without they also was taking me too. We were in such bad shape they took all three of us in the same ambulance, because they felt they could not wait for another one to arrive. Dad was conscious but was still groggy from his concussion. They took us to a small hospital not far away. Once they had us medically stable, they transferred us to a bigger hospital more able to handle our medical problems just inside of Lexington.

The old man hitchhiker sitting in the back seat never got a scratch.

Dad and I recovered first, but still it took us a 2-week hospital stay. Dad was wrapped so tight for his ribs he said he could hardly get a breath. But finally, after a few days he was able to get on his feet and go visit mom on another floor. He visited her several times a day. Dad was doing for her whenever the nurses could not. He would also be looking in on me.

Dad said I was the first to get moving around. The doctors sewed my tongue back on, and dad said I had never quit talking since. Every time he went to see me, I was somewhere down the hall eating ice cream. The doctor had put on my chart to let me have all the ice cream that I wanted because it was good for the stitches in my tongue and eased the pain, and since I would not eat solid food because it hurt but would eat the ice cream. So, I was taking advantage of the doctor's orders. Dad said I had the nurses wrapped around my little finger and I basically roamed the halls. One of the nurses had bought me a 3-wheel tricycle with a bell. Up and down the hall, ring, ring, ring. Dad said they had to finally take the bell off, because I was driving everyone crazy with it. But the nurses could always tell where I was.

Mom was hurt so bad. She had stitches all over her face and head. (There used to be a picture of mom in the hospital bed, with all the stitches, but I do not know what happened to them). But the main problem was her leg. The doctors had discussed removing her leg. They said she would never walk again. Her leg had been broken in 2 places and when she tried to walk with me, she had shattered the main bones and ankle. But on the day before the surgery to remove her leg there was a bone specialist who came in and talked to her and dad and said he had looked at the x-rays and wanted them to give him a chance to save her leg. He said that she may still not be able to ever walk, but he would like a chance to save her leg. He said once she got her stitches out of her head and face, he wanted to set the surgery if they would agree. He asks mom and dad to talk about it and he would handle everything from there if their answer was YES to try and keep the leg. Dad and mom talked.

Dad said, "Daisy I am gonna love you either way, but the decision I think should be yours".

Mom said, "Allen I may be in a wheelchair all my life and may never walk again, but if they take my leg, I know I'll never walk again". "The doctor said I would have a lot of work to do to ever walk again, but if I don't walk again it won't be because I didn't do my part to get well and walk. If there is a chance, I think I need to take it", explained mom.

Dad agreed. He knew mom would never give up if there was a slight chance of walking again.

Dad smiled and said, "I'll call the doctor back in and you can tell him and I'm with you all the way Daisy".

Dad called the doctor back in and mom told him that they wanted the surgery to try and keep her leg. The doctor said, "now, Daisy you do understand that if I get inside your leg and feel I can't help you, then I still will have to remove the leg. But I will give it my best to try to save your leg".

Mom said she understood.

The story around the hospital was that the bone specialist doctor (wish I could remember his name, bet mom would if she was still here) cut mom's leg up the inside from ankle up to halfway up the main bone and shin bone. He took the pieces/slivers of bone out and put them together like a jigsaw puzzle. He took two stainless steel surgical screws, drilled holes and used the screws to hold the bones together. One held the main bone together and one held the ankle together. It was 10 hours of surgery.

Mom woke up after the surgery and the first thing she wanted to see was her leg and if it was still there. After Dad helped her pull back the sheets, she looked at her bandaged leg with the cast, smiled and went back to sleep.

After the surgery, the doctor told mom, and dad that he had done all he could do. But it went well. Now time will tell, but there must be time to heal before mom could even think about putting weight on that leg.

The doctor said, "Daisy it will take time. Be patient. When the bone has healed back together good enough, I will need to do another surgery and one of the screws will come out. Maybe someday the ankle one, we will take out also. We will see".

Mom was in the hospital for about 4 months. Then the doctor said "we can now let you start to try to put a little weight on it. Just a little at a time. But Daisy doesn't expect too much too quickly".

By the time 2 more months rolled around mom was able to walk a little at a time with crutches. Mom left the hospital on crutches but was still on crutches for a total of 14 months. Mom finally got off crutches and was able to walk after over a year and several months since the auto accident. Mom walked the rest of her life. The only effect left over from the accident was mom's left leg was slightly turned outward (called duck foot). When she walked her left foot always pointed out to about 11 o'clock and she wore her shoes out on the left rear outside. It was a small price to pay for being able to walk and keep her leg. Through the rest of her life, she carried babies, and worked as a nurse for 33 years, drove a car with a clutch, cleaned house and did just about everything anyone else did. The upper screw was taken out when I was five or six years old, but the one in her ankle stayed with her forever. Sometimes she said the screw would hurt her, but she did not complain much. I guess she felt it was a fair trade to walk.

Mom and Dad received an insurance settlement from the insurance company of the Oldsmobile Owners insurance company. All hospital bills were paid, and mom and Dad got over $10,000.00 in settlement. That was a lot of money then, but Dad said they should have gone to court for more for what mom had to go through. But dad and mom had never had that much money in all their life. Also, it has been stated by doctors that hitting the dashboard could have, maybe caused my epileptic seizures that started with me at 10 years old.

Dad bought a brand-new F-100 Ford Pickup truck with some of the money. He was drinking when he bought it and said when the car dealer asked him how he was going to pay for it?

Dad said, "cash"! The man became so nervous he could hardly fill out the paperwork.

But mom and dad talked it over and went back and traded it back in for a green brand new 1954 Ford sedan which was more family friendly. I think that was mostly mom's idea. This was most likely the only 2 brand new cars ever owned by mom and Dad in their whole life.

Dad was working at Firestone Tires in Lexington currently. Dad was having trouble with one of his back teeth. Dad hated to go to the dentist, but this tooth was starting to hurt so much he finally made an appointment with the dentist down the street from Firestone Tires.

Dad was going to the dentist, but oh how he dreaded to do it. But the tooth was just killing him. He took off from work for the rest of the day and as he came out of Firestone he decided to just walk down to the dentist and leave his car there. As he was walking along the street, he passed by a liquor store. Dad thought well maybe I will just get me a half pint of whiskey and take the nervousness off. So, dad went inside the liquor store and said, "hey, give me a half pint of Kessler's whiskey". The store clerk wrapped the bottle in a plain brown paper sack and handed it to dad. Dad paid the man and left the store and continued down the street to the dentist. Dad stepped between two buildings and took a look for police up and down the street and turned the whiskey up and in four gulps drank it all. Glug, glug, glug, glug went the whiskey down his throat and then he threw the empty bottle away between the buildings.

Dad came out from between the 2 buildings and headed on down the street toward the dentist office. By the time he got to the dentist office dad was feeling no pain. He went into the dentist office and told the receptionist that he was here for his appointment. It was not too long before they took dad on back and put him in the dental chair. Soon the dentist came in and dad told him he wanted a tooth pulled.

Dad showed him which one hurt and the dentist said, "OK, I'll have to numb you up". The dentist took out the needle with Novocain in it and stuck dad in his gum 3 times. Then the dentist said, "I'll be back in a moment when the Novocain takes effect". Then the dentist left the room.

Finally, the dentist came back and pulled out a small pick and stuck it in dad's tooth to see if he was numb enough.

Dad said, "hell that hurts"!!

The dentist said, "well I guess you aren't numb enough, yet. Let me put some more Novocain in your gum".

Dad said, "OK".

So, the dentist took out the needle with Novocain in it and stuck dad in his gum 3 more times. Then the dentist said, "I'll be back in a moment when the Novocain takes effect". Then the dentist left the room.

Then after a while the dentist came back and pulled out the small pick and stuck it in dad's tooth to see if he was numb enough again.

Dad said, "hell, that still hurts"!!

The dentist could smell the whiskey on dad's breath, and he said, "Well Mr. Flatt, I think your alcohol is overcoming my Novocain.

Dad looked up at him from the chair and said, "aw hell, pull it anyway"!!

The dentist asked, "are you sure"?

Dad said "yah, pull the son of a bitch! It's killing me"!!

So, the dentist started to clamp down on dad's tooth. But it was not coming out easy. The dentist, trying to get a good angle, got up almost in dad's lap with him laying back in the dental chair and began to pull with both hands. As the dentist began to pull, Dad grabbed him by the wrists with his hands. The dentist would pull, and dad would hold on to his forearms. The dentist was lifting dad almost off the chair. They wrestled for almost 5 minutes. By the time the dentist got the tooth pulled both the dentist and dad were standing up on the floor out of the dental chair. Both men had sweat dripping off their foreheads and noses.

Dad said, "that was a tough son of a bitch, wasn't it"?

The dentist said, "yah, that's what's called earning your fucking money"!!!

Both men had a good laugh, before dad paid and left the office.

26. 1955-MY BROTHER TERRY FLATT IS BORN.

It is 1954 and we lived in Lexington, Kentucky. Mom had been off her crutches for only a few months and she realized she was pregnant. Mom told dad and everyone was excited. I do not remember when they told me, or if they ever did.

Terry was born January 18, 1955.

I do remember barely when they brought Terry home from the hospital. Back then mothers and the child stayed in the hospital longer than they do today.

Dad said, I had been asking where mom was, and he would explain that mom went to get me a new brother, or a new sister. I had said, "no I want a new brother not an old girl"!!

But dad explained that GOD decided which one it would be, a boy or a girl. I prayed for a brother.

I was at a friend's house that was babysitting me while dad worked, and mom was away.

Dad came and got me and brought me home into mom's bedroom. Mom was in the bed, and I was sure glad to see her. I just barely can remember this.

Mom said, "Ernest, I got a surprise for you". Then she pulled the covers back, and there was Terry. I looked at him in amazement. He was so small. Best I remember I was a little tongue tied and embarrassed for some reason. Maybe it was because I wondered if God had answered my prayer.

I asked mom kind of sheepishly looking back and forth to dad, "is it a boy, or girl"?

Mom answered with a grin, "it's a boy". "Is that ok", ask mom?

Dad just stood and grinned with his legs spread apart rocking back and forth puffing on his unlit King Edward cigar, all proud for his part in the miracle.

"Yeah", I answered moving closer to the bed. "What's his name", I ask mom?

Mom answered, "Terry Glen Flatt"!

"His last name is the same as mine", I grinned.

"Yes, it is. All our names are Flatt at the end. Now if you want to, we can take him back to the hospital and get a girl" said mom with a grin.

"No, we need to keep him, we can play together", I explained!

Mom said, "Yes, when he gets a little older you can play together. But right now, he is a little baby. You will need to always protect him and love him because you're the older brother".

"I will mommy", I answered with a big grin looking at Terry as he held my finger with his little fist while sucking on a pacifier.

Many times, down through the years Terry, and I would disagree like brothers do, but as long as I was around no one else ever messed with him. I always remembered my promise to mom to love and protect him. And Terry feels the same way about me. That is the way we were raised. Fight one FLATT and you had to fight 'them' all.

Later that year mom and dad both got a job at the Kentucky State Hospital for the Insane. Both were working on the violent wards. Dad as an orderly worked on the male violent ward mom on the female violent ward as a nurse's aide. These wards were for the patients that had been institutionalized because they were violent toward almost everybody, or somebody. Dad and Mom said there was a fight almost every day between patients on those wards. Then staff had to restrain them, and they would then try to fight staff.

There was a patient dad told me about nicknamed Soup Beans. I asked dad why they called him Soup Beans? Dad said because he would eat all the soup beans he could get. He dearly loved soup beans. He would eat soup beans 24 hours a day if he could get them.

I ask, "well dad eating soup beans would not be enough to get someone put in a mental hospital would it"?

Dad answered, "no, son! But soup beans was also a sex manic. Whenever a woman came onto the ward she had to announce "Woman on the ward" before she came through the last cell doors. This gave us time to find soup beans. We would get between the female nurse, or female doctor, or whomever female that came on to the ward. Soup beans would sit, and not take his eyes off the female as long as she was insightful.

While he was staring at the female, he would be sucking air through his teeth, and rubbing his palms/hands together between his legs, while opening and closing his legs. He also would do this as if he wanted to rape the female, and he was about to lose it if he could not. He would continue this if the female was still insightful. The rest of the time Soup Beans was just as normal as anyone else except he loved to eat large amounts of soup beans.

One day Dad asked another orderly, with seniority, named John, "John what do you think Soup Beans would do if he could really get to one of those women"?

"I don't know Allen; he probably won't know what to do with her if he had her. He has been locked up here since before I started here", answered John the orderly.

Dad told me a story about Soup Beans. Dad said, "one day a new female doctor came on the ward. She did NOT call out "woman on the ward"! Before she came through the last cell doors. Dad said everyone started calling "where is Soup, for the orderlies had to find Soup Beans. But, the new female doctor came on in through the last set of cell doors that they had at each end of the ward. This put her on the ward hallway. The orderlies did not have time to find Soup Beans, make him sit down in a chair, and get between him and the female doctor. All at once Soup Beans came running out of a door that the female doctor had just passed. Soup Beans jumped on the female doctor knocking her to the floor, and ran one of his hands right up between her legs, hunching her all the time. When the orderlies pulled him off her, he pulled her panties right off. He had gotten a hold of the front of her panties with the hand he had run up between her legs and pulled her panties off as the orderlies pulled him off her.

After they got Soup Beans off the female doctor and locked in his room, Dad looked over at John the orderly and said, "Well that answers that question"!

John asks, "what question Allen"?

Allen said looking at John with a smile, "Soup Beans ain't bluffing"!!

John looked back at Allen and said with a grin, "you got that right, and I got the proof!

Then John pulled out of his pocket the pink panties that Soup Beans had pulled off the new female doctor.

Both men had a laugh together as they went down the hall.

"You gonna give them back to her", ask Allen, talking about the new female doctor?

"Only if she will let me put 'em back on her", joked John with a big grin!

Allen grinned and said, "if you ain't careful John, you'll be in here with Soup Beans"!

Both men laughed again as they went down the hall to get back to their work rounds.

Dad said they were not supposed to hit the patients, but Dad said on the male ward the staff would sometimes smack the patients lightly because they would not do as they were told. A patient could really try the staff's patience sometime. It was a different time than today. The administration staff would look the other way as long as the treatment that was not allowed to the patients was not done right in front of them, or marks were not viewable. People were always getting fired for smacking a patient, and leaving a mark, or a supervisor just happened to see it happen. Dad said sometimes it took a smack like correcting a child to get the patients to calm down. Dad was finally fired for smacking a patient just as the head nurse entered the room. Dad said he had never left a mark on a patient or hurt them. It was just to get their attention and get control of the situation. When he got fired at the hospital is when he went back to working for Firestone changing truck tires. Working for Firestone he liked better anyway.

Mom stayed at the hospital all the way up to 1957 when we moved to Dayton, Ohio. Mom went to a nursing school they had in the evening, and they would even let her give shots in the Kentucky State Hospital. Nursing seems to be more to Moms liking than Dads.

In 1956, mom was at work. She worked on the 3rd shift at the hospital and dad worked the day shift at Firestone. They did this because they could swap up watching Terry, and I and not have to pay for babysitting. Mom would lay down for a while when me, and Terry's naps were taking place in the mornings. And then, later in the day she would do housework, and wash, while keeping up with us in the day. She would clean the house, feed us, and then would start supper, and it would be done by the time Dad got home from work. Then she would lie down, until time for her to get up and get ready to go to work at 11:00 pm. Looking back I do not know how she did it. But she never complained, or hardly ever missed work.

I just barely remember this, but I do remember this certain time. Mom had made us all supper and had gone to bed. Dad waited until mom had gone to work about 10:00 pm and Dad packed us all up and we all went out to a bar just up on the corner, and Dad got a 12 pack of beer. He got me a coke-a-cola, and some potato chips. Then we came back home, and Dad was drinking his beer. I had finished my small 8 oz. glass bottle of coke, and I asked him for a drink of his beer, and he said, "You won't like this old beer". But he gave me a sip just the same. I made a face like it was nasty. Dad just laughed and said, "I told you"! "You don't need any more of this", said Dad.

As I said mom was at work, it was Friday night, and Dad normally would let us stay up late on Friday nights so him, and Mom could sleep as late as possible on Saturday mornings. I would usually get up first to watch "Howdy Doody", and "The Big Top" a TV circus show.

But this Friday night I was sneaking around, and every time Dad was not looking, I would grab me another sip of his beer. Finally, after several sips I began to get dizzy. So, I lay down and went to sleep. I woke up later that night and got sick. I threw up all over the kitchen floor. Dad saw me get sick and thought I had caught a bug. He felt sorry for me and took me in and put me in his and Mom's bed. I got sick again and threw up all over their bed. Dad was wiping my head with a cool washcloth and he had to change all the bed covers to clean ones. I do not guess Dad ever knew I had been sneaking his beer. But it was a long time before I ever drank alcohol again. I was nineteen or twenty years old before I ever tried alcohol again.

Also, I remember us living in a half of a double in Lexington, Kentucky. As you came up on the porch one family lived in the first door to the right. Our family's front doors was straight back from the porch steps. One door faced North and the other door faced East. In an L angle to the porch

The family that lived next door had two boys. One of their boys was older than me by 5 years. The second son was the same age as I was. I was about six, Tommy was six and Jeff was Eleven years old. Tommy and I got along simply fine when we would play together by ourselves. But when Jeff was around, Jeff was a bully! He would hold me and tell Tommy to beat me up. I would go crying to mom and she said she would talk to their mom.

One time we were outside, and Jeff threw a rock at me and hit me right in the top of the head. I was stunned until the blood started to run down into my eyes and then I became scared. Then I began to cry and ran to Mom. I had to have stitches. I still have the scar to this day up in my hairline.

I think mom thought it was just kid's trouble. But this time she saw I was really hurt. I came to her so often complaining she started watching out the window. One day she saw Jeff hold me, and let Tommy hit me in the mouth, and it bloodied my mouth. After cleaning me up she went to the front door and knocked on the other family's door. You could step out on the porch, and their front door was just to the left, right there.

Mom only had her princess slip on so after she knocked, she just stepped back in our doorway. You could talk from doorway to doorway. The doors were at an L shaped angle from each other.

The lady came to the doorway, and mom told her, "Juanita, Jeff is holding Ernest when they are outside playing, and putting Tommy up to hit him in the mouth".

Juanita asked my mom, "Are you sure Ernest is not causing the trouble that's what I have been told"?

"No Juanita, I watched them through the window and Jeff was holding Ernest's arms behind his back and telling Tommy to hit him in the mouth. They bloodied Ernest's mouth", said mom. Now, Tommy, and Ernest, get along fine when Jeff is not around", added Daisy!

"Well, my boys say Ernest is causing the trouble", answered Juanita in a smart-aleck tone.

Both women were standing in their doorway talking back and forth.

Mom said, "Juanita I stood in the kitchen doing dishes, and saw Ernest, and Tommy playing, then Jeff came up, and grabbed Ernest's arms behind his back, and was telling Tommy, hit him". "I heard him say to Tommy, hit him". "Hit him in the mouth with your fist", explained Daisy!

Juanita said, "Well I don't think my boys would do that"!

Mom began to get mad, and said, "Juanita I heard it with my own ears, and saw it with my own eyes"!

Juanita said, "They are just kids, we need to leave them alone".

Mom was getting hot. She said, "Juanita I don't have a problem with letting kids play, but when one is 5 years older, and holds a younger one, and lets the other child beat up on the other one, I can't stand still for that, and you shouldn't either", explained Daisy getting louder!

"Well, I think we should just leave them alone, and let them play," said Juanita sarcastically to mom!

Mom looked at her and said, "Well, I tell you what I am going to do Juanita, from now on every time Jeff holds Ernest, and lets Tommy beat up on him, I am gonna beat up on you, and see how you like it"! "Do you understand" ask mom very sternly, staring straight at Juanita without blinking?

Both women were standing in the doorway. Juanita jumped back into her apartment doorway, and closed the screen door, and locked it with a metal hook.

Then she said through the screen door "Daisy you can go to hell"!

Mom jumped out onto the porch in just her princess slip and jerked the screen door open, breaking the hooked lock, and pulled Juanita out on the front porch, and knocked her down, and whipped the shit out of the woman right there on the front porch in her princess slip. Mom wore the woman's head out. I was there and saw the whole thing. Mom fought like a man. She was country and did not play around once it came to blows. She was serious. Just like Grandpaw Griffin was.

Finally, Mom said as Juanita crawled back into her side of the house, "Juanita remember this is what I am going to do to you every time Jeff holds Ernest, and lets Tommy beat on him"! "Do you understand", asked mom to Juanita? Juanita just nodded yes as she crawled back to her apartment with her nose bleeding.

Juanita found out Mom was not bluffing. Mom did not start fights, but just like Grandpa Griffin she sure would finish one. Mom was willing to talk, and work something out, but she was not going to put up with any bull shit.

That was the last time Jeff held me, and let Tommy beat me up. So, Juanita must have believed what mom said as true.

27. 1957-THE FLATT FAMILY MOVE TO DAYTON, OHIO.

In 1957 Dad had got laid off work at Firestone in Lexington, Kentucky. Dad had not been able to find another job. Jobs were scarce in Kentucky. Dad had talked to Uncle Orlie on the phone. Uncle Orlie, dad's full brother, (both born of the same mother) lived in Dayton, Ohio, and told dad that jobs were plentiful in Dayton, Ohio. Dayton, Ohio was 53 miles north of Cincinnati, Ohio right on the Kentucky and Ohio border. Kentucky was on the south side of the Ohio River and Ohio was on the north side of the Ohio River. The Government was in the process of building the Interstate System we all use today. Interstate 75 was not finished at this time.

Uncle Orlie suggested that Mom and Dad should consider moving to Ohio. Uncle Orlie said, "move up here and I can put in a word for you at the Dayton City Transit bus lines where I work. I do not know if they will hire you even with my recommendation. But there are jobs all over up here".

The jobs had become more plentiful up north than in the south.

Dad and mom talked it over and things were getting tuff in Lexington without them not having two pay checks.

Mom said, "if I can get a job at one of the Dayton hospitals with all my experience, we could make the move, but you need to get a job first before I quit mine".

Dad said, "how about me going up there and seeing if I can get a job first and then once I have got a job you could quit yours and we will all move up there".

Mom said, "yes and I could give a notice and leave on good terms. Also, you go find out where the hospitals are and get me an application from each one and I will send it back".

"Sounds like a plan", said Dad.

When Dad went and got Mom and came to Dayton with Terry, and I, Mom went to work as a waitress at a restaurant while trying to get a job at a hospital. Dad did not get a job with the Dayton City Transit bus lines, but he did find a job at a tire company changing tires with no problem. So, in 1957- the Flatt Family moved to Dayton, Ohio on Green Street. The first apartment we had was upstairs of a house. The people that lived downstairs were named the Hamilton's. There were cockroaches so bad at the apartment upstairs above the Hamilton's that mom put this white powder in the cracks of the walls with a pump sprayer with a metal flat nose and the roaches would come out of the walls and fall dead. I had never seen so many cockroaches coming out of the walls, then they would fall dead on the floor. Mom would sweep them up with a broom and dustpan. But mom made the place livable.

We later moved to a half of a double in Dayton on further up Green Street. 65 Green Street and lived there several years. Later mom got a job at the Capri Motel cleaning rooms with Aunt Noreen, dad's half-sister who also lived in Dayton.

28. 1958-RITA NORENE FLATT IS BORN.

In 1958, I did go to school one part of a year at Doe Creek in the same 2 room schoolhouse that my mother went to as a little girl. One room was grades 1st thru 4th, and the other room was 5th grade thru 8th grade. I believe I attended part of the 3rd. grade there. Doe Creek Elementary School was its name. I remember there were also outside toilets, and kerosene lamps. Course this was nothing new to me, Grandma Griffin's house also had outside toilets, and kerosene lamps.

I remember the outside toilets at the school. There was also a time that one of the 8th grade boys turned over the boy's toilet. He pushed it over the hill and there was a square hole dug out in the ground. It was full of shit from everybody going to the toilet.

Of course, everybody had to go up to look at it. There was one boy standing and looking at the hole full of shit and piss, when he got to close. One of the other bigger boys tried to push him in, but he sidestepped and got away. Then everybody started trying to push someone into the hole. Finally, one boy got to close and one of the bigger boys caught him off guard and pushed him into the hole. He went face first right into the hole full of shit and piss. The boy crawled up out of the hole begging someone to help him, but everybody just ran from him because he had shit from head to toe. He was crying and begging for help.

The girls and the boys were just hollering and screaming, "OOOOOOO" and running away.

Finally, he started to vomit, then everyone ran from him even more. The vomit was just shooting out of him and he was still crying and begging for help. Finally, the teacher came and took him down to the creek to clean him off. Everybody lost their playground privileges for 2 weeks after that. Mainly because the teachers could not find out who had turned over the toilet or pushed the young man into the hole. I think the student who went into the hole was out of school for several weeks.

Rita Noreen Flatt was born October 29, 1958; we lived on 65 Green Street.

Every time mom would have a baby after Terry was born Dad would sneak me into the hospital to see Mom. I do not know if it was because Terry and I were driving him crazy or because we missed mom, or if it was just mom missed us. But I would stay until the nurse caught me, then the nurse would make me leave. In those days you had to be at least 12 years old to come up to the rooms and visit. Dad would visit and figure a way for us to sneak in without the nurse seeing us. Dad and I found out that we could get away for a short visit with Mom before the nurse would find out I was there and make me leave. Sometimes I could even get to see my new sibling and Mom always seem to enjoy seeing me and I know I enjoyed seeing her. Terry was still too young to try to sneak in and keep the noise down. In Those days, a woman would usually stay in the hospital for about a week after having a baby.

Well, I was 8 years old when dad and mom brought Rita home from the hospital. Terry was only 3 years old and this time it was me that got to smile at how he was so embarrassed to see his new little sister. I can remember him looking at her little hands and smiling from ear to ear. Course I was too. Dad as usual just watched, as he rocked from heel, to toe, with his arms crossed all proud of his growing family. Dad and mom loved their children.

Rita, later on in life married Nick Monnin from the family that had the fruit farm (Monnin's Fruit Farm) in Vandalia, Ohio where we helped mom pick strawberries when all of us were children. Nick Monnin had a child by another marriage. Her name was Nakina Nicole Monnin.

111

I remember when I was in about the 4th grade I was standing in line at school and another student pushed me out of line. The female teacher saw me as I was trying to get back in line and she came and grabbed me by the arm. She said to me, "I am tired of you students getting out of line. Now get back in line now"! She then shoved me back in line. When she grabbed me by the arm, she had long fingernails and they dug down into my arm.

When I got home that evening my mom noticed that I still had the marks of the teacher's fingernails on my arm.

Mom said, "How did you get those marks on your arm"?

I said, "My teacher did it"!

My mom said, "Why did she do that, and how did she do it"?

I told mom, "I was standing in line at school, and another student pushed me out of line. The teacher saw me as I came out of line. As I was trying to get back in line she came over and grabbed me by the arm and dug her long fingernails into my arm. The more she dug the more I tried to get loose. She said to me, "I am tired of you students getting out of line. Now get back in line now"! She then shoved me back in line.

Mom looked at me and said, ``We are going back up to the school"!

Mom took me out to the car, and we went back to the school. I could tell she was truly angry. Now usually if I was bad at school, and got a paddling at school, I would have got another one once I got to home. But the teacher digging her nails into my arm that morning and leaving marks still there when I got home after school my mother was just not going to stand for. Mom was about as mad as I had ever seen her.

When we got to the school and went in. Mom took me to my classroom. But it was empty. No one was there including my teacher.

Mom said, "Let's go to the office"!

We went to the office. There was a secretary, and she asked mom what she wanted.

Mom told the secretary, "I want to see the principal"!

The secretary said, "Yes and what is it concerning"?

Mom told the secretary, "Because my son's teacher has abused my son, and I want to see him now"!

Then mom showed her my arm with the fingernail marks.

The secretary realized mom was not joking and meant business. And when she saw the marks, she went off to find the principal glad to give the problem to someone else

The secretary said to Mom, "Have a seat please, I'll go find the principal".

In a few minutes, the secretary came back with the principal and took mom and I into the inner office.

The principal asked mom what the trouble was. Mom showed the principal my arm with the fingernail marks that was still quite easy to see.

Mom asked the principal, "Where is his teacher"? Mom looked at the principal and said, "She needs to be here to explain these marks"!

The principal made a phone call but could not get a hold of the teacher. Then he left to go see if he could find her.

In a while he came back and said, "Mrs. Flatt, I have looked in the teachers' lounge and she is not her. One of the other teachers told me she has left for the day. But I will be talking to her first thing in the morning. I will most likely write her up, and it will be put in her file. If she does it again, she will be fired. This is the way we handle things like this".

Mom told the principal, "OK I will give you a chance to handle this, but if it does happen again to my child you will not have to fire her because I will come back here and handle it myself! You know Principal Andrews; it is a good thing she was not here, because it gave me a chance to calm down. You can tell her when you see her that I said it was a good thing she had already left because I may have beat hell out of her. I know kids can be a pain sometimes, but this I will not put up with. If she puts her hands on my child again like this again, I will come back, and we will see if she can put her hands on me. And she cannot! No, I don't think so"!!!

The next day after school, Mom asked me, "What did your teacher say to you"?

I said, "She held me in the class after the other students had gone out and asked me why I told my Mom that she had hurt me".

Mom said, "And what did you say"!

I told mom, "Well I told her, cause you did"! "Then I showed her my arm"!

"What did she say then", asked Mom?

"She said go on out and play"!

Mom said, "OK".

29. 1960-LILLIAN DARLENE FLATT IS BORN.

We moved to Clover Street above a family we did not get along with. They lived downstairs and we lived upstairs. Their daughter my age was named Sue. I believe their last name was Bellamy.

The thing I remember most was one-night mom and dad and the 2 adults, John Bellamy and his wife Lois Bellamy were arguing about something. I don't remember what it was about. But Dad got into a fight with John. Dad was drinking, and John got the best of Dad, but did not hurt him much. Anyway, this made hard feelings between our families. And we lived upstairs, and they lived downstairs. So, there were harsh words between the adults on occasion.

Mom was 4, or 5, months pregnant with Lillian, my youngest sister at this time. Lois had been nasty with Mom figuring she would not do anything because of being pregnant. Mom took it for a while maybe because of this. But Lois did not know Mom like she thought.

A week or so later, Mom, and Lois were sitting on the porch that we shared, one day. Both were sitting in chairs with their backs against the front of the house. Lois said something about John kicking Dad's ass. Then she made the mistake of thinking mom would not fight because she was pregnant.

Then she said, "If you weren't pregnant, I would kick your ass too". This was too much for Mom to bear. She had enough of Lois' nasty mouth.

Mom said, "Well don't let that stop you"! And at the same time Mom who was sitting on Lois' left side came around with her left fist and busted Lois right in the mouth. Lois fell backwards because she had been leaning her chair back against the wall of the house. Down she went Lois, as Mom pregnant and all, hit her 3 more-time one hand after the other. Well, it took all the fight out of Lois. I am sure she had never run into a woman like Mom who was not afraid to fight like a man, pregnant, and all.

As Mom was standing over her Mom shook her fist in Lois' face and said, "Bitch I may be pregnant, but I sure as hell ain't drunk so you can't take advantage of me like that son-of-a-bitch of a husband of yours did Allen. Tell him to try it again when Allen is sober, bitch"!!!

Mom left her bleeding from the mouth and nose, lying on the porch as she went back up the steps toward our apartment.

Mom said as she was walking toward the steps "come on Ernest, back upstairs"!

Mom said once she got back upstairs, "I had to get her fast because, after all, I am pregnant". Then she had a big laugh. So, did I.

Then a few days later, Dad kicked John's ass the next time they got into a fight, and Dad sent him to the hospital for stitches. Dad was sober this time, and John had more than he could handle.

Dad told Mom, "We got to move before we have to kill John, and Lois". Mom must have agreed because we moved a few days after that.

Lillian Darleen Flatt was born in Dayton, Ohio on September 11, 1960. We had moved back to 65 Green Street, we had half a double house with a basement, first floor, and a second floor. Nobody lived above us.

Well, I was now 10 years old when Dad and Mom brought Lillian home from the hospital. Terry was now 5 years old and this time it was me and Terry that got to smile and look at our new youngest little sister. I can remember Terry and I, both looking at her little hands and smiling from ear to ear. Rita was glad to see

Lillian, but she was young, and I am not sure she can remember it. She was about 2 years old. Dad as usual just watched and rocked from heel to toe, with his arms crossed, and his unlit cigar in his mouth, all proud at his growing family. Which were now 4 children and 2 adults. As I have said before Dad and Mom loved their children. We grew up believing that family was especially important and came first. Not that, family members did not make mistakes, but when a mistake was made by a family member it was expected for that member to make amends, apologize, and then be forgiven. That did not get us free from the hour-long scolding, or spanking, or disciplinary treatment we had coming. But we never stopped loving each other. Mom and Dad believed in spankings, but not beatings. I can remember all of us at one time or another getting punished by a "switch" from a tree branch. But every one of us grew up and did not get into any major trouble while we were growing up.

(Lillian later in life married Steve Combs. Everybody liked Steve Combs, especially Dad. Dad and Steve got along simply great. They were great friends). More like best friends than father in law, and son in law.)

We moved to E. Fourth St. in Dayton. This is the last time Mom and Dad agreed to live above or below someone again. We moved in and lived above a couple that was deaf and mute. They had 2 boys one my age and one Terry's age. But the boys were not deaf and mute so we could communicate with them and became good friends to Terry and me.

The man that was deaf and mute was everybody called Dummy. But it should be understood that in those days that was not meant as something bad. I do not think we ever knew his real name. We knew the name of his wife, it was Connie, but Connie could read lips and say somethings, so it was easier to communicate with her. Dummy could only grunt and point But sometimes you could figure out what he meant. But only sometimes. And the sons were Frankie and Johnny and as I said they could hear and talk and do sign language.

Like I said we lived upstairs. One night we heard a big noise from downstairs. Someone was screaming but we could not understand what was being said. So, Mom and I ran to the top of the stairs that lead up to our upstairs apartment. The door down at the bottom of our stairs that went out to the porch was never locked, but the one at the top of the stairs that went into our apartment was always locked.

Connie was crawling up the stairs, screaming probably for help from us. Blood was coming out of her mouth and nose. The blood was running all down the front of her blouse while she screamed for bloody murder. Dummy was right behind her punching her every time she would stop. I stood at the top of the stairs and Mom ran halfway down the stairs to where Connie was being hit by Dummy. Mom looked Dummy right in the eyes and shook her index finger sideways while mouthing the words, "NO, NO"!!

Dummy dropped his head, and fists, and turned and went back down the stairs and out the door to the porch where his front door was. Mom brought Connie up to our apartment to clean her off and see how bad she was hurt. Connie could read lips a little and speak a little. She was hard sometimes to understand, but Mom and Connie seem to always work it out.

About the same time Mom had got the blood cleaned off her and found she was just bleeding from the nose and her lip was busted then someone started knocking on our porch door. The door was not locked, but whoever it was did not try to open it. Just knocked.

I could hear Dad calling from the front room window, "Daisy the police are out front, someone must have heard her screaming, and called the police. That is most likely them knocking"!

We all went downstairs and there was the police cruiser with the lights flashing at the side of the street.

Once we got out there on the sidewalk there was a neighbor named Wayne from next door talking to the police. He was basically talking his head off about what had happened.

Dummy had gone inside his apartment and was for the moment settled down.

Finally, the police decided to go back up on the front porch to talk to Dummy.

The 2 officers went up on the porch and knocked on the door sill. "Will he be able to hear us?" said one of the officers to Dad.

"I doubt it", said my Dad. "He can understand you if you write it out", Dad explained to the officers.

"Thanks" said one of the officers in return back to Dad.

So, one of the officers opened the door to the apartment just a little. When he did Dummy saw him. The officer motioned with his finger for him to come out on the porch. Dummy came out on the porch and was very calm. The officers were about to question him about the evening's problems by writing on a pad. Suddenly the neighbor Wayne came up on the porch uninvited. He started in again talking and pointing at Dummy. Dummy kept looking back and forth from the officers to Wayne the neighbor. Dummy didn't know what he was saying, but he knew it wasn't anything good about him by his actions and pointing.

It seems Dummy had done some Olympics boxing in his younger days and was surprisingly good.

Suddenly Dummy had enough. In the blink of an eye, Dummy hit the neighbor Wayne 3 times with the same fist before the officers could have time to react. Wayne's head went back, punch, punch, punch. And down he went to the porch floor. Blood was just flowing from his nose. He was out colder than a cucumber.

The officers grabbed Dummy and knocked him down to the porch floor on his belly. They pulled his arms behind him and handcuffed them behind him. Then they pulled him up to his feet and took him to the police cruiser. They took him away to jail and called the ambulance for Wayne and to look at Connie.

Connie came over the next day with some money and asked Mom and Dad if they would go bail Dummy out of jail. So, Mom and Dad and Connie went down and bailed Dummy out of jail. As far as I know Connie and Dummy got along from then on up until we moved and lost track of them.

Mom finally did get a job at Saint Elizabeth Hospital. She started out in the emergency room on days, but later on transferred to the night shift in the mental ward. She stayed there until she retired 33 years later.

We moved to Albany Street not too far from St. Elizabeth Hospital where mom was working. We were next to a large city park with a swimming pool. We swam in the pool all the summer long. While we played in the park and swam in the pool, we made a lot of great memories that we still think about today.

Terry, Gary, Danny, and I, use to walk across the Miami River on the Washington Street Bridge and go to NCR, National Cash Register Company on Saturdays and get to watch a free movie at their theater on a street that was just next to the Miami River. And when we would leave the National Cash Register after the movie, the employees who were dressed in National Cash Register blazer jackets would give us a free candy bar as we went out the front door. The National Cash Register Company did this every Saturday for many years. I don't remember how we found out about it, but it became an ever Saturday event for us.

In 1913 the Miami River flooded Dayton; Ohio plum up to the top of the stop signs on Main Street. After that, they built flood walls along the riverbanks and the river has never flooded downtown Dayton again. The Miami River still runs through Dayton, Ohio but so far has stayed in its banks to this day in the downtown area. There are still areas that flood, but not downtown. Island Park used to flood ever so often. Mom and dad used to take us to that park and cook out and let us play. We loved that park because it had a real fire truck, and a real jet airplane that you were allowed to climb and play on.

While we were living at Albany Street a friend of mine named Tony, had a guitar he wanted to sell. Tony was a couple of years older than me. I was 10 and he was 12, and he smoked, but was out of money. The guitar only had 3 strings and was just a cheap guitar, but I thought it was the prettiest guitar I had ever seen. Tony wanted to sell the guitar to get some cigarette money. I went and asked Dad if he would buy the guitar for me. Dad asked Tony how much he wanted for it. He told Dad he wanted just a dollar because he wanted to buy some smoke makings or cigarettes. At that time, you could get a pack for about 25 cents. Dad told him he would give him a dollar for it but only if I wanted to learn to play it.

I told Dad "yeah I'll learn, if you will teach me"!

Dad said, "Well I will have to get a set of strings for it, it only has 3 strings and is supposed to have 6 strings". "But you will have to practice". I said "I will"!

So, dad bought the old wood finished acoustic guitar without a name on it for me for a dollar. Then Dad went and bought a new set of strings for it. He wanted to see if it would tune up good himself. He put the new strings on the guitar and tuned it up the best he could get it to tune. It didn't hold tuning very well, and had to be tuned all the time, but I couldn't tell anyway. Then Dad began to show me a chord. G chord was the first. He told me if I wanted to play, I had to practice till my fingers stopped hurting. I agreed. I do not think Dad thought I would stick to it. But I surprised him. I practiced all the time as soon as my homework was done till bedtime. The homework part was Mom's idea. Homework first, supper second, practices the guitar third. I must have driven Mom and Dad crazy until I finally started to learn to play.

Finally, I learned 3 chords and began to sing songs Dad had written out for me. The first song I ever learned to play, and sing was a song in G chord named "Wondering, Wondering" by Ernest Tubb. I think Webb Pierce was the first to record it but I learned it off an Ernest Tubb album my Dad had. I was 10 years old and had learned to play good enough that Dad went and bought himself a new jumbo Epiphone guitar so we could play together. The Epiphone was made by Gibson Guitars but cost less than a Gibson. Dad was enormously proud of his new guitar. Sometimes with him watching, he would let me play it, but I had to be careful not to bump, or scratch it.

I could play the songs I had learned but still had not developed a good enough ear to tune my guitar. So, I had to get Dad to tune my guitar for me. Also, the guitar I had did not stay in tune very well. So, Dad had to tune it a lot for me. And he would get upset because it would not stay in good tune.

One Saturday morning I got up to practice my guitar, and it was out of tune. I had started to be able to tell when it was out of tune bad. Dad had been drinking the night before and had a hangover. Mom, and Dad, had been arguing because of his drinking. So, I took my guitar to Dad to have him tune it. Like I said, Dad was nervous, sick, and hung over. Dad was sitting in our living room chair across the room from the couch where Mom was sitting. As Dad was tuning my guitar a string broke and stuck him in the finger. Dad jumped because it startled him, more than hurt him.

Dad said, "This cheap son-of-bitch won't stay in tune". He threw my guitar on the floor. The guitar slid across the linoleum floor to the couch right at Mom's feet.

Mom was mad anyway, so she jumped up and did an Indian War Dance right on the back of my guitar. And as she stomped the back out of my guitar she looked over at Dad and said, "See, I can get mad too"!!

She wasn't mad at me; she was mad at Dad for his drinking the night before. But I stood there in disbelief with my mouth open looking at my pride and joy guitar in pieces.

As I began to cry all I could say was, "You broke my guitar"!! "You broke my guitar"!! Then I began to pick up the pieces with tears coming down my face. I am sure Mom felt awfully bad for losing her temper at Dad, but she never said a word. Mom did not apologize easily.

Dad would let me play his nice guitar sometimes, but he had to be right there to watch me and it was not the same as having my own guitar. His guitar played so much better and tune so much better than my old one did. But as I said it just was not the same as my own guitar.

About 2 weeks later Mom, and Dad, came in late about 3am in the morning. They had gone to a friend's house to play Hearts. I had stayed home to babysit the other kids. After Terry, Rita, and Lillian had fallen asleep, I took the little ones to bed, and went to bed myself.

Dad came in and woke me up.

"Ernie wake up", said dad. "We got something for you", as dad turned on the light, with a great big grin on his face.

I was trying to wake up and get use to the light in the room. I was rubbing my eyes when I looked beyond Dad, and saw Mom holding something behind her back with a grin on her face also.

Dad said, "Are you awake"?

I said, "Yeah", as I rubbed my eyes again trying to get the sleepiness out of my eyes.

I looked at Dad, and Mom from the bed and they both had smiles on their faces, and I was wondering what was up. Then Mom brought her arms from behind her back and in one hand there was a small size, starburst finished, flattop, Gibson acoustic guitar. It was not brand new, but it looked like it was. They had bought this very lightly used guitar for me from a gospel group called the Hoskins Family. I came up out of the bed with a bound and a grin from ear to ear. I was no longer half asleep anymore.

As I played the new guitar it was in perfect tune and held it tuning perfectly. It played just like a brand new one. As good as Dad's brand-new Epiphone he had just bought just a few months ago. I played this guitar for many years after that. It tuned good and stayed in tune. But most of all, this told me that Mom was deeply sorry for breaking my old first guitar. What I never told her, but wish I had, was that I had forgiven her just minutes after it happened. Maybe she knew it but, I wish I had told her. Dad told me one time that Mom would never say she was sorry, but that she would always let you know she was sorry in some deed, or action. Dad was always quick to apologize for his mistakes, I guess because he had to apologize so often. Dad would go on a drinking bender, and once he got himself straight, he would go back to church, and kneel at the altar and ask forgiveness in front of all the whole church, and GOD. Dad was right, she would not say she was sorry, but she would make it up in some way. And Mom was always there for her children, and family whether her children/family was right or wrong. But be ready to hear about it from her if you were wrong. She could fuss for hours. Sometimes you would feel like maybe the whooping would be better. At least she would get it over quicker.

I remember the family used to bang on the bathroom door to use the bathroom while I was practicing my guitar. I liked to practice in the bathroom, because if you played and sang against the shower wall you could get some reverb bounce back. So, if someone wanted to use the bathroom, they had to first run me out. As soon as they were done, I would go right back in the bathroom to practice again. Sometimes things would get a little smelly, but I would go right back to playing and practicing.

I remember, because the park was just at the end of the street just 3 doors away, past our house, the Mr. Softy ice cream truck would pull up, and stop right in front of our house to sell ice cream. The street ended right at the park

This particular time when the ice cream truck pulled up all of us children, Terry, Rita, Lill, and I ran into the house saying', "Mom, Dad, can we have some ice cream"? "Mr. Softy, Mr. Softy", we all hollered.

But Mom said, "All I got left is milk, and bread money, so No"!

We all turned around and went back outside and sat on the porch steps and watched all the other kids getting ice cream just at the edge of the street. Dad came to the screen door of the house and saw us sitting on the steps with our mouthwatering. So, Dad went back into the house where Mom was.

"Daisy", he said, "Come here I want to show you something"! Dad took Mom to the front screen door and said, "Look at that", and pointed toward us children sitting at the end of the porch on the steps, watching all the other kids get ice cream.

Mom looked at all 4 of us sitting on the steps with our mouthwatering and said sadly to Dad, "But Allen, all I got left is milk money, and bread money"! "I hate that ice cream truck" added Mom with tears in her eyes.

Dad said, "But Daisy, if you can get them some ice cream, I will go borrow some money from my boss "Woody" tomorrow". Woody owned the Lawn Service my Dad worked for at the time.

Mom looked at Dad and said, "OK"!

Dad spoke up through the screen door and said, "You kids come here".

Mom spoke up also and said, "Do you kids want some ice cream"?

Dad told this story years later and said "The kids almost tore the screen door down getting back into the house. Then the kids went out to the ice cream truck and got some ice cream and your Mom and I thought it was the best money that was ever spent. From that time on we would buy ice cream at the store every time we got groceries, because it was cheaper than the ice cream truck".

I remember those times after the Mr. Softy Truck, we would get ice cream from the store, and we had big bowls of ice cream because it was cheaper so we could get more from the store. Sometimes with bananas, nuts, and chocolate syrup. Usually, it was Neapolitan flavor. Vanilla, Chocolate, and Strawberry in the same container. Usually a gallon, to 5-quart container.

I went to the Holler in Kentucky for a summer visit with Grandma Griffin. Grandma Griffin and Uncle Ben Griffin, Aunt Evelyn Griffin, and their children Cousin Larry Griffin and Cousin Sue Griffin all went to Doe Creek Baptist Church. Benjamin had not been born yet. Uncle Ben Griffin was a Deacon and I usually went with them to attend church. While at church one Sunday morning there was an announcement that there was going to be a Summer Vacation Bible School to be held at another church, not very far away from Doe Creek Baptist Church. They announced on a Sunday morning that if anyone wanted to go to the Bible School that was being held at Pine Hill Baptist Church then they would come with a bus and pick them up each day for a week. A friend of mine named Tommy Horn and I usually sat together and both of us decided to go to the vacation Bible School.

"I'll go if you go," said Tommy to me.

"OK, I'll go if you go" I said to Tommy! So, we decided to go together starting Monday to Vacation Bible School for a week.

Tommy and I usually would sit in the very back row of the little country church so we could whisper back and forth to each other.

On this day there was a woman named Pliney Brandenburg that would usually get up to testify. We always stopped to listen to her because she stuttered but would testify for 10 or 15 minutes. We thought it was funny to listen to her.

Pliney started out, "I---m, ssoo, glad tooo be here. Pra, issss, e, yeh, eeee the La, La, La, Lord when I die he takkkes meee!

I looked at Tommy and he was starting to giggle, which did not help me from trying to not giggle also.

Pliney continued, "I, I, I, am so, so, so, glad to serve the devil"! "I, I, I, mean, mean, the La, La, Lord"!

That was it! Tommy and I had to head for the back door before we laughed right out loud. Out the door we went snickering and snorting all the way. It was not long before Uncle Ben came out after us.

Uncle Ben being a deacon came out to get on us and make us go back inside, but I believe looking back he just wanted to get out before he laughed too.

He talked to us about being polite in church. That, Tommy, and I, should behave especially polite when sister Pliney was testifying. After his talk to us we went back inside the church. This gave us all time to get it together.

Monday morning Tommy and I went and caught the church bus that took us to the other sister church, Pine Hill Baptist Church where the Vacation Bible School was being held on the other side of the county.

On one of those days, we were at the Vacation Bible School and the preacher was preaching. I do not remember what. But I started to listen. When the preacher was done and doing the altar call, he said "If the Lord is moving in your heart then come on up"!

Tommy whispered to me, "Ain't nobody gonna go up there".

But Tommy never knew the Lord had been moving in my heart.

I whisper back at him, "Do you wanna bet"?

At the same time, I got up, moved down between the pews, stepped out and started up the center aisle. With each step it seemed that I got faster. By the time I got to the altar it seemed I was almost running. Looking back, I must not have run because the church was a small country church and not long enough to run much. But when I got to the altar, I fell down on my knees and began to cry. The preacher came by, and in a low whisper said in my ear, "Son is Jesus moving in your heart"? "Do you believe in Jesus, and that he has saved your soul"? "And do you believe he is the SON OF GOD", asked the Preacher?

I answered, "Yes", with tears in my eyes.

The preacher prayed an extra prayer for me, and the other ones that had come forward after the alter call was over.

The preacher announced, "All these young people that have come forward today have given their hearts to Jesus, and they have all been saved by Jesus. But now it is not over, each one of you needs to go back to your church where you usually attend to be baptized".

I was to go back to Doe Creek Baptist Church, and I wanted Uncle Ben Griffin to baptize me. This was because he had always been a Godly influence on me at that time in my life. Grandma read the Bible to me and Uncle Ben and Aunt Evelyn always watched out for me and taught me about Jesus.

But when I told Mom and Dad about getting saved, and wanting to be baptized, Mom and Dad was not sure I knew what I was doing. They came to the holler specially to talk to me, and Uncle Ben, and Aunt Evelyn. Then they told me that I did not have to be baptized to be saved.

I said, "I knew that, but wanted to". Then I had to sit down with Dad, and Mom, and Uncle Ben, and Aunt Evelyn, and they all began to ask me questions. Wow, I was surprised I must have been listening in church more than I realized. I began to answer questions they ask, and I must have answered correctly because Mom, and Dad, allowed me to get baptized. And Uncle Ben agreed to be the person to Baptist me.

Then next Sunday I went before the church, and after church we went to the edge of the river, and I was baptized. This changed my life. I still made mistakes because I was still young, but God was never far away in my life from then on. I also believed God had called me for something more. I just did not know what.

Once we got back to Ohio, we found a Baptist church and I transferred my membership from Doe Creek Baptist. I went to church every time the door was open unless I was sick. Mom, and Dad, Terry, Rita, and Lillian, everyone in our family had started going to church also. Dad and I started to play and sing in church. Dad never preached before anyone, but he wrote several sermons at home that were very good.

There was a man that lived just up the street named Fred that had a drinking problem. The man up the street had been on a bender. So, Fred's wife Wilma came and asked Mom if Dad could come up and talk to her husband about the Lord. Dad had done so good going to church and that he had not drank any alcohol for some time. That caused Wilma to start to have faith in Dad. Everyone was proud of how Dad had been leaving the booze alone.

Wilma said to mom, "Daisy we are so proud of how Allen has been doing. Could he come down and talk to Fred? Fred has been on a bender. Maybe he could talk to Fred about the Bible and help him to leave the booze alone".

Mom said, "sure when he gets home from work, I will ask him if he will come down to your house. We are so proud of how Allen is not drinking", smiled mom.

That evening when Dad came in from work Mom told him about the request to come and talk to Fred down the street. Dad said, "sure right after supper I will go up and talk to him".

After supper Dad went up the street and knocked on the door. Wilma came to the door and was glad to see Dad.

"Where is Fred", ask Dad?

Wilma smiled and said, "he is here in the living room watching TV". "Fred, Allen is here"!

Dad stepped into the house and the living room.

The house was a shotgun house that went all the way to the back where the kitchen was.

Fred was sitting in a chair facing the TV with his back toward the kitchen end of the house. Dad sat down in a chair facing Fred, which was facing the direction of the open door that led to the hall toward the kitchen.

Wilma went back down the hall to the kitchen to finish her work and give them some privacy.

"Fred you know I thought I would come down and talk with you awhile", said Allen.

Fred picked down the hall to see where Wilma was and to make sure she was still in the kitchen. Then he reached down and behind his chair and pulled out a fifth of Kessler's whiskey.

"Well Allen do you want a drink of whiskey", ask Fred.

"Oh no", said Allen! "I just came down to talk to you about the Lord".

"Well Allen I am glad you did," said Fred as he took a big drink from the bottle. Then he placed it back behind the chair.

"Allen, my wife gets on my case and I have told her that Jesus drank wine, said Fred.

"Well, Fred that is true, but Jesus did not drink to get drunk", answered dad. Dad began to explain that wine was a drink most people drank in that area back then because of the water being bad and hard to get. He also showed him scriptures about not drinking a drink that bubbles and is hard.

Fred looked down the hall again to see if Wilma was still in the kitchen. She was. Then he reached behind his chair and pulled out the bottle again.

"You sure you don't want a drink", ask Fred.

"N-no", stuttered Allen. "I am trying to stay off the stuff".

"Well, I sure ain't", said Fred as he took a big gulp.

Fred put the bottle back.

After talking a while longer Fred looked down the hall again to see if Wilma was still in the kitchen. She was. Then he reached behind his chair and pulled out the bottle again.

"Are you sure you don't want a drink, Allen", ask Fred holding up the bottle.

N-no", stuttered Allen. "I am trying to stay off the stuff".

"Well, that's your stuff luck", said Fred.

Fred put the bottle back behind the chair. They talked a while longer.

Are you sure you don't want a drink, Allen", ask Fred?

Dad could not stand it anymore. He rose up slightly and looked down the hall to see if Wilma could see him. She was still in the kitchen at the other end of the house.

Allen said, "well, just one little drink wouldn't hurt". "Go ahead and give me one"

Fred reached behind his chair and got out the bottle happy to have someone to drink with.

Both of them looked down the hall to check out where Wilma was and then both took a big gulp.

In about 10 minutes they both looked down the hall to check for Wilma and took another big gulp.

About 30 minutes later Wilma was in the kitchen and heard a lot of noisy talking, laughing, and singing coming from the living room. She stopped what she was doing and went into the living room. They were passing an almost empty bottle back and forth between them. She could tell that they both were drunk as skunks. She grabbed the almost empty bottle from their hands.

She said, "you two are drunk and you ain't getting anymore booze". "And I am going to bed"!!! Off she went with the almost empty bottle to her bedroom mad as hell.

"Well, that's the end of our drinking", said Allen.

Fred put his finger across his mouth from his nose to his chin and said, "Shu, Maybe, not", smiled Fred as he reached down behind his chair again and pulled out a brand-new full bottle of Kessler's Whiskey that the seal had not been broken on, yet.

Both men looked toward the hallway in the direction Wilma had disappeared. When they were sure she was gone they broke the seal, and each had a big gulp.

That night they both slept together drunk in the same bed, passed out.

Wilma told mom all about what had happened the next day.

Wilma said, "it was like sending the fox to watch the chickens"!

Dad later on told what he could remember. I remember him telling some friends about it. Dad did not go back to church for over a month. When he did, he went to the altar to ask for forgiveness. The longest dad ever went without drinking was 3 years.

Ernest, Terry, Gary and Danny use to go almost every Saturday to the "House of Horrors" movie theater on Xenia Avenue in Dayton, Ohio and watch 3 to 4 full length scary movies where they would also have a live monster show up. I think it cost about 25 cents admission for each one of us boys to get in. Mom, Dad, and Uncle Orlie and Aunt Lillian I believe used this as some adult time.

I remember when we used to go and visit in Irvine Kentucky. One time our family went to Visit Uncle Ernie Wells and Aunt Eddie. They lived on a farm and had 4 boys and one girl. This time we got there, and all the boys were down at the creek swimming. I ask mom if we could go down there too.

Mom said, "yes but you have to take Terry with you, but you boys cannot go swimming".

We said "OK"!

Then Terry and I took off down to the creek. When we got to the creek all of my fellow cousins that were home at that time Jimmy, Donald and several of their friends started trying to get us to come in the water.

I told them, "My mother wouldn't let us".

They all told me, "Take your clothes off and your mom would never know"!

Terry wanted to come in, but I would not let him because he could not swim yet. So, I made him stay on the bank and I pulled all my clothes off and jumped in. This made Terry mad that I would not let him come in. So, Terry stomped all around the bank mad cause he wanted to get in the water too. Then he pulled off his clothes and jumped in too. I made him get back out. This made him even madder, so he threw all my clothes into the creek. Even my shoes he threw in. So, I got out and he jumped in with all his clothes on to get away from me. We were both soaking wet. So, when we got back to the farmhouse mom was so mad, we got our legs switched and we left because mom was so mad.

Another time we went to Irvine and some of our older fellows/cousin's swam the river at Ravenna, KY., a little town just outside of Irvine. I would not let Terry swim it because I felt he was too young. I was afraid he would get halfway and get tired and drown and I could not save him. This time Terry listened to me and did not swim the river.

Terry told me later on when he was older, he went back and swam it himself just to prove he could. I don't doubt it because when he got older, he was a better swimmer than I was. Terry was always better at sports than I was.

It was 1960, and I went to bed one night, and the next morning I woke up in the Hospital. I did not remember how I got there, or what happened. Dad told me the story sitting alongside of my hospital bed.

"Son you don't remember anything from last night, do you", asked Dad?

I said, "No, Dad, nothing"! "I do remember yesterday that while I was riding my bike the sky seemed very gray, and I was having trouble seeing good".

Dad said, "It was about 10:00 pm Ernie and I was about to go to bed when I heard a noise from upstairs that was coming from your room. I went into your room and you were having a seizure. Then you would calm down and go right back into another seizure. So, I called an ambulance and while I was waiting for the ambulance you had about 3 or 4 more. The ambulance drivers said you had 3 more on the way to the hospital. I called your Mom who was already at work at the hospital and she met the ambulance at the emergency room. The doctors said you were having one seizure right after another seizure, and that if they did not stop the seizures your heart would give out. You were shaking and jerking so bad that you were throwing the Interns in the emergency room plum across the room. They finally got you strapped down to the bed. Then they gave you a needle in the arm with Demerol to calm you down. The doctor said we almost lost you.

I spent several days in the hospital and they ran all kinds of tests on me. They determined I had a brain tumor, but they could not operate. They began to try different medications to try and control my seizures with medications. They found that Dilantin and Phenobarbital did not stop the seizures but I had very few seizures on these medications than I had before without medications.

So, I took Dilantin and Phenobarbital all the way up until 1985. Then they took me off both drugs and put me on Tegretol. This drug seems to control my seizures and I only had one in 1991 and to this day that is the last seizure I have ever had.

You know 1960 was a big year for me. My youngest sister was born. I learned to play the guitar and decided to make music a career. I was diagnosed as an epileptic and began to take medication for it the rest of my life. But most of all I learned who Jesus was. And got saved by him. I also came to the realization that someday I would preach the Gospel of Jesus Christ.

ERNEST FLATT & TERRYFLATT-brothers about 10 & 5 years old.

30. 1961-THE BOYS CLUB IS WHERE WE HANG OUT.

1961 we lived on Albany Avenue next to a park. Terry, and I, our cousins Gary and Danny talked mom and dad, and Uncle Orlie and Aunt Lillian into letting us join the Dayton Boy's Club. At that time, only boys were allowed. You couldn't join until you were six years old, so Terry, and Danny, just made it. We used to go every Saturday all day. We would make things in the wood shop, play pool, lots of different games, basketball, boxing, and swimming. Everyone swam in the nude because it was only boys. The pool was very large and started at 3 feet deep and went to 4 foot deep then there was a divider to the deep end. "Non-Swimmers" and "Tadpoles" could only swim in the shallow end. All of us boys, me, Gary, Terry, and Danny, learn to swim at the Boy's Club. There were different levels, and you had to take a swim test to move up to the next level. With each level you had to be able to accomplish certain swimming tasks to gain the level increase. There was the "Non-Swimmer", the "Tadpole" these first levels only allowed you in the shallow end of the pool. the "Goldfish", the "Sailfish", the "Swordfish" and the "Lifeguard" gave you the ability to use the whole pool including the diving board. I acquired the level of a "Goldfish". That was as far as I cared to try for, because once you became a "Goldfish" you were allowed to swim the whole pool and dive off the diving board. That was good enough for me. I think all of us at least became "Goldfish". But there was no doubt that the best player in the big game room among use four, especially billiards, was my brother Terry. He won all kinds of awards.

I got involved in the wood shop. I still have a wooden bowl, and a stop sign shaped, wooden, jewel box I made for Mom. I also made a lamp on the lathe out of a bowling pin, but I do not know what happened to it. But all of us boys sure learned a lot about sportsmanship and fairness at the Boy's Club and we have never forgotten it even today. We will always remember and thank the Boy's Club of Dayton, Ohio. Our folks knew what they were doing when they signed us up at the Boy's Club. It kept us out of trouble and gave us a place to have fun and hang out. Not to mention it was much better than a babysitter. I still donate to the Boy's Club today. I still owe some of the values I learned in life to my time at the Boys Club. They taught me leadership, fairness, and how to be a man at the Boys Club, not to mention how to swim, and do wood work, play sports and a good work ethic.

31. 1962-DAD AND I JOINED THE DAYTON MUSICIANS CLUB.

In 1962-I started playing music in front of people other than family at age 12. Dad and Mom and the family used to go to friend's houses that played music. We would sit in a circle, and take turns playing songs. Everybody played, but when it came your turn you got to choose the song and sing it. I had gotten good enough that I was allowed to join the circle. When it came my turn, I would usually choose a Buck Owens song. He was my favorite at that time. There was a man that played drums that started coming. His name was Raymond Rogers. He was a very good drummer and played regularly at night clubs around Dayton. He liked playing with Dad and tried to get Dad to come out to the clubs he was playing at, and sit in.

Dad and I also joined the Dayton Musicians Club, and we were invited to go play at the shows they would have. You did not get paid but it gave me a lot of experience playing in front of big crowds. Dad would a lot of time be the MC because he was the most experienced of everybody. They liked the way Dad would tell jokes and introduce the acts. Dad had a lot of experience on radio and at being a professional entertainer, and it showed. The president of the DMC was Don Young.

Dad told a story about himself. There was this one time when Dad was working for Woodruff Tree and Lawn Service. He came home and was raw around his genitals and butt hole.

Dad slept in his boxers, or nude and we did not have air conditioning, so our windows were usually open with just a screen. Before going to bed and taking off their clothes they would turn off the lights and let up the blinds for good airflow. Dad asked Mom if the mineral oil was still beside the bed on the stand so he could put some on himself.

Mom said, "Yes I think so. It should be on the stand beside the bed".

Dad did not want to turn on the lights, so he felt around until he felt the bottle. He opened the bottle and poured some into his hand.

Dad said, "His thinking was to pour some into his hand and dash it on his private parts".

But just as he poured it into his hand, he thought it felt a lot runnier than Mineral Oil was normally, but he wanted to be quick so as not to spill it. So, he dashed it between his legs on his genitals, and butt, very quickly.

"I-I-I-Ouch", Dad screamed!!! He was screaming and making a lot of noise.

So, Mom turned on the light to see what Dad was making such a commotion about. Dad was in the middle of the room dancing around screaming. Then he grabbed a Funny Book, (some people call them a comic book) from the nightstand and started fanning his privates in the middle of the room.

Mom began to laugh at the sight.

Mom said, "Allen what is the matter"?

Dad hollered as he kept fanning his private parts, and dancing in the middle of the room, "I am on fire, Daisy"!!!

Mom looked at the bottle, and Dad had got the 97% Rubbing Alcohol bottle by mistake.

Dad kept fanning in the middle of the room. Mom began to laugh again. Dad did not care that the light was on, or if anyone saw him. He kept fanning with the funny book.

Dad told the story later, "The next day he was all well around his private parts. But the pain, and cure was worse than the problem"!!! Dad always said, "it was a rough damn game, but it sure cured my rawness"!

32. 1963-ERNEST AND TERRY STEALING CIGARETTES.

In **1963**-Our family still lived On Albany Street in Dayton, Ohio right next to the big city park. There was a big swimming pool we got into everyday of the summer. One-time Terry and I stole 2 of mom's cigarettes and went to the park to sneak and smoke them. We did not know how to smoke. We were just showing off for some of our friends. We could not even inhale the smoke and it would make us cough. We were on the other side of a building trying to hide to smoke the cigarettes when dad started to holler for us.

Dad hollered across the park, "Ernie, Terry, come here"!!!

We didn't realize it, but the smoke was coming around the corner of the building and dad could see it. When he hollered for us a second time, we looked around the corner of the building right toward dad where the smoke was coming from. Then we jumped back behind the building.

I said, "oh, shit dad is hollering for us"!

We both put our cigarettes out with our feet. After putting out my cigarette I went around the corner and was walking toward dad just as though nothing was wrong. I was walking across the huge park toward dad ahead of Grant. When I got to Dad, Grant was a long way back.

Dad looked at me and said, "were you smoking"? I was stunned. I asked myself, how did he know?

"No", I answered, with big round eyes.

Dad said, "you know I could see the smoke coming from around the end of the building".

Dad gave me a look that told me he knew, and I was busted.

Dad said, "Now don't lie to me, was you smoking"?

I dropped my head and said, "Yes sir".

"Where did you get the cigarettes", dad added with a stern look.

"I took them from mom's purse", I replied.

"Uhm, was your brother smoking also", ask dad?

"Yes sir", I said with my head down.

I looked around and Terry was still a long way off enough that he could not hear what had been said. He knew we were in trouble, and he was taking his time getting to dad. Maybe to think about what he would do or say.

"Well, you stand right over there and don't say anything, I want to see if your brother will be truthful to me. I stepped over to the side of dad facing Terry as he approached dad. Hoping Terry could tell by my face, we were in trouble.

Once Terry got close enough, dad asked in a stern voice, "was you smoking"?

Terry looked at me, and I wanted so bad to give him a signal, but dad was watching.

"Don't look at him, look right here at me", pointed dad at himself.

"Now were you smoking behind that building up there", dad asked again.

Again, Terry looked at me, you could tell he was afraid to answer, but I couldn't even twitch an eye.

Terry said, "NO SIR"!

My head dropped.

Dad looked at Terry and said, "Well, Ernie has already told me that you both were smoking".

Terry gave me a dirty look as if to say you dirty dog.

Dad punished us but I do not remember what it was, but I am sure we did not like it. I do remember that we also got punished from Mom for stealing her cigarettes as well. I do not remember what the punishment was for taking Mom's cigarettes was either, but I am sure we didn't like it as well.

33. 1964-1965- PLAYING MUSIC IN NIGHTCLUBS & MEETS DEANNA FAY BANNER.

We moved to 324 Morton Ave, Dayton, Ohio 45410 and liked it much better. We had a whole house. Terry and I went to Patterson Elementary School.

Terry and I decided to play at some night clubs. Terry played a snare, and I sang and played my guitar. We made a few dollars from tips and I feel in love with performing.

Terry moved on to sports, but I kept the music going. There was nothing else I wanted to do for a living than play music. I knew from this day on that was what I wanted to do. Any job I took was a back seat to music. By this time, I was in High School, performing every chance I could get.

One day Raymond Rodgers, a drummer dad and I, had played music with at the "singing/playing song circles", and the Dayton Musicians Club Shows, came by our house.

He came by our house and to ask Dad, "Allen how about you, and me, putting together a band"?

Dad studied and said, "Well Rodger it's just too much work putting together a band".

Raymond Rodgers usually went by Rodger. Most everybody called him Rodger including Dad and me.

Then Rodger said, "I'll take care of it all. I will get the musicians and book the night clubs. We will start off slow maybe a Friday or a Saturday night, a couple nights a month. Then if it works out, we could work into a Friday and Saturday night regular every week. You are the front man, singing and playing guitar, I'll play the drums and be the band leader and take care of everything else if that's the way you want it".

"How about it, Allen," asked Rodger?

I was sitting and listening hoping dad would do it. Rodger added, "We will all make the same money".

Dad said, "Rodger I just can't do it. At my age I need my sleep, and I have to work on Saturdays".

I think Dad was afraid that if he started playing in night clubs that he would start to drink again, and it would cause trouble between him, and Mom.

Rodger seemed disappointed and with his head down he said, "Allen I need someone who could put on a good show and sing a lot of songs. You were the only one I have met that fits the bill. I know a lot of musicians, but I do not know any front men. Especially as good as you".

Dad studied for a minute. Then Dad said something that really got my attention.

"Rodger why don't you let Ernest do it", ask dad?

Rodger's head popped up and looked at me. I was laying on the couch and when I heard Dad say what he said, I raised up and sat upright on the couch. Rodger began to study me. He had heard me play and sing a lot at the Dayton Musicians Club shows.

Rodger asked looking at me, "Do you think he can do it"?

"Well Rodger you have heard him, do you think he is good enough", ask Dad? "And as you know, him and I have done shows together before at schools, and clubs, and we have gone to nightclubs, and sat in before", spoke dad.

"Well yes", said Rodger, "I just didn't know if you would let him by himself"! "He would be a great way to get people talking about us, and word of mouth is the best way to advertise", studied Rodger.

I was sitting there taking notice like a dog, and someone had just pulled out a steak.

Dad said, "Well of course, we are going to have to ask Daisy and she is at work, and you will have to take full responsibility for him while he is at the club. He doesn't drink and he is fairly level headed. We would expect you to watch out for him. But most of all we have to convince Daisy. This is Friday night, and I think we are both off this Sunday if you want to come back and talk to the two of us. That will give us a chance to talk between the 3 of us".

Rodger said, "That will be just fine. Ernest you think you could put on a show", Rodger asked me?

I was on top of the world and almost hollered "YES"!!!

"Well, you understand you will have to listen to me, and ride with me", said Rodger.

"NO PROBLEM, SIR", I answered!!!

"Well, I guess it is up to your mom then" said Rodger. He added, "There's no doubt in my mind that you can do the job, because I have heard you before and have always been impressed with you. It just never crossed my mind that your folks would let you".

Dad repeated, "Well as I said we will have to convince his Mom, and she will have the final say.

I will talk to her tonight when she gets home", Dad said turning to me. "Ernie you need to let me talk to her, so don't say anything until I talk to her. You make her mad, and she will just say no".

I said, "OK dad, I will leave it to you". This was OK with me anyway. Dad was a good talker and knew just how to present it to Mom.

Roger said, "Well goodbye Allen, I will call you or come by Sunday". Then he shook Dad and my hand, and then was gone out the door.

Later that night when mom came home from work, I could hear dad and mom talking in the other room, but I could not understand what was being said. I wanted to hear so badly, but Dad had said let him handle it. He knew Mom best and Dad could sell a refrigerator to an Eskimo if he really wanted to. So, I stayed up in my room and ease dropped as much as I could. I was so nervous to hear what the answer would be. After about 30 minutes Mom called for me and asked me to come and sit down in the living room. Boy was I nervous. Dad was smiling a little, that was a good sign, but mom looked serious.

Mom asked, "So Ernest you want to play music in a nightclub with Roger. Is that right"?

I answered, "Yes momma I really do"!

Mom looked at me as if she was studying me and said, "Well, Ernest if your Dad, and I were to agree there has to be some rules. And you must follow them if you want to get us to keep letting you play music in clubs".

"OK, I will follow the rules", I answered.

"Just a minute Ernest, you haven't heard the rules yet", said Mom. "Do you want to hear them first", ask Mom?

I said, "Yes", as if it really mattered, though it really did not. Because I would have done anything at this point to get to play music with a band.

Mom said "OK".

Then Mom continued, "Number one you cannot miss school for any reason, or the playing music stops". Then Mom stated, "Do you understand, school comes first"!

I nodded my head yes and said, "Yes mama".

Mom spoke and said, "Number two is you are going to be making money, and since you are making money you will be required to give half of what you make for room, and board, and food, now that you have got a job. The other half you can use to buy clothes, shoes, or boots, guitar strings, whatever you want to wear to school, and whatever you need to play music".

"Do you understand", mom asked as she watched me nod my head yes again? The money was not even a worry for me. I would play for nothing at that time.

"Number three, I know you don't drink, or we could not trust you to do this at all, but you should never start".

"Yes mama, I won't", I answered. This was true. I was proud that I did not drink and had learned from my Dad that drinking gets in the way of being successful in the music business. Plus, I was taking drugs for my seizures, and alcohol killed my medication.

This was a promise I kept all the way to after graduation from High School, and when I was 19 years old when I was on tour in Tule, Greenland in 1969. I drank too much champagne, and beer at a party. I thought the Champagne would not get you drunk; I was wrong. There was a Danish man that worked on the base at the party. He said he would chug 2 beers for every one that I chugged. I was already high on the Champagne and agreed to the challenge. The next day I was so sick I could not get out of the bed, I had thrown up. Then after getting sick the Jack Green Band, or I should say the "Jolly Green Giants", came through and told me goodbye. I was so embarrassed, and sick that I never drank alcohol again until 24 years old.

"Ok if you can agree to these rules then I think your Dad and I will trust you but remember rule #1 you can never miss school because you stayed up late", said mom. "You still owe me a High School Diploma, understand young man", ask Mom looking straight at me?

"Yes mama, I understand", I answered so happy I was about to bounce off the ceiling. I left the room walking on a cloud.

Dad smiled and said to me, "OK, I will call Rodger and ask him to come by. Your Mom wants to talk to him too".

That Sunday we had a meeting with Rodger and Mom made sure Rodger understood that he was to take care of her oldest baby boy. Then she made sure that I understood that Rodger was in charge or else. I knew what else was, "it meant the music stopped".

Rodger told me that he was going to start finding other musicians and setting up some practices. Then he would start booking gigs. Rodger found Ralph Rodden to play guitar. Ralph was an older fellow but played well. He played an electric Fender Stratocaster. He always had a cigar in his mouth. Also, he did some face fucking, while he was playing, but played very well. He liked to play Buck Owens songs and could play them just like "Don Rich". Don Rich was Buck Owens' guitar player, fiddle player, and harmony singer. So, we got along great. Then Rodger found a bass man by the name Joe Petcock. Joe could sing a few songs himself and he could sing harmony with everything I sang. We had our first practice, and everyone just fell right into the groove. Rodger told the other fellows that they were going to build the show around me. Everyone seems to agree with me being the front man. So, Rodger said he would begin to book us some gigs.

In a few days Rodger called and said we had a gig that would start in 2 weeks at the Green Lantern on Springfield Pike in Dayton, Ohio. I was so excited. Rodger owned the PA, and it was a good one. A Fender PA that could take 6 microphones, or instruments. But we only needed 3 microphones. Back then musicians did not mic the instruments, unless they played a big venue, like a memorial hall. Rodger sang a couple of songs and did some harmony too. Rodger would run the PA while he was playing drums, and never miss a lick. In those days, the PA consisted of a power amp mixer combo and 2 columns of speakers. We did not even have monitors in those days, and we did not mic any instruments in a nightclub. We would just run vocals through the PA and turn the columns slightly inward toward the singers.

Rodger said that we would get a Saturday night gig at the Green Lantern and if we did good the club owner would bring us back in for a Friday and Saturday night twice a month.

So, we got together and worked on some comedy, and 4 sets of songs. I had learned some comedy routines from Dad, and we were using them now. We were doing good and having fun at practice, but the proof would be once we played in front of a crowd. The musician's families liked us, but again the proof would be in playing in front of a crowd.

We showed up at the club on our first night and everybody was a little nervous. Maybe I was more nervous than anyone else, but I made sure I did not show it. I wanted the other musicians to believe I was professional. After all they were all more experienced than me. The club owner had agreed to my age and let me play as long as I did not drink alcohol and Rodger watched over me, but he wanted professionalism just the same. And of course, it was promised that I would not drink alcohol even behind his back. This was no problem because I did not drink, did not want to, and had too much to lose. Mom would have killed me and stopped the music.

Once we got to the club, we moved all the equipment inside and Rodger introduced us to the club owner. I think this was mainly for my sake. Then we all went on stage and tuned up and took a sound check before the people started to come in. Man, we were hoping we would have a crowd. So far, we had the people that worked there and the families of the band at a table of their own. We also had a special guest. Dad said later in the night he would sing some songs with us. Everybody in the band liked Dad and considered him a real pro.

We started playing the first set and there were only the people that worked there, and the families of the band for a crowd. So, we were concerned about If anyone would come out.

Then about 9:30 pm all of a sudden, the place began to fill up. Also, we began to get applause. And then requests for songs and believe it or not we knew all of them. These people liked Buck Owens and I knew all of his. I also knew a lot of Carl Smith, Marty Robbins, and Ray Price and that is what they wanted to hear.

By the second set the place was rockin' and we were on top of the world. We were getting tips, and everybody was having a ball. Dancing and whooping and hollering, and they did not want us to stop. And when Dad came up on the third set, they acted like Ernest Tubb had just come in. They could not believe how much he sounded like Ernest Tubb.

The band, including Dad and I played a total of 3 sets. Then the last set had come to an end.

"Folks we want to thank you for treating us so nice tonight, but it has come to the end of our evening", I said at the end of the last set. "Please request that we come back and see you again real soon, just ask Bill the club owner to have us back", I said trying to sell the crowd on us.

Rodger spoke up on his mic from behind me and said, "Yeah folks just ask for Ernest Flatt and the Country Hillbillies"!

All of a sudden, my mouth fell open. I turned stunned and looked back at Rodger. I could not believe they were giving me top billing. Rodger was grinning from behind his drums.

Then Joe the bass man grinning from the other side of the stage stepped up to the mic and said, "well I guess we got a name, Ernest Flatt and the Country Hillbillies"! "Let's hear it for Ernest Flatt, have you ever heard anyone sing as good as him at any age", he asked the crowd?

The crowd went crazy with applause. I did not think things could have gotten any better. But then stepping up on stage the Club Owner Bill spoke into the microphone.

He said, "folks you wanna hear them play another set", he asked the crowd?

The crowd went crazy again with applause and whistles.

"Well fellows if I pay you another set will you play for these fine people", shouted Bill into the microphone?

Of course, we all said "yes"!!!

"But before they play another set, would you like for me to bring them back again", ask Bill?

The crowd again went into a large applause, whistles, and screams.

"How about every other week", shouted Bill into the mic?

The crowd again went crazy. Bill turned and pointed at me and said, "Play it Boys"!!!

We jumped into a Wynne Stewart song.

"They Call Me A Playboy", I sang with a cold kick off. "While I'm making' my rounds, chasing the bright lights of every night spot in town", I sang.

The song was a western swing, bouncy 4/4 song. The dance floor filled up and the stage was completely surrounded by women clapping to the music. I was hooked. At that moment I knew what I wanted to do for a living.

Dad had been in the music business and was able to get in backstage when certain artists would come to Memorial Hall in Dayton. All together Dad had taken me backstage to meet in person, Ernest Tubb and all his band; Hank Williams Jr when he was still doing only his dads' music.; Mack Wiseman; Carl Smith; Jimmy Dickens; Carl, and Pearl Butler which I later got to back up in Minneapolis, Minnesota in 1973 at the Flame Cafe.

One time we were backstage going down steps, and I looked and coming up the steps toward us was Marty Robbins. He said "Hi" and we both answered "Hi". Dad Looked at me after Marty had gone on by, and said, "Who was that"? I said, "Dad, don't you know who that was"? Dad said, "I don't think so"! I said, "Dad that was Marty Robbins"! Dad said "Oh, I didn't know what he looked like". "He must have come after I left Nashville, I didn't know what he looked like but I have sure heard of him", replied dad.

Later during the show, we were backstage, Marty Robbins had a small 6 string Martin guitar about the size of a ukulele. As Marty was getting out the Martin, Dad asked, "Marty when did you start playing a ukulele"? Marty held the small Martin guitar up, looked at it and said, "Yesterday". Then both of us laughed. Marty went out on stage and put on a fantastic show.

When Marty came off the stage, he shook hands with several people and came over to where Dad, and I were standing. His guitar case was there beside us, as Marty was putting away his guitar, Dad asked, "Marty how much does one of these small guitars cost compared to a big D-28 Martin"? Marty held up the small Martin guitar just above the case and studied. Then he answered, "I am sorry to say just as much as a D-28". "Isn't that awful". Then he laughed, and shook his head, as he put the little guitar away. Marty Robbins was always one of my favorites from then on.

There was a place just outside of Dayton, Ohio, called Wild Cherry Park. They had outdoor country concerts from time to time, with grand Ole Opry Stars. So, at Wild Cherry park I met Ernie Ashworth (Talk Back Trembling Lips) and it just so happened that Dad taught him to play guitar. There was also another outdoor venue called Chautauqua Park. They had a nicer covered stage with a curtain and a backstage area. Dad got me backstage at other times, to meet Porter Wagoner, and then Bill Anderson.

Then one time I was backstage, and here came walking up backstage before the show time was, Conway Twitty! Dresses in Bermuda shorts, a t-shirt, and flip flops. All I could do was just stand there with my mouth open, and watch him talking to another man about the size of the crowd, as he smoked his cigarette. I was amazed. This was Coway Twitty, Rock Star, then a Country Music legend They were looking through a peephole in the curtain.

One time he took me to Cincinnati's Memorial Hall, which was 53 miles south from Dayton, to see Buck Owens and the Buckaroos. Buck Owens was tops at that time. Opening for him was a newcomer named Merle Haggard, Bonnie Owens, and his band the Strangers. I was on cloud nine. Dad could not get us backstage because he did not know anyone with the show. But I stood, and watched Buck Owens and the Buckaroos sign autographs at the edge of the stage at the end of the show. Buck Owens even got down and walked around with us. He was just a little taller than I was. I knew every Buck Owens song that was out. What a great night. I have many great memories because of Dad and Mom.

Not too long after starting to play music in night clubs I met and started dating Deanna Fay Banner. Deanna was the daughter of Avery Banner, and Ethel Banner. Avery and Dad had played music together several years before. Dad ran into Avery and they started to talk about old times and about how they used to play music together and the good ole times. At one time Avery and the Banner Family had a family band and played music together. They had a large family and 2 or 3 of them played and sang.

Dad also told Avery how I played music and was pretty good. Avery asks Dad, Mom and the family over to play some music and have supper one Saturday night. I was not playing in a club that night and Dad asked me to go along to play some music. Dad said, "Avery liked to play, and I am sure we will play some music. Avery played dobro and old fashioned Hank Williams electric steel guitar".

Avery was a mechanic by trade and I guess a very good one. I think he worked on large equipment. Like bulldozers and such. He didn't have much education but was very smart. I remember he built a paddlewheel boat in his garage motor and all. When it was done he took it to the lake and rode the family around to show it off to everybody at the lake. Avery was very good with money, in spite of his lack of education. Then not long after that he sold it, and went looking for another project. He was always fixing up old cars, and selling them, and such.

After I got there, I found out Avery had several daughters and several sons. Avery likes to play music and take a nipe from time to time. So as the night went on Avery would get more likeable and happy. Sometimes if we did a song exceptionally well, he would stand up, and jump up into the air and hollow, "YepHee", just like an old cowboy might do. It seemed he would jump almost 3 foot in the air as he hollered out.

Avery and Ethel's youngest daughter was 2 years older than me, but was still at home and not married. Her name was Deanna Fay Banner. Although she was older than me, she seemed to get a crush on me after she heard me sing, and I fell for her too. I remember her looking in the face like Donna Reed, but with dark hair. She liked Carl Smith and I just happen to know a few Carl Smith songs. I was kind of backwards still, but she made the moves to be friendly, and I liked it.

She went to a co-op high school where she was studying school for 2 weeks and worked at Inland a Division of General Motors for 2 weeks. Then she would start with the rotation of school and work all over again. She was very smart and pretty. She reminded me of Donna Reed in the face. I used to walk about 6 blocks to the bus stop, and catch the city bus, and ride all the way across Dayton Metropolitan Area to the end of the bus lines, and then walk about 4 miles to get to her house to be able to see her. I would sometimes do this a couple of times a week, and almost every weekend. Not too long after we started dating, she got her own car and began to pick me up. We would go to the movies, bowling and to eat out, that is if I was not playing music. I usually did not have much money because mom made me pay rent. But Deanna would a lot of times pay for me, and her both, and drive too. She was very kind to me. As a matter of fact, she bought me clothes and things. One time she bought me a trench coat just like the spy's wear. That was just because I said I liked it in a movie. Another time she bought me a pair of Justin Cowboy Boots to wear to play music because my old boots were worn out.

My mother became uncomfortable with Deanna spending so much money on me. So, she went and talked to Ethel about it. Ethel Banner was Deanna's mom.

Ethel said to mom, "Daisy don't worry about it. If she did not spend it on Ernest, she would just blow it on something else. If she did not want to spend it on Ernest she would not. We like Ernest and we think he is good for Deanna. They both seem to care a lot about each other".

I remember one day I came in from a date with Deanna. Deanna had dropped me off because she had to get home. We always used the back door on Morton Avenue. When I walked in by myself, mom and dad, Uncle Orlie and Aunt Lill were playing a card game in the kitchen around the eating table. They usually played Canasta, Spades, or Hearts.

I said my hellos to everybody. Dad began to tell Aunt Lill and Uncle Orlie about the trench coat I was wearing, and that Deanna had bought it for me and that it had cost over a hundred dollars. Then he began having me show off the Justin Boots that she had bought me. They cost about $75.00. In those days that was a lot for a pair of boots. They were very nice and fancy.

Dad and Uncle Orlie were big kidders and joke tellers.

Uncle Orlie said, "Son I need for you to pull your pants down, so I can see what you got down there". Dad and Uncle Orlie laughed out loud.

Aunt Lill said, "Oh Orlie, you don't need to embarrass the boy".

Uncle Orlie laughed and said, "Oh I was just joking with him, he knows I am teasing".

Aunt Lill was right, my face had turned beet red, so I tried to smile and made my way out of the kitchen and went upstairs.

Terry, my brother and I had been doing the dishes after supper as part of our chores since Terry was about 7 years old. There was almost a 5 years difference between our ages. But because we would be doing the dishes and then we would get into arguments we had been taking turns to do the dishes for a couple of years. One night it was my turn, then the next was Terry's turn.

Dad would always start the breakfast in the morning and just as he was getting breakfast done Mom would come in from her night shift and finish it. Then we would all sit down for breakfast, and after breakfast was over all us kids would go off to school. Dad would go off to work. And Mom would do the dishes and then go lay down to sleep until close to supper. Which she would have ready by the time we all got home. Then after supper Mom would lay down again until time to get ready for her 11:00 pm shift. Which she had to leave for work by 10:00 pm

But back to breakfast, Dad needed the dishes clean so he could do breakfast the next morning. This time was my turn to do the dishes.

I was about 14 or 15 years old and we had finished supper and there was something special on TV I wanted to watch.

So, I ask Dad, "can I watch this TV program before I do the dishes, I promise I will do them after the TV show"?

Dad looked at me and said, "OK but Ernie you know I will be very upset if I wake up in the morning and that sink is full of dishes and I can't get to doing breakfast on time".

I said, "Yes sir, I won't forget"!

"You, better not because I am going to bed, or in the morning I will be whipping you all the way down the stairs from your bedroom", said Dad firmly.

Well, I fell asleep in the chair watching the TV show. When I woke up it was in the middle of the night, and I was half asleep. So, I got out of the chair, turned off the TV and went to bed. Forgetting about the dishes in the sink.

The next morning, I woke up as Dad jerked the covers off me. I had nothing but my shorts on. As the covers were jerked off, I felt the cold air on my body, and then the feeling of Dad's belt across my legs as I jumped out of bed.

Dad was hollering, "I thought I told you what would happen if you didn't do those dishes. Get down to the kitchen and get them dishes done"!!

I was dancing with each smack of the belt and crying. Dad whipped me all the way down the stairs, through the living room, and into the kitchen. Finally, once I was in front of the sink and the water was running, he stopped whipping me. I stood there crying washing the dishes.

As I was standing there crying Dad said, "first get me a biscuit pan and skillet done so I can get the Biscuits, and Gravy going". "I told you last night that I needed these dishes done so I could get breakfast ready before time to go to work", dad hollered!. "Your mom is gonna be home in a while, and this is gonna throw us behind". "Get it done"!

I cried as I got the dishes done in my underwear.

I look back on this and realize that Dad was mad, but not near as mad as he led me to believe because there was not a mark on me, so he had chosen his licks with the belt very carefully. Finally, Mom came home, and she helped me get the dishes done. She said it was to speed me up, but I think it was because she felt sorry for me. But she still felt I deserved it. Looking back on it, I do too. I learned a big lesson; It was the last time I ever fell asleep without my chores being done again. Especially the dishes!

I started high school at Stivers High School on east Fifth Street September 1964-the family lived on 324 Morton Ave. Dayton, Ohio 45410.

I had a friend across the alley from Mom and Dad. His name was Howard Shank. He played a little music, and when we would go out to the clubs where I played, he would teach me to drive his cherry 56 Ford 3 speed on the column. That is how I learn to drive a stick.

I had been driving dad home from bars because dad was too drunk to drive safely since I was about 12 years old. But it was always an automatic transmission until Howard showed me how to drive his 56 Ford stick.

Deanna, my girlfriend, had a girlfriend from school named Dianna. My friend Howard Shank was about 25 years old. Dianna and Deanna had now just become 18 years old. Howard and Dianna started to get a crush on each other. So that he would be able to neck with Dianna, Howard would let me, and Deanna sit up front and I would drive. Although, I did not have a driver's license I had driven dad home before. But Howard taught me to drive his stick shift. A 1956 Ford and trusted me. So, I would drive, Deanna and I, also Howard and Dianna around on a double date using Howard's car. I was just 15 years old.

34. 1966 –ERNEST GETS HIS DRIVERS LICENSE.

I got my learner's permit-driver's license just as soon as I turned 16 years old. I passed the written test with no problem.

I was a good driver and took and passed drivers education in school. I took the driver's test just as soon as the law would allow. Which was Oct-1966. I was very excited to take my driver's test.

As I remember Dad had promised to take me. We woke up and when I looked outside there was 2 foot of snow on the ground. Dad tried to talk me out of going.

Dad said, "We can go another time Ernie".

I said, "Aw Dad, I've been waiting a long time"!

Dad said, "Well son it is going to be slick, you might fail, or wreck my car, or even get hurt".

Afraid Dad was not going to take me, "I said Dad I will be really careful and drive slow".

Dad said, "Ok, we will drive there and see, I got good tires, but if I think it is too slick, we are coming back. I do not want you sliding my car and getting' hurt".

Again, I said, "I will be careful".

We got to the driver's test station with Dad's old 1956 Oldsmobile. Dad's car was very heavy, and Dad said it handled well on the roads. They had put out salt on the streets and it was doing good on the road. So, Dad agreed to let me take the test if they were giving it that day. Once we arrived Dad asked the Highway Patrol officer if they were going to have the driving test today.

He said, "yes".

Dad wondered later if the officer thought Dad was getting ready to take the test. Because when he found out it was me, he had a strange look on his face. I took the test and took my time. When it came to the parking test, I used what I had been told in drivers education class and I put it right there perfect the first time. The officer gave me a 100 % on parking and 80% on the driving, because he said I drove too slow. But I passed! Not too many people can say they passed their driving test in 2 feet of snow.

Dad said on the way home, "I think that Highway Patrolman just didn't want to act scared and went along with it when he thought it was me taking the driving test. But after he found out it was you; he had a scared look on his face". Then Dad laughed big and loud as he let me drive home. Dad said, "Wonder what he would have said if he knew how many times you drove me home when I was drunk"? Dad laughed loud again.

I remember Dad would let me borrow his old 56 Oldsmobile to go to the store. Sometimes he would let me take Terry, and my cousins Gary and Danny to the drive-in to see a movie. I remember one night on a Saturday Terry, Gary, Danny, and I went to the drive-in movie and decided to stop at a place they call Frankenstein's Castle at the edge of Dayton. It was a rock round building with a winding stair on the inside and looked like a castle tower on the outside. It was about 3 stories high and was at a park. People called it Frankenstein's Castle and would go there to make out. I had found it, and seen it first when Howard Shank, Dianna, Deanna, and I went there after a date. I told Terry, Gary, and Danny about it after the drive-in let out. They all begged me to take them there.

Once we got there we went up to the top of Frankenstein's Castle and looked around. You could see the city lights of Dayton from the top of the Castle. Everything else though was very dark. Finally, we went back down to Dad's old Oldsmobile to leave. There were 2 older fellows there, older than me, looking at Dad's car. They looked to me like college age not High School, but who knows.

All of us got into the car and these 2 fellows came closer and asked, "What size motor you got in this old Oldsmobile"?

I answered, "I don't know, it is my Dad's".

One of the guys said without really asking, "Let me look at it"! Then he started to raise the hood.

After raising the hood, the 2 fellows began to talk between themselves about how big the motor was. All the others, Gary, Terry, and Danny were in the car, so I got out and told them to stay in the car.

One of the fellows told the other, "Let's pull all his wires out".

I spook up and said, "Fellows, please don't do that. This is my Dad's car, and he will be very mad. The fellows in the car are my brother and cousins and I am responsible for them. We just came back from the movies and they wanted to see Frankenstein's Castle. We don't mean any harm".

One of the fellows looked at the other one that had said, "Lets pull out all the wires"!

Then he said, "Naw, they ain't done anything to us"! Then he closed the hood.

I said, "Thank you"!

Then we got the heck out of there. But man, we were all scared. I was thinking how mad Dad was gonna be for me taking the younger boys somewhere I was not supposed to be at. Plus, we would have to walk to find a phone to call Dad. We did not have cell phones back then. So, when the older fellows left, I felt lucky.

Dad later on traded the 1956 Oldsmobile in for a 1959 Ford six cylinder. Dad's old Ford car was not very fast being a 6 cylinder, but he let me drive it a lot. I went over to see Deanna driving Dad's old 59 Ford car. Deanna was staying at her sister's house. Her sister's name was Margie. Margie was married to an older fellow named Charlie that I liked a whole lot. As a matter of fact, everybody liked Charlie. A lot of the neighborhood teenagers like to hang at Margie and Charlie's house. Charlie would take us to the lake and ride us around in his speed boat, play board games with us, and he liked to hear me sing and play. His favorite song was "The Race Is On", and he would always ask me to sing it. Charlie liked to drink beer, but he would not allow us to drink any even if we wanted to. I did not drink so I did not care.

I went over to see Deanna and she was not at Margie's. After knocking on the door and getting no answer all of a sudden, I saw a neighbor teenager about my age that I had met at Charlie's and Margie's house. We started talking and he asked if I would take him to the store. I agreed, so we went to the store.

On the way back we came to a hill called Meeker Hill. Allen and I started to talk about how fast Dad's car was.

I said, "Dad's car is only a 6 cylinder and it will only do about 80 miles an hour flat out".

Allen asked, "Wonder how fast you could get it up to down Meeker Hill"?

I said, "Let's give it a try".

So, we turned around at the top of Meeker Hill and took a running start down the hill.

We were up to 80 miles an hour right in the middle of the road, when we started down the hill. Meeker Hill was on a small country road of 2 lanes. All of a sudden, I looked up and saw a car with a family coming at us up the hill. It scared me, and I jerked the wheel to avoid them. I could see their scared faces in the wind shield looking back at me. A dad was driving, his daughter was in the middle, and a mother was on the passenger side. As I jerked the wheel the 1969 Ford went off the side of the road in the gravel on the right. I missed the Families Car but as the ford got in the gravel it began to slide sideways to the right. The right side of the car contacted several small trees. I steered the car back on the pavement and began to straighten up the old car. But by this time the car was beginning to bounce so severely that I went off the left side of the road into the gravel. The car began to slide to the left. Again, the left side of the car was sideswiping several small trees. Again, I fought the wheel and brought the vehicle back onto the pavement. Both the right and left side of the car was smashed in all down the sides by the small trees. But by this time the car was picking up speed and was sliding toward the right side of the road again. I looked through the windshield of the old Ford and saw a big tree about 3 to 4 foot across coming right for the front of the Old 1969 Ford. I turned the wheel as hard as I could, but we kept sliding toward the big tree. The car turned enough that it contacted the tree at about the middle of the front end on the right side of the Ford. The car swung around 180 % to the left and a bunch of small trees just curled the back end of the car up under the right rear corner of the trunk. Finally, the car came to a stop facing straight across the road with the back end in the ditch.

I was still hanging on the steering wheel.

The hood on a 1969 Ford opened the opposite way from back to front. I looked up and the hood on the old car was bent all the way forward on the car like a spear sticking out. Then I looked at the windshield and there was a round busted place about the size of someone's head in the middle of the windshield on the passenger's side. The first thing that came to my mind was Allen had hit the windshield. I was afraid to look.

So, I began to ask in a soft voice, "Allen, are you OK"?

Allen did not answer.

Again, I ask a little louder, "Allen, are you OK"?

Again, Allen did not answer.

So, I looked over toward the passenger seat and did not see Allen.

By this time, I was almost shouting, "Allen, Allen, are you OK"?

All of a sudden Allen stuck his head up from the back seat, and said "Yea, I'm OK"!

The back of the seat where he was sitting had broken and he went into the back seat.

Man was I glad he was OK.

I ask, "Are you sure you're OK"? "Are you bleeding, there is a big hole in the windshield"?

Allen said, "No it wasn't me, I got thrown into the back seat when the seat broke"!

Up to this time I did not know just how bad the car was damaged. I tried to get out the driver's door and it would not open. I had to lean toward the passenger's side and kick the door until it finally opened. When I got out of the car, I got sick at my stomach as I stumbled around the car. Every side of the car was destroyed. The driver's side was damaged from the front to the back. The back end was curled up under the trunk just like a giant had bent a toy car up under. The right side was also swiped from the front to the back. The front end was smashed in on the passenger's side from the center of the radiator over to where the 2 right side headlights used to be. Out in the middle of the road was the car battery. This was what had busted the windshield. At this point I began to throw up.

After I threw up, I began to say, "Dad is going to kill me". I said this over and over again.

About that time the man in the car with his family came backing down the hill.

He said, ``Are you fellows OK"?

All I could say was, "I am so glad I was able to miss you folks"!!

After he found out that we were OK he asked if we wanted a ride to a phone to call someone.

I ask, "Yea, could you give us a ride to my girlfriend's sister's house".? "It is not far".

He gave us a ride back to Margie and Charlie's house and Margie had come home. I ask to use the phone. I called Dad and he asked how bad it was and could I drive it? I told him I did not think so.

I waited at Margie's house for Mom and Dad to show up. It seemed like it was a long time before anyone came.

All of a sudden Mom came through the door and started saying, "Ernest are you OK, Are you hurt"?

I said, "No I'm OK".

She said it several times and at the same time she started checking and feeling my limbs.

Her and Dad had seen the car first before getting there.

Mom said, "Are you sure you are not hurt"? "Nobody could have been in that car and not got hurt", she said.

Again, I said, "No I'm OK".

Mom said, "Ernest I have seen the car and you have to have been hurt"!!!

Once again, I said, "No, Mom, I'm OK".

I saw Mom's more scared at that moment then I had ever seen her before, and it hurt that I had caused it.

Mom took me back up to the wreck. When we got there the Highway Patrol was there talking to Dad. As I walked from Mom's car to up where Dad and the Highway Patrolman were standing, I thought, Dad is going to kill me. At the least be very mad at me, and I deserve it.

I reached Dad and he turned around and looked at me and said with a great big puff on his cigar and a grin, "Well how you are doing daredevil". "Are you OK"?

I answered surprised, "Yeah Dad, I'm OK but I messed up your car".

Dad said, "You sure did. You wrecked the shit out of it". He continued, with a smile, "I thought I would come and pull the fender away from the tire and drive it home". "But that ain't gonna happen. I'm just glad you're OK".

Later after we got home Mom and Dad took my driver's license. Mom kept my license for about 4 months. But they would let me drive to the store to do errands for them. Finally, one day I asked why I was allowed to drive to the store for them, but could not drive any other time?

I said, "It's not fair Mom, because I could have a wreck going to the store to run errands just the same as going out on a date". I said, "Mom I have learned my lesson"!

I did not know it but after I said that Mom wrote to "Dear Abby" in the newspaper. Dear Abby had a syndicated column in the newspaper where she helped mostly women with romance and family problems.

"Dear Abby" wrote back in the newspaper, "Mrs. Flatt if you think your son has learned his lesson then your son is correct. It is not fair for your son to drive to the store for convenience to run errands for the family. But Mrs. Flatt, if you feel that your son has not learned his lesson then he should not drive at all. Even to the store".

After the article came out in the newspaper, mom gave me a copy and said she was going to trust me and give my license back to me. I began to drive on dates and such again and of course to the store.

35. 1967—ERNEST PLAYS MUSIC AT SAM'S PLACE.

I had a small Country Band with steel guitar, lead guitar, bass guitar and a drummer and of course me. I played rhythm guitar and did most of the singing. We got a job playing music at a place called Sam's Place in Dayton, Ohio on the corner of Wayne Ave. and East Third Street, Thursday, Friday and Saturday nights. Each of us made $15.00 a night. That was enough after paying mom for rent to make money to buy school clothes. Of course, my favorite clothes were western clothes, and still is today.

The drummer of the band was the youngest of the other members. He was the brother of an old school friend of mine named Allen Perkins. The drummer's name was Gary Perkins. Though he was younger than me, he was a pretty good drummer. And did a great job.

The guitar player was a fellow from Waco, Kentucky not too far from where my Mom was born. Just outside of Irvine, Kentucky. His name was Charlie Fritz. He could play all the Buck Owens and Merle Haggard songs just like the original guitar players on the records. Charlie had a finger pick in' style and was able to roll the chords just like Merle Haggard's guitar player. Charlie used a thumb pick with the end cut off and he would stick a thin regular pick between his thumb and the thumb pick. Then he would play the strings also with his fingernails like they were finger picks. He also played a Fender Telecaster which had the sound in Country Music that was most popular at that time. I was 17 and Charlie was 24 years old. You can probably tell we worked good together. As a matter of fact, as my music jobs got better, I would always find a way to get Charlie in. I ended up getting Charlie a job with Gean William's Country Junction Show in West Memphis, Arkansas. Also, I got him a job with the Clyde Beavers Show in Nashville, TN. I will talk more about these jobs later on.

36. 1968- A BIG YEAR FOR ERNEST FLATT

I graduated high school at Stivers High School in May 1968-not a great student but with grades good enough to keep Mom off my back so I could continue to keep playing music.

Deanna Banner and I had been dating off and on for 4 years. Sometimes we would argue and break up but we always seem to get back together. I remember one time we broke up for about 3 or 4 months and I had gone and got another girlfriend. Then one day I got a call from Deanna and she wanted to meet and talk. By the time we finished talking I went and immediately broke up with the other girl. She was a pretty blond, but I cannot remember her name.

Nov. 2nd, 1968, Ernest Allen Flatt marries Deanna Fay Banner. She looked great as she came down the aisle at the church. Looking back, we were both young and maybe too young to get married but we did anyway. When we were not angry at each other it was a great marriage, but when we were arguing it was bad. But we argued from the beginning when we were just going together. We stayed married for 9 ½ years. But I am getting ahead of myself.

We got an apartment off of Riverside Drive in Dayton, Ohio. We were cleaning it and getting it ready to move into after we got married. I was working second shift at a metal heat treating company, called Metallurgical Heat Treating. It was the second shift and I would meet Deanna over at the apartment and we would work and clean on it to get it ready then I would head to Dad and Mom's house to get some sleep so I could go to work the next afternoon.

One evening I started toward the folk's house after painting the apartment and I turned on to Riverside Drive and that was the last thing I remember until I woke up and I was being helped into the emergency room by 2 police officers. They had my arms around their necks and were leading me in the doors of the emergency room. I had been knocked unconscious. I had a car wreck on the way to Dad and Mom's house. I was driving another of Dad's 1959 Fords. It seems I had fallen asleep and the front tire hit the curb, and it jerked the car sideways. I hit my head against the side window, and it knocked me out. The car continued over the curb, and clipped the guide wire to a telephone pole, broke it in half. Electric wires went everywhere around the car. The car continued into a garage and crashed through it.

The cops said, Ihad knocked out all the electricity in that part of town.

The Police officer told me later what happened at the scene.

The cops also said that when they got there, I was trying to start Dad's car.

One cop asked me, "Son what are you trying to do"?

I answered, "I'm trying to start this car so I can go home"!

He said to me, "No you're not, your hurt"! He said, "Your bleeding, and going to the hospital"!!

I said, "The hell I ain't, I got to go to work"!!

Because I was awake and not cooperating, they took me to the hospital in their car. It seems I had been thrown out of the car and landed on a rock on my left side. I must have got up off the ground and got back into the car trying to start it. The cops said I was lucky I did not step on one of those electric wires on the ground.

As I said I came to myself, as we were coming through the doors of the emergency room. I had a place on my left side where the rock had scraped me and left gravel in my side.

It was not long before Mom and Dad showed up. This time Dad was really upset because I had totaled out his second car in 2 years. He chewed me out good this time.

Finally, The doctor came in and told Mom out in the hall, that I had gravel in my side and he was going to have to scrub me with a steel brush, medical soap, and bring the gravel to the surface and then pick it out. He told Mom it was going to be very, very painful but it had to come out or it would cause infection.

They came back into my room.

Then Mom and Dad went out to the hall and Mom told Dad, you are going to hear him scream in a minute. Then she told Dad what the Doctor had told her. She told Dad, "I have seen this done before it is rough".

After the doctor came back into my room with a nurse, he then told me the same thing he had told Mom. He told me to grab the rails of the bed and hold on. He gave me a rubber thing to put between my teeth, took a pan of hot water, soap, a steel brush, and then began. He would brush awhile, then pick awhile. I was so glad when he would pick. He said he had to brush to get the gravel to the surface. When the Doctor would brush to bring the gravel to the surface, I believe I left my fingerprints in the bed rails from squeezing so tight. But I never said a word, though I wanted to. I didn't scream, I didn't holler. But I wanted to. Man, it did hurt!!!

I didn't like the second shift job at Metallurgical Heat-Treating straightening lawn mower blades after they had been heat treated, because it kept me from playing music, but once I got married, I needed a full time job, and Dad worked there too in the day time, and had helped me get the job, and I didn't want to let him down.

I played music in night clubs around Dayton with my band on weekends when I could. There was a lead guitar player named Charlie Fritz that was very good, and sang great harmony with me.

There was a country music show on TV late at night. It was called the Gene William Country Junction Show. It was coming from Jonesville, Arkansas. They were having a 6-state area talent contest. Gene, and Carol Williams were coming to Dayton, Ohio and you had to do an interview, and audition.

Deanna said to me, "Ernest, why don't you send in, and request an audition for the contest".

I said, "Well they may not like me".

Deanna said, "You won't know unless you try".

I said, "Ok I'll give it a try"!!

I sent in a letter and waited for a reply. This was long before shows like the "VOICE" came along.

Finally, one day a letter arrived. The return address on it was The Gene Williams Country Junction Show, West Memphis, Arkansas. I was so excited I could barely open the letter. In the letter was an invitation to meet with Gean Williams and Carol Williams at the Holiday Inn on Wagner Ford Road in Dayton, Ohio. It said to be prepared to do 2 songs and bring your own back up.

"Alright", I shouted as I called Deanna at her work to tell her. The appointment was 4 weeks away.

Deanna and I waited for the appointment day to come. The 4 weeks passed so slowly for Deanna and I. Especially for me.

Finally, the appointment to meet with Gene and Carol came. Deanna and I were to meet them at the Holiday Inn on Wagner Ford road. Once we got to the Holiday Inn there were a lot of people waiting to be interviewed.

Gene and Carol came out and passed out applications and said to fill them out. Gene was the boss and Carol was his wife. Gene was a man about 6' 1", with light brown hair. Dressed in an olive-green business suit and a pale-yellow turtleneck sweater, with alligator cowboy boots. Carol was a beautiful, well built, platinum, blond woman with a Dolly Parton look, but not as big at the top. But still built very well. Gene did all the announcing, booking, producing, and commercials on the TV shows and live shows. But Gene did not sing or play at all. His background was as a Radio and TV announcer. Carol Williams would sing from time to time on the TV shows and fill in as secretary for Gene. She wore a bright red country dress that showed all her beauty and with the dress was a pair of matching red high heel shoes.

After the applications were filled out, they asked everyone to sing a song. Everybody just played an instrument and sang a song without a band. It was my time, and I sang a song with my guitar that was up tempo. While I was singing, I noticed Gean, and Carol was whispering and looking at me. Deanna must have noticed also. Because when I was done with my song Deanna whispered in my ear with a smile, "I think they liked you".

Gene got up and announced that he would be getting in touch with us if he felt that we were right for the contest. He would be choosing 2 to 4 people from Dayton to enter the contest. As everyone was leaving, and shaking Gene, and Carol's hand it became my turn, Gene leaned over to Carol, and whispered something. Carol nodded her head.

Then she turned to Deanna, and said, "Darling come over here a minute, I need to ask you a question".

Then Gene whispered in my ear, "Hang around for a few minutes".

Then he continued to shake hands with the rest of the people.

I walked over to where Carol, and Deanna were talking.

Deanna whispered to me with a smile, "They want us to hang around, I think Carol likes you".

After everyone left Gene, Carol asked, "Ernest how many songs can you do"?

I answered, "Honestly I don't know. A bunch. I can sing different songs all night for 4 or 5 hours and never do the same song twice".

Gene grinned and looked at Carol and winked. Carol smiled.

Gene said with a smile, "Ernest we have decided we want you for the contest which will be held in Little Rock, Arkansas. We will send you a letter with an invitation to appear. Will that be a problem for you to make it down there"?

I smiled back at him and said, "No problem at all"!!

Then Gene looked at Deanna and said, "Who is this pretty lady"?

Just as I was about to answer, and say I was sorry for not introducing Deanna when Carol spoke up and said, "Gene this pretty lady is Deanna Flatt, Ernest's lovely wife".

Gene said, "Glad to meet you Mrs. Flatt" as he stuck his hand out to shake! Deanna took his hand, and they shook. Then Gene asks, "What do you think about your husband being in the music business"?

"I always knew it was just a matter of time", replied Deanna. Then she added with a smile, "He already plays on the weekends and it is all he has ever dreamed of, besides me of course". Then we all had a big laugh.

Gene asked us if we would like to go to dinner with them and we excepted the invitation. After dinner was over, Gene and Carol walked us out to our car.

As we got to our car, Carol said, "I need to get something for a headache. It has been a long day; do you know where a pharmacy is"?

I said, "Yeah, go up Wagner Ford road, this way" as I pointed to the right. "When you come to North Dixie, make a right. It will be on the right", I explained.

Gene and Carol said "goodbye" again and walked over and got into a Brand new 1969 4 door Fleetwood Cadillac that was crème yellow on the bottom with a tan vinyl top.

We said "goodbye", and they drove away.

Then we drove away in our 1968 Super Sport Chevrolet. Red, with a Black vinyl top, with a 327 High Performance Engine. We thought our car was sharp until we saw Gene and Carol's Cadillac. Man, that Cadillac was sharp.

After they left, I wondered if the statement Carol made about "something for a headache" was for real, or just to see if I would offer drugs. But I did not because I did not do drugs or drink. But who knows, maybe she did have a headache?

Later on, I got the invitation in the mail for the contest. As we were making plans to go to Little Rock for the contest, I received a call from Gene Williams, and he asked if we could come down on a Thursday and perform on his TV show. The TV show was called the Gene Williams Country Junction Show and was tapped on a Thursday and showed on a Saturday The contest was on Saturday also. Of course, we said yes. Deanna, and Mom, and I agreed to drive to Little Rock, Arkansas to attend the TV show and contest. Mom and Deanna did all the driving so that I would be rested for the show and contest. The TV show was just like I had seen on TV. The entertainers and band performed in front of a backdrop that looked like the outside of an old store. The background set made it appear they were performing on the porch of an old fashion store like you would see at a road junction in the old days. The band, the Country Junction Boys backed me up and was great. Gene always had a good band. I sang "Truck Drivin' Man". The show was filmed at Channel 8 in Jonesboro, Arkansas. Gene announced me as one of the contestants and invited everyone to come to Little Rock for the performance.

THE DAY OF THE CONTEST

The contest was held in an arena at the fairgrounds and it was packed to the brim with people.

I sang "They call me a Playboy"! The crowd seemed to really like me. When the judges started calling off the names of the top 10, as well as the other nine contestants, they called off "Ernest Flatt"!!!! I was in the top 10. This made my hopes go up. Then it was announced that the top 10 had to do another song. Then the judges would vote again for the 3rd place, 2nd place, and 1st. place. I was backstage waiting my turn to do my second song. When Sandy Manuel the drummer for the Gene Williams Show stuck his head through the curtain and said "Hey, Ernie, do that song you had done on the TV show"! "Truck Drivin' Man"! "And we will kick up the speed a little", said Sandy with a big smile. Sandy Manuel the drummer really liked my style.

Then the announcer, who was a DJ from the top country radio station in Little Rock, introduced "Ladies and Gentleman, here is Ernest Flatt"!!!!

I stepped up the 3 steps from behind the stage, and through the curtain. As I stepped through the curtain out on-stage Sandy had already started to count the song "1, 2, 3, 4", and the rhythm of the band started, I began to strum my rhythm on my acoustic guitar. As I got to the microphone it was time for me to sing. "I stopped at a roadhouse in Texas", (The crowd went crazy with applause) "A little place called Hamburger Dan". "And I heard that old jukebox a playing", "A song about a Truck Drivin' Man".

When I finished the song, the crowd gave me a standing ovation, it was easy to see I got the best applause of everybody. Then I waved and went to the crowd and took a bow and went back through the curtain and down the steps to behind the stage. Once I got behind the stage, I began to pace back and forth while I waited for the rest of the finalists to sing their song.

Finally, all 10 of us were waiting to see who the judges would pick for the top 3 winners. The judges were well known people from the area. One was a TV news anchorman from one of the largest TV stations in Little Rock, one was a reporter from the biggest Little Rock newspaper, another one was a Preacher/Pastor of a large local church, and the final one was a member of the Chamber of Commerce. I really did not think I would be lucky enough to win the 1st place spot. But I was hoping I could just place 3rd or 2nd to save face with my family. After all 2nd or 3rd would not be too bad over a 6-state area contest. And most of the entertainers were very good. There was even a girl that danced with a 15-foot snake around her neck, while dressed in a "I Love Genie" TV show outfit, singing "When You Wish Upon A Star".

The announcer went and collected a piece of paper from the judges at the edge of the stage.

Then the announcer walked back to the center of the stage and spoke into the microphone to say, "Ladies and Gentleman, I have the name of the winner from the judges for the 3rd place of the Gene Williams Country Junction Talent Contest. The winner for 3rd place is--------"!

There was a long pause.

Then the announcer said in a loud voice, "Jeff ----Martinez-----"!! the crowd began to applaud, as well as the entertainers backstage. They all began to congratulate Jeff. Then Jeff Martinez went up the steps and through the curtain to accept his 3rd place award with a big smile on his face.

I was thinking, well I did not get 3rd place.

The announcer went and collected another piece of paper from the judges at the front of the stage.

Then the announcer walked back to the center of the stage and spoke into the microphone for the second time to say, "Ladies and Gentleman, I have the name of the winner from the judges for the 2nd place of the Gene Williams Country Junction Talent Contest. The winner for 2nd place is-----"!

Again, there was a long pause.

Then the announcer said in a loud voice, "Sherrie ----Ranch-----"!! the crowd began to applaud for the second time, as well as the entertainers backstage. They all began to congratulate Sherrie and pat her on the back. Then Sherrie Ranch went up the steps and through the curtain to accept her 2nd place award with a big smile on her face.

I was thinking again, Well I did not get 2nd place. I was thinking, I lost. So, I might as well leave from behind the stage. I started walking toward the exit with my head down. Disappointed!!

Although I could not see him (I was told later what happened), the announcer went and collected the final piece of paper from the judges at the front of the stage.

The announcer walked back to the center of the stage and spoke into the microphone for the third time to say, "Ladies and Gentleman, I have the name of the winner from the judges. For the 1st Place winner of the 6 State Area, Gene Williams Country Junction Talent Contest. The winner for 1st Place is-----"!

Again, there was a long pause.

Then the announcer said in a loud voice, "Ernest ----Flatt-----"!! The crowd began to go crazy and applauded for the third time, as well as the entertainers backstage.

Suddenly I stopped walking toward the door. I thought to myself, "Did I hear correct"? "Can I trust my ears"? "Did they just call my name"? "Or did I just imagine it"? "Did I just win 1st Place"?

Suddenly, the entire entertainer group that was backstage, began to congratulate me, and pat me on the back. I still could not believe it, and I still had not made a move toward the steps that led upon to the stage.

The drummer for the Gene Williams Country Junction Band Sandy Manuel, stuck his head through the curtain with a big grin, and said, "Ernie, come on out here son, you have won buddy"!!!!

About that time somebody from backstage started pushing me toward the steps that lead up to the curtain and stage. I was stunned.

Just as I went through the curtain the announcer said, "Ernest Flatt, come on out here son, or do you want me to give this award to someone else", he laughed!!!! "Ladies and Gentleman, the winner Ernest Flatt" as Sandy the drummer pushed me toward the microphone!!!!! I was stunned.

So many flash bulbs were going off that I could hardly see the crowd that was going crazy with applause. I was getting a standing ovation. The applause went on and on. I was on top of the world.

They handed me a trophy and told me about the part in a movie, a trip to the Bahama Islands, and a recording contract with Sonic Records in Memphis, TN. I could hardly take it all in. The flash bulbs continued to pop.

Finally, the announcer said, "Ernest the crowd wants to hear you do another song, how about it"? "Will you do another song son, for the people", the announcer asked? The crowd began to applaud, whistle, and scream again.

I stepped to the microphone and was shaking as I said into the microphone softly, "OK".

Then the entertainer in me pulled it together and I said as my voice echoed in the arena "Judges---, Ladies and Gentleman---, my Dad who could not be here, because he had to work, my Mom, and my Wife, who drove me down here---, and of course Gene Williams and the Country Junction Band---, I think you so much for helping a country boy's dream come true. You want me to sing another song, OK, I sing better than I talk". Suddenly I realized I didn't have my guitar and said, "Could someone backstage hand me my guitar"? Then someone came and handed me my guitar. Once I had my guitar in my hand I began to settle down. I turned to the microphone again, and said, "Here's a Buck Owens song, Act Naturally"!!!

The crowd began to applaud my selection. I turned to the band and said, "G, chord fellows".

Then I started the rhythm out on my guitar and the band fell right in. I sang, "They're gonna put me in the Movies".

The crowd began to roar with whistles and applause. What a great day this was for me and my family. Wish Dad would love to have been there, but he had to work. But Mom was able to take time off and told him all about it.

As it turned out I won the Gene Williams Country Junction 6 State Talent Contest and got promised a recording contract in Memphis, TN. Also, a contract to do 2 songs in a country music movie called "THE SOUND OF COUNTRY MUSIC", Produced and Directed by Al Gallaway Productions. Also, I was promised a trip to the Bahamas Islands, and a large screen TV.

Well, I did not get the TV as promised at all. And we did not make it to the Bahamas Islands we only got as far as Miami, Florida. The movie was supposed to be filmed in the Bahamas Islands, but something happened, and we did not go beyond Miami, Florida. We spent 6 days in Miami, Florida practicing for the movie and having a good time on the beach. Then we went back to Memphis, TN. and filmed the movie in a theatre. I do not remember the name of the theatre. The background set was like we were on the outside of an old barn. Then our part of the movie was sliced into a movie with Big Country Stars that were inside of the barn.

Also, I did get the recording contract with Sonic Records, but the recordings never got released except in the movie.

37. 1969-ERNEST GETS A FULL TIME MUSIC JOB.

I got a phone call from Gene Williams at home one evening and he said he was watching the first showing of the movie "The Sound Of Country Music".

He said, "Ernest guess who I am watching right now"?

I said and asked, "I don't know, who"?

He said, "I am watching you on a 75´×50´ screen"!!!

I said, "Great, Out of sight"!!!

He said, "We are showing it at a Drive in here in West Memphis, Arkansas. And we are full. We are going to do a live show at intermission on top of the Concession Stand".

"Ernest, we want you to come to work for the Gene Williams Show as soon as possible".

Then Gene asked, "Are you interested"?

I said, "Sure am"!!

We discussed salary and he promised me $100.00 a week and he would pay all expenses including motels, travel expenses, and Income tax.

I ask him to give me one day to decide.

He said, "OK, but I need to know as soon as possible. I want you because you're in the movie, but if not, I will have to hire someone else".

I promise to let him know next day. The reason I wanted the time was I wanted to talk to Dad and Deanna.

I called Dad right away and told him about my offer. I asked Dad if he thought I should take it.

Dad said, "Well son that is something you have to decide for yourself. But one thing is for sure if you don't give it a try you will always wonder all your life if you passed on your one chance to make it".

Right then I decided to take the job.

I called Gene and he said, "There is a boy from Richmond, Indiana about 30 miles away, that is coming down for a recording session, and his parents said you can ride with them for free. All your family has to do is drive you to Richmond, Indiana and meet them at the Walmart tomorrow their time at noon".

Then he gave me their phone number and said, "Call and make arrangements with them. Although all arrangements are already made just in case there is a problem. Call me if there is a problem. But there shouldn't be".

I said, "I am on my way"!!!

That is when I found out that all things in the Music Business happen real fast. Bookings and such, and you have to be ready to jump on the opportunity.

So, I got a full-time job with the Gene Williams Country Junction Show. Later on, Deanna and I moved to West Memphis, Arkansas just across the Mississippi River from Memphis, TN. We were taping 2 TV shows on Thursdays to be aired on Saturdays and Sundays. The shows were 1-hour television shows, 2 shows a week in Jonesboro, Arkansas on Channel 8. The TV shows were filmed on Thursday's while traveling by tour bus doing shows on the road the rest of the time. We were gone all the time.

Gene asked me if he knew a good guitar player because the fellow he had was leaving. (The guitar player that was leaving was Alton Yancey. Alton Yancey later on hires me for the Lynne Burns show.)

I said "Yes". "If I can get a hold of him there is a good guitar player back in Dayton, Ohio named Charlie Fritz.

Gene asked me, "Is he any good"?

I said, "Yea, he plays just like Merle Haggard and Buck Owen's guitar players"!

Gene said, "Try and get a hold of him, I'll pay for a plane ticket to get him here right away".

I called my Dad, and he brought Charlie over to Mom, and Dad's, family home where I was to call at a certain time so Gene could talk to him. He hired Charlie sight unseen on the phone just by my recommendation. Gene sent him a plane ticket, and Charlie went to work playing lead guitar for Gene Williams. Charlie and I were still traveling with the "The Gean Williams Show" on the road. We were all living in West Memphis Ark. just across the river from Memphis, TN. recording at Sonic Recording Studio in Memphis, TN, and visiting Sun Records Studio where Elvis Recorded in Memphis, TN. We got lots of experience working with the Gene Williams Country Junction Show.

I remember one time the other musicians and I got into a water fight in a Holiday Inn. We started out with glasses of water and ended up throwing trash cans full of water at each other. The beds and floors were soaking and wet. When you stepped on the carpet the water came up over the soles of our boots. We were lucky we did not get in trouble from Holiday Inn. It was not unusual for musicians to pull jokes on each other. Like one musician might catch another musician asleep and put shaving cream all over them. I fell asleep on the bus one time and when I woke up there was a girl that I did not know standing over me laughing. I looked and the other members of the band were at the front of the bus just outside of the front door laughing. I had shaving cream all in my hair and up and down my arms. Man, I was mad. Mainly, because it embarrassed me, because of the girl.

Back then everybody wore Beatle Boots because they looked like cowboy boots but were cheaper to buy than cowboy boots. Sometimes our pants legs would hang on the top of the Beatle Boots, and Gene was bad about dropping a lit cigarette down in our boots. Sometimes he would do this right in the middle of the taping of one of our TV shows. I cannot remember how many times I pulled off a Beatle Boot without even unzipping it after he dropped a cigarette in my boot.

Charlie Fritz, and I were working for the Gene Williams show. We were out west where a friend of Gene's had a ranch in Oklahoma City when we decided to go fishing. They had told us about where there was a lake, and where to go to fish. They loaned us some fishing equipment, and we were off to fish.

I was fishing from a bank that was up on a small hill with a small artificial fish, with three hooks on it. Charlie was fishing closer to the water on a lower bank with some kind of artificial bait. I had my line on the reel hang up several times.

So, I said to Charlie, "Charlie you may need to not get down in front of me like that, I have had my reel hang up several times, and I don't do this very good.

Charlie answered back, "Oh I have been watching you, and you are doing well. I'll be alright".

I was going to throw my line way out into the water. So, I pulled back my pole and let go. The reel hung up again and I hit Charlie right in the back of the neck with the artificial bait. Two of the hooks stuck him right in the back of his head right where the neck started.

I could not get the hooks out of his neck because of the spurs. That ended the fishing. Charlie was in pain so we had to load up and take him to a hospital so the doctors could cut the spurs off and get the hooks out of his neck. They gave him a tetanus shot and some pain pills. I apologized to Charlie and he said he forgave me and that it was just as much his fault as mine.

Then there was another time we were out west playing a show with the movie in a small town in Arizona. Everybody went over to the pool hall and Gene and Charlie were gambling playing a pool game. Gene was fair at pool, but Charlie was pretty dang gone well. Gene was teamed up with Charlie and they were beating everybody in the hall and taking their money. Gene was backing them with high stakes money. Every time they would win Charlie would get him another shot of liquor. Finally, Charlie started to get drunk and began to miss more, and more, shots on the pool game. Gene noticed this, and figured it was time to quit. But Charlie did not want to stop. So, Gene decided to go back to the motel.

Gene told me, "Ernie, will you drive Charlie back to the motel, he doesn't want to quit"?

I told Gene, "I will drive him back to the motel".

Gene said, "But don't let him drive the equipment van, he is too drunk"!

I said, "OK"!

Charlie kept playing pool and drinking. He did not want to stop although he was now losing, I kept trying to get him to leave and go back to the motel, but he wouldn't stop.

We had got paid, and Charlie was playing with his own money now. He had lost all he won with Gene and was now losing his pay.

Finally, Charlie lost everything he had and was drunker than "Cooter Brown" as the saying goes.

"Charlie let's go back to the Motel", I asked him again.

"Charlie said, "No I can beat these fellows. You got any money", he asked?

"I don't have any money left", I lied.

"Well, I got enough for one more drink", said Charlie.

"Well Charlie I am going to get the van and bring it around and pick you up, while you drink your drink", I said. "The van is behind the Theater", I explained! "I'll meet you out front of the poolhall, when I come around, I have to circle the block". "You just wait on me out front, till I come around", I added!

Charlie said, "OK"!

I left to go get the van which was behind the theatre. I was not gone more than 5 minutes. I circled the block, and when I got back around to the main street where the pool hall was there was no sign of Charlie and the pool hall had closed. I was confused.

I rolled the window down, and I hollered loud, "Charlie, Charlie"!! Still there was no Charlie. So, I circled the block again looking for Charlie.

Just as I was about to turn the corner, to go around the block again I heard Charlie holler, "Ernie, Ernie"!

I stopped the equipment van and saw Charlie rounding the corner running. He had run all the way around the block. Actually, it was more of a stagger run toward the van. I was afraid he was going to fall down so I got out of the van and started walking toward him. Just as I got to him, he took a swing at me, and began to curse me. I side stepped the wild swing.

"You son- of –a-bitch, you tried to leave me", Charlie cursed at me as he swung at me again.

I side stepped the swing again, and said, "No Charlie, I told you I was going to get the van"!

Charlie swung at me again. Side stepping his swings as drunk as he was, was not a hard thing for me to do. He was very drunk, and I was stone cold sober. So, I side stepped his swing again. This time he fell down in the middle of the street. I went over to him and tried to talk to him.

"Charlie, I didn't try to leave you, you're just drunk, I went to get the van to drive us back to the motel, now stop getting upset", I begged!

But he did not listen, he got up and immediately hit me in the mouth. When he hit me, it made me mad and I knocked him to the pavement. The moment that I did I was sorry for hitting him. I went to help him up. But he would not take my hand.

"Charlie", I said, "take my hand and let me help you up and settle down"!

Finally, he took my hand and as I got him to his feet, he called me a "Motherfucker" and came out of his pocket with a small pocket knife. Just as he started to swing at me with the knife, I saw it and knocked it out of his hand. He then hit me again in the side of the head. This did not hurt nearly as much as it made me mad. I swung on him and knocked him back to the pavement on his back. Then I jumped on top of his chest and I began to hit him with my right on the left side of his face, and then I hit him with my left on the right side of his face. I hit him like these 4 or 5 more times then I let him up. After I got to my feet, I kicked away the knife, then once he got up to his feet danged if he didn't come after me again.

He was saying, "I am gonna kill you". "Nobody whips me like that, you son-of –a-Bitch"!!!

About that time the police came on the scene and took both of us into custody and to the police station.

Once we got to the police station which was just down the street, they were talking like they were gonna arrest me because I had whipped Charlie. But they told Charlie to go into the bathroom and wash the blood off his face. But as soon as Charlie saw his face, he became mad again and started raising hell, and slamming the bathroom door, and beating on it. That is when the police realized how drunk he was. All this time I was sitting still not causing any disturbance.

One of the policemen told Charlie to settle down or he was going to arrest him. I told the police officers that I had not had anything to drink and that I was just trying to get him to the motel when he attacked me. I told him we were entertainers, and he was playing pool and just drank too much. But I would like to take him back to the motel if they would let me.

The police officer told Charlie to let me take him back to the motel or he was going to lock him up. Charlie agreed to let me take him to the motel.

Once we got to the van and was on our way to the motel, Charlie fell asleep. We got to the motel and Charlie staggered in and went to bed.

The next morning when we woke up Charlie was all black and blue and swelled up. Gene wanted me to take him to the hospital. So, I did. Gene was acting like I was the one who had done something wrong for whipping Charlie.

We got to the emergency room and there were some cops there and they tried to get Charlie to file charges on me. But Charlie was sobering up now and told them, "No I was drunk, and it was all my fault". It took several days for Charlie to heal. He had to wear makeup and sunglasses on stage when we would do our shows. I felt so bad for what I had done.

I stayed with Gene's show for several months after that.

Then Finally, I became upset with Gean Williams because Gene had promised to pay me a flat pay which included the income tax. When it came time to file income tax Gene went back on his word and refused to pay the income tax. So, I was not happy.

One day I received a phone call and was offered a job with the Lynne Burns show. Alton Yancey used to play lead guitar with Gean Williams and knew how Gene could be. And now he had his own show with his wife Lynne Burns. Alton was an excellent lead guitar player and Lynne was an excellent performer, and singer. Alton was the band leader, and boss. One day he called me at the TV station while we were filming a TV show. Alton said he had seen me on the TV show since the contest and liked what I did. He offered me a job with him and Lynne Burns. They were putting together a show to take on the road with Wynne Stewart. He wanted me to play bass guitar and sing. We would be on the road and was gone for 8 weeks at a time. And off 2 weeks at a time.

In late1969, Deanna got tired of being by herself, and me being gone all the time. So, she moved back to Dayton, Ohio from West Memphis, Arkansas.

Because of me leaving the Gene Williams Show and going to work with Alton Yancey and Lynne Burns I got to go to Tule, Greenland for the 1st time.

Tule, Greenland is an Air Force base 500 hundred mile from the center of the North Pole. We caught a plane out of New York City. I think the airport was called J.F.K, airport then. We flew to Iceland, then changed to a military plane to Tule, Greenland. While we were on the plane to Tule, Greenland we were issued a parka with fur around the hood like the Eskimos wear. We were to keep them until on our way back home. We would be there for 2 weeks. The shows were booked for 3 weeks. So Tule got a new band/act every 2 weeks. We got there and found out that Jack Green and the Jolly Green Giants were there with us for a week. We all stayed in the entertainer's barracks. You could put a glass of hot water outside and it would be frozen solid in 5 minutes.

In Tule, Greenland you had Phase 4 which was a warning of a possible snowstorm or blizzard.

A Phase 3 was a warning of a sure snowstorm or blizzard and you should be planning to go back to your barracks.

A Phase 2 was a warning of a possible snowstorm or blizzard and to go back to your barracks immediately.

A Phase 1 was to stay where you were at and ride out the storm wherever you were.

Also, in Tule, Greenland and certain times of the year it was dark 24 hours and other times it was daylight 24 hours. We would do jokes on other entertainers in the middle of the night and tell them they were late for their show. But it would actually be when the clubs were closed. They would not know until they got to the club and found it was closed and about 6 or 7 in the morning actually instead of the evening.

There was a Taxis service that moved everybody around free of charge. Musicians as most people know like to pull jokes on each other. One of the jokes was after a musician had gone to sleep and slept for a few hours we would go in and wake them up. They would think it was AM when it really was PM. When we would wake them up, they would get a Taxi and rush to the club thinking they were late, to find out the club was closed in the middle of the night or very early morning. This was a common joke that everybody got played on them at least once unless you had a watch that showed AM & PM on it. Guess that is why Military uses 24-hour time.

The last night that Jack Green and the Jolly Green Giants were there we had a big party. There was a Danish contractor that said he would chug 2 beers for every one that I chugged. I was not a drinker to start with. I remember drinking 3 beers. The next morning, I awoke in my bed in a pool of puke and was sick as all get outs. I never drank again after that until I was past 24 years old. Everybody told me I was so drunk that I was staggering down the barracks hall bouncing from wall, to wall. Then every time I came to a door I would crash into a room when I hit the door.

Three of the musicians grabbed me and threw me into a cold shower and held me under, until I begged to let me out. The water was Ice Cold. The only thing I remember of the evening after drinking the 3 beers was the very cold shower. But the next morning I was sick as a dog. I woke up and there was throw up all over my bed, and I was so sick I could not get out of bed. All the Jolly Green Giants came into my room one at a time with a smile on their faces to tell me goodbye. I am sure one of the musicians in our band put them up to it. I would have been ashamed if I had not been too sick to care. But I sure learned a lesson about drinking games. I never drank again until I was 24 years old.

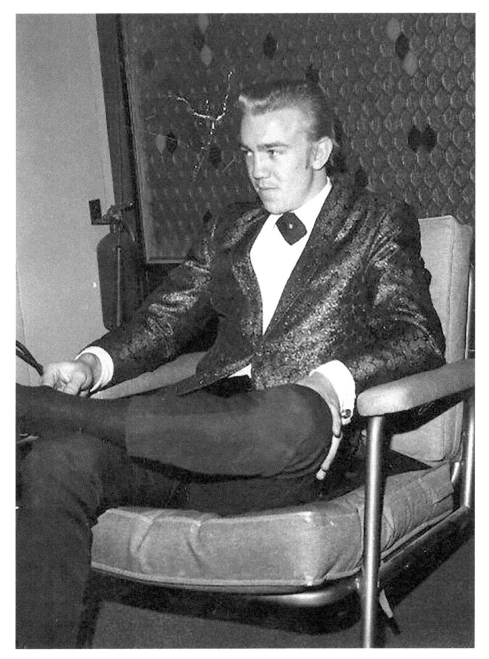

ERNEST ALLEN FLATT, SR.-1970 IN GREENLAND BEFORE A SHOW

38. 1970-ERNEST GOES ON A USO TOUR-OVERSEAS.

Working with Alton Yancey and Lynne Burns I got to play music with Wynne Stewart and many other country stars and go with them overseas for 6 months on a USO tour to entertain troops in Vietnam. We played many large clubs and Fair Dates. Opening for big name country acts. We would be gone for 8 weeks and then come home for 2 weeks then go back on the road again. This went on for about 4 months or better. Then we got a job with Wynne Stewart. He was the one that recorded "It's Such A Pretty World Today", and many other hits. Wynne hired "The Lynne Burns Show" along with Ralph Mooney, a well known steel guitar player. He was putting together a show to go on a 6-month USO tour to Vietnam and other Military Bases to entertain American Troops in the Far East. Everything was going well when all of a sudden Wynne Stewart had to back out of the tour. It had something to do with contract interference between his record company and the tour booking agency. But he said he could fix it up so we, The Lynne Burns Show, could still go on the tour without him and Ralph Mooney. And everybody would get a raise in money for the tour. We all agreed it would be "The Lynne Burns Show" and she would be the Star and Front person. Her husband Alton Yancey and guitar player would be the band boss.

The tour left Los Angeles, California, February 27, 1970 and included the **Republic of Korea** for one week, the **Philippine Islands** for one week, **Thailand** for 2 weeks, and **South Vietnam** for about 16 weeks. **Hong Kong** for just one day, and one night as a layover for a shopping spree. The booking agency put us up in a real nice hotel downtown Hong Kong. The Hilton Hotel.

We landed first in **Hawaii** after leaving California and spent a day and night in a hotel right on the beach and flew out the next morning. Man, it was pretty. The water was so blue. We only got to sightsee for just a short time.

We flew to Korea and lost a day. We did not even know where it went. It was now March the 2nd, 1970. We lost the 1st. of March because of the International Date Line.

Then we landed in **Soule, Korea.** Our schedule was for one week.

We stayed in the Soule Hotel. We were told by our tour manager to tip the bellboy when he took our bags up a couple of bucks and he would help us with anything we needed. I gave my bellboy a two-dollar tip and every time I went out the hotel door, he was waiting to help me with anything I needed. I began to believe he was sleeping outside my door. It turns out that my bellboy was a college student on a break, and I had given him about 4 weeks to a month worth of pay as a tip.

The first day we got on a train and traveled up to the DMZ border to do a show for our troops.

My last day in Seoul, Korea we had off and my bellboy asked if he could take me to a real Korean Restaurant. It was a restaurant where tourists did not go very often. I agreed and said "OK". We went to the restaurant and he ordered for us in Korean and a chef came to the table and cooked the food right in front of us. It was very tasty meat, veggies and rice. We had a very good meal, of course I could not understand anyone but the bellboy. He said someday he wanted to come to America to go to college there.

The next morning, we loaded for the airport and I said goodbye to the bellboy and tipped him another 2 bucks. I noticed the food from the Korean restaurant was good, but I could still taste it sometimes when I burped the next day. Somebody told me I may have eaten DOG.

We had been in South Korea for 1 week. We went to the airport and caught a plane for the Philippines.

We landed in **Manila Bay, Philippines,** and traveled doing shows around the Philippines for one week. I remember one night we had a Pilipino Band that opened for us and they were amazing. They were a Beatles Copy Band. They all had Beatle haircuts and Beatle suits, Beatle Instruments, and sounded just like the Beatles. Man, they put on a great show.

After their show as we were coming on stage and they were going off, when I spoke up and said, "Man you fellows sure did put on a great show. You sounded just like the Beatles"!

All the guys in the Beatle Band just looked at me with a blank stare.

Then their manager spoke up and said, "They no speaky English".

I looked surprised and asked, "None at all"?

The manager answered, "No English, not a word, they no understand you"!

"But they sang every song the Beatles do", I said astonished!

The manager said, "Yes, but they know not what they sing".

Everybody in our band was totally amazed.

We were on our way to **Bangkok, Thailand**. We spent 2 weeks traveling all over Thailand giving a show for the troops. We traveled by bus, train and truck. One night we stayed in a hotel right across from Laos. We could look out our hotel room and see across the river into Laos. We were worried that we might get invaded, because at that time Laos and China were getting pretty testy with the United States and Thailand was our Allied partner. But as it turned out we did not have any problems.

Finally, we left Bangkok and flew to **Saigon, South Vietnam**. Once we were on the plane flying toward Vietnam, we were informed by the road manager that because of the Black-Markets in Vietnam we were not allowed to have US cash money. That it would be taken from us by customs and not returned until we were leaving Vietnam. Because I had been sending money home I had about only $230.00. We each had to place our US cash in an envelope and seal it with our name and passport number on the outside. The road manager said as far as our salary we would be able to get a certain amount of our pay each month in MPC (military money) to spend only on our military bases for toiletries and such. We could get all the **Piasters** (Vietnamese money) that we wanted, to spend off base. But we were informed that Piaster would go up and down in value and that we might lose money in the transaction. We were informed that it was not a good idea to trade very much of our salary off to Piasters. All the rest of our salary got sent home.

Once we got to Vietnam, we were put up in the Saigon Hotel where we lived for about a month while we did shows around Saigon. We would fly on military C-130's cargo planes. Our equipment was all brand new furnished by the Booking Agency except for our guitars. All our equipment would be loaded on a cargo skid with a webbed net pulled across it. Then the skid would be loaded up the tail of the plane and sat right in the middle of the plane. There were fold down seats on each side of the C-130 that we sat in.

When the plane would take off as soon as the wheels were off the ground the pilot would point the plane straight up until it was high enough that snipers could not shoot at us. It was somewhat of a wild ride. But our equipment never moved. When they would land, they would come straight down under power and then at the last minute flatten out and land just like they were landing on an aircraft carrier. This made it a lot less likely that we would get shot at from the area around the landing base.

When we were not riding in the C-130 plane, we were riding in a Saunooke, or a Huey Military Helicopter gun ship. Once we were on the ground at our destination, we were usually moved by military deuce and a half trucks to where we were to perform.

After we left **Saigon** we were moved to **Da Nang** where the Booking Agency put us up in a Villa. A villa was a part of a city block where the front was a street and then there was an alley up the middle. On the left side were a row of villas surrounded by concrete block walls 10 foot tall and on the right side of the alley where another row of villas surrounded by concrete block walls 10 foot tall. Each Villa had a concrete block wall on every side that opened with a door only into the alley. At each end of the alley there was a security gate with armed guards. The gates got closed after 10:00 pm or past 2200 hours military time, and the armed guards would not let you in.

See diagram of Villa layout below. The lines are concrete block walls.

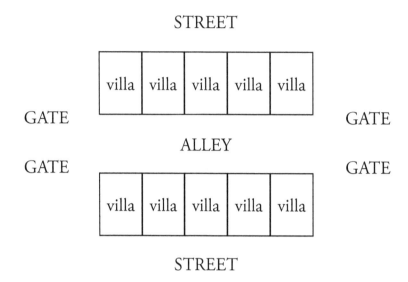

STREET

GATE   GATE

ALLEY

GATE   GATE

STREET

One night we came back from a show late, past 10:00 pm. The Vietnamese Guards all dressed in black had already closed the gates for the evening. We came back in the back of a deuce and half with a Sargent and 1 Corporeal, 1 Private as armed guards and a Private as a driver. When we got to the gate the Vietnamese guards would not let us in. And the Vietnamese Guards did not speak English. It turned into an argument between the Sargent and the Vietnamese guards behind the gate. Suddenly from somewhere from behind the gate a Vietnamese Guard locked and loaded his weapon.

All of a sudden, the soldiers from up on our deuce and a half hollered at us:

"GET DOWN ON THE TRUCK BED, NOW"!!!

Then they both locked and loaded their M-16's and took aim. The Sargent, who was in charge, drew his Colt 45 1911 and jumped from the back of the deuce and a half and got between the Vietnamese guards, and soldiers.

He began to holler as he put his gun away, and put up his empty hand saying, "HOLD IT", he said to the Vietnamese Guards. Then he turned to his soldiers, and put up his hand and screamed again, "HOLD IT".

Then the Sargent walked up to the gate and began to SHOUT to the Vietnamese, "Give me someone who can talk English before this gets out of hand. English! English!

Does anybody speak English", shouted the Sargent a question at the guards?

Finally, a Vietnamese officer came from inside one of the villas that could speak English and they began to talk.

The Sergeant said, "These people are staying in your second villa there on the left, they are tired, and just want to be let in to go to bed".

Then the Vietnamese Officer that had come from in the villa began to shout to the guards and said something we could not understand in Vietnamese. After that, the Vietnamese guards began to open the gate. We were all down on the bed of the deuce and a half truck because we were scared and did not have any guns. We began to get up carefully. Looking around wide eyed.

The soldiers and the Sargent began to talk, and the Sergeant said, "Man this was about to become Dodge City all over again".

We all agreed with a sigh of relief.

One night coming back to the villa in downtown Da Nang we were in the back of the deuce and a half when we heard 4 shots. Bang, Bang, Bang, Bang. When we heard the first shot of gun fire, we all fell to the truck bed and the driver down shifted and gave it the gas and got out of there. No one knew where the shots came from, who was shooting, or who the shots were shot at. But we did not want to hang around to see. No one got hurt.

Each time we moved further north the danger became greater because we got closer to the border between North Vietnam and South Vietnam. We were doing an average of 3 shows a day. We were 2 weeks ahead of the Bob Hope Show and were hoping he would catch up with us. Thinking maybe we could see his show or even see him.

After we left **Da Nang** we were moved to **Chu Lai.** By the time we got to Chu Lai we had become so hardened that when we would have a rocket attack, we would not even go to the bunker. At first, we would go to the bunkers, but they were always so full there was not any room. So finally, we would just go sit out on the steps of the Barracks where we were being housed and listen for the rockets. The Vietnamese were not very good shots with their rockets and usually if they hit what they were shooting at it was an accident. But even a blind hog gets an acorn sometimes. So, we would just sit and listen and watch until the attack was over. Most of the time the rockets were always hitting way over on the other side of the base where the planes and runways were.

One time we saw a fighter jet go down in the distance. We did not ever know what brought the Fighter Jet down. But the pilot parachuted out. We saw the plane crash in a ball of fire to the ground and then we saw the chute open and the pilot come down.

We left Chu Lai one day in the back of a Huey Helicopter. I was sitting next to the gunner on the left side in a fold down canvas seat with my feet dangling out into clear blue sky. The drummer Teddy (I cannot remember his last name) was sitting on the right side next to the gunner on the opposite side of the chopper. The 2 girls (Lynne Burns and Wendi Rivers) and Alton Yancey were inside the chopper with our equipment.

After the show we were on our way back sitting in the same seats, when the pilot decided to give the girls and us a fun ride. He was flying just over treetops. Up, and down, sideways. It was better than any rollercoaster ride. It was hard to hear because of the chopper blades. The gunners, pilot and co-pilot all had headphones and mics so they could talk back and forth. Then all of a sudden, the gunner turned to me and hollered we are receiving fire.

The gunner locked and loaded his 60-millimeter machine gun hanging on the left side of the Huey Helicopter. There was also one on the right side of the helicopter.

The gunner said later on that he asked the pilot "are we gonna fire back".

The pilot said, **"HELL NO, WE ARE GETTING THESE PEOPLE OUT OF HERE"!**

All of a sudden, the helicopter shot upward very, very, fast. Gaining altitude at such a fast rate, it was as if we were in a very, very, fast elevator. We were gone upward, man, in a second. We could really feel the G's on us.

Once we landed, we found out that our chopper had six holes up in the lower front. One round went right in between the pilot and co-pilot but missed everybody. This did scare us a little, but it was done and over before we knew how bad it was.

One good thing about Chu Lai was we could swim everyday if we got back before dark. Chu Lai had a very nice beach. We did get a lot of Rocket Attacks in Chu Lai. The gooks used handheld rockets that did a lot of damage but were not very accurate. As I said before, every time we went to the bunkers, they were always already full. We were told that the rocket that would get you was the ones you did not hear. So, the drummer and I would just go sit on the steps of our barracks and listen to the rockets go over.

At night we would watch the helicopters with a tracer bullet every 6 rounds, working out the premier to keep the enemy from trying to get in. It would look like a steady stream of red laser. Somewhat like a ray gun just eating up the jungle edge. Then we left Chu Lai to go to Whey, which was very close to the North Vietnam, South Vietnam border. We did not stay there very long but did not have any trouble.

Then we went back to Saigon after about 4 months which was the capital of South Vietnam to get ready to catch our flight to go back home.

The booking agency gave us a day and night off in **HONG KONG**. They put us up in a very nice Hilton Hotel right downtown. I bought 2 suits; tailor made for me for $45.00 apiece. They were sent back home to me by mail. Then I bought Deanna 2 rings. One was gold with a diamond, and one was gold with an onyx stone. Both cost only $35.00 each, but they were appraised back home for over $100.00 apiece. Honk Kong was awesome.

On the way home we landed in **Taipei China** to re-fuel, but the Chinese would not let us off the plane. The Chinese Soldiers surrounded the Plane with machine guns to make sure no one got off until we were re-fueled and on our way. That was the first and last time I was ever on a plane while it refueled.

We started back to the USA from China, to land in San Francisco, California on August 27, 1970. We were in the air 19 hours and had a time change. We actually arrived in San Francisco before we took off in China. We gained a day. It was August the 26th, 1970. When we landed, I kissed the ground. We were sure glad to be back. We had been gone from the USA for approximately 6 months.

We had a layover to change planes in San Francisco to get a plane to Los Angeles. While we were on the ground for the layover, I tried calling Deanna. I had been sending money home and would need money for a plane ticket from LA to Dayton, Ohio. We were not allowed to have cash money in Vietnam because of the Black-Market value of US Money. So, I only had the amount that they gave me back when I went into Vietnam that they had taken from me. I thought Lynne and Alton would give us a ride back to Arkansas, but they decided to stay in California and go to Disneyland. I wanted to go home, and I had spent all my money in Hong Kong that I had except for a few bucks. Once I got to LA my plane fare home would then be my responsibility and I did not have it. But I called several times and could not get a hold of Deanna. I even tried calling Margie her sister and still did not get a hold of anybody. If I could get a hold of my wife Deanna, she would have the money I had sent home and she could send me money to get home.

Finally, I called Dad and Mom in Dayton, Ohio and told them my problem. Dad said for me to call him when I got to LA because my plane was about to leave.

Dad said, "I will try and call some of her family and see if I can get a hold of her".

I said, "OK".

When the plane landed in LA, I found out the airport was huge. There was a building for each airline. So, I found a phone and called Dad and Mom collect because I was running out of money.

Dad and Mom said to find out how much the ticket would cost and call them back to collect, then they would Western Union me the money. I found out how much money the plane fare was gonna be and where the Western Union office was at. It turns out the Western Union office was 3 buildings away. A good 2 mile from where I was at. And I only had 2 hours before the plane I needed left. Also, I would need someone to pick me up at the Dayton, International Airport. Once I left LA I would fly to Cincinnati, Ohio where I had a layover to change planes for 2 hours. Then I would be in the air for 15 minutes to land in Dayton.

So, I called Dad again and told him my problems.

Dad said, "We still have not got a hold of Deanna so we are sending you the money in about 15 minutes, and we will send you enough extra for Taxi to get back from the Western Union Office, and some food. Your Mother is afraid you are hungry. But we cannot help you getting over to the building where Western Union is". Dad said, "You will have to run to the Western Union Office. Call us before your plane takes off so we will know you are OK".

I told Dad, "OK"!!!

Then I took off to the Western Union Office, running some, jogging some. When I would get tired, I would keep walking. Finally, I got to the Western Union office and got the money Dad and Mom had sent just like they said. I could always count on Dad and Mom.

I was gonna run back but there was a taxi stand right outside the Western Union Office and Dad and Mom was true to their word and had sent me about 40 extra bucks.

I ask the Taxi Man, "Can you take me back over to the American Airlines Building"?

He said, "Sure"!

I said, "How much"?

He said, "Aww, 5 bucks".

I smiled and said, "Let's do it, I am short for time and I still need to buy my ticket".

The Taxi had me back to the American Airlines building in just a short time.

I purchased my ticket and called Dad and Mom back. I told them, because mom was always on the other phone when we were talking, what time I would be leaving and what time I would be in Dayton.

Dad spoke up and said, "Son don't worry about coming to Dayton we will meet you in Cincinnati, there is no use in you waiting 2 hours. We can pick you up and be home in an hour".

I said, "OK, have you gotten a hold of Deanna yet"?

Dad paused and said, "No not yet but we will keep trying. See you in Cincinnati. We Love You"!

I answered, "I love you folks too"!

I could not understand why Deanna was so hard to get a hold of. But it never entered my mind that she was with someone or mad at me.

I got on my plane and in about 4 hours I was landing in Cincinnati. I got off the plane and there was Mom, Dad, Terry my brother, Rita, and Lillian my sisters. There was a lot of hugging' and kissing'. I had not seen them in 6 months and was so happy to see them.

Then I looked at Dad and said, "Did you get a hold of Deanna"?

Dad dropped his head and said, "Yeah son I got a hold of her".

I said with a smile looking around, "Well where is she"?

Dad dropped his head again and said, "Ernie, she got mad because you called us instead of her and said she wasn't coming".

I looked at Dad in dis-belief and said, "Aw, you're kidding', where is she"?

Then I started looking behind several concrete posts because I thought Dad was teasing and she was hiding.

Dad dropped his head again and said, "No son she didn't come, she got upset because you didn't call her, but called us instead"!

I looked at Mom's sad face, and then around at Terry's, Rita's, and Lill's sad look.

I said with tears in my eyes, "But dad didn't you tell her, I tried several times to get a hold of her, and was running out of time"?

I then realized that they were not teasing.

Dad answered with his head down, "Yeah son, we explained all that to her. But you know how she is when she gets mad"!

I could not believe that Deanna would not want to see me after I had been gone 6 months. But it was true. I decided to not ruin the moment with my tears and decided to deal with Deanna and my relationship later after I got back to Mom and Dad's house. So, I wiped the tears from my eyes, and decided to be happy to get to see my Dad, Mom, Brother, and Sisters.

So, I said, "Well I am glad to see all of you all anyway"!

My Mom gave me a big hug.

So, we left the airport with a smile on our faces for the ride from Cincinnati to Dayton, Ohio. But inside I was very unhappy. I am not sure that I ever got over this for the rest of Deanna's and my marriage.

Home Sweet Home, back in the Good Ole USA.

Once I got back to Dad and Mom's house, I started trying to call Deanna. I could not find her. I finally got a hold of Margie, Deanna's sister, she said she did not know where Deanna was. I thought that sounded strange from Margie. I even wondered if Margie was lying to me. Deanna also was not at her Mom and Dad's house according to Randy, her younger brother. So, I was told anyway. It was hard for me to understand that none of her family knew where she was. It did not feel right, like everyone was hiding something.

It was 3 days, and nights before Deanna finally called Mom, and Dad's phone, and I answered. I was never able to get her to tell me so that I would understand why she was so mad, and why I could not get a hold of her, or where she was for the whole time, I was looking for her. But we did make up and started to see each other again. You see I do not give up on marriage easily.

While I was on the road, I got to know some people and there was a man in Nashville that had a couple of hit records and had said when I got back from the USO Tour for me to call him and he would hire me to play bass for him and front his group. His name was Clyde Beaver and lived in Hendersonville, TN. just outside of Nashville, TN. In the next county north from Davidson County, called Sumner County. So, I called him, and he offered me a job on the phone to start right away.

Down through the years I learned that most all music jobs seem to come about all at once, and right away, and you had to jump at the opportunity.

Deanna and I talked about it and we decided to move to Hendersonville, TN where I would take the job and she would look for a job. Deanna could always find a job because she was so good at accounting, and office work. She could type very fast, and accurately, as well as use an accounting calculator very fast and accurately. So, we loaded up and went to Hendersonville, TN. because Clyde Beavers wanted me right away.

As soon as I got to Hendersonville, TN. The Clyde Beavers Show needed to go on the road that weekend. I had gotten Clyde to agree to let Deanna go with us on the road because I had been gone so long. We were gone for a week. But we had to pay for our own motel on the road because we would need an extra room. We agreed. It also gave Deanna a chance for a mini vacation.

After being home for a week it was time to go on the road again. So off we went again. This time we were leaving without Deanna going with us because she was going to hunt for a job. Also, I think she now understood that it was not so great unless you were playing in the band. So, we rented her a motel by the week.

The band was gone for 2 weeks.

When we got back to Clyde Beavers' office in Hendersonville, TN. Clyde's wife was there with a note for me to call this unknown phone number.

Deanna answered the phone at the other end and asked me, "Well now that your back when are you coming home"?

I said, "Home! The motel, Where"?

Deanna spoke with a smile in her voice and said, "Mr. and Mrs. Beavers said they will drop you off".

Clyde and his wife drove me to Shiloh Springs Road to a small mobile home park and dropped me at the mobile home park.

Clyde's wife smiled and said, "I believe Deanna is waiting for you in that mobile home right there", as she pointed to a brand-new mobile home just to the side of Clyde's Cadillac Deville.

What I didn't know was Deanna had already taken some of the money I sent home from the USO Tour and bought us a brand-new Mobile Home, had it delivered, and was already living in it, at a Trailer Park at the edge of Hendersonville. It was on Shiloh Springs Road. As I knocked on the door Deanna came and opened it with a big grin on her face.

She said, "Welcome home stranger! I sure do hope you like it"!!

I said, "Well give me a kiss and a hug first"!

After the kiss, hug, and looking around I ask, "More important do you like it"?

She answered, "Only if you do. We can always take it back for another".

Then she began to show me our new home.

The mobile home was 2 bedrooms, 12' wide and 24' long. It had all new appliances including an air conditioner, orange and brown shag carpet, and was very nice. I liked it, it was great, and Deanna had handled the deal all by herself. It was a real big surprise for me. The master bedroom took up the whole back end of the trailer with windows in an arch across the end of the trailer and just off the master bedroom was a full bath. The hallway leading from the living room went back to the master bedroom and had another bedroom and another full bath. The living room and dining room as well as kitchen was separated by a bar. All the curtains, carpet, and furniture were matching colors. It was great.

I went to Tule, Greenland 2 more times with the Clyde Beavers Show. We opened for more well-known country acts at fairs, arenas and large clubs.

I was on my way to Michigan on North US 75 to do a show and was traveling in a car with 3 other musicians. It was dark and rainy, and a car went by us going way too fast. We all made a comment about how fast the other car was going and how dangerous it was. We could see the red taillights getting farther and farther in the distance, to the point that we could barely see the taillights.

As we were talking and looking at the taillights in the distance, all of a sudden there was a ball of fire in the distance. The ball of fire separated, and one ball of fire went to the left of the road in the median strip of the freeway, and the other ball of fire went to the right of the road on the shoulder.

Somebody in the car said, "Lord there has been an accident. Hurry up and get there"!

We increased the speed of our car up and arrived at the scene of the accident. One car was destroyed in the back end where the other car had hit it in the back. It was engulfed in flames and burning faster and faster.

The car on the right side was in the grass pointed toward the median. The front of the car was destroyed. The car was smoking, but not on fire yet.

We all jumped out of our car when it came to a stop. The other three ran to the car in the median that was on fire. I ran to the car that was on the right side of the road. I approached the driver's side window, and the car was starting to be filled with smoke, so I could not see the driver or inside of the car.

I began to holler, "Buddy, where are you? Buddy where are you"? At the same time, I was pulling the car door open, but it was stuck. I pulled again with all my might and finally the door came open and I fell down. I got up and went back to the driver's door and began to feel around on the driver seat but couldn't find anybody.

I started to holler again, "Buddy where are you"!!

Then I heard a voice saying from the other side of the car, "Over here"!!

I said, "Where are you"?

The voice said, "Over here on the ground"!!!

I ran around the car and there lying on the ground beside the car was a young man about my age. About that time the car burst into flame, and began to burn a full flame, hotter, and bigger.

I kneeled down beside the young man and told him, "Buddy, can you walk we have to get away from this car it is going to blow up"!!

He said, "I don't know, but I will try".

I asked him to put his arm around my neck and I put my arm around his waist and we began to walk away from the burning car that the flames were getting bigger all the time. We were about 60 feet from the car when "BOOM"!! The car blew up. It knocked us both to the ground on the grass. I checked myself and was OK. Then I was trying to check him in the dark to see if he was OK.

I said, "Buddy are you OK"?

He answered, "Yeah I'm OK"!

I took off my white, cream colored trench coat and covered him up. About that time, I heard sirens off in the distance. Finally, the 2 ambulances arrived. The medics came and started to take care of the young man. Then they took him off to the hospital.

The Police took our statements, and we went on our way. This is all we ever knew about what happened to the young man.

39. 1971-ERNEST ALLEN FLATT, JR. IS BORN.

Deanna and I were still living in Hendersonville, TN. just outside of Nashville, TN. when we decided to try and have a child. We wanted to try because Deanna had always had problems with her monthly cycle. So, we discussed it and she went to a doctor and found out that she had to have one ovary taken out. This left her with only one ovary and her chances of getting pregnant slim. The doctor told her to keep a record of her temperature and when it was just above average have sex and not move for 15 to 30 minutes. Deanna would take her temp and call for me to have sex, and naturally this was fine with me. Then one day after going to the doctor we found out that we were pregnant. We were so happy.

Nine months later Deanna said, "you need to take me to the hospital"! I grabbed the pre-packed bag, put it in the car, and then I got Deanna and we drove the route to the Madison, Memorial Hospital we had rehearsed. Madison Memorial was closer than going all the way to Nashville from Hendersonville. Madison Memorial Hospital is just on the outskirts of Nashville. I tried to not be nervous, but it was tuff. We arrived at the hospital safe and sound.

But it was false labor pains, but everything was OK with the baby and Deanna.

After the third time of making the trip to the hospital and having only false alarms I was a pro and I think Deanna was too. We made jokes about this baby not wanting to be born. But we were really getting scared because I had taken off from the road so that the baby would not be born while I was away. But we were starting to run out of money and time. Soon I would have to go back on the road.

Then finally on the third trip over about 1 trip a week to Madison, TN., on Dec. 25, Christmas Day 1971 we got the best present that either of us had ever gotten before. Our baby boy was born healthy and strong, and cried his lungs out.

We had talked about what to name him but had not come up with a name yet. But our time had run out.

While in the room Deanna was holding our new baby and asked, "What are we gonna name him"?

I said, "I don't know. You choose".

Deanna said, "How about, Ernest Allen Flatt"!

I looked at her stunned.

Then I ask softly with a lump in my throat, "They will call him JR. ----are you sure you want to do that to him"? Besides, we will get our names mixed up and never know who people are talking too, are about", I added.

She smiled and said, "Well, it was just a thought".

Then I remembered I had a cousin named Little John Carter, son of Dad's sister. Also, I had a cousin named Billy Well, after his Dad, Bill Wells married Emma (Mom's sister).

So, I said, "You know we could call him Little Ernie", I have a cousin named Little John Carter after his Dad. Everybody calls him Little John".

Deanna said with a smile, "Little Ernie, I like it".

"Little Ernie it is then", I said softly as I leaned and kissed him on the head.

I did not fight too hard, besides I was so proud that I couldn't say no.

Everything was great until it was time to take Little Ernie home. The doctor said he had to stay a few days because of yellow juntas. But he was OK. But Deanna should go on home without him.

Deanna cried all the way home. But everything was fine when we went back each day to visit and then finally after 3 days, he was released to 2 smiling young faces as we carried him home for good.

I was so proud of "Little Ernie".

And so, Ernest Allen Flatt's family/generation begins.

40. 1972-ERNEST GETS A RECORDING CONTRACT.

After leaving Clyde Beavers, I freelanced with several different artists for a short time and met Judy Lee, she became my manager and booking agent.

I did a package show with a lady named Barbara Allan. At that show I impressed a couple of ladies that were Writers, Managers, and Recording Artists, Betty Amos and Judy Lee. Betty Amos was the one that wrote the song, "I'm Tired of Playing Second Fiddle To an Old Guitar" that was a hit and recorded by Jeannie Shepard.

Judy Lee was Betty Amos's guitar player and partner. Judy Lee wanted to manage me and said she could get me a recording contract. She also said she would book me on the road for 10 percent. Once I got a hit record her cut would go up to 20 percent as a manager and booking agent. She also said she would help me get my own band together. So, we signed a contract, and I was off on the road.

Soon I was in Nashville, writing for Window Music, and recording for Stop Records. I recorded 4 songs for Stop Records but never got a release. The money was always spent on "Johnny Bush" which had some very good success. He sounded and his style was like that of "Ray Price".

Johnny Bush did "This Time You Gave Me A Mountain", his hit was before Elvis Presley did it. He also recorded a song written by "Willie Nelson", "Whiskey River Take My Mind", this was before "Willie Nelson's" hit on it. But they put <u>My Recordings</u> on a back burner because I was still an unknown and they were a small label that had just hit big.

Finally, Judy Lee decided we should look for another label.

Betty Amos asked me to do a demo recording on two of her songs. One was called, "What You Always Wanted to Know about It but Were Afraid to Ask". There was a bestselling book out at that time called "Sex, What You've Always Wanted To Know About It, But Where Afraid To Ask". The other song was a country waltz called "The Will to Love". I went in and recorded the demos and the man that owned the record company really like the songs and my recordings, so he signed me to a contract.

This record label owner had earlier bought the record company Mega Records when Sammi Smith was signed to it. He went out and got a song from Kris Kristofferson called "Help Me Make It through The Night" and had Sammi Smith recorded it. He put a lot of money behind this song and Sammi Smith and made the record label a big name and then sold it for a big profit. In the process he made Sammi Smith a big star.

He had bought Candy Records and intended to do the same thing with me, and the song Betty Amos had written called "What You Always Wanted to Know about It but Were Afraid to Ask". The song sounded like it was about sex, but toward the end everybody found out it was about a cowboy's gun. He was planning on buying 100,000 copies and sending them to radio stations to play. Which would automatically be a hit in those days. The recordings had been done and we were waiting to get the finished records back from the pressing plant when we ran into a problem.

The A & R man named Jim Hurley ran off with a secretary, a large sum of cash, and several tapes, belonging to the record label. This made the Label Owner man very angry and he decided to bankrupt the company which left me, the musicians, Betty Amos and Judy Lee without anything. This put me back on the road to make a living doing concerts without a recording label.

41. DEANNA MOVES BACK TO OHIO.

Deanna again moved back to Dayton, Ohio-because I was gone so much on the road. She did not want to be alone in Hendersonville with me being gone on the road so much. So, she asked me if she could move back to Ohio where she had family and friends and would not feel so alone.

I had Randy Parton, Dolly Parton's brother on the road with me playing bass guitar. He was an excellent bass guitar player, good singer, and a good friend.

One time we came in off the road, and because it was late at night when we got into Nashville I was invited to stay the night at Carl Dean's house which was Dolly Parton's husband. Some of the Parton's were there, except Dolly Parton, and Carl Dean were not there. But I was invited to come in, and sleep till morning before I headed back to Dayton, Ohio.

Dolly Parton's mom (I don't remember her name) said, "Ernie why don't you stay till morning, and I will make Gravy & Biscuits before you hit the road. Then you will be fresh, and I won't be so worried that you'll fall asleep while driving back to Ohio".

Mrs. Parton was a friendly country woman that reminded me in a lot of ways of my Grandma Griffin except a little younger, and her hair was darker, and not gray. She was a round woman that wore a plain, printed, country dress.

I could not turn down the invite, so I lay down and got some sleep. The breakfast next morning was great. I met Stella Parton, one of Randy & Dolly's sisters, and Floyd Parton, one of Randy & Dolly's other brothers. Stella later on had a couple of hits. Floyd was a great guitar player from what I heard, but in the short time I knew him I never got a chance to hear him play.

After breakfast Randy told Stella that I had, and ear infection and the doctor had given me a prescription for penicillin. Stella asked me if she could have 3 or 4 of them.

I ask her, "Why"?

She said, "Because they helped her keep the skin on her face clear"?

I gave her 4 of them, but did not understand why she would need them, because I thought she was prettier than Dolly was. She had long straight blond hair, a nice figure. Not as big as Dolly at the top. But she was very pretty.

Years later I saw Stella Parton on TV after she had a hit and it looked like she had done something to her eyebrows that made her look different. But I never saw Randy again. I heard he was entertaining at Dollywood, Pigeon Forge, TN. in east Tennessee. But each time I went there with my family I never was able to see him.

42. 1974-BAND GOES TO LEBANON, PA.

I was in Nashville and between jobs when my Manager/Agent Judy Lee asked me to take a gig for a man in Lebanon, PA. He had lost his band and wanted us right away. We had played this club before. It was a nightclub that also had strippers that danced on our breaks. We had worked there before, and he owned a half of a double just across the street that the strippers and the band stayed in. It was part of the deal to furnish us our living quarters while we were playing at his club. This was not an unusual deal for some club owners. They would do this and expect to pay less, because the band leader (which was me) would not have to pay for motel expenses for the band. The strippers stayed downstairs, and the musicians stayed upstairs. Well, the musicians were <u>supposed</u> to stay upstairs, and the strippers were <u>supposed</u> to stay downstairs. But everybody had their own bedroom. I am not sure that there was not a lot of use of the stairs through the night.

Judy told me to get the contract signed before we unloaded our equipment.

Once we got there, he signed the contract, and we unloaded our equipment. We played the first week and he would not pay me what the contract promised. We got into an argument and I chased him around the desk in his office with a mic stand. We cussed at each other and argued for over 30 minutes. I told him if he did not pay me what he was supposed too, then we would load up and leave. But he still would not pay the rest of the money. So, we loaded out equipment back up and went back to Nashville. I paid for the gas up there and back home, and then I divided the money that was left between each Musician in my band.

But when I got back to Nashville the lead guitar player I was using at the time said his dad wanted to talk to me. His dad had a talent agency in Nashville. I was called into his office and raked over the coals.

"You're going to pay my son what you owe him for the whole 6 weeks you promised", he said!

"I don't have it", I said.

"You are going to pay him, or you may not like what happens here", he shot back in a threatening manner.

I returned, "I told you I don't have it. The money the club owner paid me was not enough for even one week. He broke the contract. So, I took enough to pay for the gas up there and the gas back to get us home. Then I divided what was left equally between all of us. You can threaten me, and it still won't change what you get, because I don't have it". I added, "I am going to file suit against him through the musician's union, and if the union is able to collect then everybody will get their money, including me"!

He said, "I am going to call your manager then"!

I said, "Well call her"! "But it ain't gonna make any difference unless she pays you. Cause I ain't got it"!

He called Judy Lee and I could only hear his side of the conversation. Finally, he handed the phone to me and said, "She wants to talk to you"!

I took the phone and said, "Hello".

Judy asked, "Ernie do you have the money to get this asshole off my back"?

I said, "Judy I already told him I don't have it. The money the club owner paid me was not enough for even one week. He broke the contract. So, I took enough to pay for the gas up there and the gas back to get us home. Then I divided what was left equally between all of us. I can't pay what I don't have". I added, "I am going to file suit against him through the musician's union, and if the union is able to collect then everybody will get their money, including me"!

Judy said, "Well if you ain't got it, you ain't got it".

"Well Judy he is threatening me, but I don't believe he knows who he is messing with", I said mainly for a bluff because he was listening.

Judy said, "Let me talk to him again".

I gave the phone back to him and he and Judy began to talk with him again, I could not hear what Judy was saying but the last thing he said to Judy was "Well we'll see you in court"!

Then he hung up the phone and said to me, "I'll see you in court too".

This made me mad, and I said in a sharp tone, "If you will look at the union bylaws you will find that I have a right to see if the union can get my money for me. Then I will be required to pay everybody involved. But until then I can't pay what I don't have"!

"Now I have sat here, and listened to your intimidation, and shit long enough. Now I am getting up and taking my ass out of here. You have a damn good day, because I got to head toward Ohio, and I barely got enough gas money out of my share to get there. We have all lost unless the union can get us our money".

Then I got up, and went back to my van, and went to Dayton, Ohio.

I stayed on the road working with my own group and because I was missing my family so much, I started working out of Dayton, Ohio doing my own booking. Since the failure of Candy Records my bookings had gone downhill and Judy Lee was not coming up with as many bookings as she used too and could not connect me with another recording label. So, little by little I decided to start booking myself and my band, I put together a new band in Dayton, Ohio. But first I started out just finding work for myself.

Someone called me and needed a front man singer, and bass man. I played a job in a small club downtown Dayton. This is where I met Marc Glascoe a good guitar player and Bob Urey a good steel guitar player also a drummer named Mike Walsh. I got to the gig and Marc and Bob, and Mike was there to finish up the band. We played a set, and everything went well, we worked well together.

I ask Marc, Bob, and Mike on break, "Where are you guys playing next"?

Bob answered, "Wherever you are going to be at"!!

Mike, replied, "Yeah, man let's start a band together"!!

Marc spoke up, "We're with you, wherever you want to go"!!

I looked amazed at all three of them, "OK I can find us some gigs"! So, we started a band. Marc stayed with me for over 8 years. We finished the night and were rocking the house. There was a cute little girl that kept looking at me over her boyfriend's shoulder from the dance floor as I sang my songs. I was not interested, but I played the part and smiled at everyone. He and she must have got into an argument about something and she left. I was told that she said she thought I was cute, and this made him mad and they got into an argument at the table where they were sitting.

At the end of the night, I went to pack up to leave, in one of my hands was my bass guitar in the case and in the other hand was my mike stand. As I stepped out of the club door which came out on the sidewalk in the corner of the building, I stepped down the 3 steps and onto the sidewalk. Then I turned to walk up the street. I noticed out of the corner of my eye this same fellow from the club that was dancing with the girl that had left angry and mad; he was crossing the street to a car on the other side of the street. He opened up the trunk of the car and got something out. He walked back out to the middle of the street holding something behind him. Once he was in the middle of the street, he took a stance with his legs apart and produced a sawed-off shotgun from behind him.

Then he pointed it at me and said, "Hey motherfucker, I am going to blow you all over that wall"!!

I stopped and realized he was talking to me. I thought if he comes close enough, I could grab him and knock his head off. So, I put down my guitar and my mike stand to get my hands free.

I looked at him and asked, "Who are you? And just what have I done to you to make you mad at me"?

"I just don't like you", he answered!

I studied him hoping he would come closer, but he stayed in the middle of the street about 20 feet or so away.

"Well, that's not much to hold against a fellow you've never met before", I said to him making sure he did not realize I was scared and shaking.

"You've been flirting with my girlfriend", he said in a nasty voice.

"Buddy, I don't even know who your girlfriend is", I lied. I had seen them dancing together, but I had not flirted with her anymore, than any other girl in the club that night.

"I am gonna blow your ass all over that wall behind you", he growled pointing the sawed-off shotgun at me.

I looked at him and thought, He is going to shoot me, or he is not, but I ain't crawling for nobody.

I looked him dead in the eye and said to him, "Buddy I don't want your woman. I have a wife and a son waiting for me at home. So, I am going to pick up my guitar, and my mike stand, and I am going home to my family. Now you are gonna shoot me, or you ain't, but I am leaving"!!

I took a deep breath, then I bent my knees, reached down, and picked up my guitar and my mike stand, then I turned and began to slowly walk toward my car that was parallel parked down the street from the club. With each step I took I was expecting to hear a gun blast any second. But with each step I took, I got closer to my car. I did not want to look around at him, but out of the corner of my eye I saw him go back to his car and put the shotgun back in the trunk and close the lid. Then he got into his car. After starting his car, he squealed his tires and came down the street and spun his car in a circle facing back the other way, as I was putting my things in my trunk.

He jumped out and said, "Fuck you"!

I looked at him and said as I closed my trunk, "Buddy what have I ever done to you"?

He answered and said, "Haven't you ever met someone before you just didn't like"?

I looked at him and said, "Well, I have now"!!!

Then I got into my car and drove away. He fell in behind me with his car. I was wondering if he was waiting to get me in a secluded part of town so he could shoot me. One thing for sure was that I was not going to lead him to where my house was so that he would know where I lived. Knowing where my car and property was, he could do any number of things to me in the middle of the night. He could do vandalism or burglary to me at his whelm during the night. I turned right, then left, then right again trying to get him to lose interest. He continued to follow me about halfway to my house, and then all of a sudden, he turned off and I never saw him again. So as soon as I was sure he was gone, I gunned my old car and headed for home watching my rear mirror. I guess he was just checking to see if I was telling the truth about going home. But what he did not know was once he let me make it back to my car, I now was in possession of my 38 specials, and it was a good thing he went his own way. Because his shotgun was in the trunk, and my pistol was in my hand as I drove toward my house. I played this club several more times, and every time, I had my gun on my person, but I never saw this fellow, or his girlfriend ever again. Which was fine by me?

GRANDPA FRANCES FLATT & AUNT GENEVA.

43. 1975-MUSIC IS STILL FULL TIME BUT ONLY IN THE TRI-STATE AREA.

1975- Deanna and I bought a house on Wolf Road. The house on Wolf Road was a house that both Deanna and I really liked. It was a brick Ranch, with three bedrooms, a detached garage and with a nice fenced in backyard. That was a bedroom for Deanna and me, a bedroom for Little Ernie, and a bedroom for me to make into a studio for recording.

I started working for Lamar Outdoor Advertising Company while also playing music. The company put up what we call billboards. The company called them Highway Bulletins. I was the assistant Construction Foreman and Dick Wells was the Construction Foreman. We became good friends.

I had taken the job because Deanna had some surgery and could not work. Also, we had wanted to buy a house and needed the extra income. Therefore, I took the job and actually liked it. So, I was playing music on the weekends and working 5 days a week with Lamar Outdoor Advertising. I was also the operator of an 80-foot boom crane for the company. The boom was on the back of a truck. Sometimes we had to lift bulletin sections up to the stringers on poles, or sometimes on to roofs of buildings, 60 or so feet above ground.

Dick had an 800 cc. Z1 Kawasaki that could outrun just about anything on the road. He gave me rides all the time. We would talk about how cool it would be if we both had a motorcycle to ride. Then I would not have to ride on the back of his. One time I rode on back with him and we were going so fast that the motorcycle was only touching the cracks of the highway. The lines look like one continuous line. I looked over his shoulder and we were doing 130 miles an hour.

One day after getting a highway bulletin job done, and on the way back to the shop. We stopped at a Honda Dealership just to look at the motorcycles. The owner of the Dealership saw us pull up with the crane on the back of the truck. We were looking at the motorcycles and he came over and pointed out a Brand-new Honda XL 250, Semi Street and Semi Trail. It had a 4-stroke engine and turn signals, a headlight and tail light, and semi knobby tires.

The Dealer owner asked, "How do you like this one"? "It is only $1400" but I will knock it down to half price" said the dealer.

We both agreed it would be perfect for my first motorcycle. But I knew Deanna would not agree to let me buy it because we could not afford it.

"Well sir I would like to buy it so we could ride together, but I can't afford it right now".

"You can sure afford this one", said the dealer owner.

"Not unless you are going to give it to me", I joked in return.

"Well almost as good", smiled the owner.

"What do you mean?", said Dick his interest climbing.

Then the dealer said something that made Dick and I take notice and look at each other.

"I couldn't help but notice the crane on the back of your truck", said the dealer.

"And it just so happens I need a sign and a metal post put up. The concrete foundation is already in place out front and the metal post is lying right beside it. All you would have to do is set the metal post on the foundation and bolt it to the concrete foundation. The bolts are already installed in the concrete. Just put the nuts on and tighten them up with a large socket and ratchet. Then Lift the sign-up top of the post and put the

4 bolts and nuts into the sign to hold it to the post and you are done. You 2 can do this job in about 30 minutes to an hour. Then I will sign the title over to you 2 fellows and the motorcycle is yours. Take it with you"!

This made Dick and I look at each other in amazement. But I wasn't sure Dick would do it because we could be fired.

Dick said to the dealer, "Let us go talk about it for a minute outside".

The dealer said, "Sure".

Dick and I went outside and looked at the foundation for the sign and there lay the metal post with a plate and bolt holes at the top and bottom.

Dick turned and said, "We could do this job in about 30 minutes".

I looked at Dick and said, "Do you think we could get away with it"?

"Sure", said Dick. "We just need to get it done as fast as possible so we can drop off the motorcycle at your house and tell them we got hung up in traffic".

"Do you think we can get it done fast enough", I asked?

"Piece of cake" smiled Dick looking at the pole and concrete foundation. "You are good with the crane and I'm good at installing. It will be just like we usually do", replied Dick.

"Here's the deal. I will own half of it and you will own half of it. You give me at least $25 a week until you pay off your half and then I will sign my half over to you. That way you got something to ride and we can ride together". "Is it a deal", ask Dick?

I asked, "What is the cost of the motorcycle we are using"?

"Half price, like the man said, that would be about the cost of installing the sign" answered Dick.

I smiled a big smile and said, "$700.00, my share?

No, $350.00 is your share, $700.00 is half price from the dealer. He said he would drop it to half price" said Dick.

OK, if your game, I'm game", I said!!

Then I asked Dick, "When are we gonna do it"?

Dick said, "Friday afternoon we will be down this way and most of the bosses will be in their weekly meeting. We will send the other workers back by themselves like we did today and stop on the way here and knock it out"!

"OK", I said, starting to get nervous.

We went back in and told the dealer he had a deal.

That Friday we started back to the shop alone just as Dick planned. We stopped and had the post and sign wired up and installed in 23 minutes. The dealer signed the motorcycle over to us and we left with it up on the bed of the truck with the crane.

We dropped the motorcycle off at my house on Wolf Rd. and headed on back to the shop.

I started wanting to get the motorcycle paid for so it would be all mine. So, I paid it off way ahead of time, and Dick signed it over to me. One weekend we took off and rode all the way to Dick's dad and mom's house in Kentucky. Dick said, "Because I am so much faster than you, you take the lead"! I could only run 80 miles an hour flat out on my Honda 250cc.

I said "OK"!

I ran it wide open all the way down there. 80 miles an hour was the most it would do. All the way down there and all the way back. It was a long ride but fun. When we got down there Friday night, we stayed all day Saturday and then we started back Sunday so late that it got dark on us just outside of Cincinnati, Ohio and by the time we pulled off the freeway in Dayton, Ohio I was so cold I could barely put my legs down to hold my motorcycle up when we stopped at the first red light at the end of the exit ramp. Dick said Goodbye to me and turned for his home and I waved and turned for my home. Though it was cold we each made it home OK.

44. 1976-ERNEST'S FIRST 45 RPM RECORD FOR CLARK RECORDS IS RELEASED.

In Cincinnati, Ohio Ernest Flatt and the Gold Rush Band, recorded the song **"Baby's Gone To Live With Another Man"** A-side and **"Train"** on the B-side and it became # 1 in Irvine Ky. This was most likely because my cousins on my mother's side were calling in to request the DJ to play the recording.

I wrecked my motorcycle and broke my left arm running into a garage. As I said before I had a brand new 250 Honda XL-semi-Street and semi dirt bike. It would run 80 miles an hour flat out. My friend Dick Wells had an 800 cc, Z1 Kawasaki that could run like a drag racer. We would ride together. But I had trouble keeping up with him. He would slow down for the curves and then zoom, he was gone. So, I would take the curves as fast as I could to try to catch up with him.

He and his wife had busted up a few months before. This day Dick had a girlfriend riding on the back of his motorcycle with him. Like I said he and his wife had broken up. But really the extra weight still made no difference, he would slow down and then zoom, Dick was gone. Finally, I took a turn onto a street too fast. So fast in fact, that I could not lean the motorcycle enough to make the turn. And so, I crossed the corner curb and sidewalk with my motorcycle. There was a house on the other corner of the street. My motorcycle hit the curb and jumped into the air and came down in the fellow's yard. You cannot control an airborne motorcycle unless you are a trick rider. When I landed, I was in the slick grass, and with the brakes locked I was just sliding on the grass and could not steer or stop. Instantly I realized I was out of control and not stopping. I looked before me where I was going and there was a chain link fence and a garage coming at me.

In a second it went through my mind, "Should I lay the motorcycle down"? "Should I hit the chain link fence, or should I hit the garage"? "The chain link fence may cut me all to pieces", was going through my mind.

I remembered when we were at the hospital emergency room the time Sonny Crowden got beat half to death by an intruder, there was a young man they brought in that had wrecked his motorcycle into a barbed wire fence. The fence just rolled all around him. I remembered how his mother acted when the doctor came out and told them he had died.

"But the garage would be unmovable", I thought! All this went through my mind in just a few seconds. But before I could make up my mind, the front tire of my motorcycle went between the garage wall, and the fence end post. I bounced off the garage like a rag doll. I didn't feel the hit. I was just stunned, and in the blink of an eye I was on the concrete driveway on one knee, and one foot. I was wearing a helmet and I believe it saved my life. Because the crash, really, really rang my bell.

Dick Wells had heard the crash and turned his motorcycle around and came back. As he pulled up and started getting off his motorcycle he said, "Ernie are you ok"?

As Dick got to me, I was wobbly, but getting up to both feet. Still stunned and not feeling anything, I looked over at my motorcycle and said, "Yeah, but my motorcycle is all messed up".

Dick left me and began to walk over to where my motorcycle was sticking between the fence post and the garage with the front forks, and wheel all bent up.

I was so stunned that all I could do was walk in a small circle in the driveway. As I walked in a circle, I suddenly realized there were drops of blood on the driveway where I was standing. I called over to Dick and said, "Dick I must be hurt there is blood on the driveway. See where it is coming from"!!!

Dick left the motorcycle and came back over to me and began to check me out. He took my helmet off and had me sit down on the driveway. He said, "The blood is dripping off your left-hand fingers let me see up your jacket sleeve". When he asked me to raise my left arm, I suddenly realized that I had no control over my left arm. When he pulled my left arm up to look up the sleeve of my riding jacket the most awful pain shot up my arm.

Dick said, "Aw your arm is broken, I can see the bone sticking out"!! Dick said, "You need to go to the hospital"!!!

I said, "But, what about my motorcycle"?

Dick said, "We're not far from my house, you sit over here in the grass with Beth and I will run on my motorcycle and get my car to take you to the hospital. I'll also call Deanna"!! "Beth you stay with him and keep him still"!!

I said again, "But what about my motorcycle"?

By this time Dick realized that I had my bell rung pretty good. Dick said, "Ernie I will come back and get it and take it to your house, but right now we got to get you to the hospital, OK"?

Dick came back with his car and took me to the hospital. By the time he got back I was beginning to hurt. Deanna met us at the hospital.

It turned out that I had a compound fracture, and the bone was sticking through my arm just above my wrist. It was almost like I had 2 wrists. The doctor set the bone, stitched up where the bone was sticking out, and then he put my arm in a cast from my elbow to around my thumb.

Because of the cast being around my thumb I could not play bass guitar with my band which was part of my income. I hired 3 different bass guitar men and thought they did fine. But the band did not like their style of playing. Plus, everybody was making less money because of the extra man. I was still doing the lead singing. Because I could not find a bass guitar man that pleased the rest of the band, I cut my cast off from around my thumb so I could play.

I still had the cast on my arm; it just did not go around my thumb anymore. I played the bass guitar until time for me to go back to the doctor and have my cast cut off.

When I went to the doctor, he was not happy. The doctor cut my cast off and my forearm had not healed because of the constant movement of my fingers while playing my bass. When the doctor took my cast off it was like I had a second wrist just 1/3 of the way up my forearm. The doctor was angry.

He said, "Son the bones did not heal. I am going to have to do surgery on you. I will have to take some bone from your hip and graft it around the bone where it did not heal. To try and get the bones to heal back together. Then I will also have to put a pin in your arm from the wrist to your elbow. Now you will not be able to play bass. And don't cut the damn cast off this time"!!!

I said, "Yes sir I won't".

After the surgery I bought a Fender Rhodes bass keyboard. I learned to play the bass keyboard with my right hand until I was able to play bass guitar again. I took tape and put on the keys of the bass keyboard and wrote the notes on the tape. I lay the bass guitar across my lap and learned the notes that it took to do a 2-4 bass line. Then I studied the notes and pattern it took to play a 4-4 walk. Once I had learned the patterns everything fell into place. But I still could not take my eyes off what I was doing. So, I had to pull the mic boom stand down to where I could sing and still be able to see the keyboard. I didn't like this because I wanted to make eye contact with the audience. About the time I had begun to learn to look up from the keyboard at the audience it was time to get my cast off again and I went back to playing my bass guitar. To this day I can play bass keyboard with my right hand.

LILLIAN FLATT singing on the show in Parkin, Arkansas. Ernest Flatt on bass & Sandy Manuel on drums. Notice lill has a broken arm. Us Flatt's are always breaking something.

45. 1977- ERNEST & DEANNA'S DIVORCE BECOMES FINAL.

Deanna Banner, Flatt and I got into an argument about something, and she left me for 3 days, and nights. I told her that true to what I had told her before, that I was not taking her back this time.

She had not been able to be found for 3 days when I came back from the USO tour in 1970, and once before after an argument she had left, and I could not find her for 3 days.

We were living on Wolf Road and she just up and left. My band was playing at the NCO club on Wright Patterson Air Force Base in Fairborn, I found out later that she had made a date with a soldier while dancing to my music at the NCO Club. Then she went missing for 3 days and nights.

I was so mad that I went out to a club and got another girl on the rebound and brought her back to the house. Then Deanna came back to the house and started calling this girl a whore. I told her, "Don't call her a whore she is here where you are supposed to be".

Deanna started to cry, and we began to talk. I was a sucker for tears. So, I told the other girl to leave and Deanna and I got back together.

At that time, I told her when we got back together that the next time that she left again that it would be over. That she might as well get a divorce. I was not sure, but I even wondered if she had found someone else, maybe the soldier at the NCO Club or whatever, while she was gone during that time. Of course, she would not admit it if she was. I was just feeling she did not want to be with me, and it was over.

This may have affected our marriage from then on, but I was trying to hold our marriage together for everybody's concern. But especially for Little Ernie's concern. Also, I didn't and still don't believe in divorce except for fortification as per the Bible.

Well true as before the third time she finally called me after 3 days. I told her to go ahead and get a divorce because apparently, she didn't want to be with me anymore. She said she did not have the money for a divorce. I told her I would help her pay for it if we got the divorce. She went and got a lawyer, and we got a divorce, or actually a disillusionment of marriage. This was degreed on 10/25/1977.

It bothered me most when Deanna and I divorced that I would not be able to spend as much time with Little Ernie as I did before the divorce, like when Deanna and I were still together. I knew that it was over between Deanna and me, but I loved Little Ernie very much and it hurt me that I was not going to be able to keep the family together for the sake of Little Ernie.

Then after a while I met a girl at one of my club music dates. A club called THE MUG & JUG in Piqua Ohio. Her name was Gwen Ward. She was a small girl that was cute as a button. Gwen moved in with me on Wolf Road, while Deanna and I were waiting for the marriage to be finalized. Gwen had nothing to do with the breakup of Deanna and my marriage. But I believed from the way she talked that Deanna thought she did. But I met Gwen after Deanna, and I had already separated.

On about the day I met Gwen Ward, in October, my song/recording "Baby's Gone To Live With Another Man" was accepted for the WONE Radio album project-and played on the Radio.

Then one day I received the final divorce paper from the court ending Deanna, and my marriage. All I could think about was not being able to go to Little Ernie's room, and kiss him good night.

Not too long after that Gwen, and I got into an argument. She said she was going to leave me. I began to feel sorry for myself. Missing Little Ernie, and now Gwen was going to leave. I felt I could not keep a family together. I was a failure.

I went into my music room and took two bottles of Epilepsy pills, Phenobarbital, Dilantin and drank 5 cans of beer, and began to write my mother a goodbye note. I did all this in about 30 minutes.

I do not remember too much, but I was told I came out of the music room to get another beer and was swinging on the fridge door. Then I started for the living room. Gwen said I was swinging on the swinging doors between the living room, and the kitchen. Then I collapsed on the carpet on the floor in the living room, unconscious.

Gwen called Marc Glascoe my lead guitar player and said "Ernie has collapsed on the floor".

Marc asked Gwen, "What is the problem with him"?

Gwen said to Marc, "We got into an argument, and he has collapsed unconscious on the living room floor"!

Marc said he would be right there.

It took Marc twenty to thirty minutes to drive across town to the house on Wolf road.

Marc said he got there and when he looked at my lips, they had turned blue.

Marc said to Gwen, "Call an ambulance, now"!!!

Marc began to do CPR until the ambulance got there.

The ambulance came along with the police. The medics were in such a hurry that they clipped my side when they took scissors and cut my Farrier Fawcett T Shirt off of me. They had to shock me 2 times on the way to the hospital to restart my heart. They got me to the hospital and pumped my stomach. I was unconscious for 9 days and nights. The doctors told my parents that **IF** I awoke, the doctors were not sure if I would be OK or NOT. The doctors told my Mom, and Dad that I may have brain damage, be paralyzed, blind, or not able to speak, or hear.

I was told, the whole 9 days, and nights, my Mother never left my side, except to shower and eat.

The first time I woke up the doctor was by my bed with my Mom. She stood in the background. The Doctor had a black beard and black hair.

The Doctor then spoke gently and asked, "Ernest do you know where you are at"?

I studied and looked around, then I studied some more. After several seconds went by, I was trying to think through the fog. After I looked around a lot, then fog cleared enough that finally I asked, "In the hospital"?

I had been in a hospital so many times after a seizure episode that the question was not hard to figure out, but it still took me a while to get through the fog and answer.

The doctor then asks another question, "Ernest do you know how you got here"?

I studied some more through the fog and asked with a slurred speech, "I don't know an ambulance maybe"?

The doctor said "Yes"!

Then the doctor asked, "Do you know why you were brought to the hospital"?

I studied long and hard, but the fog would just not let me through. I had no idea of time.

Then I ask again with slurred speech, "Did I have a seizure"?

"No", answered the doctor!

"Think hard, take your time Ernest", the doctor said looking at mom and back at me. Mom began to cry.

I studied long and hard, but the fog would just not let me through.

I studied long and hard again, but the fog was blocking me trying to not let me through.

It seemed like several minutes passed. I was becoming scared because I could not remember.

Finally, the fog cleared just enough to let me remember before I collapsed.

I spoke with slurred speech, "I took too much, some-of- my- pills".

The doctor looked at mom and then back at me and said, "That's good that you are starting to remember".

The doctor then did a physical on me checking my reflexes, eye movement, grip with my hands and such.

Once I woke up my Mom, and Dad looked as if they had aged 20 years, and I had done that to them. Up to that time Mom and Dad were just Mom and Dad, but I noticed gray hair and wrinkles for the first time on them. I had done that and was sorry. Then I began to cry.

Mom, I am so sorry, I said.

My Mom asked me as she kissed my head, "please Son, promise me you will never do this again".

I said in a slurred voice, with tears in my eyes, "I promise Mom".

Then I went back to sleep.

I woke up again and there was an orderly at the foot of my bed. He had a beard and black hair and I thought he was the same doctor from when I first woke up.

The orderly asked, "Ernest do you know where you are at"?

I began to cry out, "Oh NO, I have done it again"!!! "I have done it again"!!! "Mom I am sorry"!!!!

I thought the orderly was the doctor and I had tried to take my life a second time after promising Mom not to. I was so out of it that time was folding in and out on itself. Finally, I realized that I had just woken up and was still in the hospital and I had not broken my promise to Mom. This was also only an Orderly that just happened to have Black hair and a Black beard just like the doctor from when I woke up first.

After I realized that I had not broken my promise, I settled down, then I went back to sleep again. I slept a lot for several days.

One time when I woke up, I told the nurse, "Get this fucking tube out of my dick or I will pull it out". I had a catheter inside me.

Mom told me later on that I would not have been able to pull it out because there was an inflated balloon up inside of me.

For 3 months I was in the hospital not able to comb my hair. If I tried to comb my hair I would rake toward the back of my head with the brush, then I would Rake my hair, back forward with the brush. I was not able to have the motivation to raise the brush off my head. I was so stoned they would not let me stand.

To this day I have kept my promise and realize that this was the most stupid thing I had ever done in my life. The lesson I learned was when you die is decided by GOD. If GOD is not ready for you to go, you will not go. If you try to take your life and GOD is not ready for you. You could still wake up and be alive. But you could still be alive and paralyzed, and only able to move your eyes, but, alive with all the same problems and more. If it is GOD's will you do not die, you will not die.

I got out of the hospital and got strong again. But it took me 6 months before I was able to go back to playing music thanking GOD for his love of me, and the love of my family.

Gwen, and I, had been going together for almost 8 months when we decided to get married. Gwen, and I, went to the marriage license bureau in Dayton, Ohio to get a license to get married. When we got there the lady at the bureau looked up our records and found out that Gwen was not divorced from her first husband in Kentucky. Besides that, she had married a different man on her second marriage, which apparently wasn't legal.

Gwen said, "I know I am divorced! My first x husband went and got the divorce"!

The lady from behind the desk said, "Do you have your divorce papers"?

Gwen said, "No"! "But I know I am divorced", she added.

"Here is a number in Kentucky you can call", said the lady behind the desk handing Gwen a piece of paper with a number on it. "You can use the phone booth out in the hall. Tell them to call me", added the woman behind the desk.

The lady at the license bureau gave us a phone number to call in Kentucky and a number for them to call her back. Gwen and I went out to the hall to a phone booth and called the number.

Gwen said to the person on the other end, "My fiancée and I wish to get married and the lady at the marriage bureau here in Dayton, Ohio said that I was still married". "I know that my ex-husband got a divorce, he told me he went down and got it started, and I paid the fee"!

The lady on the other end must have said something to upset Gwen, because she started crying

I said, "Gwen what is the matter"?

Then Gwen handed the phone to me.

I took the phone and was talking to a woman on the other end. I explained that Gwen and I wanted to get married. The lady on the other end said, "No, she cannot get married. She is already married. Then she named Gwen's husband, which Gwen claimed, was her ex-husband.

I said "Mam, she says she is sure she is divorced from him".

The lady on the other end said, "No she is still married! Her husband came in to get a divorce, but never paid the fee, nor did he follow up on it, and they are still married".

I said, "Are you sure"?

She answered, "Yes I am sure. I am looking right at the paperwork. She is still married and will have to get a divorce if you two wish to get married"!

I said, "thank you". Hung up the phone and began to laugh out loud. That is when I realized I had dodged a bullet, and maybe did not really need to get married, and get back into what I had just got out of with Deanna. I began to laugh again, over, and over again. I just could not stop laughing. Gwen just cried more and more.

We did not stay together much longer after that.

But the day we broke up it went like this.

Gwen asked me to drive her to her mother's house in Piqua, Ohio. So, we loaded up in my car and went to Piqua where her mother lived.

When we got there Gwen's sister asked if I would drive her over to her boyfriend's house to get some money from him to pay a bill. I pulled up outside the house and Gwen's sister went in and came back out with some money to pay a light bill. We stopped on the way back to Gwen's mother's house to pay the light bill at the electric company. She went in and came right back out, then we went back to Gwen's mother's house. We were not gone more than a half hour to 45 minutes. When we got back to Gwen's mother's house, Gwen's mother met us at the door and asked us where Gwen and her daughter were. We both said she was here when we left. So, we started looking for Gwen and her daughter which stayed most of the time with her grandmother in this very same house.

I went around the block on foot hollering for Gwen but did not find her. Then I got in my car and drove around the block several times and then widened the search another block or two and still did not find her.

When I got back to the house something did not seem right. Then I noticed that no one was as upset as I was. This seemed even stranger. After about an hour and a half I realized something was amiss. Then I told her mother and sister that I needed to go back home to Wolf Road and if Gwen came in and wanted to talk to me tell her to call me.

I went back home and never heard from her.

Later I found out that Gwen and her daughter were across the street from her mother's house in the Hospital watching me go crazy looking for them. They were looking through the Hospital window from across the street.

Maybe she wanted to leave me, and was afraid I would try to stop her, or commit suicide, or whatever. But it sure made me mad that she could not just have been straight and told me to my face. I would have had more respect for her. Anyway, that was the last time we ever dated.

Later on I saw her again in a night club in Troy, Ohio. My steel guitar player and I were out trying to find a gig for our band. She tried to get me to come back after I dropped the steel man off. But I dropped my steel man off and then went home to the one I loved "Ellis". I heard later on that she married a drummer that played for me a long time ago. The drummer was going to college to become a lawyer. I heard he was helping her get her divorce.

One day we were all in my 1969 Blue Dodge Coronet car going somewhere together. Seating in the back seat of the car were my younger siblings, my brother Terry, my oldest sister Rita, and my youngest sister Lillian. I was driving, and dad was in the front passenger seat.

Dad looked over at me and said, "I need to make a phone call. If you see a phone booth, would you pull over".

I saw a phone booth and pulled over. I decided to back the car into the parking spot right in front of the phone booth, so the back of the car was toward the phone booth. Then dad got out of the car to make his call in the booth. I just left the car running so we could listen to the radio.

In those days there were not any cell phones, and the phone booths were on every other corner. The booth had glass all the way around and was basically a tall glass box with a phone on the back wall. In the front of the phone booth was a folding door with glass in it. The door had a hinge on the side and in the middle and the door folded inward to the phone booth then you slid it to the side. So, you had to step sideways and pull the center of the door toward you and slid it sideways to open it.

As I said Dad was a large man. My dad was a big man. He was about 6′ 1″ and weighed about 245 pounds.

On the back wall of the phone booth, where the phone hung, was a metal shelf. It was used to set things on and to read a phone book. The shelf was in the corner just opposite the door and just under the phone.

As my brother, my sisters, and I, sat there we were listening to music on the radio. After several minutes went by, all of a sudden Dad got back into the car.

Dad jumped back into the car and he said, "Couldn't you all hear me hollering"?

I answered, "No sir, we were listening to the radio"! "What", I asked?

I looked at Dad and he had sweat all over his face and pouring off the end of his nose. His shirt was soaked through with sweat.

I ask again, "What happened Dad"?

Dad said, "I went into the phone booth to make my phone call. I figured I would leave the folding door open because it was so hot inside the phone booth. I reached into my front pants pocket to get out my change. When I pulled out my change my hand hung on my pocket and I dropped all the coins on the concrete floor. So, I bent down to pick up my change, and when I did my ass pushed the door to the phone booth closed".

My brother, my sisters, and I, all began to snicker but were afraid to upset Dad, so we were trying to hold it in. We were imagining Dad with his head down, and butt up in the air.

Dad continued, "So I thought I will straighten up and open the door. But my head got hung under the metal shelf in the phone booth, and my ass was sticking up against the door that was closed".

By this time my brother, sisters, and I were having a very hard time holding back the snickers. But we did not want to offend Dad by laughing at him.

Dad continued his story, "Every time I would rise up, the back of my head would hit under the damn metal shelf, and my ass would bang up against the glass on the door. I was kicking, and raising hell inside of that damn phone booth, thinking I will have to kick the damn glass out. I was stuck, and I was hollering for you kids!

"HELP ME GET OUT OF THIS DAMN PHONE BOOTH"!!

By this time all of us were laughing full out loud.

But Dad didn't care, and loved to tell a joke, so he continued on.

"I didn't know you couldn't hear me for the music, and I was hollering, and cussing, and kicking the hell out of the glass in that phone booth. But it must be a safety glass because it would not break. The sweat was just rolling off me. And I was stuck with my head down under that damn shelf and my ass, up in the air against the door, and that phone booth was rocking, I was farting', out of wind, and couldn't get my breath, and I was trying to tear that phone booth up. I thought the phone booth was going to turn over"!!

By this time, we all were laughing so hard we were rolling in the car's seats and holding our stomachs. We had forgotten about caring where we were rude to Dad or not. Dad was even beginning to chuckle a little now then as he told the story.

Finally, I stopped laughing, and got enough wind to ask, "Dad how did you finally get out of the phone booth"?

Dad said, "Well as I said, I was farting' and it was stinkin', and I was out of breath. I thought I was gonna pass out. So finally, I was afraid I might pass out, and just in case I did, I got down on my knees so I wouldn't fall, if I did pass out. But, once I was on my knees, I was able to get my head out from under that damn shelf, and turn around on my knees, on that concrete floor. Then I was able to stand back up and open the door.

"Well. Did you make your phone call", Lillian asks from the back seat with a grin?

"Hell no", Dad almost shouted!! The sweat was still dripping off the end of his nose.

"Well, do you want to make it now", asks Terry? Then with a snicker almost unable to keep from laughing.

"Hell no"! "I ain't going' back in that phone booth from Hell. I'll wait till we get back home", answered Dad.

"Phone booth from hell", said Rita with a big snicker.

Then we all started laughing again, and so did Dad as I eased the car back out on the street.

46. 1978- ERNEST MEETS ELLIS ANN SMITH.

One day I was over at mom's house and my Dad asked me if I would take him downtown Dayton, Ohio to take care of some business.

He asked, "Hey Ernie will you give me a ride downtown? If you can give me a ride downtown, then I can just run in and take care of my business. And, if you will drive me down then I will not have to find a parking place it is not going to take me long. I will jump out and you can circle the block till I come back out. If I come back out and you are not there, I will just stand there till you come back around".

I told Dad, "OK I can take you down, Dad"!

I drove Dad downtown and let him out on Main St. Then I drove around the block, and as I came back to the spot where I had let Dad out, he had not come back out yet. So, I drove around the block again. As I came around the second time, I looked at the spot where I had let Dad out and he still had not come back out yet. So, I drove around the block again and just as I turned the corner to go out of sight, I saw Dad come out of the building, but it was too late. So, I went on around again.

As I was going around the block again Dad stood outside of a Pawn Shop that was there with his back up against the window. He had backed up against the window because it was starting to sprinkle rain and he could get under the awning. He was looking up and down the street waiting for me while he puffed on his cigar. I got caught by a Traffic Cop and it took me a while longer the last time.

When I drove around once again to the spot where I had let Dad out, he jumped back into the car and was laughing.

"Go, Go", Dad said as he got into the car laughing.

I asked as I drove away, "What's going on"?

Dad began to tell me, "Just as I came out of the building, I saw you turn the corner. So, I thought I would wait in front of the Pawn Shop window under the awning because it was starting to rain. I backed up with my back to the Pawn Shop window and was smoking my cigar and looking up and down the street for you. Finally, I saw you coming. Suddenly I felt a fart coming on, so I looked up and down the street and did not see anyone. I did not want to fart in the car, so I raised my leg just as you pulled up and farted a big, long, loud stinkin' fart. It was one of those wet sounding long ones. All of a sudden, I looked down to the right of me and there was a fellow with his head right even with my ass. He had snuck up and I did not see him. He had bent down looking at something in the Pawn Shop window right even with my ass. But I swear I did not see him. On top of that, I had even raised my leg so there was nothing I could say that would convince him that I had not done it on purpose"!

I began to laugh and said, "Well what did he say or do".

Dad said, "Nothing, he just stood up, made a bad smelly face, and walked away. Then I headed toward your car.

We both drove away laughing. Dad had a way of getting into funny situations and he made them even funnier by telling them. He was an old radio man and knew how to tell a story and would be able to picture everything.

I was playing music at a north Dayton, Ohio nightclub on N. Dixie Drive, when in walked a girl that I saw from across the room, and fell head over heels in love with her. But before I could get over to her to talk to her, the fellow that I had playing bass guitar was already there and sitting beside her. Her name was Ellis Ann Smith. Cliff was the name of the fellow I had playing bass for me. So, I went over, and the other girl that was a friend of Ellis' started to hit on me. Her name was Julie; I was not really interested but wanted to be next to Ellis. So, I went along, and we all went out for breakfast at the end of the night.

Later on, a couple of months down the road, my band was playing at a different club when in walked the same two girls, Ellis and Julie. This time Cliff was not there. I was playing my own bass guitar. So as soon as break came, I went over to the table. Julie immediately began to hit on me again. She asked me to dance, so I danced with her.

When I got back to the table I said, "Now, it is time for me to dance with you", I said looking straight at Ellis as I put my hand out.

So, Ellis got up and I took her hand, and we went to the dance floor. She was so sexy; her waist was so small I could reach around her with just one arm. She had on this black, high waist, pants that really showed off her figure and flat stomach. I was smitten.

As soon as we got far enough on the dance floor so Julie could not hear, I told Ellis, "I have wanted to ask you out to breakfast, but I cannot get a word in edgewise with Julie around".

Ellis said, "Yeah I know she can be that way".

I looked at Ellis in her eyes and said, "I want to take you out for breakfast after I get done here tonight, but just you"!

"Ok", said Ellis, "I will take care of it. We are going to leave when you go back to play, but I'll be back later by myself".

I said, "OK, but are you sure you are coming back"? "Really", I ask?

"Yes, I promise", answered Ellis.

So, after the dance was over, I said goodbye and the band, and I went back to play another set. Ellis and Julie got up and waved good-bye as they left. I was wondering if Ellis would really come back. I hoped she would.

But sure, enough later in the night she came walking back in. I went over to her table and explained how happy I was that she had come back. I bought her a couple of drinks and we danced on my breaks. Once I played the last set, we left to go to have breakfast. We stayed at the restaurant until almost 6:00am. This went on for almost every night for 2 weeks.

Finally, I asked her to marry me because I loved her, and because we both needed to get some sleep and we wanted to be together. So, we became engaged to be married. The date was set for February 17, 1979. This was selected by Ellis. And just to show you how smart Ellis was, she selected this date because she figured I would never forget it because it was also my dad's birthday. She was right. I have never forgotten the date. Every year it comes around. I remember this date is the day we got married.

I always felt like I was very lucky to get a girl like Ellis. I felt she was beautiful and to me she was very sexy. I could almost reach around her waist with both my hands. I also felt she was very smart. I never had a desire for a dumb woman. She had 2 years of college and rode horses that jumped the fence. Her horse was named "Half-A-Deck". She said the horse was named "Half- A-Deck" because sometimes the horse acted as if it was playing with only a half-a-deck for a mind.

Ellis's parents were very educated, financially successful people compared to my side of the family. Ellis's Mom was an ex-English teacher and was very strong minded. Ellis's Dad got his Engineering Degree in the service. Both were very good people. They would not take anything from someone that they did not earn, themselves. They did not believe much in Jesus and the word of God, but they were honest, good people. They believe not speaking good English meant that you were not very smart or educated. I did not fit the idea of what her parents had in mind for her to marry at all. They were from the North, New York State in fact, and my family was poor country southern people from Kentucky and Tennessee. By the time I had met Ellis her family had moved from New York State and now lived in Centerville, Ohio just outside of Dayton. The place they lived in was about a $200,000.00 house or more. The house was all brick with a dining room and Kitchenette. They had two Living Rooms, one with nice white furniture for guests and the other with nice furniture for everyday use. They had three bedrooms and at least two baths. Also, they had a 2-car garage and two fireplaces. Ellis's Dad worked for General Motors and was a Buyer that wore a suit and tie at work every day. He was what factory people would call a "SUIT". Ellis's Dad and I got along fairly well, or at least we could talk, but Ellis's Mother seemed a lot of times to be rude to me, and sometimes I was rude in return. It would be fair to say she did not care too much for me. But Ellis said she was that way to everybody. She used to be an English teacher, and was fairly blunt.

Ellis's Dad's name was Shelton Smith, Sr. Her Mom's name was Shirley Jane Scorse Smith.

Ellis Ann Smith had two brothers Shelton Smith, Jr. and Sullivan Smith. Ellis was the youngest.

47. 1979-ERNEST MARRIES ELLIS ANN, FEB. 17,1979.

The day we got engaged, Ellis and I had a talk. I had asked her to get married and she had said "Yes". This made me very, very happy.

Ellis asked me if I wanted to really get married, because it had not been long since I had gotten a divorce from Deanna and the affair with Gwen had not lasted and it had not been over for very long.

I said, "Yes unless you don't want to". Then I said, "I want to marry you if you want to marry me. I love you. I am not the kind of man that is happy without someone that I love being beside me. But I do have one request, be sure that you can treat Little Ernie just as if he was your own child".

Ellis answered, "I am sure, I can treat Little Ernie just as my own child, but I want to be sure you want to marry me".

I answered, "There is not a doubt in my mind that I love you and want to marry you, if you love me and want to marry me too".

So, we agreed on the date of, February 17, 1979 to have our marriage ceremony. Well Ellis came up with the date because it was my Dad's birthday, and she was sure I could remember it. She was right.

Ellis had some money saved and wanted a big wedding. I did not have that kind of money. So, Ellis began to put it all together she handled it all. She was really good at handling the important things for a ceremony. She did ask me to find her a flutist. She even pronounced it correctly. I would have said a flute player. I was amazed.

I ask, "Why a flutist"?

She explained, "I want a flutist to play the wedding march".

"Really", I said confused! "OK, I'll get you one"!

To be honest I thought she was out of her mind. The Wedding March on a Flute? I imagined the flutist playing the flute as if it would be played on a march for the Revolutionary War. "Here comes the bride"! "Here comes the bride", I thought! Fast like a March!

But, if that is what she wanted, that is what she would get. So, I called a good guitarist friend of mine named Rick Bashore. Rick taught guitar at Dayton Band and Equipment, he knew all the musicians in Dayton, and he got me in touch with a flutist.

Ellis had told me to just get a number from the flutist and she would call him, or her. She did not want to spoil the surprise. So, I found her a flutist that had heard of me and was very excited to get to play for us. So, I gave her the number of the flutist. Ellis called the flutist and made a deal to play at the wedding.

The day of the wedding Ellis had handled everything. I had a Baby Blue Tux and had got my hair curled. That was still the style then. Because I had not talked to Ellis ahead of time, and discussed it with her, I found out later on that Ellis did not much like it. She most likely would have told me <u>not</u> to have my hair curled.

My brother Terry Glen Flatt was my best man.

Ellis sent someone from the back of the church to ask if I had the Wedding Ring. Suddenly, I was in terror, because I had forgotten the Wedding Ring on our kitchen table at our Mobile Home that we rented together. What were we going to do? It was too late to go all the way back across town to get the ring.

Ellis sent her engagement ring back by someone to give to Terry. So, we would get married with her engagement ring. Ellis must have thought I was really dumb. I sure felt stupid. But it was easy to forget the ring because I was so excited. More excited than any music show I had ever done. But out of all the things Ellis had taken care of, she had done great. But of the 3 little things she had given to me to do, I had only got one right, the Flutist. I had forgotten the Wedding ring on the kitchen table and tried too hard to look special by curling my hair. I should have just got a regular haircut and put my tux on. Oh, and yes, and remembered to get the ring. I felt so stupid that I had let the love of my life down!!

Then it was time for the wedding to start, my brother Terry and the ushers, and I was standing up front of the church. Suddenly the Flutist began to play very, very, very slowly, the Wedding March. It was very beautiful, slow with vibrato, not at all as I had imagined. The arrangement was not at all as I had imagined. And this was the idea of my beautiful wife to be! Wonderful!!

Suddenly there was Ellis with her Dad coming down the aisle. Her dress was not typical, it was extraordinary. It was a crème-colored white. It was smooth, straight, thin, silky but not shiny. Her wedding gown showed off her figure. It had a Biblical like hood that covered her head to around her face. The hood was trimmed in a small white feather like material around her face. She had a train that flowed behind her of the same material as the dress. I believe it was also trimmed in the white feather like material. She was so beautiful it took my breath away, most everybody else's too. Terry whispered to me with a smile on his face, "And she's got a good job too"! At that time, I had been given the gift from GOD of True Love that would last forever.

The reception party was great. I met a lot of Ellis' family I had never met before. And of course, Ellis met a lot of my family. My Dad was not at the wedding; he had gone on a drinking bender that very weekend. We all missed him but maybe he did not want to show up loaded afraid it would have embarrassed us in front of Ellis' family.

Ellis and I had already moved into a mobile home trailer park and after the wedding we felt even more at home.

48. 1979-TRAVIS LEE FLATT IS BORN.

Ellis informed me that we were going to have a baby. The moment Ellis found out she was pregnant she stopped smoking, and if you knew Ellis you know what a feat that was for her. She also stopped drinking any alcohol at that moment. By the way she did this for every child she had.

Very quickly we realized that the mobile home was way too small. So, we began to look for a real house. But everything cost too much.

Then the day came that we had to take Ellis to St. Elizabeth hospital, the baby was on the way. We did not want to know ahead of time if it would be a boy or girl. But we had picked out 2 names, Travis Lee Flatt was the boy name, I do not remember the girl name. Maybe Ellis does. We went to the hospital and time went by. We had agreed for me to stay in the delivery room.

I was not in the delivery room when Little Ernie was born. They did not have the Fathers in the delivery room much back then. The father just paced back and forth in the waiting room.

But in the delivery room, I never saw a woman handle giving birth on TV or Movies any better than Ellis did. When the contractions would come, she would grit her teeth and push with all her might. She was going to do her part for sure.

Ellis had agreed ahead of time she would not take any pain killers because she did not want to harm the baby. Ellis kept pushing and pushing, but the baby was not passing because it was so big. Finally, after not being able to pass the child the doctor said the baby's heart rate was going down. The doctor looked at Ellis and me between contractions and said, "Ellis I know you wanted to have this baby without drugs, but I am going to have to give you drugs to do an episiotomy before we lose this baby"!

> episiotomy-(e-pez-e-ott-a-me)- *(means the* vagina is soft and designed to stretch *to* allow the baby to be born. *This* means making a small cut at the lower end of the entrance to the woman's vagina to allow easier birth of the child).

The Doctor continued to explain to Ellis, "I am going to have to cut you to get the baby out and this means give you drugs"! We both agreed. I do not think after pushing for so long that Ellis was hard to convince. She had done her part as best she could. She had been a real trooper.

They gave Elis some drugs that put her in la-la land. Then the doctor cut Elis and reached in and pulled out a baby boy, just as blue as a pair of new blue jeans. The doctor smacked him on the behind and he did not cry. Then the doctor took a suction machine and sucked out his nose and mouth. Then he smacked him on the behind again. Finally, the baby began to whimper/cry. The doctor jumped up and wrapped the baby in a blanket and said, "I am going to ICU"!!! And with the baby wrapped in the blanket out the door he went with no more exclamations. His assistant began to sew Ellis up. Ellis was kind of out of it, but I was sitting there beside my wife wondering if we had just lost our first-born baby. It makes me want to cry to think about it to this day. I thought how would I be able to tell Ellis? But I believe God knew how hard it would have hurt us to lose Travis.

But **Travis Lee Flatt was born-Oct.14, 1979** and did continue to live. He was a tough little, big, kid.

The next time we saw Travis Lee Flatt was in the Intensive Care Unit for babies and he had gotten his color back. He was no longer blue. Travis weighed 11 pounds and 12 ½ ounces and was 23 inches long when he was born. Now he had started to gain more weight.

They kept Travis in ICU and my mom Daisy Flatt, who was a nurse at the same hospital on another ward, visited every night. She worked the 3rd shift and would visit at the beginning of her shift, and at the end of her shift before she would go home. The nurses started saying here comes Grandma, get Travis out of the incubator for her. Mom would sit and hold Travis and kiss his forehead.

Dad came by the hospital, and me and him, had to look at him through a window. He was laying there with his pecker lying over on his leg. Dad said, as he always does, with a joke, "Look he's a Flatt alright; it is laying plum over on his leg. Makes me ashamed of myself"!!! Then he gave a big laugh and swirled his unlit cigar around in his mouth. As he smiled looking at Travis proud as a pow paw could be.

The day I took Ellis home, we found out Travis was going to have to stay longer in the hospital. Ellis of course cried, because she had to leave her first son in the hospital and go home. I had to promise to bring her back each day. As if I could have kept her away.

Travis stayed in the hospital about a week before they would let him go home. The day we took him home we were very happy to go and get him. He had a troubled birth, but fast became large and healthy. What do I mean? Well, he was large when he was born. I guess what I mean was he got bigger and stronger by the time we took him home. I was not long till he was about to catch up with his brother Little Ernie, and Little Ernie was not small for his age. We just called him that to be different from Me.

The same year Travis was born Ralph "Peewee" Middlebrooks (one of the original OHIO PLAYERS) went to work for Ernest Flatt and the Cotton Mouth Band, the CMB playing Saxophone. Once Peewee went to work with us, our show stepped up about 3 levels. Peewee was an excellent entertainer and fit right in with our band. We were playing Country, Southern Rock, and even some Bluegrass, and M-TV tunes. Our show got better, and so did the size of the clubs, and of course our pay. So, we had some costumes made for us. Of course, we had flashy western outfits made for us. When we were playing Rock Tunes, we had a ZZ Topps kind of look. Course this was when ZZ Topps wore western outfits. Of course, we still did the traditional country songs.

49. 1980-ELLIS AND I BUY OUR FIRST HOUSE

Ellis and I bought a house on Norman Avenue in Dayton, Ohio. It was a 2 story, 1 bath, white house with 3 bedrooms upstairs. Downstairs it had a living room, dining room, a kitchen and a room just off the kitchen in the back of the house. I believe it was used at one time for a breakfast table. The stairs wound in a half circle with one landing as it went up to the second-floor bedrooms. Just off the dining room there was a door that went down to the full basement. In the basement there was only a furnace, a laundry sink and a place for a dryer and washer, but lots of open room.

At the other end of the basement, I put carpet on the floor and walls for a practice/recording room for me and the band. There was an outside door which led to the basement from outside so that the band members did not have to bring their equipment through the house.

While we were living at Norman Ave, I bought a used motorcycle. It was a Honda Dream 350 cc. It was just like the one Elvis Presley rode in the movie "Roustabout" except his was red and mine was gray. It ran very well, and I bought it for $300.00. I had not had a motorcycle since I had wrecked the Honda 250 cc semi street and semi dirt bike. I rode it everywhere. Finally, one day I was on the freeway doing about 60 miles an hour, on route 4 just a way from interstate 75, when my back tire blew and went down. I had both feet sliding along on the pavement, and because of the back tire being flat and rolling up, the back end was wobbling side to side. I was easing on the front brake and trying to slow down the motorcycle. You could **NOT** have driven a 10-inch nail up my butt with a sledgehammer. In that short period of time, I think I said several prayers. I was all over the road, luckily no one else was around or I may have hit them. Finally, I came to a stop and pushed the motorcycle to the side of the road. That is when I realized that if you ride a motorcycle you better watch the wear on your tires.

I remember one time on Norman Avenue we had a band practice and once we got through, I went upstairs and Ellis was sitting on a foot stool very close to the TV and the TV was very, very loud.

I looked at her and jokingly said "Can you hear it"?

She turned and looked at me and said, "Just barely when your band is playing downstairs"!!

I suddenly realized how loud the band must be. All I could do was laugh. But she did not laugh. I do not think she thought it was funny.

Then I said, "Sorry"! "We're done for tonight". She still did not laugh, but looked relieved, and moved back to the couch as she turned down the TV.

That was when I realized I needed a studio with sound proofing for practice. No long after that we started to practice at the clubs when we could.

We had to buy the house on a land contract and had 5 years to be able to get re-financing for the house. Financing was hard for me to get because I was a musician, and Ellis did not make much money at her job. Musicians work by contract, and banks count this as not dependable. That is unless you are making over a hundred thousand a year and can put down a large amount of money.

We lived in the house about 5 years but still were not able to get a loan. So, we lost the house.

50. 1981-ERNEST AND THE COTTON MOUTH BAND

Ernest Flatt and the Cottonmouth Band had played several times in Springfield, Ohio at the "Charlie Star". We had also played a big club in Columbus, Ohio called the "Charlie Horse". But the "Charli Star" was a lot closer to home than the "Charlie Star"

The Cotton Mouth Band opened for the band "McGuffey Lane". This was in a club in the "Urban Cowboy" days that held 8,000 people when full. It had a mechanical bull, video games and pool tables. At the other end in another room, there was another stage where another band would play, usually a rock band.

When we opened for McGuffey Lane on the Friday Night the club was full. We came out and did a fantastic show for our part. When we left the stage, we got a standing ovation, and the McGuffey Lane Band was waiting at the bottom of the 4 step stairs as we came down off the stage. They all congratulated us on our performance.

The next Saturday night we found out just before we were to go on stage that they had hired a Female Singer to go between us and them. Her and her band was passing through from Nashville, so they hired her act to put between us. That was actually a compliment because the night before they had to come out to a crowd already pumped up and could not put on their show with their own build ups. So, they put this Country Girl that had a record being played on the radio between us and them. That put a laid-back show between us and them so they could pump up the crowd themselves for their own show.

On or around December 1981 Ellis found out that she and I were pregnant again.

51. 1982-LACEY FLATT IS BORN-AUG. 29

One time we played at the Texas Saloon and our opening act was male strippers. The whole audience was nothing but women. The strippers came out and put on a 1 hour and ½ show then we had the stage. Talk about a wild night. Some of the fellows got grabbed by the butt as we made our way to the stage. We were the only males except for employees in the building. All the women were drunk and wild. We had a good Elvis night. We kind of got a feeling as to what Elvis went through. But we put on a good show.

As always about the last 2 months before the baby was born Ellis had to stop working and I would have to go out and find a second job so we could make ends meet. This time I got a job at Carefree Aluminum loading trucks with Aluminum windows and doors and no insurance. We were still living at Norman Ave. when Lacey was born.

On August 29, 1982 Lacey Elizabeth Flatt was born in Dayton, Ohio at Saint Elizabeth Hospital the same place Travis was born at and where Grandma Daisy Flatt worked. Lacey's birth was pretty much without any physical problems.

Her birth was very exciting to the Flatt Family because she was the first female born in her generation. She was the first girl born since her Aunt Lillian Darlene Flatt which was now Lillian Combs. Lacey was so beautiful right from the beginning. We still lived on Norman Ave. in Dayton, Ohio. I was still playing music for a living and Ellis and I did not have any Medical Insurance.

We only had medical insurance when Ellis was able to work, and of course every time we got pregnant and she could not work we lost our medical insurance. Back in those days there was not any Federal required pregnancy leave to keep the job. Musicians could only afford insurance if they had a hit record or worked for a star. Of course, I could not afford Medical Insurance and every time we had a child we would go deep in debt. Plus, children needed to go a lot to the doctor, a lot, so unless Ellis was able to work, we were usually in debt to doctors and hospitals. But we continued on hoping I would get a break and a hit. The band was actually doing very good, but we never got out of the struggling musician category. We were paying our bills but always needed more money and of course we as usual would go in debt to the doctors and the hospital. I am not sure, we were both young, but being a little older than Ellis, I believe I began to notice this quicker than Ellis. But I believed that someday we would have a hit record and things would change.

My Dad used to say, "I love all my children, and I wouldn't take a million dollar for any of my children, But I wouldn't give a penny for another one just like any one of them"! I began to take on that same idea. But Ellis and I were always struggling for money.

LACEY FLATT, TRAVIS FLATT, and LITTLE ERNIE FLATT

52. 1983-SIT DOWN GIG AT THE KRYSTAL PISTOL

In July 1983 Ernest Flatt and the Cotton Mouth Band took a sit-down job of 6 nights a week at the Krystal Pistol Night Club in Fairborn Ohio. Good steady pay, and sometimes we would play somewhere else on Sundays or Sunday Nights for more extra money, kind of like overtime. This made for good steady money. I remember several times we played 28 or more days in a row without a break. We were like Zombies playing music when we worked this much. We were all so tired, but we needed the money for our families. But with all the performing/practicing we were getting better at our show.

1983-Sept. 3, 4, 5, 1983 Ernest Flatt and the Cotton Mouth Band won the Piqua Heritage Festival, out of 60 bands there ended up being 16 bands as finalists which did the show on the last day.

Our turn came to play, and I told the band, "We get so many requests for" DIRTY LAUNDRY", although it is not a country song, let's do it anyway"! So we took a chance and decided to perform the EAGLES SONG and Peewee Middlebrooks danced into the crowd with his saxophone and the cordless mic I had bought him. We brought the crowd to their feet.

There ended up being 6 bands that placed in the top 6:
1ˢᵗ place was "Ernest Flatt and the Cottonmouth Band"
2ⁿᵈ place was "The Other Bunch"
3ʳᵈ place was "Legend Creek"

The other finalist in alphabetical order were:
"Country Showman Band"
"Home Brewed Band"
"Stillwater Band"

Saturday, October 8, 1983-Ernest Flatt and the Cotton Mouth Band opened for Terri Gibbs at Mary's Country Lounge in Miamisburg, Ohio. We did a great job and Terri Gibbs was impressed.

Oct.31, 1983, Ernest Flatt and the Cotton Mouth Band played for the Troy Business Association in the Middle of Troy, Ohio's town square- at the Strawberry Festival. We even got a newspaper article done about us. A picture was taken by a newspaper reporter of Pee Wee dancing and playing his saxophone in the crowd down the street with a little girl dancing beside him and the caption said, "Wow, mister, how are you doing that"?

Wednesday, February 22, 1984, Ernest Flatt and the Cotton Mouth Band opened for Johnny Paycheck at the Texas Saloon in Troy Ohio, 1375 S. Union Street. The Texas Saloon held about 500 people. We had been playing the Texas Saloon for some time, usually 2 weeks at a time. We left the crowd screaming and wanting more. When we came down the steps Johnny Paycheck and his band were waiting and asked, "Man where did you guys come from"?

I shook Johnny Paycheck's hand and said, "Johnny we are playing at the same place you use to play. We are the house band at The Crystal Pistol in Fairborn, Ohio".

Johnny Paycheck replied, "No kidding, that was a long time ago for me"!

Our show was a lot faster moving than Johnny Paycheck's show was. Then we went back on after his show was done and we still kicked it. But he was the one that brought the crowd in and he had the hits. We knew it but were proud of our performance.

53.   1985-ERNEST RETURNS TO GOD

I was at the Holiday Health Spa doing a workout. I was sitting with my feet and legs over in the Hot Tub after working out. All of a sudden, a gray-haired old man came over and sat down beside me. He put his legs over in the hot tub also. He asked me after a few seconds, "Son what is on your mind"? "You look like you have got something on your mind", he continued.

"Well," I said, "I just can't seem to be happy".

"Do you know Jesus Christ", he asked me?

"I was saved and baptized when I was 10 years old, but I guess I have been running from GOD for many years, about 25 years", I replied.

The old man said he was a retired Pastor and now his job was to help Christians to overcome the demons of Satan. He said down through the years the Lord had used him to build many church buildings and start congregations. He also said that his son was Pastoring a church in Midway, Ohio just outside of Dayton. He then asked, "Why do you think you were running from GOD"?

I explained that I was a musician/entertainer and had not been going to church as I should have. I explained, "I play music for a living and a lot of times it is in Night Clubs where people drink booze. I keep thinking I will make it and never have to play NightClubs again. But so far it has not happened".

"My wife and children don't deserve to be broke all the time just for my dream of making it in the Music Business", I explained.

He said to me in a soft voice, "Maybe son, you are performing music for the wrong master"! "Maybe doing music for the Real Master, the one that gave you the gift in the first place, is what you need to put your efforts to"!

This really hit home for me.

He then invited me, and my Family to come Sunday Morning and visit the church where his son was the pastor. It was a Church of the Nazarene.

I went and talked to Ellis, and we both agreed to go visit the church in Midway, Ohio. We went and visited and started going to church regular. Then I began to make plans to stop working music for a living. But I had music contracts that I had to fulfill before I could stop.

I explained to the entire band that I was stopping once all the contracts were fulfilled. That I was not booking any more gigs. But I do not think they believed me. So, I was playing 6 nights a week and going to church on Sunday.

Our last contracted gig was on New Year's Eve, Dec. 31, 1985 in Franklin, Ohio. Then I stopped playing music in clubs.

Ellis and I were living in an apartment in Dayton, Ohio with our children, Travis and Lacey. We were having trouble finding regular jobs and we were on Welfare. My phone rang off the wall with offers of music jobs and it was hard, but I turned them down because I was not going to work in bars again.

Welfare gave Ellis an assessment/test to determine what her aptitude and interests were. It turns out she scored high as a Travel Agent/Hospitality Worker. They ask her if she would like to be trained as a Hospitality Worker or a Travel Agent.

She said, "Yes she would"!!

So, Welfare set Ellis up for vocational training. They set her up for classes, and trained Ellis to be a Hospitality Worker/Travel Agent. Like a Vacation Planner. The deal was she was to pass the course and they would continue to pay her while she completed the course and got a job.

Welfare gave me a test and offered me training to do what my aptitude and interest was in. The deal was the same as the one they gave Ellis; it was to pass the course and they would continue to pay me while I completed the course and got a job. The assessment/test determined I was best suited for Music, naturally, and, also as an Electrician. They said if they gave me vocational training would I want to be an Electrician.

I said, "Yes"!!

They set me up for vocational training at Montgomery County Joint Vocational School, 8 hours a day 5 days a week for six months. I passed the course with high marks. Then they got me a paid job as an Apprentice Electrician with an Electrical Company for on-the-job training.

After this was over Ellis and I decided to visit friends in Nashville, TN. While we were there Ellis looked into the newspaper, made some calls for interviews, and Ellis got offered 2 jobs. I put in an application at Opryland Hotel as an Electrician. They said they would let me know.

We decided to let Ellis go down to Nashville and start both jobs. One job was in the daytime and the other one in the evening on the second shift. So, Ellis loaded up her old car and moved to Nashville. She got there and moved into a motel and went to work in Nashville without the kids and me. We talked on the phone all the time. I think there is a possibility that Ellis liked being on her own more than the kids and I liked being away from her. I guess only she would know for sure.

54. 1986- ERNEST AND ELLIS MOVE THE FAMILY TO NASHVILLE, TN.

At the beginning of 1986- I had quit music for a living and had not been able to find a job. Ellis was out of work also because we both had stopped working in Night Clubs. She no longer was bartending. We were on welfare to pay our rent and be able to feed us all. The devil was trying to get me back into music. I was offered music jobs in NightClubs almost every day. It was hard to turn them down. Welfare offered to send both of us to be vocationally trained. Ellis was trained to be a Travel Agent. I was given an assessment the same as Ellis and found out that I had an aptitude and interest to be an Electrician. So, the State of Ohio sent me to a Vocational School to be trained as an Electrician. After our training we both went to work but did not make much money. But it was a living.

Ellis & I went to Nashville, TN. to visit a friend. Ellis began to look at newspapers and found lots of jobs. While we were there Ellis put in for 2 jobs just to see and got offered both of them.

Ellis and I talked once we got back home and we decided to let her go down by herself and take these jobs. But she would be there by herself until I could get a job then we would move the family down to Nashville, TN. But not to play music. It was tough but Ellis loaded up and went to Nashville, TN. by herself while I stayed home with the children.

Ellis was staying in a motel room. Then finally when she could afford to, she rented a one-bedroom apartment with just a bathroom and bedroom over across the river from downtown on 16th street. In the meantime, I was trying to get a job at the Opryland Hotel as an Electrician on the phone but was not having any luck. I told the man at Opryland Hotel that I needed the job badly and would make a good employee. I told him how my wife was down there and working. But I could not come until I had a job because of my children.

Finally, the man that does the hiring for the Opryland Hotel told me, (I guess he got tired of me calling everyday), "Mr. Flatt, I would hire you in a minute if you lived down here, but I just can't hire you when your address is in Ohio. Call me when you get moved down here".

So, I asked Dad if he would move into our apartment and watch Travis and Lacey while I went to Nashville and tried to get a job. I told Dad, "Dad I just about got the job, but he won't hire me unless I have a Nashville address and live down there. Also, Dad you will be watching my children, so I need you to stay sober while you are watching my babies".

Dad agreed he would stay sober and said "Son you go get that job for your family, I'll take care of your children, you don't worry about anything as far as these kids. They are in good hands". Dad kept his word while I was gone. Dad was retired and loved his children and grandchildren. So, Dad kept his apartment, but moved some of his stuff into our apartment, and I packed and loaded up for Nashville. I called several times after I got down there, and Dad was always sober and proud to be taking care of his babies.

So, I called Ellis and told her the plan and said, "Move over I am a coming"!

I got to Nashville and moved in with Ellis. I put an application in with the Opryland Hotel and got an interview and was told that they did not have any more positions available in the Electrical Department they had just filled them all. My head dropped.

The man I had been talking to on the phone said, "But, Mr. Flatt because of your vocational training in electricity and because we want you so bad, would you take a job in our Heat and Air Department"?

I said, "Of course, I want a job"!

I was hired to start next Monday.

I went to work for Opryland Hotel in Nashville as a Heat & Air Mechanic. It took Ellis and I, three whole months to earn and save enough money to rent a house for the whole family. We had to pay the first month's rent, the deposit, the electrical deposit, the water/sewer deposit, and of course food for everybody. I also had to rent a trailer to carry down all our furniture and such.

We rented a house on Gallatin Road just at the edge of Nashville. We rented the whole downstairs for our family. We were living in Inglewood on Gallatin Rd. I had an old 1976 Dodge van that we took to Ohio and rented the biggest U-Haul trailer they had and then loaded the trailer and Van with everything we had, and then we moved to Nashville, TN. Ellis, Travis, Lacey and I loaded up. Just about 25 miles outside of Nashville the old Dodge van began to lose power. Every time we came to a hill the old van would lose power and barely make it up the hill pulling that big trailer loaded down. Sometimes we would fall all the way to 30 or 40 miles an hour to make it over the hill. We would just barely make it to the top of the hill then we would pick up speed going down the other side. Then we would just barely make it to the top of the next hill. And we were on a US 65. From hill to hill we prayed to get over. God helped us and we made it all the way there to our new residence on Gallatin Road. But I was still praying because I only had enough money left for gas to and from work until the next pay day. I was wondering how would I have enough money to get the van fixed or how would I get to and from work? We were too new at work to miss work. We had not built up any sick or annual time yet. Ellis' work was the other direction from me and both of us needed a vehicle. All these things were going through my mind.

As soon as we got to the house we had rented, we took the trailer off the van. The van began to run just fine. I guess the old van just felt the trailer was too heavy. Thank God for helping us because we did not have the money to get the van repaired. I needed the van to get to work and Ellis needed her car. We had used every bit of our money to rent the house and make the trip back to Nashville. I had brought back groceries from Ohio to get us by, but we were broke until the next paycheck. Ellis got paid every week, but I got paid twice a month, on the 15th and last day of the month.

I worked at the Opryland Hotel in the Heat & Air department for 6 months. They offered insurance and benefits. Most likely the best job I have ever had since music. But they just did not pay enough. I worked 2:00pm to 11:00pm 5 days a week.

There was a man that worked at the hotel in Heat & Air (his nickname was called "Chief", he spent 20 years in the Navy as a Chief Boiler Operator on a ship). He had 10 years with the Opryland Hotel as a Boiler Operator, 20 years with the Navy as a Boiler Operator, and 10 years with the State as a Boiler Operator. He was getting ready to retire and he suggested that I put in an application with the State and told me how to go about it. He said, "You'll make more money an hour and have even better benefits with the state".

So, with his advice I put in an application with the State of TN. After a month or two I received a call from a man with the Department of Correction at the TN. Youth Center in Joelton, TN. He asked me to come in for an interview.

I said, "Sure".

I dressed nice as I had been taught and I went up for the interview. The man interviewed me and then said he would let me know. Time went by and I heard nothing. I believed that I did not get the job.

Then one day just before time to go to work I received a call from the Superintendent at TN Youth Center Mr. Murray. He wanted to talk to me about doing a second interview for a job.

Mr. Murray asked, "Mr. Flatt I am sorry to ask you, but could you come in again for another interview"? "The reason I am asking is, the man that interviewed you the last time is very sick and is in the hospital and I am not sure he is coming back, and I need to fill this position. Could you come up tomorrow morning for another interview if you are still interested".

"I sure am, and I sure could", I answered.

So, we set up a time at 9:00 AM. I would be able to do the interview and still go to work at the Hotel.

I went to the interview the next morning and was hired to start in 2 weeks at 2 more dollars and hour more than I was making at Opryland Hotel. So, I gave a 2 week notice to the hotel.

Finally, I went to work for the State of TN, Dept. of Corrections, TN. Youth Center in Joelton, TN. just outside of Nashville, as a Building Maintenance Worker 2, Nov. 1986. It was just before Thanksgiving, and I was only making $987.00 a month. The pay was paid 1/2 x 2 times a month. This took me a while to get used to. It was not much money, but I was glad to get it and have a steady job with benefits. I had sick leave, annual leave, and Medical Insurance. This meant a whole lot with children. Ellis worked at Ramada Inn as a night desk manager. I cannot remember if she had benefits, or not, but mine with the State was much better

We lived there at Gallatin Rd. till 1987, just after Grant was born. By the way, the van that we moved from Ohio with was still running and running fine.

LACEY ELIZABETH FLATT.

55. 1987-GRANT FLATT IS BORN-JULY 3.

1987-Grant was born-July 3; we lived at 3815 Gallatin Rd. Nashville, 37216, in the Inglewood Area. The day Grant was born was a wild, rough day. Grant was born in the early morning. The birth was fairly normal without problems. Grant and Ellis were still in the hospital.

But after Grant's birth I left the hospital to pick up Travis and Lacey. We had a church get together in Inglewood just down from the house where we lived. Ellis was still in the hospital and so was Grant. There was what church people call a big "dinner on the ground", a horseshoe game, and everybody including the kids, were playing games in the yard, volleyball, and such in the yard of the pastors house right next to the church.

I was playing horseshoes with the men of the church, when I heard someone yell, "Hey, Ernie, Lacey is hurt"!!! "The dog bit her"!!

I stopped playing horseshoe right away and started to run over to where Lacey was. She had been in the yard playing with the Pastor's daughter.

I ran over to where Lacey was, and she was on the ground and someone was holding the pastor's dog by the collar. I looked at my daughter and I could see her skull, then the blood started to come. She also had a bite on her face, on her cheek and she was crying. I prayed under my breath, "Oh Lord help us", while at the same time trying to get my breath. Then I grabbed up my Baby Girl in my arms and said out loud, "We're going to the hospital"!! Then I began to holler out loud, "TRAVIS!!, TRAVIS"!!!

One of the church men put a towel on her head to help with the blood that was coming, as I was carrying her to the car.

Another church man said, "Where are your keys brother"? "I'll drive you"!

I said, "In my pocket".

He got my keys out of my pocket as I was walking to the car carrying Lacey. I hollered for Travis again.

The man that got my keys out of my pocket, said, "You hold your daughter brother, and I'll drive you".

I said "OK, but DON'T stop for lights. Look both ways and if it is clear go through".!!!

He said, "OK"! "I'll get us there safe and fast"!!

The towel was beginning to get red and soaked with blood. Travis began to cry from the back seat. Lacey was whimpering a little, but under the circumstances she was doing pretty good. But she could not see the blood like Travis, and I could. I was really worried and concerned.

I summoned all the faith I could from God, and I said, "Travis, your sister is going to be fine once we get to the hospital, so you just try and relax, I got the towel on her head". I was bluffing to help Travis. That seemed to help Travis, but the fact was I was just as worried as he was. The brother from church that was driving our car did as I asked, he slowed for the lights, made sure it was safe, and then went through. We got to the emergency room in less than 10 minutes, and when they saw the blood on the towel right away, they took Lacey away from me and to the back. They had me answering questions to fill out papers.

I kept saying, "How's my daughter"?

They kept saying, "She is fine, the doctor is seeing her now. You can see her when the doctor is done".

Finally, the doctor came out and said, "Mr. Flatt, we have stopped the bleeding. That was the most important thing to do first. We are going to need to do stitches, but first we need to do x-rays and check her out for skull fractures. But understand we have time to do the stitches, and I am going to make the stitches real close and tight, and I am really good. So, don't you worry about your daughter, because when I am done, and she is older you will not be hardly able to tell the scar is there. It is close to her hairline and everything is going to be OK. We need to check her for a skull fracture. Once the x-rays are done, we will know more about that. And, then you can go back to see her.

After the x-rays they let Travis and Me back to see Lacey. Her head was all bandaged.

The doctor came in while we were visiting Lacey and said, "Mr. Flatt I got good news, she does not have a skull fracture. But we will have to take her into surgery and put stitches in. But as I said before I am good, and I will put them close together and tight. I am going to put her to sleep to keep her from moving around. I'll take care of her Mr. Flatt"!

While Lacey was being sewed up, I called Ellis and broke the news as gentle as I could. I had to phone call Ellis, because she was still in the hospital from earlier in the morning giving birth to Grant Charles Flatt, our new son. Ellis took it well considering the circumstances.

Lacey ended up having 50 stitches on the inside and 100 on the outside.

The dog had bit her cheek which took 4 stitches, it was more of a nip. The big cut was on the left side of her head right up at her hair line. The big fang sliced her head open like a knife right at her hairline. Her head was bandaged for weeks.

As it turned out Lacey and the Pastor's daughter were playing and screaming, and the dog was tied up in the corner of the yard and thought Lacey was hurting the pastor's daughter. So, he attacked Lacey. I found out later that the dog was part wolf and part German Shepard.

When the pastor came to the hospital to see about Lacey, I told him he better do something about the dog, or I would. He turned the dog over to the Human Society. But they would not tell me if the dog was put down or not.

I called Mom and Dad up in Ohio and told them the story. When Mom and Dad found out about it up in Ohio one was on the main phone and one was on the extension.

Dad told me as soon as they hung up the phone from talking to me that he looked at Mom and said, "When are we leaving to go down there"?

Mom looked at Dad and said, "Just as soon as we can get something in a suitcase"! Dad answered "Right". Dad said they both began to pack and were on the road in 30 minutes. Mom and Dad drove all night and were there by breakfast. They stayed for several days. They wanted to see Grant and once Lacey got hurt that was it. They were coming to Tennessee.

GRANT CHARLES FLATT-age 17.

56. 1989-THE FLATT'S BUY A HOME

In 1989-Ellis and I bought a home in Cheatham County just outside of Nashville, and moved to 250 Bandy Road in Ashland City, Tn. 37015. This was a nice quiet area in the country. It was a brick, 3-bedroom house, with 1 and ¾ acres of land. We bought it through the Farmers Homeowners federal program where the house payments were based on our total family income. We started out paying $250.00 a month. As our pay went up, we finally got to the highest our payment could be, at $350.00 a month.

One night I heard a noise from the kitchen in the middle of the night. I ask Ellis, "Did you hear that noise"?

We both were listening and heard the noise again. I got up and sneaked out into the hallway in my whities tighties. As I went down the hall, I was very quiet, and slow. I was trying to let my eyes adjust to the dark. Finally, I was on the edge of the kitchen and could not see but could still hear the noise. I was trying to see but could not.

Finally, I decided to turn on the lights and take a chance. I had my 44 magnum Smith & Wesson gun in my hand. I reached over and turned on the kitchen light. There was Grant, my 3-year-old son on top of the refrigerator with a block of Velveeta Cheese and a butcher knife about 10 inches long trying to cut him some cheese. He loved cheese.

He had pulled out the drawers of the cabinets and climbed the drawers like a ladder to the top of the counter. Once on the counter he climbed up on the refrigerator and was trying to cut himself a slice of cheese. He looked at me with a big smile and said, "Hi Daddy, I want some cheese"!!!

I looked at him with that big butcher knife and said in a nice soft voice, "Give the knife to Daddy" as I walked slowly to him. Once I had the butcher knife in my hand, I growled, "WHAT ARE YOU DOING"!!!

I put the knife over into the sink, I reached up and took him down from the refrigerator, hugged him and took him into the bedroom to tell Ellis what had happened. We had to tie his bedroom door shut until I went and got a lock so I could lock him in so he would not get up in the middle of the night.

Ellis noticed that Grant was crawling around on the floor but was favoring his right hand. He was only crawling with his left hand. After she mentioned it to me I started noticing also. We took him to the doctor and the doctor put him in the hospital for tests. It turned out he had an infection in his wrist. So, they had to do surgery on his wrist. The doctor said this was normal for young babies. Babies could get an ear infection and it would settle in their wrist or hip or any joint. They did surgery and kept Grant in the hospital for about a week. Every time Ellis and I would go to see him he would be off down the hall somewhere playing with one of the nurses, riding a big wheel. Grant had the nurses wrapped around his little finger. They just loved him. But after a week he went home and has done fine ever since.

In 1989 I was working for the Tennessee Prison for Women when I met Doug Leslie. He kept inviting me to church so finally I agreed. Ellis, Travis, Lacey, Grant, and I decided to go to Grays Point Baptist Church with Brother Doug Leslie and his family. Doug, Sherrie, Freddy, and Amy Leslie. We became good friends and we started to go to church at Grays Point Baptist church in Joelton, TN.

I also began to sing with a gospel Group called "The Redeemed Singers". But it did not last long because the leader was out for himself and not GOD. Enough said about that.

Brother James Humphrey was the pastor at Gray's Point Baptist Church in Joelton, TN. This is where I met Brother Dennis Green and Sheila Green, his wife. They had three sons Little Dennis, Nick, and Chris.

It was not long before I was leading singing for the church services. Then Brother Doug, Sister Sherrie, Brother Clay Dowell and I started a gospel group called "The Lambs of The Flock". Everybody could sing good, and Sister Sherrie, Brother Clay Dowell and I could write good, ordained songs. We started to travel to other churches to sing. Then Brother Dennis Green joined us and began to play bass guitar. We needed more musicians so Travis, my son began to play drums, and did very well.

I wrote a song God gave me called, "Thank You Lord For Loving Me".

Brother John Adams came to me, and said, "You all should record that song, it gives everybody such a blessing that hears it"

I said, "we would like to but it cost money none of us have", I replied.

Brother John asked me, "well how much does a recording cost"?

I explained, It would be best to do an album, we have a lot of songs already written. the more songs you do the cheaper per song it gets. There would be a cost for hiring a recording studio, session musicians, and then for the actual making of thealbum. And everybody was doing the Cassettes at this time. and I didn't know how much that would be, but I could find out. He asked if we wanted to record an album, then find out how much money we were talking about and let him know, and he may produce it for us.

I found a fellow

in Ashland City, TN. who was a session musician that had a studio in his home. He said he would do the whole 10 songs/album and play all the instruments himself, while using a drum machine or the drummer, for a flat fee of $100.00 a song. Then we would take the recording to Nashville, and hire a duplicating company to make the boxes, covers, and cassettes, or finished product. I set up a meeting with the Session Musician and Brother John Adams. They met and Brother John agreed to the deal. As a matter of fact, he paid for us to record a whole album of 10 songs. We sold them at the singings God sent us to, and made back Brother John's money. We had ordered enough that we sold about half, and he made back his money. He said to sell the rest for money to sponsor the Gospel Group and spread God's Word in song.

Brother John Adams was a retired Vice President of Commerce Union Bank, and knew how to handle money. He was about 68 years old.

brother John Adams then heard me preach one night, and came to me and asked if he could sponsor me to sign up to a, by mail, Bible Course, from "LIBERTY UNIVERSITY" whose Chancellor was Jerry Farwell the TV preacher. The whole course was done by mail. I told him I would be very interested. So, Brother John gave me the money to enroll him, and me in this course. Once we finished we were certified and have a certificate on file with Liberty University which is a great Christian College in Virginia. Both of us passed with flying colors.

Little Ernie lived with us until he was 17 years old and then he moved out. He moved in with his friend Clinton. I came home from work one day and he had all his things packed and told me he was moving out.

ERNIE FLATT, JR.

57. 1991- DAD (JOE ALLEN FLATT) DIES AUGUST 14.

Then I was set aside again for another year to be Ordained. This was more complicated. I was to be watched by 6 preachers from the area, preach every time I was asked at a moment's notice. Also, I had to have the 6 preachers that had been watching my life and actions to stand up for me at my Ordination and sign my Certificate of Ordination on that night. This was a way of saying you can trust this man I trust him and God Trusts Him. This was a great honor for me. I still have the certificate of Ordination on my wall with the signatures of the 6 Preachers on it.

I preached everywhere I could. I remember even preaching at the Cheatham County Fair one year and many, many churches.

WE had not lived at Bandy Road in Ashland City very long before Dad died on August 14, 1991. One day after my birthday.

I will never forget the phone call I got from Mom telling me that Rita had gone to his apartment and could not get him to answer the door. Dad lived in an apartment complex for senior citizens. She went to the apartment manager and the manager said any time they had to unlock a tenants door they had to call the Police.

So, the Police were called, there was a smell that Rita smelt at the front door when they opened the door. The Police ask Rita to stay outside while they went in. They recognized the smell. Rita had to stay outside while the Police went into the apartment. The Policemen came out and told Rita that her Dad was dead. Rita then called Mom and tried her best to tell her the news. Dad had been dead for 4 days before they found him in his apartment.

Then Mom had to phone call me in Tennessee to let me know. How hard that call must have been. I remember she said, "Are you sitting down"? "I got some bad news", she began. "Rita went over to see your Dad because no one had seen him for over 4 days. His car was there but she could not get him to answer the door. She went to the Apartment Manager and he said that the Police had to be called to use a security key and enter the apartment". She went on to tell me the story of how the police entered Dad's apartment and found him. Then they told Rita. Rita was crying when she called Mom. How hard it must have been for Rita to tell Mom what the Police had told her.

I called Ellis at work to tell her what Mom had told me, and she came home from work at Riverbend Maximum Security Institution right away. Travis, Lacey, Grant, Ellis, and I left for Ohio immediately after packing. I drove as safe as possible, but 80 miles an hour all the way there. Never saw a cop, but we didn't care if I did. No one slept. Made it there in 5 hours, 385 miles, never stopped this time even for the rest room.

After we got there, I watched TV every waking hour without knowing what I watched. People would say "What are you watching"? I would say, "I don't know"!! I am sure it was the same for everyone else. I spent over one whole week when Dad died barely knowing where and what I was doing. Dad's death was unexpected. Yes, he drank, but he always seemed to be super strong. Then he was gone. They had to do an autopsy on Dad because Ohio Law says you have to do an autopsy on everyone that dies outside of a hospital. He could not be buried until the autopsy was done and a reason for death was determined by the coroner. The body had to be released to the funeral home before there could be a funeral. As it turned out this took about 5 days to a week.

Everyone in the family gave Ellis praise for helping make phone calls, answering the phone, lining up appointments, and all things to help with the arrangements of the funeral. She jumped right in just like a family trooper at a time when none of us could, even Mom. I do remember making plans for Dad's funeral and going to the funeral home and gravestone place.

At the gravestone carver's place Dad's stone was a Black Shiny flat stone, with his name and birth and death on it and it also had a guitar on it.

I was studying the stone when Mom asked me, "Ernest what is the problem"?

I said, "Nothing Mom, it doesn't matter".

Mom said, "Yes it does son, what is the matter"?

I said with tears in my eyes, "Well Mom, Dad played a guitar with six strings, not four strings. The stone has a tenor guitar on it with just four strings instead of six strings". Everybody agreed, and Mom asked the stone carver could that be changed.

The stone carver said, "Yes, that can be fixed with no problem"!

When we went to the Funeral Home, we sat around a big round table and the Funeral Director walked us through the whole ceremony, cost and all. Mom had an insurance policy on Dad to pay for his funeral. But we were still on a budget. We got Dad a nice shiny black coffin, but we got the best vault (the coffin went into) they had. A Vault was required by Ohio Law. It was waterproof and all. We also decided on a Cadillac Limousine, to take Dad out in style. Dad would have liked that. We were also informed that Dad's coffin would be closed and not opened. Because he had been dead for 4 days and he could not have an open coffin.

I had to be talked out of going to the morgue to see Dad. Mom asks me not to go to the morgue to see Dad. The funeral director asked me not to go to see Dad.

He said "Son he has been dead for four days when they found him, Son you won't see your Daddy. Remember him the way you remember him now".

I said, "Is he going to be that bad looking? I can handle it! I need to see that it is him for closure"!

The funeral director paused and looked down at the big roundtable we were all sitting around and said, "Son I doubt if you will be able to tell if he is a black man, or a white man by this time". He said, "Son you will not see your daddy there". "Remember him the way you do now, please"!

Mom spoke up and promised me a copy of the death certificate once she got it if I would not go to the morgue. So, I said "OK"!

I got the copy of the death certificate a couple of months later at home in Tennessee from Mom by mail just as she had promised. I read every page, looked up every word I didn't understand in the dictionary. The thing that convinced me it was Dad was the death certificate discussing his Tattoos on his arms. He had 2 boxing gloves on his right forearm from the Navy, and a tattoo of a heart with a ribbon across it on his left upper arm. All us kids knew better, but thought Dad was so strong he would live forever. I guess this is when we kids of our generation, realized for sure, that this was not so. Everybody dies. Up to this point the closest one to die from our generation that we were close to was our cousin DannyEdwin Flatt. Danny had died 03/23/1977 while in the military.

Mom had been smart enough to have a life insurance policy on her and Dad. Just enough to pay for the funeral for them. But we didn't have enough to buy a plot. Mr. Lambert, the next-door neighbor, offered us a plot to bury Dad.

I told Mr. Lambert, "Thanks, but we need to bury Dad someplace where Mom could be buried by him when her time comes". They had divorced but both stayed unmarried.

Mr. Lambert said, "Well hell, I'll give you two plots. I got 4 of them. But I am not sure they are very good, because I was drunk when I bought them". It seems he had bought them when they were first building the cemetery, and it didn't look like much.

So, the Lamberts next door gave us 2 plots, one for Dad and one for Mom. As it turned out it was at Memorial Gardens out on North Dixie Lane, one of the nicest cemeteries in Dayton, Ohio. The Lamberts were wonderful people and neighbors.

And eventually they were buried right next to Mom and Dad in the other 2 plots. They lived next door in life and were buried next to each other in death.

Mom had to come up with the cash for opening and closing costs of the graves. Through this happening, I learned you got to have a burial plot, and opening and closing costs, as well as the funeral costs for anyone that may die in your family. The funeral home will wait for the insurance money to arrive for the funeral cost, which is the most, but the burial plot, and the opening and closing you must have up front.

I never got the chance to tell Dad how much I loved him before he died. And that I understand him better now. But I did go to sleep on the couch one time in Tennessee on Bandy Road, Ashland City, TN. and then someone knocked on the door. I went to the door and opened it. There stood Dad just outside my front door.

I asked, "Hey Dad what are you doing here"?

He never answered but came into the house and sat down at the table smoking his cigar.

I asked again, "Hey Dad what are you doing here"?

He never answered, but again puffed his cigar blowing the smoke into the air. I could smell the smoke from his cigar.

I asked one more time again, "Hey Dad, what are you doing here"?

Again, he never acknowledged me or answered but blew his cigar smoke toward the ceiling.

I said, "Well the hell with you, if you are not gonna answer me"!!!

Then I lay back down on the couch with my back to him, when all of a sudden, I woke up on the couch.

I turned immediately toward the kitchen table, but Dad was not there. I sat up on the couch with my legs hanging off and my head in my hands shaking all over. There was no doubt that Dad had just visited me. It was so real, I felt awake the whole time. I know one thing for sure, if it should ever happen again, I will not be so rude, and say what I said. I have always since then, wished I could take back what I had said.

There was never any doubt that Dad or Mom loved their children with all their hearts. I have always hoped I can make my children understand this also. We are all just doing the best we can and just like Dad sometimes there are demons in our lives. But we always have GOD on our side. And even with our praying and believing sometimes we just need a break from reality. We can't always give our children everything we want to give them, and we just hope that they end up better than us. I guess what I am trying to say is, with the continuing larger weight of the world coming down on our shoulders, how do you overcome the devil's tricks, even though you know the things that are right (GOD's WAY) through the reading of God's Word. Especially when the whole world is rejecting what we know is right. God help us!! God teaches us in his word, but we are human beings battling against super non-human demons that can enter our brain, our being, and our bodies, thank GOD not our souls. Thank GOD, not our souls! Jesus, please help us to overcome!!! We are just weak sinful humans!! But GOD made a way for us to be forgiven. Through his Son Jesus Christ. Thank GOD!!!

Grant was about 4 years old when one night I was watching' the kids while Ellis worked the second shift at Riverbend Maximum Security Institution. All of us, Grant, Lacey, Travis, and I had just finished eating supper. I had made supper, cleaned up and now was tired. As I was watching TV in the living room, and the kids were back in the bedrooms playing at Bandy Road in Ashland City.

Then all of a sudden Travis came into the living room and said, "Dad Grant is hitting' me"!!!

I said, "Ohh, he is just a little boy and can't hurt you, go on back and play, I'm trying to watch the news"!!

After a while Lacey comes in and says, "Dad Grant is hitting us"!!!

I said, "Oh, I already told Travis he is just a little boy and can't hurt you guys, go on back and play, I'm trying to watch the news"!!

About that time Travis came from around the corner and said, "But Dad, he's got a baseball bat"!!!

I said "Oh, that's different", as I jumped up and headed down the hall to the bedroom.

As I went through the door, and into the bedroom, Grant was jumping up and down on the end of the bed with an aluminum baseball bat all cocked back and ready to drill somebody with it as they came through the door.

I went through the door and hollered, "What are you doing boy"?!!!

He swung the bat just as I came into the room and hollered. I had to reach out and grab the bat to keep him from clocking me with it. I spanked his butt and put him to bed. I think Travis and Lacey were glad I did because he was a goanna clock somebody. He almost did me. We learned from this experience that Grant was a tuff little bugger.

One day Travis, Lacey, Grant and I were going down to the creek to just do a walk up and down the bank for a bit. The creek was a good walk down a small wagon road behind our house in Ashland City, then down a small hill to the creek. Travis was riding his bike with another neighbor older boy just ahead of Lacey, Grant, and Me. Travis and his friend went down over the small hill and out of sight. Travis had got to going too fast and hit a rut that had washed out of the road. This caused him to flip his bike. By the time I got to him he was crying, and his mouth was bleeding. I took him down the hill to the creek and had him wash his mouth out with water from the creek. But he kept crying. He was trying to push his bike back up the hill to go home with all of us. But he kept crying. I carried Grant to the top of the hill and sat him down and told him to wait for me there. Then I went back down to the bottom of the hill to help Travis get his bike back up the hill. He continued to cry. Finally, we got back to the house and Travis was still crying. All at once, I became worried because I knew Travis was tuff, but he would not stop crying. I had to call Ellis at work, and she did not trust the small hospital we had in Ashland City and suggested we take him to Nashville. She said she would meet us at Baptist Hospital Emergency. So, we got into the car, and I drove him to the emergency room at Baptist Hospital in Nashville.

When we got to Nashville they did x-rays and determined Travis had broken his jaw. They had to wire his jaw shut for a couple of months. I felt so bad because I had made him push his bike home. But I thought he had just busted his mouth, or I would have gone and got the car.

58. 1993- MOM / DAISY GETS HURT AT WORK AND HAS TO RETIRE-TRAVIS HAS BRAIN SURGERY.

Mom was at work at Saint Elizabeth Hospital. She was working the mental hygiene ward when a patient broke free from an orderly and ran down the hall. Mom was washing down a wall when she heard the orderly holler from the other end of the hall. She looked up and the male patient was right up on her. He grabbed her arm and swung her in a circle, and right back into the wall she was washing down. It broke her right arm and broke her right leg. She had to have her arm set and had to have a hallo put on her leg for some time. Mom never worked again.

Her health went downhill from there. Maybe it was because of being bed ridden for so long, or a diabetic, with high cholesterol, and high blood pressure. But she never worked again.

The thing that really bothers me is the administration of Saint Elizabeth Hospital in Dayton, Ohio where she had worked for 33 year, and they tried to get out of giving her retirement to her. She had to get a lawyer to make them do the right thing. And they were supposed to be religious. It was run by the Catholic Church.

Mom was going to her Doctor Herman C. Knoll, but she was not getting any better. Dr. Knoll was a good doctor and had been the Dr. For me when I lived in Ohio. But then Mom had a stroke. The whole left side of her face became paralyzed. She had to sit with a machine that shocked her face over and over. Finally, she had feeling back in her face except for the corner of her mouth. She would take a drink of water and it would run out the corner of her mouth. But this didn't stop Mom she kept shocking her face with this machine till she finally got all her feeling back in her face. But Mom seemed to get weaker and weaker. One of the signs she was getting weaker was she was not able to clean the house like she used too.

Also, in 1993 Travis was watching Lacey play a basketball game at her elementary school. Travis was in the stands sitting next to me and the whole family when he became dizzy. I helped him outside thinking maybe he was just hot. Once we got outside Ellis and I decided to call an ambulance. The ambulance came and got him, and Ellis insisted that he go to Nashville to Vanderbilt Hospital. They did a lot of tests on him and determined that he had a brain tumor, 2 centimeters long about 2 centimeters deep in his brain on the left front side of his head.

The doctor was the head of Neurosurgery at Vanderbilt. The doctor said the tumor had to come out because it was growing, and he would die if it was not removed. But the doctor only gave him a 20% chance of coming through without being blind, paralyzed, deaf, or dead. But he was going to die anyway unless it was removed. But he said we had some time to decide. We decided to talk to Travis and let him be a part of the decision.

We also took the no choice decision to GOD. We went to church and everybody prayed. Everybody called other churches and members at other churches all over the country prayed for Travis also.

I went to work, and the switchboard called me to the phone and said I had an important emergency call. I called back and it was the Neurosurgeon Doctor/ Professor from Vanderbilt He said he needed to talk to me and Ellis. He said he had someone that he wanted us to meet with that may have good news for us. We agreed to meet later that day. Ellis and I left work and went and got Travis out of school. We went to the Hospital and met a young surgeon that was one of 5 Doctors in the world that was able to do computer guided surgery. He told Travis, Ellis, and me that he could do the surgery and give Travis an 80% chance of coming through it with no problems. The way I saw it, after we took the time to pray, GOD sent us a Doctor that had totally turned the odds the other direction. From 20% chance of no problem to 80% with no problems. We made the arrangements for the Operation.

Travis's surgery was set for Wednesday, so Pastor James Humphreys of Grays Point Baptist Church called a special prayer service on a Tuesday Night for Travis. Brother James said, "We can wait until Wednesday night because the surgery was Wednesday morning. So, we would have a special prayer service on Tuesday not Wednesday for Travis. This way we put it in the hands of the LORD". We had the service Tuesday night before the surgery, everybody came, everybody prayed. Travis got up and gave God the praise before the surgery had even happened. I was so proud of my son.

On Wednesday morning at 5:00 am in the morning we all showed up at the hospital, Ellis, Lacey, Grant, and I. I believe the kids were just as worried about Travis as Ellis and I were. Several church people, Pastor James Humphreys, Brother Charlie Osborne, Brother Dennis Green, Brother Doug Leslie all came to the lobby, stayed all day, and prayed for Travis while he was in surgery.

Travis's brother, my oldest son, Ernie Jr., drove his car all night to get there from Dayton, Ohio. He had to drive around Kentucky to get there for the surgery. There was a snowstorm and they had closed Interstate 75 through Kentucky. So, Ernie had to drive around the east end of Kentucky to get to the east end of Tennessee. Then in a blinding snowstorm made his way on Interstate 40 to get to Nashville. It took him all night driving through a Snow, and Ice storm, but with God's help he got there.

When he got there he said, "There just wasn't no way I was not going to be here"!!

Travis was in surgery for over 8 hours. Then finally the Neurosurgeon came down to talk to us. I noticed as he began to talk to us there was a Gold Cross hanging around his neck. He had just come from Travis's surgery.

He started out by saying, "Well Travis is fine. He is sitting up in his bed eating some ice cream. I could not have gone any better. It was textbook right. No problems at all. We got all the tumor, now we still have to check him out for a few days to make sure there are no problems with eyesight, hearing, muscle coordination, and mental memory and such. But I don't expect to find anything wrong. It went as great as we would want it to".

We all kept saying "Praise God"!!

The doctor continued, "The brain does not have any pain receptors for itself. So, therefore, Travis is not in any pain whatsoever".

"When can we see him", said me and Ellis!

The doctor said, "You can go up right away. Like I said, though I will want to observe him for a couple of days, and then he can go home and do anything he wants except sports, or something where he could injure his head, and/or pull his stitches out".

We went up to see him in his room, and sure enough he was eating ice cream with a big grin on his face.

The next day Thursday he was walking up, and down the hall with one of those poles on wheels, and a plastic IV in his arm.

On Friday, the Doctor said, "There is no reason to keep you here so you can go home".

Travis was so very happy to go home.

Sunday morning Travis was playing drums in church, with his head all bandaged up, but not missing a lick on the drums. I wish for Travis to remember how many people prayed for him. And to never forget the blessing GOD gave him, because he was serving him, and believing in him. Travis has never had a seizure again.

Ellis and I realize how close we came to losing Travis. GOD gave us all a blessing, especially Travis.

E. FLATT FAMILY
Bottom-left to right-GRANT FLATT, ELLIS FLATT, ERNEST FLATT
Top-left to right-LACEY FLATT, TRAVIS FLATT

59. 1994-ERNEST ALLEN FLATT PASTOR-CHRIST COMMUNITY CHURCH.

While I was leading singing at Gray's Point Baptist Church, I was being set aside for one year to get my Preaching License, then for another year I was set aside to be Ordained. I was preaching anywhere; anyone would let me. Then I met Brother John Krance. Brother Krance was a retired preacher, and now was called as an Apostle for the Lord. He would go around, find a church that was closed down, and find a preacher to take it over, and get it back open again. Brother Krance heard me preach somewhere, and began to watch, and listen to me. Everywhere I would preach he would show up to hear the word that God gave me to give that night.

Brother Krance came to me one night and asked, "Brother Ernest, would you like to Pastor a Church"?

I told him, "Brother Krance, I can't Pastor, I have been married twice in my life".

Brother Krance said, "If I can set down with you at your home, and while using the Bible prove to you that you can be a Pastor of a Church would you be interested"?

I said, "Yes, if you can get it from the Bible, then I would be interested"!

Brother Krance asks, "Well then, I will need a time when you, and your wife will both be available. Will you give me a chance"?

I said, "Yes I would"! We set up a time when Ellis and I both could be available, and Brother Krance came by and in less than 1 hour he had convinced both of us that I was the husband of one wife.

Brother Krance said before he left our house that he was going to start looking for a church for me. It may take a while, or it may come quick.

Brother Krance took me to several churches but none of them did God tell us was a fit. Finally, he took me to a small country church on River Road in Nashville, TN. just off Charlotte Pike. This little church was built in 1824, before the Civil War. It originally was called Watkins Chapel. It had been left by the landowners for anyone to use for a Church or a School. It had been used by several Pastors down through the years as different churches. But now it was abandoned and needed to open back up. Brother Krance had gone and got the keys and permission for us to look at it.

We went down to look at the church. It was like a "Little House On The Prairie Church". Nice, but old. It had wooden floors, pews, pulpit, stage, bathroom with running water, electric heaters all around the outside walls, song books, and several ceiling lights that hang from the ceiling, along with ceiling fans. The toilet pipe was run straight out to the old outhouses that were right beside the creek. This would have to be fixed or code would get us. Also, it did not have any air conditioning.

Brother Krance asked me, "Well what do you think"?

I said, "Let me pray about it and I will make a decision as to what God what's me to do".

Brother Krance said "OK"!

On my way home I was driving, and Ellis was in the passage seat. I was praying as I drove.

Ellis asked, "Well are you going to take the little Church"?

I looked at Ellis and said, "You know if the church had air conditioning and the toilet fixed, I would take it in a minute"!

Then Ellis spoke back at me and said, "Oh you are just scared"! But it was not Ellis' voice it was a man's voice. I just about ran off the road, before getting my composer.

Then I looked at Ellis again and asked, "What did you say"? This time I was looking straight at Ellis when she answered.

Again, came the male voice from Ellis, "I said you're just scared"! Ellis's mouth was moving as she talked but I could tell she had no idea what I was hearing. She thought she was just talking.

I pulled the car over and was looking at her saying nothing, in amazement. She just kept looking at me as if wondering WHAT? I continued to look at her in amazement.

I finally said to God, looking at Ellis, "You know I am going to take that little church"!

In her own voice, Ellis replied to me softly and sweetly, "OK"!

I turned the Buick Station Wagon toward home. When I got home, I called Brother John Krance and told him what had happened. He said it was a sign from God. I agreed. I told him I would take the little church. I am not sure when I told Ellis about what had happened and how God had used her, if she believed it had happened or not, but I believe she believed that I did. I guess that was good enough for then.

Brother Krance went and got the papers, put them in my name and filed with the city government.

He asked me, "Brother Ernie, what do you want to call the church"?

I thought for a minute then said, "Well I want Christ in it. And it needs to be a Community Church". So, I said, "How about, Christ Community Church"?

Brother Krance said, "Christ Community Church it is"! He got the electricity put in the church name, helped us get a tax-exempt number from the Federal Government and get everything set up for the church.

I took the church over as Pastor Brother Krance guided me when I asked, but told me I had to pray and let God guide me. We had a lot of cleaning to do and fixing things, but we opened up in 3 weeks. Brother Krance helped me up until he died about 4 or 5 years later, but he always made me make the decisions with prayer to God. He would only advise. I remember he always said, "Be on time, lead the flock into the church house, and lead the flock out of the church house"! Be at the front when they come in and be at the back when they leave.

Brother Less Schutt and his family came down as the first family to join. He also became the first Deacon. Brother John Adams and Sister Mattie Adams also started coming to our little church. Brother John Adams became an Elder. Less' wife became the first treasurer. Then Ellis, my wife became the second Treasurer after Less' wife resigned.

The Warden of Riverbend Maximum Security Institution gave us a Heating and Air Conditioning Unit that we installed in the church. It was a used one but worked well.

Alan Jackson gave us enough donation so that we were able to have installed vinyl siding and new windows on the church. His donation was given to us to use a picture of the church on the front of his Album called "Precious Memories". We told him we would not charge him for using the picture of the church, but he insisted that we sign a contract and accept the donation. His album became the #1 Country Gospel Album of the year. but I must say all the credit was his. He did a wonderful Gospel Album of old sacred songs. He later made it into a Video DVD with more songs added. He also put out a Karaoke Version. Our church picture is only on the original CD. I have even got a wooden plac with the picture of the CD cover on my wall. They sold the Pac and the CD at Cracker Barrel. My Mom's favorite restaurant.

In 1998, I bought a Brand-new Dodge Ram truck. It was Red with silver along the bottom. It was a 6-cylinder, short bed with one seat cab. Although it was new it had that 50's look to it. I guess that is why I liked it so well. After all, at that time I was a Dodge man.

LACEY FLATT, ERNIE FLATT, TRAVIS FLATT-on the porch at a=Ashland City, TN.

60. 2000-APRIL 04, MOM / DAISY FLATT DIES AT VANDERBILT HOSPITAL IN NASHVILLE, TN.

Due to heart problems and the fact that Mom was not getting any better, we as a family decided to take Mom to Nashville, TN. To Vanderbilt Hospital because the doctors and hospitals in Dayton were not helping her and she was getting weaker all the time. The doctor in Nashville put her in Vanderbilt hospital immediately after he examined her. She was there for 3 days and was actually feeling a lot better. The Doctor said he had to get her stronger to do the surgery to help her. I believe she looked better than I had seen her look in years. She had fixed her hair, put make up on and had finally quit smoking cigarettes. I believe she felt very good compared to the way she had been feeling 3 days earlier.

I received an emergency call on my cell phone while at work from Mom's Doctor at Vanderbilt Hospital.

The Doctor said to me on the phone, "Mr. Flatt you need to come out here to the hospital".

I asked the Doctor, "I am at work, do I need to come right now"?

He said, "Yes Mr. Flatt your Mom has taken a turn for the worse you need to come right away".

I said, "I will be right there as soon as I can get there".

Then he said, "Mr. Flatt, take your time and be safe".

I said, "Yes sir I will".

I hung up the phone with the Doctor and immediately called Ellis at her work. She said she would meet me at the hospital. I started for the hospital and began to think about the last thing the Doctor told me.

"Mr. Flatt take your time and be safe".

I began to realize that the tone in his voice had changed from the way he had been talking. I didn't realize it at the time, but I believe Mom was already dead by the time he called me. He began to realize I might rush and get in an accident. But he didn't want to tell me on the phone that Mom was already dead. I called Lillian my sister on the way to the hospital and told her I would call her as soon as I knew something about Mom.

When I got to the hospital Ellis got there just as I was pulling up. We went in and the lady at the lobby counter told us to have a seat. After a moment she told us the Doctor wanted to talk to us and lead us to a room. There was nothing in the room, but a table and some chairs.

She said, "The Doctor will be right with you, please have a seat".

Then she closed the door. Ellis, and I were in the room by ourselves.

I looked at Ellis and said, "I don't like this"! She nodded in agreement.

Then the Doctor came in and sat down across the table from us.

He said, "There is no easy way to say this, so I am gonna just say it".

"Your Mother has passed away".

I said in shock, "My Mother has died"? My Mother had always been so strong, and then I remembered how strong Dad had been. But Mom had been so sick lately.

He dropped his eyes and nodded his head yes.

He began, "Today we took her to the operating room, and cleaned out her carotid artery in her neck. She was awake and doing very good. We were happy with the results. So we decided to take her back to her room. On the way back to her room she was talking to the orderly and just suddenly quit talking and lost consciousness on her gurney. The orderly wheeled around, took her right back into the operating room", said the Doctor.

The doctor then said, "We worked on your mom for 55 minutes. I got her heart to beating, but just could not build any blood pressure. Her valves in her heart were just fluttering/worn out and would not close off to build blood pressure. I just could not get her to build any blood pressure", he said as almost an afterthought. "Her heart valves were just worn out from all the high blood pressure. I am so sorry. I wish I could have seen her a year ago, maybe we would have been able to do something more".

Ellis and I were sitting there with tears in our eyes and I asked, "When can I see her"?

He said, "Let them get her cleaned up from the surgery and you can go right in and see her"

Ellis said, "I will help make the calls to Ohio while you see her".

I said in a whisper, "OK".

Finally, the Nurse came in and took me in to see Mom. She was still laying on the operating table and she just looked like she was asleep. The Nurse left me alone with her. I looked at her and held her hand as tears came to my eyes.

Then I said, "Well Mom you don't have to hurt anymore. Mom I love you and always will". Then I said, "Mom, we were just trying to get you some help".

Then I kissed her on the forehead and said, "Goodbye".

We had to make arrangements to get Mom back to Ohio for the funeral. The Funeral Home that had done Dad's funeral took care of all the arrangements with the TN. Morgue people, and came down and got Mom, and drove her back to Dayton, Ohio. Rita, Lill, and Terry handled all the particulars of the funeral because of me living so far away. And Mom had left Rita as the executor of her affairs. Rita did a great, and tuff job, of handling Mom's affairs. That is why, I am trying to get as much of my affairs together before my time comes. The older I get the more I think about these things, and don't want my children to have to deal with this, any more than necessary.

I bought a brand new, bronze, 2000 Dodge Ram with an extended cab. It had 4 doors, but the back doors were suicide doors and shorter than regular doors. It was an 8-cylinder, 5.2 liter with a short bed.

Also, that year Ernie, Jr. bought a 2000 Harley Davidson Custom Sportster. It was a pretty light Greenish Blue color with a bunch of chrome on it.

I went to visit in Ohio, and Ernie borrowed a Kawasaki 550 cc for me to ride and we went riding. This brought back my old desires to have my own motorcycle and ride again. I had not had a motorcycle since I owned one on Norman Avenue. It was a Honda 300 Dream like Elvis rode in the movie "Roustabout", except his was red, and mine was gray. I don't remember the year it was, 1985, maybe?

I had been running sound for the Cheatham County Fair each year which included the Fairest of the Fair beauty contest.

Lacey had entered the Cheatham County Fairest of the Fair Beauty contest about 2 years in a row and finished in the top but never won 1st place. She always looked gorgeous.

Finally, the third time she had a beautiful white dress, and answered all the questions perfectly. So, in August the year 2000, Lacey Elizabeth Flatt won the Fairest of the Fair Beauty Pageant and became "Miss Cheatham County". This also got her a spot in the Miss Tennessee Pageant. She went to Nashville at the Opryland Hotel for the Miss Tennessee Pageant. Lacey was just as beautiful as any of the other women in the Pageant, but it was easy to see that the other girls in the pageant had spent thousands on their dresses. We couldn't afford that. Lacey did not make it to the 10 top finalists, but this was only because at this level (Miss Tennessee) it was very political, and the families had to have a lot of money to spend. Lacey looked just as good as the rest and answered the questions just as good. But the judges were all newspaper, TV, and political people. I think she would have been in at least the top 10 if it had not been one sided.

MOM/DAISY GRIFFIN FLATT-in later years.

61. 2001-HAYLEE FLATT IS BORN AUGUST 10.

I remember that Haylee, my first Grandchild, was a little early being born. I just happened to be in Dayton, Ohio when she was born. I don't remember why I was in Dayton at that time, maybe to celebrate my birthday with Ernie and Sharon and the rest of the family. But while I was there Sharon Flatt (my daughter by marriage) had to be taken to the hospital, because Haylee was on her way into this world.

Sharon had some problems with Heather Miller's birth, (her first child by her first husband) and now she was having problems with Haylee's birth and Haylee ended up being a little premature. We were all worried about Sharon and Haylee. After a few days Sharon was weak but doing better. But Haylee had to be kept in an incubator. We could only get to take her out for a few minutes at a time. I got to hold her for a little while and she was smaller than most dolls that little girls have. I don't remember her weight, but she was very small, but very beautiful. I was just amazed at my first grandchild. Ernie and Sharon of course were very proud and should have been.

Haylee stayed weak for some time, but when she began to grow, she grew fast and strong. By the time I came back for Christmas she was big and strong as any other baby and still the most beautiful baby around.

2001 was also the year I bought my first 2000 Harley Davidson Custom Sportster. It only had 700 miles on it. I had gotten some money from Mom's estate and I used that money to start looking to buy a motorcycle. I bought it from Little James Humphreys. It had a Windshield and extra-large seat, and lots of extra chrome and high-performance parts on it. Screaming Eagle exhaust and Carburetors. I added saddle bags because I like the Heritage Softail look. It was Maroon Red with Black Harley Color scheme.

Grant would jump on the back of my motorcycle any time I was going on a ride. Lacey liked to ride too, but not as much as Grant. Ellis rode a couple of times but did not seem to care much for it. I figured it was because her brother Sullivan had been in a bad motorcycle wreck back when he was younger. Grant and I would ride to the movies, on back roads just anywhere. Grant loved to ride; he was my little riding buddy.

We loaded the Sportster up on my truck, strapped it down and went to Ohio to ride with Ernie. My Sister Lillian's son rode with Ernie, Grant rode with me, and Lillian rode with a friend of hers that had a motorcycle. We had a ball. We rode all over the Dayton area.

I would ride with Dennis Green around home because he had a Harley, and we would ride together. One day I went over to Dennis' house to see him and he was not home. I left his house to go back home and it was a beautiful day. I came to the end of Peter Pond Road where the stop sign was and turned right on Bear Waller Road and headed home. I was cruising along at about 40 miles an hour and that is the last thing I remember.

When I woke up, I was on the x-ray table at the hospital. There was Brother James Humphreys, Ellis, and a State Police Officer. They began to tell me I had a motorcycle wreck. I didn't remember anything.

The doctor told me, you have 8 ribs broken on the right side, your right pinky finger is broken. Plus, your right lung has collapsed. Also, we are not sure, but you may have a brain concussion. We are going to transfer you to another hospital in Nashville".

I asked, "How is my motorcycle"?

The police officer said, "It was taken to your house by James Humphreys Jr."

Brother James spoke up and said, "Little James took it to your house. It is gonna need to be repaired".

Then I remembered that my gun was in my zipped inside pocket of my motorcycle jacket which I didn't have on. I then began to worry about a child finding it and getting hurt.

I looked at the Officer and asked, "Where is my gun"?

The officers stopped talking and his face got very serious and asked, "What gun"?

"The one I carry in my inside zipped pocket of my leather motorcycle jacket", I replied to the worried looking officer. "I don't want a child to find it", I added! Then I added, "I have a permit to carry in my wallet"!

The officer reached over to a chair and got my jacket. He unzipped the inside pocket and pulled out the small, Northern Arms, Black Widow, 22 magnum, stainless steel, revolver, with black rubber handles. He pulled it out as if the gun was nasty with just his index finger and thumb.

The officer added, "Is it Loaded"?

I answered, "Wouldn't be much good if it wasn't"!

After he was able to see it good and was more comfortable with it he began to unload it.

Then he said as he was unloading the gun, "Mr. Flatt I will have to see your permit"!

I said, "Yes sir, it is in my wallet".

He replied, "Your wife has your wallet down the hall"! He had now unloaded the gun and asked, "After I call and check this out will it be OK to turn this gun over to your wife"?

I said, "Yes, she is a Correctional Officer, works for the Department of Corrections and understands guns".

He said, "OK", and went out down the hall with the gun to find Ellis and my permit.

I did not remember, but I was told by the State Trooper, what the witnesses said a 13-point Buck deer came from the woods and butted me on my motorcycle. I went airborne over the deer and did a somersault down the highway. They say the scratches on my helmet were caused by me hitting the antlers of the deer. The witness said I flipped 3 times and slid for over 30 yards. The motorcycle hit the deer and broke his front legs and he ended up in the ditch, trying to get up. But he couldn't. The State Trooper went over and shot the deer in the head to put it out of its misery. The Trooper said he gave the deer to a poor family for food.

Like I said before, I didn't remember anything until I woke up on the x-ray table at the hospital. I don't remember at the scene, the deer hitting me, hitting the pavement, the ambulance ride or anything until I was on the x-ray table. The last thing I remember was turning right at the STOP sign at Peter Pond Road, and Bear Waller Road, to head home.

I was transferred to another hospital down in Nashville by ambulance. Once I had a room, they did a whole lot of tests on me. Finally, the Doctor came in and said he had to re inflate my right lung. To do this he had to cut my side and insert a tube into my lung. He cut my chest between 2 of my ribs, just under my right arm. This was scary but didn't hurt much. The doctor sprayed something on my side and then took a scalpel and cut me open about an inch or so long. Then he took the tube with a squeeze pump on the end and stuck it in the cut and squeezed one good pump. This inflated my lung.

He said, "Lungs sometimes when hit hard with the ribs will deflate, and the only way to get them to Inflate back up is to pump them up. The tube goes through the lung tissue and the hole in the lung will heal really fast".

I was so sore on my right side from being bruised, I could hardly move. My whole right side was starting to turn blue form under my right arm all the way down to my hip.

The doctor said, "If you think you are sore now, imagine if you had not, had those leathers on. I would still be picking gravel out of your side, butt and leg, and the road rash would be almost unbearable. Also, here is your helmet and do you see these 3 scratches on your helmet, well if you had not been wearing it we would not be worrying about your side or lung because you may not be with us. God was watching over you, Son"!

I spent about 3 days and nights in the hospital before they let me go home. I was off work for over a month. My whole side had now turned totally black from under my right arm all the way down to below my hip.

I was sitting on the bed at home with my shirt off when Ellis came into the bedroom. She said, "What is that"?

I said, "What's what"?

Ellis looked at me and said, "Don't that hurt, go look into the mirror in the bathroom"!!!

I went into the hall to the bathroom and looked into the mirror. There it was, my collar bone was sticking up just before the shoulder. It was not sticking through the skin, but it was definitely sticking up.

Ellis said, "See don't that hurt"?

I said, "No, actually it doesn't"!

Ellis said, "You need to go to the doctor".

I said, "OK".

I went to the doctor, and he sent me to a bone specialist. He did x-rays and determined that my collar bone had been broken from the Motorcycle wreck. But it had not hurt, because of how much pain I was in, from all the other things that had been broken, and all the hurt I was in. The bone specialist decided not to fix it because it did not hurt. He said, "If it should ever start to hurt, then we could do surgery, and fix it. But we will have to put screws in to hold it in place until it heals, and also scrap the bone so it will join again". So, it was decided to not do the procedure at this time. Mt collar bone is still broken to this day.

Sometime later the motorcycle insurance man came to my garage to appraise my Harley which is where Little James had taken it. The appraiser said, "You are very lucky, these kinds of accidents, motorcycles and deer, happen a lot. But 80% of the time they are fatal. We can fix your motorcycle, replace your leathers, and helmet, but of course we cannot replace you. You were very, very lucky"!

My motorcycle was made as good as new by the insurance company. They sent it to a Harley Dealership. When I got it back, they had made my motorcycle look and operate brand new. All my leathers were replaced with better leathers by Harley Davidson Leather. Also, my Helmet was replaced by a better helmet. But by the time I was well enough to ride my motorcycle it was cold weather, and I didn't get to ride much.

Tennessee Preparatory School where I worked closed on July 31, 2002. Everybody at TPS lost their job including me. I had been trying to get a job teaching the same class at Tennessee Rehabilitation Center in Smyrna since May 2002. But TRC did not want to pay me the same amount of money I was already making. I was changing departments from the Department of Children Services, to the Department of Human Services. I should have kept my same money, but the Department of Human Services wanted to pay me $700.00 less a month. Mainly because the 8 teachers that were already at TRC were being paid less.

At about this time, Ellis, Lacey, and Grant moved out, and Ellis filed a divorce against me for Incompatibility. Then I got me a Lawyer and we began to have a Divorce Battle in court that was because she wanted half my retirement although she had already got hers and spent it when she was asked to quit Riverbend Maximum Security Institution. Also, she wanted custody of Grant, although Grant had told me that he wanted to stay with me. I told my lawyer that I had done nothing and wanted to file charges against her for adultery, but my lawyer said I could not file charges against her because she had filed first. It made no sense to me. But I was not going to let her take half of my retirement and take Grant just to get child support. I knew I would take care of him, and I have.

TRAVIS LEE FLATT & RACHEL FLATT

62. 2002-ERNEST STARTS TEACHING AT TRC, SMYRNA

Finally, on August the 23, 2002 I had to take the job at TRC with $700.00 less a month.

Grant and I had to move to Smyrna because I could not take a pay cut and still drive all the way from Ashland City where my house was to TRC to work each day. TRC wanted me for teaching Building Maintenance Trades and Groundskeeping. I would be teaching 2 classes for less money.

Moving was hardest on Grant. He had gone his freshman year of High School in Ashland City at Sycamore High School. He was so good at soccer that he had played ON the freshman team and the varsity team his first year of high school. He had lots of friends and now he had to move. He didn't like it much, but seemed to understand, and he hung in there. Remember I have said earlier that he was a tuff little bugger.

So, we moved to an apartment in Smyrna on Lakeside Drive. We ended up living there for 4 months. The apartment had 2 bedrooms, upstairs and a full bath. Downstairs there was a half bath living room, kitchen, and a dining room. Money was tight, and I didn't have a garage to keep my motorcycle in, so I was renting a storage shed to keep it in. Finally, I had to let it go. I just couldn't pay the storage, payment, etc. I gave it back to the bank and they sold it for more than I owed on it. But Grant, and I, both were sad that the Harley was gone. We really missed it. I lost all the money I had put down on it. But I just couldn't afford it anymore. I couldn't even afford to put tags on it and buy insurance

Every time a motorcycle would pull up beside us Grant would say, "I sure do miss our Harley Dad"!

I would just look over and say, "Yeah, me too"!

Grant began to make friends at his new school, Michael, Chris, and David became his best friends. They would come over to the house and hang out. Of course, they were friends at school too and watched each other's back. They told me that no one messed with Grant cause, Grant didn't take any shit from anybody.

But Grant could never get in on the click for the soccer team. The coach would put Grant in the game, and he would score and then put Grant right back on the bench and play the other players that were in the click. Their parents were putting more money into the program than I could afford. In return the coach was playing favorites, even though Grant could out play the other players. Grant never missed a practice and kept trying to impress the coach all the way up till his senior year. Then in his senior year Grant came to me and said, "Dad, I have had enough! I don't like to be a quitter, but this Coach just will not give me a chance. So, I am not going to do soccer this year"! I didn't want him to quit but I understood.

I went to Dayton, Ohio to visit Ernie Jr., Sharon, Heather, Haylee, Lillian, Jesse, Rita, Nick, Shawn, Layton, Logan, Terry, and Damon.

Lillian and I were on our way to Terry's house on US 35 when up in front of us a Ford Bronco spun and hit the concrete barrier in the middle of the interstate, then the Bronco flipped and rested upside down. I was driving and pulled over to the side of the road. I told Lillian to call the Police and I ran to the upside-down Bronco. When I got to the Bronco there was a Young Black girl still in the driver's seat hanging upside down. I crawled into the Bronco and all that was holding her in her seat was the shoulder and seat belt that was still fastened.

She was a slim, young, black, girl weighing about 110 pounds. She was scared to death and shaking all over. If she had undone the seat belt she would have fell and hit her head on the roof of the Bronco.

I ask her, "Are you OK"?

She screamed and answered, "Yeah"!!, "Get me out of here"!!!

I told her, "Don't undo your seat belt until I am ready and in place. I am going to lower you down so you will not hit your head"!

I reached up and got her by the shoulders and braced her.

Then I said, "OK, undo the seat belt".

She unsnapped the seat belt and I lowered her to the roof of the Bronco. Once I got her down, she was so excited she crawled right over top of me to get out of the Bronco. She got out of the Bronco and then I got out of the Bronco. We walked over and I got her to sit down in a safe place. About that time, we heard the scream of the distant sirens coming. The Police and an ambulance pulled up.

I told Lillian, "Let's get out of here because they will hold us up for an hour and we really don't know anything"!

Lillian said, "OK"!

So, we got back into my truck and went on to Terry's house to visit with Terry Flatt, my brother.

63. 2003-ERNEST & ELLIS' DIVORCE IS FINAL-DEC. 17, 2003.

Ellis and I fought in court for 2 years for a divorce settlement. Ellis had moved to New York with Lacey. While they were there Ellis reconnected to an old boyfriend from her past. While we were in court she began to live with her old boyfriend. We continued to fight in court through our lawyers. They were the only ones making any money. Ellis wanted to get married to her old boyfriend, she had before I met her. I believe she was catching grief from her boyfriend to get the divorce over with, New York law would not allow this, also TN. law would not allow it either. Anyway they could not get married while we were still married. Finally, Ellis agreed to make a settlement with me that if she would leave my retirement alone(she had already used her retirement with the State of TN.) and let Grant stay with me then I would agree to the divorce, and she would too. She was to pay $20.00 a week for child support. I did not want it, and she was not making much money, so I told the court $20.00 a week was enough, and I was going to put it into a bank account for Grant.

This was the same year that all nine of us teachers at TRC joined together and made up a bill and took it to TN. State Congress and got our pay raised back up equal to the other teachers in TN. That would raise my pay backup $700.00 a month. But to do that we had to sell it to TN. Congress at Legislative Plaza in Nashville to all the Congressman. Get Senators and Representatives to get behind it so we could have a bill to change the law and have them vote on it. Jean Chambers, one of my co-workers, knew how to write the bill, all nine of us vocational teachers signed it and it passed unanimously. Although the head people of the Department of Human Services sure didn't like it. The bosses of the Department of Human Service and Tennessee Rehabilitation Center fought us all the way. But Senator Jim Tracy, Marsha Blackburn, and Diane Black told all the bosses, now that the law had passed, that they better leave us alone or there would be a lawsuit coming from their office. They never bothered us after that again. But they did take our Longevity Pay by using a loophole. Longevity Pay was a perk we got for $100.00 per year of service, once a year, on our hire anniversary. We would get this extra check once a year up to 30 years which would equal $3,000.00. Then that was as much as you would ever get, $3,000 from then on, every year, but no more than that. You didn't start getting the longevity pay until you had 5 years in. That would be $500.00. Then next year you would have 6 years and you would get $600 for longevity. This started looking really good when you got up to about 10 years or more. $1,000 dollar was nice for Christmas, and my anniversary was on Thanksgiving every year. So, it was our Christmas money.

64. 2006-BOUGHT A HOUSE FOR GRANT & I

Grant and I lived in the apartments for 4 years before we could afford to buy another house. On 732 Dellwood Drive we bought a house just behind the apartments. It was in a housing plot called Lakeside Homes, just behind the apartment complex where we lived. Grant had made some new friends and He didn't want me to move to LaVergne or Murfreesboro. The houses were $10,000.00 cheaper in LaVergne or Murfreesboro. These were the next towns north and south. But Grant wanted to stay in Smyrna because he had made friends there and I didn't want to uproot him again and change schools on him.

The house we bought was what I was told was called a zero-lot line house. Our house and another house were separated by a soundproof firewall. Kind of like a condo. We had 3 bedrooms, 2 full baths, a kitchen with appliances, a living room, a single car garage, and the backyard had a 6-foot-tall privacy fence all around it. Grant took one half of the house with 2 bedrooms and a bathroom. He took one bedroom and made it into a computer room and one bedroom was his bedroom. So, he had his side of the house and I had my side of the house. We shared the living room and kitchen. My side of the house had the main bedroom, with a walk-in closet and a bathroom just off the bedroom. I also had the single car garage. I divided the garage with a wall and a door and took half the garage and made it into a Home Recording Studio. We had carpet all through the house except the bathrooms and kitchen.

Grant, and I, eventually got tired of the light colored carpet that we couldn't keep clean, and we installed Laminate wood flooring in every room except the bathrooms and bedrooms. Grant's computer room also got the Laminate flooring because all his friends came in and out and it was the first room where the carpet got dirty. We put an easy to install and easy removal rug over the laminate flooring that covered most of the living room except around the outer edges. This made the house look so much better than before and easier to keep clean.

I was still Pastoring at Christ Community Church, but the church attendance had fallen off so bad that only 2 families were keeping the little church open by the grace of GOD. We were also talking about closing the little church. Grant and I lived so far away, and Brother Leslie Schutt the Deacon then went through a divorce when his wife left him just as my wife had left me. The Devil was really coming against us and our little church. Eventually, we voted to close Christ Community Church on River Road.

I had heard the big tree out in the front of the church had been hit by wind, and the wind had blown off a large branch. The big branch had fallen through the tin roof, and crashed down into the church. The last I had heard was that someone had taken a bulldozer and dozer it down. I finally went back by there to find out if it is true, or not. I could not even tell the church had ever been there. It was all grown up, and no remains of the little old church were even there except where the driveway came up to the road. Lots of good memories were shared at that little old church for sure.

All THE FLATT SIBLINGS
(back row) TERRY GLEN FLATT, ERNEST ALLEN FLATT, Sr.
(front row) LILLIAN DARLENE FLATT, RITA NOREEN FLATT, MONNIN

65. 2009- BOUGHT A SILVER CHRYSLER 300 TOURING CAR.

ERNEST FLATT SR. with his new chrysler car.

It was Sunday and I was thinking my 2000 Dodge Ram truck was getting a lot of miles on it. So I began to think maybe I should get something more dependable in case I needed to go to Ohio for an emergency or something. So I prayed about it to the LORD and realized, OK, I can get something better but I could not afford a new vehicle at this time. I just had one income and now that Ellis and I had separated financially things were tight. But I did need something more dependable. I could trust my old truck around town and the Nashville area, but not on a long trip to like Ohio. Maybe the old truck could make it, but it was getting a lot of miles on it and things were bound to go wrong with it. So I considered going and looking at a used vehicle. So I went with Grant after church to see if there was a car available at CarMax. I needed a newer vehicle because my old truck had started giving me trouble and I just needed some more dependability. The salesman was showing us some cars online he had on the lot.

Grant spoke up and said, "Dad, you've been saying you really like those Chrysler 300's, why don't you ask him if he has got one of them.

I smiled and said, "Well son, I don't think I would be able to afford one of those"!

"Well," explained the salesman! "Let's look and see", he added as he clicked on the computer. He spoke up and said, "You know I got 6 of them, you want to go look at them and maybe test drive one", he asked me.

I said, "sure if you think I can afford one for the amount of payment I said I could pay", I replied. We went out and Grant wanted me to get the 8 cylinder Hemi engine one. But they had one with 28,000 miles, clean as a pin, with a 6-cylinder engine. It had been owned by a company as a fleet car. So, all the regular maintenance had been done on it. It had white crème colored leather interior and was painted Gray metal flake. So, I test drove this one, wondering if the engine would be powerful enough with a six cylinder engine. I realized immediately that this car was plenty fast, and strong enough for me. Plus, it would get better gas mileage than an 8 cylinder. It also had a stick, automatic shift, transmission. You could shift it by putting it in low, and moving the shifter to the side to change gears, or just put it in drive and go. So, I took the car. And paid it off 2 years early.

(My son Grant is still driving the car today. As a matter of fact, Matt, my son-law, still has my old 2000 Dodge Ram truck, he pulls his boat with. It is still going strong.)

2011-12

HAYLEE FLATT-Ernest Flatt, Sr.'s first grandchild

66. 2012- ERNEST SR. BOUGHT A 1911, ARMSCOR

The Rock Island Armory in the Philippines is an Armscor Corporation. The 45 caliber was made in the Philippines, 45 caliber, semi-automatic, black matte, handgun with the same specs as a 1911 Colt like what was used in World War I & II. This gun was the same military specs. Parts were even interchangeable with the 1911 Colt 45 caliber semi-Automatic pistol that the specs came from. But it was built in the Philippines and is about half the price of the Colt 45 1911 made in the USA.

Grant and I both liked the Colt 1911 that was used in both World Wars by the American Soldier, and the Colt model/brand was very expensive, and the Armscor model was about half price. So I bought one from the Armscor Rock Island Corporation in the Philippines online. It had to be sent to a Gun Dealer in the USA. So it was sent to Bass Pro Shop at Opry Mills Mall in Nashville, TN. where I picked it up, after a background check was done. I have been very happy with it. It shoots good and straight.

67. 2013-I BOUGHT GRANT AN ARMSCOR 45-1911, AND LACEY A SMITH AND WESSON 38 SPECIAL SNUB NOSE

Because he liked mine, on February 20, I bought Grant my youngest son, a Armscor, High Standard 1911, 45 caliber handgun assembled in Texas. A handgun with the same specs as a 1911 Colt like what was used in World War I & II. The difference between my 45 1911, is the parts were manufactured in the Philippines by Armscor just like mine. But Grant's handgun was assembled in Texas with the Pilipino parts under the "High Standard" brand. But it is the same gun, and cheaper than a Colt Brand 1911 semi-automatic handgun. We got it at Speciality Arms dealer in LaVergne, TN. So we did not have to send off for it and they did the background check on Grant and put it in his name right there.

(LaVergne Tennessee, is pronounced la-vern-e due to being french, but everyone in TN. pronounces it la-vern, Tennessee. FYI)

On February 21, 2013, I also bought Lacey a 38 special., recessed hammer, snub nose, Smith & Wesson, stainless steel, 5 shot Revolver with Pink Grips at Specialty Arms in LaVergne, TN. I felt that for lacey a safer gun would be a revolver. Because she was not around me as much for me to train her. But she wanted and still wants a semi automatic gun. I now think she could handle one after seeing her shoot. I also later bought her a Black Widow 22 magnum revolver, 5 shot pistol, by North American arms. It is a hideaway gun/back up gun. I already had one and she liked it. Grant gets all my guns when I pass, so I bought another Black Widow to give to Lacey when I pass.

Later on I bought Travis a 9mm semiautomatic pistol. It is a Beretta, we bought it at a Pawn Shop in Smyrna, TN, used but in great shape. I don't remember the date, but I believe it was close to one of his birthdays.

While I am mentioning it Ernie, Jr. gets all my instruments, Grant gets all my guns, (except the one 22 magnum for Lacey), Travis gets all my knife collection. Lacey gets my Harley Davidson Tri Glide, 2016. All this and any changes will be in my Last Will and Testament. The last Will and Testament will of course be the binding/lawfull document. I am trying to get all my affairs in order before the Lord calls me home, so there will be as little upset as possible for my Family. I do realize there will be clean up, cause I am a pack rat and don;t like to throw away anything I think I may have need of. So my children will have to deal with this. Pictures, documents, certificates, clocks, collectables, and such. Oh well.!!!!

Dad on his Harley Davidson, Tri Glide- that he got for his birthday.

Ernest Flatt at TRC-work in his office.

68. 2014-I BOUGHT 2 MOTORCYCLES IN ONE DAY

I had received my income tax return and had some money. Grant and I went to Murfreesboro for something and so we decided to stop at Bumpus Harley Davidson just to take a look at the new motorcycles. When we got there a salesman approached us and asked what we were looking for.

I told him I didn't have much money and was just looking around.

He asks me, "How much can you come up with"?

I told him, "We are just looking around, but I like the Heritage Softail".

He said, "I have a used Heritage Softail upstairs, let me show you"!

He took Grant and I upstairs and he showed us a 1998 Heritage Softail and said the payments would only be about $150.00 a month. I became interested but I needed a motorcycle for Grant also.

He showed me another motorcycle they took in on trade, a 1985 Honda. It was a 1985 Honda Sabre V-65 1100cc. He said he wanted $900.00 for. I became interested even more. I had $1200.00. I was thinking I need 2 motorcycles so Grant and I can ride together. Then he took me over to see the finance lady for the 1998 Heritage Softail to see if I could get financing. It came back the Heritage Soft Tail motorcycle could not be financed because they don't finance a motorcycle that old. But my credit was approved just not for this motorcycle. I became more interested but let down.

Then the salesman said, "Mr. Flatt let me show you something that may interest you"!

He took Grant and I back upstairs to look at another motorcycle that they had taken in on a trade.

"Mr. Flatt", said the salesman. "I did show you this one before when we were up here because it was sold, but I have just found out the deal just fell through and this is probably the best deal we have here at the dealership. This motorcycle is not a Harley, but I can give you a great deal on it. Because my boss wants us to get rid of it"

He showed me a motorcycle that looked brand new and had lots of chrome on it because it was a custom, He began to tell me about it.

"Mr. Flatt, this is a 2011 Kawasaki Vulcan Custom 903cc. I can sell you this for $400.00 down, at a cost of $3200.00 and get you financing for about $126.00 a month. We took it in on trade for a Harley and because it is not a Harley, my boss wants it out of here"!

I began to think, I have $1200.00. $400.00 dollars down that would leave me $800.00.

I told the salesman, "I need two motorcycles, one for me, and one for my son, let me, and my son talk".

He said, "OK, I'll be right back while you talk".

I told Grant, "Grant If I can buy this motorcycle for $400.00 down and get you the Honda Sabre for $800.00. We would have motorcycles to ride. Now, I know that they are not Harley's, but we could ride together. If I can get them to come down a hundred dollars, and make the deal, are you OK with that"?

Grant said, "Yeah sure, OK, Dad". I called the salesman back over.

I told the salesman, "I can put down $400.00 on the Vulcan, but as I said I need 2 motorcycles. That leaves me $800.00 I can give for the Honda V-65 Sabre. $800.00 for the Sabre out the door, tax and all. This is the only way I will be interested in doing the deal. Because I want my son to ride with me."!

The salesman said, "$800.00 out the door for the Honda"?

I said, "Yes, that leaves me enough for a down payment on the Kawasaki Vulcan".

Then he said, "Let's go back to the office".

Once we got back to the office he said, "Let me talk to my manager. I'll be right back"!

After some time finally the manager came to the door of the office and asked, "$800.00 for the Honda out the door, and you are gonna put down $400.00 on the Kawasaki"?

I looked at him and said, "Yes, but I gotta have them both so my son and I can ride together"! "Not getting any one of them is a deal breaker", I said.

The manager looked at me and said, "$800.00 out the door? DEAL"!

We shook hands and the deal was done. They gave us temporary tags, and we put the Honda on my pickup truck, strapped it down and Grant drove my truck home with the Honda strapped to the bed. and I rode the Kawasaki Vulcan home. Both of us were very happy.

But the deal between Grant and I, was for him to take a motorcycle training course, and get his license before he could ride the motorcycle. And of course, motorcycle insurance. I could not have let him loose on it and take a chance he would not have a wreck without training first. This way he has taken all the safety training possible because riding a motorcycle can and is dangerous, because car drivers don't respect a motorcycle.

Grant & Maggie-on his 2013 Harley Davidson "Softail Slim"

69. 2015-GRANT GETS A JOB AT ASPEN DENTAL SMYRNA, TN

On March 22, 2015, Ernest started attending church at **True Love Christian Church** in Smyrna, TN. Pastor Shane Towe was the preacher and he was also a Maintenance Man at TRC where Ernest worked.

I received a call from Ernie Flatt, Jr. he said, "Dad Aspen Dental has been trying to get a hold of Grant. The lab tech supervisor for the Smyrna store called me and asked, "Does your brother still want a job as a Lab Tech Trainee"?

Ernie said, "He sure does"!

Then Ernie said the supervisor said, "I have been trying to call him and his answering machine keeps saying it is full. So, I told him I would call you, and get the message to Grant, and have Grant call him".

I was so excited that I called for Grant from the other room and told him, "Ernie has a message for you". When Ernie told Grant his face lit up. He had been trying to get this job for a year or two. I think we had just about given up.

After Ernie got through talking to him, Grant put me back on the phone, Ernie told me after he talked with Grant, "Don't tell Grant but I am fairly sure Grant has the job in the bag. But I don't want him to be overconfident. So please don't tell him".

Grant called the number on Monday and he was set up with an interview and test. Grant took his interview and took his bench test. He had to wait a couple of days to find out if he got the job or not. Then the supervisor called Grant and he was told to give Big Lots his 2-week notice that he would start at Aspen Dental as a Lab Tech Trainee on Monday morning on March 30.2015 at 8:00 am.

On March 29, 2015 Palm Sunday, Grant started attending church at Free Love Christian Church in Smyrna, TN.

Grant started working March 30, 2015 for Aspen Dental as a Lab Tech Trainee.

In May 2015 Grant bought a 2015 Black on Black Dodge Challenger.

70. 2016- ERNEST FLATT HAS A MOTORCYCLE ACCIDENT AGAIN

On Father's Day June 18, 2016, Shane Towe, Grant, and I went on a motorcycle ride. Earlier that day, I had adjusted my brake pedal and told myself to be careful until I was used to the new adjustment.

Shane, and Grant were ahead of me and I went around a curve and saw they had stopped at a stop sign. So, I hit my brake to slow down, and I hit it too hard because of the adjustment and not being used to it.

Well, I hit the brake too hard and the rear end came around to the left. I was not able to straighten it out and went down on the right side. I went down to the pavement and slid to a stop. I had just put-on highway crash bars a couple of weeks before, and the crash bars kept the motorcycle off my right leg. But I couldn't get up because my right leg was pinned but not crushed.

Grant and Shane were stopped at the stop sign. Grant saw that I was down and left his motorcycle at the stop sign and came running back to me and lifted my 600-pound motorcycle off me. He lifted the motorcycle so hard that it went over to the other side and fell to the left side. About that time Shane came running up and helped Grant lift it back up off the left side, to put the kickstand in place, and stand the motorcycle up.

I got up and walked around for a while, and finally went over and sat down on a church porch to get my breath. I sat there for a while but did not get any better. Finally, Shane talked me into going to the hospital. He said, "I will ride home and get my wife, and have her come back and take you to the hospital, while Grant and I take the motorcycles home. Then we will come to the hospital". I agreed.

Grant and I waited, and finally Shane and B.J. got back. BJ is Shane's wife. B.J. took me to the hospital at Stonecrest in Smyrna. They admitted me to the emergency room to do tests.

Grant and Shane got to the hospital, and by this time they had found out that I had broken ribs, and a collapsed lung. The hospital then informed me that they had to transfer me to a Nashville hospital, because they were not a trauma unit. So, they called an ambulance to take me to Skyline Medical Center in Nashville.

Once I got to Skyline Medical Center, Lacey and Matt were already there waiting for me. Lacey was upset but handled it well.

Once I was admitted into the emergency room, they did tests and came up with the same diagnosis. They had to cut me to put in a tube and get my lung inflated again. Then they admitted me and put me in a room. I stayed in the hospital for 1 week. I was out of work for about 6 to 8 weeks.

This was my 3rd motorcycle accident in my life.

Also, in 2016, we found out that Ellis had developed 4 stage bladder cancer. She was sick and went to the doctor and that is when she found out about the cancer. She had to have surgery and her bladder was removed, and all her female organs. She was having trouble with her kidneys. She had to have a bag that hung on her right front to collect the urine. She was going through some rough times. It was also ruff for me and all the kids. They were all worried about her. She came down after she was feeling better to take a trip to Florida to see Universal Theme Park. She at this time was doing better and we thought she may whip the cancer. That was right after Father's Day, June 18. The reason I can remember it was, on Father's Day, June 18, 2016 when I had my 3rd motorcycle accident. Ellis drove me to a doctor's appointment I had while down visiting the kids. I was so sore I could only walk very slowly to the car and she did the driving. I really appreciated her doing that for me.

71. 2017-MOM/ELLIS DIES & LACEY GETS MARRIED!

Later that year and the beginning of 2017, Ellis Ann Smith, Flatt, Hitchcock, the mother of 3 of my children, had been in, and out of the hospital several times. The kids have been up to New York to see her. Grant has been up to New York at least 2 times. Travis and Rachel had been up there one or two times. Lacey has been up there 3 or 4 times.

On May 2, 2017 I had a TREE'S INC. truck run a stop sign as I was on my way home from work for lunch. I was going about 30 miles an hour, when I approached a cross street. I didn't have a stop sign but the cross traffic did. There was a big tree truck stopped at the stop sign. Then all of a sudden, the driver pulled out in front of me although I had the right of way. I locked up the brakes on my 2011 900 cc Vulcan Kawasaki motorcycle, and started to slide. My motorcycle slid into the passenger door of the big tree truck. The motorcycle and I bounced off the right front door of the truck. I did not go down, but the motorcycle front tire hit the truck went over on its side and I was standing across it. Just as if I had stood up and put my feet on the pavement. It hurt my back, and my left arm. My back kept me off from work for a while. Then my arm got infected from the inside out. My motorcycle, forks were bent, cracked my windshield, bent my front wheel and scraped up my exhaust pipes. I was off work for a total of 48 hours from work. My left arm had to be lanced by the doctor because it had become infected. He lanced it and then squeezed the infection out. Then he put me on antibiotics.

About this time Lacey and Matt decided to set a date to get married in hopes to have the wedding while Ellis could still attend. This was good news. Lacey and Matt moved up their wedding date to September 2017 because we had got news from Ellis's doctor that she may not have more than 6 months left. Matt and Lacey both wanted her to be a part of the wedding. So, the date was set for September 8, 2017 to be held in Aurora, New York. This was because Ellis was not able to travel very far. When Ellis heard the news, this made Ellis very excited, as well as everyone else in the family. Ellis became so excited she began to plan the wedding with Lacey. Ellis got to feeling better and was doing a lot of the planning to help Lacey.

After about a month went by, Ellis went to have her nymph tube replaced going into one of her kidneys. They found a kidney infection. Ellis was back in the hospital again. She had a Kidney Infection that had moved into her blood system. On top of that she had developed Pneumonia. So, they put her back into the hospital. After several days she was taken from ICU to a regular room. We are all praying she can last to Lacey and Matt's wedding. It means so much to Ellis, and everybody else in the family for her to be a part of the wedding. "God, we want her to be around forever, but I think Ellis is just asking to be here until after the wedding now. LORD, please give her this time. She is a strong woman, but I am afraid she is getting tired with all the sickness. Give her strength, LORD. IN THE NAME OF JESUS".

Ellis was in and out of the hospital several more times. She would get out and then in about a week she would have to go back to the hospital again. She was fighting a tough battle. It was getting closer to the wedding date for Matt and Lacey, but Ellis was not doing much better. Lacey was talking to her Mom almost every day on the phone. But her Mom was not getting any better, and she was back in the hospital again. It was now down to the next to last week of July.

I was going to be driving my truck to Aurora, New York. Grant, Travis, and Rachel were going to be riding with me. I promised to pay the expenses, because none of them had much money, and would have to take off from work without pay.

Grant, Lacey, and I had gone and ordered, Grant's suits and mine. They were blue 2-piece suits with pink ties. Lacey picked them out, and Mat and Ryan would come and get theirs at another time.

Right after we got our suits, Ryan and Matt ordered their suits. It was now down to the next to last week of August. And Ellis was still in and out of the hospital. We were still praying she would be able to make it till September 8.

Ellis and Lacey had planned everything they could control.

August went by and I don't think Lacey and I even remember much about our birthdays, other than I got my Trike. We were all so concerned about Ellis. I am sure Lacey was from talking to her.

The insurance company totaled my 2011 900cc Vulcan Kawasaki motorcycle and paid off my loan and gave me enough to get another motorcycle. My family, Ernie, Travis, Lacey, and Grant said to me, "We know you are not going to quit riding, but how about you buying a 3-wheel motorcycle this time. A Trike".

I said, "Well let me see if I can afford one, they cost a lot".

When I went to the doctor his nurse told me that she knew someone that had a Harley Davidson Tri-Glide Ultra for sale. I wanted at least a 2014 Trike. When I called, he said he had one that was 2014 metal flake Blue. Brother Shane and I went and looked at it. I had already been approved by the credit union for a loan. I took pictures and sent them to Little Ernie. Ernie got back in touch with me and said, "Dad it may be worth what the man is asking but that is not a 2014. It is 2013 or older. This made me afraid of the deal, so I backed out.

I went to Bumpus Harley Davidson in Murfreesboro, TN. about 6 miles from home to check to see if they had any. I found a 2016, Tri-Glide Ultra, Vivid Black, with only 1024 miles on it. Almost new, barely broke in. This Trike they had was equipped with Navigation, anti-lock brakes, Bluetooth, AM, FM, Sirius Radio, Phone Hands Free, Reverse, and the engine was a 103, everything that I needed. I began to make a deal with them. They said if I would take the 3-day, motorcycle class they would pay for it and they could give me a very good interest rate to get the payments where I wanted to be able to afford the bike. I agreed. I took the class, and on Sunday, August 13, 2017, my birthday, I left with my all Black & Chrome Harley Davidson, Tri-Glide Ultra. I rode home on my Trike as proud as one could be. The LORD was really good to me I was thinking.

Finally, it was coming on the 1st. of September and time for us to drive to Ernie, Jr. house in Springfield, Ohio. Our plan was to drive to Ernie and Sharon's house and stay for a day or two to divide the trip into half, to make it easier traveling. Actually, it was Ernie's idea, and it sounded good to me.

We loaded up my 2017 Silverado, and Grant, Travis, Rachel and I started to Ernie's house in Ohio. Once we got there, we had a great bonfire, drank some Corona, and cooked s'mores. Course Ernie and Sharon and the girls are always good to us and feed us great when we visit. They are great hosts. We had a great time. Tuesday, Sept.5, 2017, we loaded up the truck and headed for New York. Ernie, Sharon, Heather, and Haylee were coming up later in their MotorHome.

I got a phone call from Lacey. She said that Ryan (Matt's Best Man), well, his wife, the mother of his 2 children had been killed. Even though they were separated, Ryan would not be able to be there and be the best man. So, Grant would have to step up and be the best man. Grant stepped up and said, "OK".

Once we got to Aurora, Lacey had a place for Grant, Travis, Rachel and I to stay at. It was right on the lake. This was a house that belonged to a friend of Lacey, and Ellis. This lady owned another larger house on the lake right next to the one she usually rented out. She let us use the smaller house for no charge seeing as it was off season, and she loved Ellis, and Lacey very much. We were very comfortable.

We found out once we got there that Ellis was still in the hospital. It was beginning to look like the wedding would have to be held in the hospital. As a matter of fact, Lacey had pretty much decided that would be how it was going to go. Although Ellis was still determined to leave the hospital and make the wedding.

Ernie and Sharon had decided to rent a campground to park their motorhome. It wasn't far from Aurora. And they rented a car. Ellis was in the hospital that was in Syracuse, New York. Another city 45 miles away from Aurora. So, we spent our days at the hospital, in Syracuse.

The first day we got to Ellis' hospital room in Syracuse, She was sleeping most of the time. She would wake up, just long enough to throw up. Then she would go back to sleep. One time everyone went to go get something to eat and I stayed with Ellis while she was sleeping. She woke up and started to throw up. I grabbed her a pan. But it was too late. She had thrown up all up the front of her bed gown. I thought, I will call the nurse once she is finished throwing up. Ellis had the pan pulled up to her chest and threw up some more. The throw up was dark, bile looking substance that smelled awful. I felt so sorry for her. After she had stopped throwing up, she looked at me and said. "This ain't no picnic, Ernie". I looked at her and said gently, "Yea, it doesn't look like it is, Mom".

Even though we were no longer married, I still called her Mom, just like the kids did. After all, she was my best friend for 24 years and still was.

They took Ellis for an x-ray later after they had cleaned her up from the bile, throwing up. She slept most of the rest of the day. They had to give her meds so she could stand the x-ray, so she slept after coming back to her room. Ellis had many friends and family that were there at the hospital. They came to see Lacey get married, but I think they came also because Ellis may not be around long. Her older brothers were there, Sullivan and his wife Debbie were there. Her oldest brother Sheldon came also. They all came from farther distances that we had. They flew in. Bill's family was there. Several friends from the lake, Aurora, NY area. Sorry but I can't remember all their names. Plus, things were a whirl with all that was going on.

September 7, 2017. The next day when we got there, we found out they had put a tube in her nose down into her stomach. She didn't like the tube but began to realize that pumping the bile out of her stomach was making her feel better. It was pumping the bile up out of her stomach and into a glass container/jar. And she was not needing to throw up and was even feeling better. She began to joke and laugh a little with everyone. We even began to think "Maybe she will be able to walk down the aisle with Lacey. But we were sure it was going to have to be held in the hospital".

Ellis' team of doctors came in and began to talk to mostly Bill, but Bill told them we were all family, and it was OK to talk in front of us. And, for us to speak up if we had any questions.

So, the head doctor began to explain. "We did an x-ray of her stomach and we have found a mass. We believe we need to keep her comfortable using any meds that is needed. She doesn't have long", explained the doctor.

Bill spoke up and asked, "How long does she have doctor"?

The doctor spoke and shook his head, "I don't know".

The Doctor spoke in questions as he shook his head.

"Hours"?

"Minutes"?

"3 days"?

"But I think we need to just make her as comfortable as possible".

Then the Doctor asked if there were any questions.

Then the doctor and his team left the room.

Then with tears in his eyes Grant went to Ellis' bed side and said, "Mom do you want anything".

"Yes, I want a cheeseburger", answered Ellis with a big smile.

Someone spoke up and said, "Well, Missy (Her family always called her Missy) we are going to have to ask the doctor to see if it is OK".

They left the room and in a little while came back and said, "The doctor said she can have whatever she wants"!

So, Grant and Travis left to go find a hamburger place. When they came back with Ellis' hamburger, she ate it all.

After she finished the hamburger, someone asked her again "Mom, Is there anything else you want"? Ellis grinned from ear to ear, and said," Yeah, a Margarita".!

Again, someone said, "Well, Missy we will have to ask the doctor again".

They left the room and in a little while came back and said, "The doctor said she can have whatever she wants"!

So, Grant and Travis left the hospital for the second time, to go find a liquor store. When they came back, they had the makings to mix up a Margarita. Best I remember, Lacy mixed it for her. Ellis drank every bit of it.

This day was the wedding day. When we all got to the hospital, the hospital had got us a big room for the wedding, and they also furnished a lady to play the piano, and an extra part to add to the wedding cake.

Ellis was very weak, so they brought her down in a wheelchair. Ellis was very determined to get out of the wheelchair to walk with Lacey, and I went down the aisle. Ellis was too weak, but she insisted on getting out of the chair. Lacey, and Bill was trying to talk her out of it but was having no luck. Ellis was having none of it. She was going to walk.

My heart was breaking. So, I knelt down beside her chair, and said, "Mom, they can put your dress on you while you are in the chair. I know you want to get up and walk with Lacey, but Mom, you're just too weak, and we are afraid you might fall. So how about Bill just push you in the chair alongside me and Lacey, right down the aisle. OK"? This seems to appease her, and she nodded her head in agreement.

ELLIS & LACEY WEARS THE SAME DRESS-for their weddings.

They got Ellis' dress on, and the music started. Lacey held my arm, and Bill pushed Ellis right alongside. Down the aisle we went. When we got to the front, I gave my wonderful daughter away. One of the proudest moments for a Father is to give away his daughter to a young man she truly loves and will make her happy all her life. And Matt Robertson was just that man. I could not have picked one for her any better.

The wedding went without any hitch. It was beautiful.

After Matt and Lacey said their vows, which was beautiful, Lacey turned and asked Austine, (Matt's little girl) to come forward. Lacey knelt down and spoke to Austine.

"Austine, I am not going to try to take your Mothers place, But I love you as much as I love your Daddy. I will always be here for you, should you ever need me. I want to give you this".

Lacey reached over and took from Grant, 2 silver necklaces with half hearts that matched together to make one whole heart. She gave one to Austine and put it around her neck and fastened it. Then she took the other one and gave it to Austine, so she could put it around Lacey's neck and fastened it. There was not a dry eye in the place.

We had to get Ellis back to her room, because the doctor didn't want her up out of bed for more than a few minutes. But Ellis stayed until she was ready to go back. You can bet on that!

September 9, 2017 it was planned for all the wedding party to go to Niagara Falls. But Lacey did not want to leave her mother, because she was feeling so weak. So, Lacey stayed, and the Wedding Party went to Niagara Falls. Before we left, I told Lacey that if I did not hear from her, then we would go from Niagara Falls back toward Ernie's house in Ohio. This was because; everyone had to get back to work.

At Niagara Falls we rode the Maid of The Mist, took lots of pictures and had a great time.

Once we got done at Niagara Falls, I called Lacey and she said her mom was sleeping, but very weak. I told Lacey that Ernie, Sharon, Heather, and Haylee all needed to head home for work, and school, and was going to head from Niagara Fall back to Ohio. Ernie wanted my group that was riding with me, Grant, Travis, Rachel and Myself to follow them back as far as Ohio and spend the night. He was so concerned about me driving and falling asleep. Lacey said that she thought her Mom was just hanging on until she left the hospital.

I told Lacey, "Well maybe it would be better for you to just go home and get a phone call later. She didn't want you to see the end anyway".

Lacey said that maybe she would leave tomorrow. I asked her if she was sure that she did not need me to come back.

Lacey said "No, there is nothing any of us can do".

I said, "OK if you're sure, then I will head back with everybody, some of them had to get back to work also".

I followed Ernie and Sharon's RV all the way back to Ohio.

MOM/ELLIS when she was still healthy-she died-September11, but, she made sure she was here for Lacey & Matt's wedding. She wasn't gonna miss that.

"SHE HAD TO GO, BUT IT LEAVES ALL OF US SAD".

Travis, Rachel, Grant and I left in my truck, from Ernie's house Monday morning after visiting Rita, and Nick up until about noon.

We were just at the edge of Smyrna, TN. when we got a call from Lacey.

Lacey said, "Dad we are about halfway home, where are you"?

I answered, "We are just at the edge of Smyrna. Why"?

Lacey answered as she began to choke up. "I just got a call. Mom has passed away, peaceably a while ago". I pulled my truck over. The phone was on the truck speakers. Everyone in the truck began to weep. Finally, I began to be able to ask Lacey, "Are you OK"?

Lacey choked out, "I am as well as can be expected".

I ask, "Is Matt driving"?

She said, "He is".

I said, "Good"!

Lacey said, "Mom didn't want a funeral, she is going to be cremated, and her ashes spread in Arizona, in the desert, where her Mom and Dad's was". "Bill is going to send me half the ashes and, Travis, Grant, and I will someday in the future take her ashes to the Desert. But that will be a long way off."

Lacey spoke slowly and said, "I am also going to have some globes made with just a little bit of her ashes made for each one of us".

I said, "I understand, I love you, call me when you get home".

Later on, Maybe a month or so, Travis, Lacey and Grant, all got money from their Mom's Life Insurance.

Grant decided to buy himself a used Harley Davidson motorcycle so he could save some and still get a Harley. Which he has wanted for a long time. So, he prayed about it for several weeks before going to look for it.

We went to Bumpus Harley Davidson to just look around after church.

Grant bought a 2013 Harley Davidson, Softail Slim, from Bumpus Harley Davidson where I had got my Trike. It had 10,000 miles on it and was in great shape. It is a Blue Metal Flake and looked great. Grant was so proud. They gave him a temp tag for his motorcycle, and he rode it home.

Grant had been riding his motorcycle for about 3 weeks. We got a call, and Bumpus said his tag for his motorcycle was in. So, we decided to stop at McDonald's in Smyrna to eat on the way to pick up his tags for his motorcycle. It was Saturday, December 02, 2017, and we had just got finished eating at McDonald's and Grant was following me. We were at Nissan Blvd. and Ken Pilkerton when the cautions light caught us. I stopped, and I heard this squealing of tires. At first, I thought it was me. But then I looked into my mirror and I saw Grant going sideways and going down on his motorcycle. Man do you know how it feels to look into your mirror and see your youngest son having a motorcycle wreck, and there is nothing you can do.

First the motorcycle back end when to the left, then went down on the right side. Grant had cleared the bike and was sliding on the pavement and so was the bike.

Then the bike bounced upright and flipped over to the left side and spun around facing the other direction. Then as the bike began to slide again, on the left side the windshield came off, and began to slide down the road. All the time Grant is sliding on his right knee and hip. He also took a hard hit to the right Shoulder.

Grant had not even paid the first payment on his new motorcycle.

72. 2018-OUR FAMILY STILL IS GOING STRONG

Grant met a wonderful Young Lady at Slaughterhouse last Oct. 2017. A prayer answered by GOD.

Then after the holidays of 2017 around Jan. 2018, they began to date. Her name is Mary Margret Spencer Henris, or "Maggie" as she prefers. And I have noticed a change in Grant to the better. Grant had been treated so badly by some girls in the past, he was lonely, and I believe a little afraid to trust anyone again. But I believe he was lonely most of all. Grant said he waited to date Maggie because he was still getting over losing his Mother. Although he said he would never get fully over losing his Mother.

Maggie brings out the best in Grant. I have noticed he doesn't drink as much as he used to do. They go to church on Sundays, sometimes with me, sometimes at Maggie's church. Grant has always gone to church with me, but now he has someone other than me to go to church with. This is good.

2018 was a good year except for holidays. Every time a holiday would come around, we were reminded that Ellis was no longer with us. Both my boys (Travis and Grant) miss their Mom, but I think it bothers Lacey the most. Naturally, she was a lot closer to her Mom than the boys. The girls were always the closest. She moved to New York with Ellis when they left Tennessee. She talked on the phone more often to Ellis than the boys did, and once she moved back to Tennessee. Lacey also made more trips to New York to see Ellis than the boys. Don't get me wrong, not that the Boys didn't love, and miss their Mom, it was just the Girls (Ellis and Lacey) were closer even when they disagreed with each other. Ellis, and her Mom, (Shirley) were the same way. One minute they were disagreeing and crying. But the next minute they were laughing together. Ellis, and Lacey were the same way.

Anyway, as I was saying Lacey took her Mom's death the hardest. Especially, around holidays, Ellis' birthday, and such. But it does seem that with the passing of time it gets a little better for all of us especially Lacey. But as I was saying the beginning of 2018 was rough around Holidays for Lacey. As a Family we tried a little harder to get together on Holidays to give each other some support.

On top of everything else with losing their Mom, my children found out that Ellis' two brothers, and one of the brothers wife was trying to cut Bill (Ellis' husband at the time of her death) and my 3 children out of the Ellis' part of the inheritance that was left by Ellis' Mom and Dad. They had a letter sent to all 4 including Bill, that wanted them to sign away their rights without even knowing how much it was, or if it was right, or not. Because it wasn't made a provision in the will what to do if one died ahead of all the rest.

Although none of it would, or should be mine, my thinking is that Ellis' part should go to her heirs. That is the only thing that is right and correct. And Ellis' heirs would be Bill, (her current husband at death) and her three children, (Travis, Lacey, and Grant). This is the only fair and common (non-greedy) thing to do.

So, all 4 got a lawyer and filed suit in Florida (this is where the GrandParents lived when they passed) to try and get the court to make the Uncles and the Aunt do the right thing.

We are waiting to see what the court declares. If the court declares that Ellis' heirs have not a case, we will move on. The Uncles and Aunt had very little to do with my children anyway, and the fact that they didn't just do the right thing to start with, is a real shame. They are smart people and could have done the common sense thing on their own. Without, there having to be a court suit. But just the same, no matter which way it turns out, I suggest to my family that forgiveness is Jesus' way. Forgive and move on.

Time to change the subject and move on.

Lacey had us all over at Thanksgiving for a great meal at her and Matt's apartment. Grant, and Maggie were there. Travis, and Rachel were there, Austine, Lacey and Matt of course were there. We had a great time and a great meal.

We did have a great Christmas 2018. Lacey got us all together at her and Matt's apartment for Christmas Breakfast. We had their apartment full! Austine was there and of course Matt and Lacey. Luanne (Matt's Mom) was there.

Travis and Rachel brought along Rachel's grandmother. We were sure glad to have her there with us. She has been so good to Travis, and Rachel down through the years. She has helped them out so many times.

Grant and Maggie were there. And of course, I was there.

Then we opened Christmas Presents together.

Austine opened her presents first. Then we all began to open presents.

Finally, after everyone opened their presents, Lacey stood up and said, "Last Dad we got one more present for you. We all went together, including Ernie and Sharon in Ohio, and bought you this present". She reached behind her and pulled out a big box all wrapped up in Christmas Paper. I was astonished.

I began to open it, pulling off the wrapping paper, till I got to a brown box. But I still didn't know what it was. So, I ask, "What is it? Is this a joke, a box in a box"? Lacey said, "Well open it"! So, I began to open the brown box. Once inside the brown box I saw a soft, black, guitar carrying case, and on the front of it was the Logo for Martin Guitars! No matter how hard I tried, tears came to my eyes. I sniffed out, "you bought me a Martin"! Lacey began to explain "I called Ernie and said "What would Dad want for Christmas? We are going to go together and get him something".

"I know what", Ernie explained to me! "Dad has always wanted a Martin Guitar; Martin Guitars are the Harley Davidson of acoustic guitars. But they are expensive, just like Harley-Davidson Motorcycles are. But if you all want to go together, I will put in too, and we will get him a Martin. I know just the one he would like, and it is one of the cheaper ones they have". Then Lacey said, "So, Ernie and I made the arrangements, but we all went together. I opened it like Ernie said to do, when it came, just to check if it was OK. It seemed OK to me".

With tears beginning to form in my eyes, I unzipped the carry case, excited to see the guitar.

When I opened the case, it was an all brown, DJR-E Martin. That stands for Doughnut Junior with a Fishman electric pickup in it. I had always said that I would like to have a small Martin guitar like Marty Robbins used to play on the Grand Ole Opry. Now just to show you, God knows what he is doing. Marty Robbin's Martin was small but had a blond front. This Martin was the exact same guitar. Except it is all brown, but it IS a Martin. It tuned good, like a Martin should. And it looks just like the first guitar I ever owned, and learned to play on, when I was 10 years old!

(Look back at 1960, chapter 29) it was the one my Dad bought for a dollar for me, and my Mom stomped all to pieces.

I am so glad to have this Martin. I have owned several guitars in my life, but this is the first Martin Guitar I ever owned. And the fact that my family bought it for me, I would not take anything for it. There are two guitars I have always said I wish I still had. The first one I had and learned on, and the Epiphone that belonged to Dad. He bought it new while I was learning to play so we could play together. Later in life, he gave to me and it was stolen in the 70's from my house on Wolf Road, in Dayton, Ohio.

When I went to Ohio after Christmas, I took my Martin with me to Ernie's house. Ernie told me the rest of the story.

Ernie said he told Lacey, "I am getting one for Christmas and I've been checking on prices. The one Dad would like is about $600 something, total".

Lacey replied, "How about you order it, since you know what it is, let me know how much we need to send you".

Ernie checked and found they had one that was brand new, but the box had been opened and he could get it for a big discount. He called Lacey back, and they agreed to order it. Ernie had it sent to Matt, and Lacey's Apartment.

I have been playing it in church ever since. This guitar is so very special to me. Priceless!!!

I ordered a Chrome Tree of Life Branch Custom fingerboard inlay from online. I installed it on the Martin, because I planned on playing it in church for GOD, in honor of my family's gift to me.

I also bought a set of strap locks, and put those on it, so my strap would not come off, and take a chance of dropping it.

I ordered one more thing. I ordered a hand made custom Lute Sound Hole cover to stop feedback when I have it plugged in to an amplifier. It is wood with my initials on it in cursive. *EAF*

73. 2019-ERNEST A. FLATT, SR. RETIRES FROM THE STATE OF TN.-DEPARTMENT OF HUMAN SERVICES

When I got out of music for a living in 1985, while still in Ohio. I went to a Vocational School, or Electrical Trades and passed.

I got my Electrical Apprenticeship and became an Electrician in Ohio. My first Job as an Electrician was with Combs Electric doing residential electricity.

When I came to Nashville, TN. in 1986, I got a job with the Opryland Hotel as a Heat & Air Maintenance man. repairing ice machines and setting thermostats, etc. My electrical knowledge got me the job because they wanted me but did not have an opening in Electrical. So they gave me a job in the Heat & Air department.

After about 6 months I got a job with the State of TN.

I started as a Building maintenance Worker #2 in November 1986 at The Tennessee Youth Center in Joelton, TN.

Then I was transferred to The TN. Prison for Women in Nashville, TN. and was promoted to a Building Maintenance Worker #3.

Then I was riffed to the old TN. State Prison.

Then I went to Riverbend Maximum Security Institution-at Nashville, TN.

On March28, 2019 was my last day at work. As a Vocational Instructor per Specialty with the State of TN. After 32 years with the State of Tennessee, Department of Human Services, I finished up as a Vocational Instructor per Specialty, teaching young adults with a disability a trade. So, they could get a job.

Since I was retired, I decided to take up a hobby, so I started to collect clocks, and make candles, and continued to work on this book. I am also working on a joke book, called "Jokes You Shouldn't Tell Around Woman"!! It is a book of dirty jokes that I heard my family tell as I was growing up

I am also working on a Flatt Family & Griffin Death and Births layout. This came about through research on the book-THE FLATT FAMILY STORIES.

I am also considering a book on Sermon GOD has allowed me to write down through the years.

And Finally, I am still a Songwriter, writing mostly Country and Gospel Songs. And I still have my own studio and still do recordings here at home.

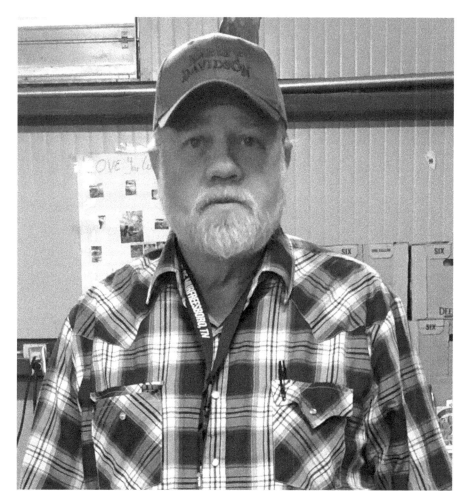

ERNEST FLATT JUST BEFORE RETIREMENT-last day of work

DAD & GRANT-at Dad's retirement party

74. 2020-COVID-19 HITS THE WORLD

In January of 2020, there was a Virus that started in China and was brought to the United Stated by travelers coming from China. By February, the virus now called CoronaVirus -19 had begun to spread to people all over the world. It seemed to be worse on older people. People began to die at an alarming rate per day.

At this time there was no cure, no tests, for it, no one including the experts knew exactly what it was. It seems to attack the respiratory immune system. So, if you had a weakness of some kind, especially a person that was older, the most in dire straits. And if the older person caught the virus, they were the one most at risk to get sick, and not recover. Or to die! The younger persons seem to either not get too sick, or they got sick, but recovered in a week, or two. But older people (like 65 and up) seem to get so bad they had to be put on a ventilator. A lot died, some barely got better after being put into ICU in the hospital. And this was happening in all states, and several countries. It was also given the name Covid-19 Virus. According to doctors there are several Corona viruses in the world. Flue is a CoronaVirus, but it is not as catching as CoronaVirus-19. Corona Virus-19 was then given the name COVID-19 for short.

Finally, President Donald J. Trump, put a ban where government says it had started

On around January 2020 Lacey, Maggie, and I all got sick. We were all sick for about 1 or 2 weeks. But at that time there was not a test for Covid-19, so we went to the doctor appointments, but the doctor's did not know enough about Covid-19 to know if we had it. The doctor just treated us for flue. Gave us antibiotics for the sinus and chest infections we had.

By the time June of the summer of 2020 came around there was a lock down in the country. A lot of businesses, restaurants, bars, churches, were closed down. Church services were done online, or not at all by a lot of congregations. Many people were laid off temporarily. Ernie Jr. was laid-off, Matt Robinson, my son in law, was laid off, Lacey was laid off, Pastor Brother Shane was still working at Tennessee Rehabilitation Center,*(where I retired from)*, but all the students were sent home. Then the State of Tennessee Department of Human Services began to work employee's at home. All stores, and businesses were only open if they were considered essential for the population. I guess the government decided who was essential, no one ever knew. But, Walmart, grocery stores, Liquor stores, gas stations/fast stop groceries markets stayed open. Fast food places went down to just drive through services. Regular restaurants had to do only carry out. Everyone was required to wear a mask over their nose and mouth. Like a doctor wears in surgery. If you went into public you had to wear one. This went on all the way up to about September 2020. Then sit down restaurants and such began to open back up but with fewer occupancy at a time. And we are still wearing the mask to this date, and it is January 2021 already. But I am getting ahead of myself.

All sports changed their schedules, and most had little, or no, crowd. Many businesses went out of business in 2020 One right after another. Most small businesses were affected the most. Just like older people died the most. They also determined from 65 years and up were most variable to the Covid-19.

Grant Charles Flatt (my youngest son) had already moved in with Maggie (his fiancé), while they were waiting to get married. She had her own apartment. So, Grant had moved out, and Travis (my next to oldest son) and Rachel (Travis' wife), had moved in with me. And had been there for a month or so.

On September,04,2020, I was at home when I got up out of my recliner chair to go to the bathroom. Travis and Rachel had gone somewhere, and I was alone by myself. When I got finished in the bathroom,

I walked back to the living room. By the time I got to the living room and sat down in my recliner chair, I suddenly realized I was totally out of breath. As a matter of fact, I could hardly get my breath. I had to breath very, very, deep on purpose, to even get my breath. I let like I had run around the block. But I had not!

I sat in the chair after I got my breath, and finally, I felt a little better.

After I rested for a while, I decided to go outside to check the mail. Well, by the time I got back from the mailbox, and it was only at the end of my maybe 16-foot driveway, I was out of breath again. So, I sat down in my chair and rested again. This time I fell asleep or awhile, maybe 30 minutes or so.

When I woke up, I felt a little better, and remembered that I had to go to Kroger's Pharmacy in Smyrna to get my medication. So, I went out to my Silverado 2019 and by the time I got up into my truck I was out of breath again. So, I sat there a minute and it seemed to pass quicker this time. I drove up to the Kroger's Pharmacy and went in. Of course, I had to wear a mask over my nose and mouth. And by the time I walked into the store I was out of breath again. I sat down and waited my turn and began to feel better again. It came my turn, and I got my prescription and left the store. By the time I got back to my truck in the parking lot, I was out of breath again! I had to set in my truck or a little bit before I could drive. While I was setting and driving, I felt fine.

So, I got back to my house, and again once I walked from my truck to my living room recliner, I was breathing hard and wore out again. So, I rested for a while. Went to the bedroom and put on some comfortable clothes (PJ's). Then I walked slowly back to the living room and my recliner.

Then as I sat there Travis, and Rachel returned home. So, I began to tell Travis how I was feeling. Travis asks, "Well, dad do you need to go to the hospital"? I said, "I don't think so, I'm OK if I am just sitting". Travis asks, "Are you sure"? "Maybe you should call your doctor or someone", he explained. Bout that time lacey called. I answered my phone and began to tell her what had been happening. She began to say, "Dad you need to go to the hospital and have yourself checked out! You might have Covid-19", she explained! "Who is there with you", she asked? I explained, "Travis and Rachel are here with me", I said. "Well get Travis to drive you to the hospital emergency room, please", she said. Finally, I said, "OK"! "But I will have to go get some clothes on and shower, but I will go", I promised Lacey. She said, "Let Travis drive you". I said "OK".

I went to the bedroom, but by the time I got to the bedroom. I don't feel like showering. I was out of breath just putting on my clothes, So when I got back to the living room, I had to set down and rest in my chair again. I told Travis as soon as I rest, we can go.

Travis drove me to the emergency room at Stonecrest Hospital in Smyrna, TN. They made me put on a different Covid-19 mask and took me in. But would not let Travis or anybody else come in. Travis said he would call Lacey.

They admitted me right away! They did a Covid-19 test on me and said I was negative or Covid-19. But my oxygen was low. They did an MRI, and several other tests on me and kept me overnight. They determined that I had a Pulmonary Embolism. A blood clot in my left leg that had gone to my lungs. They began to treat me right away. They kept me for 2 days and one night. My regular Doctor Joshua Hixson came in the next day to see me. He put me on blood thinners, and a drug to dissolve the blood clots. He said I would have to take the blood thinners for about 4 months. They determined I did not have a heart attack but came really close. I had no damage done to my heart. GOD was watching over me. But he let me go home but had me come and see him at his office in a few days.

When I went to see my doctor at his office, he said he wanted me to go see a cardiologist, Dr. Cable, to have me checked out. Dr. Cable sent me to Stonecrest to have another type of MRI done on me to check my heart. They ran the test and determined my heart was OK, that I did not have any abnormalities with my heart. Everything came back normal for my age. I have been getting better all the time and stronger.

October 10, 2020, at half past 5 in the afternoon, Grant Charles Flatt married, (Maggie), Margret Spencer Hernris, Flatt. They were married in Franklin, TN. By Brother Shane Towe at the CARNTON PLANTATION as a background. It was such a beautiful wedding. All of Maggie's Family came, and Ernie and Sharon Flatt came from Ohio, Heather and Matt, Haylee and Avery, all came from Ohio also. Lacey and Matt Robertson, Austine Robertson, Luanne Burger (Matt Robertson's mom), Travis and Rachel Flatt were there. Sister Rose from church came. Several friends of Grant also came that he had not seen in a long time. It was a wonderful wedding, although it rained off and on all day. Plus, they had a wonderful reception party under a big tent on the grounds. And Grant and Maggie have been happy together ever since.

Along with everything else in 2020, somewhere around August, it was found out that Nick Monnin had cancer. He is Rita Noreen Flatt, Monnin, my oldest sister's husband, and just like a brother to me. Nick was taking chemo treatments, but it was not working. Then on 10/16/2020 just a few days after Grant and Maggie's wedding we lost Nick Monnin. I was still getting over my Pulmonary Embolism, and my doctors did not want me to drive or very long. Around town to church was OK. But not for long trips, like to Ohio. So, I could not go to Ohio or my family, but I wanted to. Lill and Rita, Shawn and his new wife, and his boys, Logan, and Layton, all Nick's family were all there. Wish I could have been.

Then on Christmas Eve, 2020, a man from Nashville, TN. Parked a RV on Second Avenue in downtown Nashville. It was full of explosives. It exploded and damaged several buildings in downtown Nashville on Christmas Eve. Lucky, he warned everyone ahead of time, with a loud recording coming from the RV, and the police had time to evacuate several people. Few people were hurt, but the only one that was killed was the terrorist who was in the RV. The Police, and FBI are still trying to investigate and find a motive and a reason for this. One building that was damaged was the AT & T building that housed some cell phone switch gear. AT & T cell phone service was knocked out for several days after this over several states.

Several buildings were damaged and will have to be rebuilt or repaired. Several people were injured, but it could have been a lot worse. Second avenue is blocked off for the moment, till everything is inspected and safe again. Several businesses will be closed for a while.

Good-bye, 2020. Hope 2021 is better and we beat the covid-19. But as always,

GOD HAS GOT THIS!!!

75. THE FLATT FAMILY TREE

Francis A. Flatt---born---Feb. 23, 1897, Sparta, TN., White County died-09/15/1977
Maddie L. Grider, Garner, Flatt-born-Sept. 20, 1892,
Died-complications of childbirth---Feb. 26, 1923 Burl, Kentucky
Children:
Noreen Garner, Carter, by Maddie's first marriage

Children of Francis A. Flatt and Maddie L. Grider, Garner, Flatt
There were 2 children of this union
Orlie Glen Flatt born-03/15/1920
Joe Allen Flatt-born-02/17/1923
Maddie L. Grider, Garner, Flatt died from Complications of childbirth 9 days after the birth of Joe Allen Flatt on 02/26,1923

Orlie Glen Flatt born- 03/15/1920 died-02/14/1981
Orlie's 1st. Marriage-Wife Name Unknown
Marriage date: unknown
Divorce date: unknown
There were 2 son's by this union-both died in a car-bus wreck while uncle Orlie was in the military.
Orlie's 2nd marriage-Lillian Mary Homan-born-03/31/1932
Orlie Glen Flatt was married to Lillian Mary Homan, Flatt on-10/10/1952
There were 3 children of this union
Children of Orlie Flatt and Lillian Mary Homan, Flatt-married 10/10/1952-
*3 children of this un*ion
Gary Glen Flatt-born-09/14/1953
Danny Edwin Flatt-born-12/21/1956 died- 03/23/1977while in the Marines in Florida.
Debbie Lynn Flatt, Wolford- born-08/22/1967

Joe Allen Flatt-bd-2/17/1923 died-8/14/1989
(2nd son by Francis Flatt and Maddie Flatt)
Married Daisy Griffin Flatt: August 03, 1946, Saturday
(10 child by Rufford Griffin and Nancy Griffin)
Divorced: January 05, 1978, Allen & Daisy were never remarried.
Daisy Griffin, Flatt-bd-5-09-1930 died-4-04-2000

Children of Joe Allen Flatt and Daisy Griffin Flatt-married:08/03/1946-
4 children of this union
1. Ernest Allen Flatt-bd-8/13/1950

2. Terry Glen Flatt-bd-1/18/1955
3. Rita Noreen Flatt, Monnin-bd-10/29/1958
4. Lillian Darlene Flatt, -9/11/1960

1. Ernest Allen Flatt, Sr.-born 8/13/50- Marriage #1-11/02/1968-i child of this union
    Marriage#1: Deanna Fay Banner 11/02/1968 Divorced:10/25/1977
    Children of Ernest Allen Flatt and Deanna Fay Banner, Flat-
    1-child of this union.

    1a.) Ernest Allen Flatt, Jr.-bd-12-25-1971
    Marriage #1: 03/26/1994- Sally William, Thompson
    Divorced: 12/31/1997 *-no children of this union*

    1a.)- Ernest Allen Flatt, Jr.-bd-12-25-1971-1-child of this union
    Marriage #2: 09/23/2000- Sharon Cox, Flatt born-01/08/1971
    Divorced:
    1 child of this union-
    Haylee Flatt-born August 10, 2001

1. Ernest Allen Flatt, Sr.-born- 8/13/50- Marriage #2-3 children of this union
    Married#2: 02/17/1979-Ellis Ann Smith, Flatt, Hitchcock
    Divorced: 12/17/2003 -Ellis died-09/11/2017
    Children of Ernest Allen Flatt, Sr. and Ellis Ann Smith, Flatt
    3 children of this union

    1b.) Travis Lee Flatt-bd-10/14/1979
    Married:04/24/2004-Rachel Gervickas, Flatt
    Divorced:

    1c.) Lacey Elizabeth Flatt, Robertson-bd-8/29/1982
    Married: 09/08/2017-Matthew Robertson-Syracuse, N.Y.
    Divorced:
    Austine Robertson-bd-06/30/2010

    1d.) Grant Charles Flatt-bd-7/03/1987
    Married:10/10/2020-(Maggie), Mary-Margret Spencer Henris, Flatt
    At Franklin, TN.
    Divorced:

2. Terry Glen Flatt-born 1/18/55 -1stmarriage-
    1st. Marriage: 06/01/1973 - LaNoir Fay Fultz, Flatt born-unknown
    Divorced: -09/20/1976-Annulment
    no children of this union

2. Terry Glen Flatt-born 1/18/55- 2nd- Marriage-
    2nd. Marriage: 07/01/1978-Debbie Ann Stevenson, Flatt

Divorced:03/09/1989 Debbie died-12/14/2007
2-children of this union

2a). Marshall Flatt- born 02/20/1979
1st-Married: 00/00/0000- Stephanie (unknown name)
1-child- Hailey Morgan Flatt- bd-8-09-2002

2b). Aaron Flatt-born 09/17/1981
1st- Married: 00/00/0000- her name-*2 children of this union*
Children of Aaron Flatt and (Name unknown)
Devon Flatt-bd.-03/07/2002
Alexis LeAnn Flatt-bd.-09/29/2000

---

2. Terry Glen Flatt-born 1/18/55- 3rd- Marriage-*no children of this union*
    3rd. Marriage: -02/12/1994
    Yvetta Faith Patterson, Flatt
    Divorced: 08/01/2001

---

3. Rita Noreen Flatt -born 10/29/58-1st. Marriage
    1st-marriage: unknown date
    (Punchy), Keith Brian Kerg-born-07/1957
    Divorced date: unknown
    1-child of this union

    3a) Shawn Flatt-bd.01/27/1976
    Married: 00/00/0000 Stephine Atkinson, Flatt- *2-children of this union*
    Divorced: unknown date: 00/00/0000
    Children of Rita Noreen Flatt-(continued)
    Layton Flatt-bd.-10/20/1995
    Married: -12/28/2019-Ali Tangeman, Flatt- born-06/11/????

    Logan Flatt-bd.-09/13/199

---

3. Rita Noreen Flatt -born 10/29/58
    Rita's 2nd-marriage date: 05/25/1985 to Nick Monnin
    Nick Monnin Born-07/12/1960 Nick died-10/16/2020
    Marriage #2-no children of this union,
    no children of this union-but Nick had a daughter from a previous marriage:

    Nakina Nicole Monnin-born-05/06/1981

It should also be mentioned that Nick Monnin was a great part of the Flatt family. Just like a Brother/Family member to all of us. He raised Nakina, his daughter, and Shawn Flatt, my nephew just like a real man should, working hard on the Monnin Fruit Farm all his life. Then he helped raise the grandchildren, too. Never missing one of their Football games and always being there when they needed him. "Sis, you picked a GOOD ONE!!!! EAF

---

4. Lillian Darlene Flatt-born 9/11/60

> 1st. Marriage date: 10/07/1978 Steve Combs-born-12/10/1958
> Divorced:02/10/1991 Steve died-02/20/2016
> *No children of this union-But everybody loved Steve in the family. I think him, and my Steve Combs & Dad (Joe Allen Flatt) were best friends more so than son-in-law and father-in-law. They were buddies. Everybody in the family liked him.*

4. Lillian Darlene Flatt-born 9/11/60

> 2nd Marriage date: unknown day-1991 Jay (Buddy)
> Kittell Crawford, Jr.
> Divorced date: 11/25/1999 Buddy died-07/16/2011
> 1-child of this union
>
> 4a.) Jesse Crawford-bd.07/29/1994
> Married:00/00/0000

76. THE GRIFFIN FAMILY TREE-TO THE FLATT FAMILY.

(as given to me by Aunt Evelyn Griffin)

Father B. Griffin   born 08/04/1881 Mother: Mary Lynch Griffin

Rufford B. Griffin   born 8/04/1881 died—5/16/1952

Brothers & Sisters of Rufford Griffin:
Sis-Melvine Griffin   bd.-6/02/1871-died-7/1930 Married: Joe Potts
Bro-John D. Griffin   bd.-5/13/1873
Bro-Ben F. Griffin   bd.-9/28/1875
Bro-James Griffin   bd.-9/28/1877 married Malinda Sparks-sister to Nancy Griffin
Sis-Louise Griffin   bd.-9/04/1879 married: Jake Ashcraft
Rufford B. Griffin   bd-8/04/1881- died-5/16/1952
Bro-Gentry Griffin   bd-7/04/1883
Bro-Sidney griffin   bd-10/30/1885
Sis-Ida Griffin   bd.-3/07/1888 married: Estes
Sis- Julie Griffin   bd-7/08/1893
Bro-Grant Griffin   bd-6/25/1896
Sis-Delilah Griffin   bd-7/01/1896
Rufford B. Griffin   bd-8/04/1881 died 5/16/1952

Rufford B. Griffin Married: 05/26/1902 in Jackson County, KY.
Wife: Nancy Elizabeth Sparks Griffin bd-4/27/1885—died-6/03/1973

10 children of this union
Children: of Rufford and Nancy Griffin.
Ellen Griffin   bd-03/05/1903 died-11/24/1918
Cleona Griffin   bd-09/06/1905 died-12/12/1964
Providence Griffin   bd-11/11/1907 died-11/29/1950
Grant Griffin   bd-12/12/1910 died-12/27/1948
Solomon Griffin   bd-9/02/1915 died-02/07/1979
Emma Griffin   bd-2/24/1918 died----unknown
Etta Griffin   bd-11/30/1920 died-04/23/1990
Anna Marie   bd-7/24/1922 died-02/18/1998
Ben F. Griffin   bd-6/30/1924 died-03/01/1991
Daisy Griffin   bd-5/09/1930 died-04/04/2000

Tenth Child of Rufford and Nancy E. Griffin

Daisy Griffin born: 5/09/1929   died: 4/04/2000
>   Married: August 03, 1946 to
>   Joe Allen Flatt -born: 02-17-1923-died: 08/14/1989 at 66 years old.
>   Allen & Daisy Divorced: January 05,1978. Both were never remarried.
>   <u>Children of Daisy Griffin & Joe Allen Flatt: 08/03/1946-4 children of this union</u>
>   1. Ernest Allen Flatt-born-8/13/1950
>   2. Terry Glen Flatt-born-1/18/1955
>   3. Rita Noreen Flatt-born-10/29/1958
>   4. Lillian Darlene Flatt-born-9/11/1960

Ernest Allen Flatt, Sr.-born-08/13/1950- 1st marriage
>   1st. Marriage: Nov.02, 1968-Deanna Fay Banner, Flatt
>   Dissolution of Marriage: October 25,1977
>   *1-child of this union*
>
>   1a.) Ernest Allen Flatt, Jr.-born-12-25-1971
>   Marriage #1: 03/06/1994 Sally Williams, Thompson, Flatt
>   Divorced:12/31/1997 *no children of this union*

>   1a.) Ernest Allen Flatt, Jr.-bd-12-25-1971
>   2nd Marriage: 09/23/2000 Sharon Cox, Flatt
>   *1-child of this union*
>   Haylee Flatt-born. - 08/10/2001

Ernest Allen Flatt, Sr.-bd-08/13/1950
>   2nd Marriage: February 17, 1979 to Ellis Ann Smith, Flatt
>   Divorced: December 17, 2003
>   Children of Ernest Allen Flatt, Sr. and Ellis Ann Smith, Flatt-3 children of this union
>
>   1b.) Travis Lee Flatt-bd-10/14/1979
>   Married:04/24/2004-Rachel Gervickas, Flatt born-01/21/1976

>   1c.) Lacey Elizabeth Flatt-bd-8/29/1982
>   Married: 09/08/2017-Matthew Robertson born-03/27/1991
>   Austine Robertson-born 06/30/2010

>   1d.) Grant Charles Flatt-bd-7/03/1987
>   Married: 10/10/2020-Maggie, Mary-Margaret Spencer Henris, Flatt
>   Born-??/??/????

---

2. Terry Glen Flatt-born 1/18/1955
>   1st. Marriage date: 06/01/1973 LaNoir Fay Fultz, Flatt
>   Divorced: 09/20/1976
>   *No children of this union*

2. Terry Glen Flatt-born 1/18/1955
    2nd. Marriage date: 07/01/1978 Debbie Ann Stevenson, Flatt
    Divorced: 03/09/1989
    2- children of this union

    2a). Marshall Joe Flatt-born-02/20/1979
    Marriage date: 00/00/0000- Stephanie (unknown maiden name)
    1-child of this union
    Hailey Morgan Flatt- born-8-03-2001

    2b). Aaron Flatt-born-09/17/1981
    Marriage date: 00/00/0000- (her name and maiden unknown)
    2-children of this union
    Devin Jon Flatt-born-03/07/2002
    Married:00/00/0000

2. Terry Glen Flatt-born 1/18/1955
    3rd. Marriage date: unknown- Yvette (unknown maiden name) Crawford, Flatt
    Divorced: (unknown)
    No children of this union

3. Rita Noreen Flatt-born 10/29/58
    Married: 00/00/0000-Punchy (do know last name)
    Divorced:
    1-child of this union

    3a) Shawn Flatt-bd.01/27/1976
    Married:00/00/0000 Stephine Atkinson, Flatt- 2-children of this union
    Divorced: unknown date: 00/00/0000
    Layton Flatt-bd.-10/20/1995
    Logan Flatt-bd.-09/13/199

3. Rita Noreen Flatt-born 10/29/58-2nd marriage
    2nd-Marriage:05/25/1985 to Nick Monnin born-07/12/1960
    Divorced: Nick Died-10/16/2020
    no children of this union-but Nick had a daughter from a previous marriage:
    Nakina Nicole Monnin-born-05/06/1981

It should also be mentioned that Nick Monnin was a great part of the Flatt family. Just like a Brother to me. He raised Nakina, his daughter, and Shawn Flatt, my nephew just like a real man should, working hard on the Monnin Fruit Farm all his life. Then he helped raise the grandchildren, too. Never missing one of their Football games and always being there when they needed him. "Sis, you picked a GOOD ONE!!!! EAF

4. Lillian Darlene Flatt-born 9/11/60
  1st. Marriage date: 10/07/1978 Steve Combs-born-12/10/1958
  Divorced:02/10/1991 Steve died-02/20/2016
  No children of this union-But everybody loved Steve in the family. I think him and my Dad were best friends other than son-in-law and father-in-law.

---

4. Lillian Darlene Flatt-born 9/11/60
  2nd Marriage date: unknown day-1991 Jay (Buddy) Kittell Crawford, Jr.
  Divorced date: 11/25/1999 Buddy d Married:00/00/0000
  1-child of this union
  Jesse Crawfor-born-07/29/1994

The Flatt Family is Still Going Strong.
NOT THE END!!

CPSIA information can be obtained
at www.ICGtesting.com
Printed in the USA
LVHW072059050723
751517LV00003B/128